T0336565

Sponsored by *Tianjin Municipal Government 13th Five-year Plan Comprehensive Investment of Higher Education on Projects of Innovation Team of Producer Service & International Economy and Trade Featured Specialty*

Economics of Contemporary China: Policies and Practices

Editor-in-Chief: Wang Yujing

Deputy Editor-in-Chief: Liu Shuhan, Zhu Hong

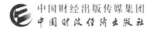 Paths International Ltd

中国财经出版传媒集团
中国财政经济出版社

Preamble

This book is principally intended for foreigners, especially for those foreign students who are studying in Chinese universities or in their home country. The purpose of this book is to help them better understand the historical background, the development process and the overall features of the contemporary Chinese economy.

China began to reform the system of planned economy at the end of 1978, and since then it entered a new era of reform and opening up and a modern socialist construction. From then on, the words "reform and opening up" have begun to appear in various governmental documents and mass media, as well, China has opened its gate wide and started to integrate itself into the world.

China definitely set the establishment of a socialist market economy as the goal of reform in 1992, and then in the next two decades, it witnessed various rounds of negotiations from "rejoining the GATT" to "joining the WTO", and finally became one of the WTO members. Since then, China's economy has grown rapidly. Its GDP, for example, turned out to be among the top 2 in the world in 2010 and its total foreign trade volume reached USD3. 87 trillion, ranking first in the world in 2012, up from nearly 30th in the 1980s. International travelers find almost no difference between modern metropolitan cities like Shanghai, Guangzhou and Shenzhen in China and New York or Sydney in developed countries. When they go back home they find they are surrounded by daily necessities labeled "Made in China" in their life. Sara Bongiorni, a reporter from Boston, Massachusetts wrote a book entitled *A year without Made in China: One Family's True Life Adventure in the Global Economy.* "After a year without Chinese goods, I can tell you this: a decade from now I may not be brave enough to try it again", Bongiorni admitted in her book.

In reality, however, many foreigners including foreign students, and even university professors, have insufficient knowledge of China. They learn from various media that China has managed to keep economic growth on a faster track in recent years and that China could keep average growth rate at about 8% even when developed countries like the United States and those in the EU fell into debt crisis and economic stagnation. They may perceive directly or indirectly the prosperity, modernity and fashion of China's metropolitan cities. They can feel the strong purchasing power of Chinese travelers and find increasing products in their supermarkets labeled "made in China". Therefore, some may wonder at the growing strength of China while others may worry about the threat posed by China's economic development. Be it wonder or worry, what they see is only one side of China.

This book will objectively present contemporary China's economic policies and practices in the course of transformation from planned economy to market economy with rigorous data and detailed information. It is well known that China began its socialist construction based on a planned economic system in 1949. The production, resource allocation and consumption were all conducted according to the plan of the government. Under the planned economy, what to produce, how to produce and for whom to produce were determined by the government. Most national resources were owned, and allocated by the government by means of fiats. Under a planned economy, the national economy was not usually affected by economic circles and the government could make some preferential policies for the development of certain industries. As traditionally an agricultural country, China had been plagued by incessant wars and conflicts ever since the Opium War. Upon the founding of the People's Republic of China (PRC), government leaders gave top priority to the development of heavy industry in order to be self-reliant and to transform from a backward agricultural country to an advanced industrial one. However, there existed many maladies in the planned economy which cannot be ignored, such as low efficiency of resource allocation, mismatch between supply and demand, lack of effective stimulation mechanism for production and high cost for plans to be made, assigned, executed and fed back to the authorities.

The course of China's economy began to change at the end of the 1970s. In the following three decades, the marketization of China's economy made remarkable achievements. According to the "Report on Development of China's Market Economy", China has preliminarily established a market economy system and has become a developing market economy entity. Firstly, the government function has shifted from serving the planned economy to serving a market economy and now the market plays an essential role in the process of resource allocation. The government has reduced its examination and control of economic projects and further standardized the investment system. What to produce and how many to produce will be determined by producers themselves according to the demand of the market, and the market entity has its liberalization in management. All this demonstrates the rule-based government behavior and the liberalization of economic entities. Secondly, China has established an economy with different types of ownership and the market access for non-state-owned enterprises has broadened. According to its WTO commitments, China has further opened the fields of finance, insurance, security, telecommunications, tourism and intermediary to foreign investment. Private enterprises have gradually entered some industries like the heavy industry, financial services, infrastructure and education, which had been closed to them before. According to the data released by the National Bureau of Statistics, the contribution proportion of the non-state-owned economy in the whole national economy has increased gradually. The ratio of added value of the non-state-owned economy in GDP, for example, rose from 53.6% in 1992 to 77.1% in 2011. Meanwhile, most of top 500 MNCs (Multinational Corporations) have entered China and pushed the competition forward. Thirdly, the market system has been perfected step by step. Not only the product market but also the factor market (capital, labor and land) has become mature. The production and operation of enterprises are market based and the financing channels have been widened. In the labor market, the market level of labor mobility and wage-pricing has increased steadily. Fourthly, a more equitable trade environment and diversification of trade entity have been formed. The marketization of foreign trade has made great progress and foreign trade has been fully deregulated. Furthermore, the marketization of finance and RMB interest rate have elevated stably and made new progress. With the increasingly fierce competition in the banking industry and the deepening monetization and financialization, the management and supervision of the markets have continuously been improved and enhanced.

There are scholars at home and abroad who have conducted research and made some academic achievements on China's economy, economic reform and development. The distinctive feature of this book is that, in the process of either conception or writing, it attempts to present contemporary China's economic performance objectively and in plain language. With three case studies attached at the end of each chapter, it intends to demonstrate an overall objective panorama of China's economic development after the planned economy, which includes regional development, industrial structure, urbanization, resource and sustainable development, exchange rate reform, finance and security market, and open trade and investment. Chapter 1 starts with the highly concentrated planned economy, and proceeds to introduce the transition from the planned economy dominated by public ownership and characterized by planned purchase and marketing by the state to the economic system reform. Chapters 2 and 3 expound the development strategy of the industrial and regional economy respectively. Chapter 4 discusses the progress and problems of urbanization, city and sustainable development, and the closely-watched real estate market in China. Chapters 5 and 6 explicate the reform of interest and exchange rates as well as the monetary policy and financial market. From a rigid interest rate and exchange rate to the currently deepened financial market, it sheds light on the evolution and establishment of China's monetary policy and modern financial system. Chapters 7 and 8 illustrate an open China covering foreign trade development, the use of FDI and the progress of "going out". The last chapter deals with an inevitable issue in order to understand contemporary China's economy: the process of China's accession to the WTO (World Trade Organization) and its influence on China.

The successful experience of China's economic development is worthy of summarizing in practice and discussing in theory. Undoubtedly, some problems such as the adjustment of industrial structure, the difference in regional development and the existence of a dual economy need to be analyzed by scholars and industrialists. Just as the development of China's economy depends on economic globalization and the international community, the research on China's economy cannot be conducted in isolation. Another purpose of this book is to make China's economy and Chinese economics "go global". It is also hoped that, by reading this book, more people in the international community can understand China and explore its economic development so that Chinese and international scholars can jointly explore the achievements and problems, challenges and opportunities of China's economic development, and the connection between China's economic development and that of the world.

Undoubtedly, the transformation from a planned economy to a socialist market economy in China is a rather complicated process, which involves the presentation of new concepts from planned economy to socialist commodity economy and to market economy, the progress from closed economy to opening up, the negotiations from rejoining the GATT to joining the WTO, the economic practices from urbanization to the establishment of the three economic circles, and the changes of economic development mode from simply pursing economic growth to exploring scientific development. All this cannot be dealt with in detail in a single book like this. We hope, however, that our book can present an objective picture of the evolution of the economic policies and practices in contemporary China and that readers can better understand the Chinese economy and its actual conditions.

We do expect readers at home and abroad to offer us suggestions and opinions for further improvement.

Wang Yujing
Liu Shuhan

Contents

Chapter 1 China's National Economy: a Market Economy
    Transformed from a Planned Economy   **1**

1.1   Highly Centralized Planned Economy   1
    1.1.1   Preliminary Establishment of the Socialist Public
       Ownership over the Means of Production   2
    1.1.2   Planned Development of the Industrial Economy   7
    1.1.3   Planned System Featuring State Monopoly of Purchase
       and Marketing and of Income and Expense   10
1.2   Transition from Planned Economy System to Market Economy
    System   14
    1.2.1   Reform of the Economy System   15
    1.2.2   Macro Economy and Industry Development under
       Reform   20
    1.2.3   Opening Up to the Outside World   21
1.3   A Fully Open and Harmonious Nation with Market Economy
    in Rapid Development   22
    1.3.1   Establishment of Market Economic System and
       Transformation of Economic Operation Mode   22
    1.3.2   The National Economy in Sustainable and Rapid
       Development   23
    1.3.3   An Important Economy Influencing World Pattern   25

Chapter 2 The Development of China's Industrial Economy   **45**

2.1   Agriculture: The Food Problem for 1.4 Billion People   45
    2.1.1   China's Reform Initiated by Food Shortage in Rural
       Areas   45
    2.1.2   A Modernized Chinese Agriculture   47

2.1.3   The Problem of the Rural People Is the Problem of
China   52

2.1.4   To Modern New Rural Area   55

2.2   Manufacturing Industry: Factory of the World   59

2.2.1   The Establishment and Development of China's
Industrial System   59

2.2.2   China's Manufacturing Industry in the Reform and
Opening up   62

2.2.3   From "Made in China" to "Invented in China"   65

2.3   Service Industry: A Perfect Embodiment of Industrial
Modernization and Urbanization   68

2.3.1   Changes in the Concept of Service   68

2.3.2   The Development of Service Industry and
China's Urbanization   73

2.3.3   Service Indusry and the Optimization of China's
Industrial Structure   76

**Chapter 3   The Strategy and Policy Evolution of China's
Regional Economy   94**

3.1   Balanced Development of Regional Economy in the Period of
Planned Economy   94

3.1.1   The Zero Foundation of Regional Economy   94

3.1.2   A New Star: Proposal and Implementation of
Balanced Development Strategy   95

3.1.3   Effects: Reversing the Imbalanced Productivity Layout   98

3.1.4   Defect: Development at the Expense of Efficiency   100

3.2   Non-Equilibrium Development of Regional Economy in the
Period of Reform and Opening up   101

3.2.1   Breaking up the Stagnant Planned Economy   101

3.2.2   Efficiency-Oriented Non-Equilibrium Regional
Economic Development Strategy   102

3.2.3   Non-Equilibrium Regional Economic Development
Strategy Focusing on Efficiency and Equality   106

3.3   Coordinated Development of Regional Economy in the
Period of Comprehensive Development   110

3.3.1   The Overall Implementation of Coordinated Regional
Development Strateg   110

3.3.2   The Strategy of Development Priority Zones and Interaction of Regional Economies   116

Chapter 4   China's Urbanization Process and Urban Problems   138

4.1   Urban-rural Gap, Urbanization and China's Economic
      Development   138

      4.1.1   Urban-rural Gap in China   138

      4.1.2   Shift towards Urbanized Mode: Changes of Rural
              Areas and Farmers   141

      4.1.3   Urbanization and China's Economic Development   143

4.2   Urbanization and China's Property Market   146

      4.2.1   Cities Merger Villages and Land Supply under
              Multi-track System   146

      4.2.2   Urban Property Market: Hottest Topic in Today's
              China   149

      4.2.3   Urbanization and Property Market: From an
              Interactive DevelopingView   152

4.3   Issues Arising from Urbanization and Population Development
      in China   154

      4.3.1   Urbanization and the Aging Population   154

      4.3.2   Urbanization and Rural Migrant Workers in China   156

      4.3.3   Issues of Urban Medical and Health Care in China   158

4.4   "Large City Malaise" in China and Sustainable Development
      of Cities   164

      4.4.1   Urbanization and City Pollution in China   164

      4.4.2   Urbanization and Urban Traffic Congestion   167

      4.4.3   Urbanization and Green Growth   170

**Chapter 5   Evolution of Interest Rate and Exchange Rate and the
             Chinese Currency Policy   184**

5.1   China in the Beginning of Interest Rate Liberalization   184

      5.1.1   The Interest Rate Policy in China before the Reform
              and Opening up   185

      5.1.2   1978 −1985: Interest Rate Policy in the Years of
              Bringing Order out of Chaos   189

      5.1.3   The"Thrilling Leap" and Ice-breaking Trip of Interest
              Rate Liberalizatio   192

      5.1.4   Icebreaking—Interest Rate liberalization Entering Abyssal
              Area   197

5.2   Exchange Rate Liberalization of RMB   200
    5.2.1   A Historical Review of the Exchange Rate Policy
        of RMB   201
    5.2.2   Distortion and Reality—Dispute on RMB Devaluation
        and Hot Foreign Exchange Reserve   205
    5.2.3   Disputes on Appreciation of RMB   208
5.3   Money Policy of China and Internationalization of RMB   212
    5.3.1   Historical Review of Chinese Money Policy   212
    5.3.2   Readjustment of International Money Policy:
        Strategy of RMB Internationalization   217

Chapter 6   The Structure and Reform of Financial System in China   233
6.1   China's Financial Industry in the Times of Planning Economy   234
    6.1.1   The Highly Centralized Unification of Financial System   234
    6.1.2   Financial Product in Short Supply   236
    6.1.3   Financial Operation Framework Centered by Credit
        Planning   237
6.2   Establishment of the Framework of Modern Financial System   238
    6.2.1   Establishment of the System of Deposit Monetary Banks   239
    6.2.2   Establishment and Development of Trust Companies   241
    6.2.3   Initial Establishment of Financial Market   242
6.3   The Deepening Development of Financial Institutions and
    Financial Market in China   245
    6.3.1   Reform and Development of Chinese Banking   245
    6.3.2   Chinese Insurance Industry Rapidly Sprang up   252
    6.3.3   The Rough Road for the Capital Market in China   254

Chapter 7   China's Foreign Trade: History and Development   287
7.1   China's Foreign Trade Development Course   287
    7.1.1   Planning Economy Period: 1949–1978   288
    7.1.2   Exploration and Practice Period: 1978–1991   290
    7.1.3   Transformation and Development Period: 1992–2001   292
    7.1.4   All Dimensional and Multi-level Opening to the
        Outside World: 2002–2011   294
    7.1.5   China's New Opening Era: from 2012 to the Present   297
7.2   International Status of China's Foreign Trade   298
    7.2.1   International Status of China's Goods Trade   298
    7.2.2   International Status of China's Service Trade   301

7.3   China's System of Foreign Trade   304
  7.3.1   System of Foreign Trade before the Reform and
    Opening up   305
  7.3.2   Foreign Trade System after the Reform and Opening up   308
7.4   Foreign Trade and the Growth   320
  7.4.1   A General Survey of China's Foreign Trade and
    Economic Growth   321
  7.4.2   Interrelationship Between China's Foreign Trade and
    Economic Growth   322
  7.4.3   China's Dependence on Foreign Trade   328

Chapter 8   International Direct Investment-the Practice in China   345
8.1   The Practice of Chinese Utilization of FDI   345
  8.1.1   The Process of Chinese Utilization of FDI   345
  8.1.2   The Characteristics of China's Utilization of Foreign
    Direct Investment   352
8.2   China's Policy on the Utilization of Foreign Direct Investment   354
  8.2.1   The Evolution of China's Policy on the Utilization
    of the Foreign Investment   354
  8.2.2   The Prospect of China's FDI Policy   357
8.3   The Practice of Chinese Outward Direct Investment   358
  8.3.1   The Development of Chinese ODI   358
  8.3.2   The Characteristics of Chinese ODI   363
  8.3.3   The Possibility and Condition for Chinese ODI   365
8.4   Chinese ODI Management   369
  8.4.1   Macro-management of Chinese ODI   369
  8.4.2   Industry Guidance for Chinese ODI   371

Chapter 9   WTO and China   380
9.1   Review of the History of China's Accession to the WTO   380
  9.1.1   The Historic Origin of World Trade Organization   380
  9.1.2   The Motivations and Benefit-Cost Analysis of
    China's Accession to WTO   383
  9.1.3   China's relations with the WTO and the GATT: From
    "Rejoining the GATT" to "the Entry into the WTO"   388
  9.1.4   China's Commitments to the WTO: Fulfillment
    and Controversy   390
9.2   The Influence on China after its Entry into WTO   392

9.2.1   The Economic Influence   393
9.2.2   The Influence of Market-oriented Reform   399
9.3   The Chinese Role in the WTO: Conversion and Prospects   400
9.3.1   China's Demand for Interests in the WTO   400
9.3.2   The Key Issues China Faced   402
9.3.3   China's Role in the WTO: Important Participant and
         Active Builder   404
Acknowledgments   **416**

In 1949, the People's Republic of China (PRC) was founded. Since then it has seen fast economic development which can roughly be divided into two stages: planned economy and market economy. China's economic development, especially the amazing achievements made after the adoption of the reform and opening up policy-so-called "the Chinese Miracle", has attracted worldwide attention.

Chapter 1

China's National Economy: a Market Economy Transformed from a Planned Economy

In 1949, after World War II and subsequent China Civil War, a new state system was established with the founding of the People's Republic of China, making China a socialist country. Having experienced a series of ups and downs in the next decades, China finally grasped the objective laws of economy and sought out suitable resource allocation patterns. Now China has successfully transformed its planned economy system into a market economy system and realized leapfrog development in the process.

1. 1　Highly Centralized Planned Economy

Given the economic and social situation of the time, and under the guidance of Marxism and influence of the Soviet Union as a model, China decided to set up a socialist planned economy as its economic system. (With the practice of planned economy, the Soviet Union realized rapid economic development. Its economic growth shocked all the industrialized countries in the West.)

According to the estimation of noted British economist Angus Maddison, the annual growth rates of China's Gross Domestic Product (GDP) and per capita GDP were 0.22% and −0.08% respectively from 1820 to 1952. By comparison, the annual increase of Europe's GDP and per capita GDP in the same period were 1.71% and 1.03% respectively. The proportion of China's GDP in relation to global GDP declined from a third in 1820 to one-twentieth in 1952, and China's real income per capita declined to a fourth of the global average level. When the People's Republic of China was founded in 1949, the gross output value of industry and agriculture was no more than RMB 46.6 billion, and per capita income was no more than RMB 66.1. Among the gross output value, that of agriculture accounted for 84.5% and industry 15.5%, of which that of heavy industry accounted for 4.5%. Therefore, it was imperative for China to revitalize and rejuvenate its national economy. At the preparatory meeting for Chinese People's Political Consultative Conference, Chairman Mao Ze-dong, then the highest leader of the country, stressed, "Chinese people are willing to cooperate friendly with people from other countries, and to recover and develop international business for the sake of production development and economic prosperity." However, the outburst of the Korean War and the ensuing Taiwan of China issue further intensified the conflicts between China and the USA. Facing a constrained international environment, China had no choice but to resort to self-reliant economic development. Unfortunately, what the old China left was an awful mess. After years of war, the agricultural production was very backward, with peasant economy playing a dominating role. Industry was extremely weak and the output of industrial goods was extremely low. Light industry was doing a little better than heavy industry, the latter barely available. Therefore, from 1949 to 1952, the main challenge facing China was to establish a national economy management framework and revitalize the post-war economy. The work focus of the ruling party was transferred from the countryside to cities. In the following 5 years after 1953, the focus of economic development was shifted from economic revitalization to transition to socialist planned economy. In this period, a highly centralized planned economy system was established. And then from 1957 to 1978, China's economy experienced winding development under the planned economy system.

1.1.1 Preliminary Establishment of the Socialist Public Ownership over the Means of Production

A. Rapid Revival of the Post-War Economy

The first step to restore China's economy was the implementation of Land

Reform, which gradually transformed feudal land tenure into farmer land ownership. The second step was to establish a state-owned economy via confiscation of bureaucrat capitals as well as collection and administration of foreign capitals; meanwhile to set up sound operation and management systems of the state-owned economy through democratic and production reforms. The third step was to restrain inflation which had affected China for more than a decade, stabilize commodity prices, and unify financial and economic administration. The fourth step was to reconstruct national capitalist industry and commerce via adjustment of relations between state and private sectors, labor and capital, and production and sales. (When the People's Republic of China was founded, the central government divided the whole country into six big administrative regions, namely, Northeast, North China, East China, Middle South, Southwest and Northwest, with each big region governing a number of provinces. The highest administrative institute of each big region was Commission of Military Affairs and Politics, one section of which was Financial and Economic Commission. The latter was also subordinate to Financial and Economic Commission, Government Administration Council. Under the Financial and Economic Commission of each region were a number of financial and economic divisions as well as regional branches of the People's Bank of China, responsible for the economic administration of the region. The planned economy system was set up on the basis of public ownership of production means.) By the end of 1952, China's economy had seen effective restoration.

In terms of agricultural restoration, most of the dikes were renovated within the three years, and 385 modern irrigation projects were completed. About 20 million people were directly engaged in the water conservancy projects and 1.7 billion cubic meters of earth work was completed, which is roughly 10 times the work required for the construction of the Panama Canal and 23 times that of the Suez Canal. In 1952, gross agricultural production reached RMB 48.39 billion and increased by 48.5% compared with that of 1949. The total grain output reached 163.9 billion kilograms, an increase of 44.8% compared with that of 1949. The Agricultural economy was restored to the highest level in history with the output of grain, cotton, sugar, red and yellow jute, and tobacco, topping all the previous records. The output of grain and cotton in 1952 even set new records, the former 9.3% higher than the best record of the history, and the latter 53.6%. However, the outputs of oil, silk cocoon, tea and fruit were still rather low. In terms of industry, the transformation of heavy industry was laid great emphasis. 3,300 new enterprises were founded, 4% of which were large and medium operations. In 1952, gross industrial output reached RMB 34.33

billion, with an average annual growth of 4.8%. The proportion of gross industrial and agricultural output increased from 30.1% to 41.5%. Imagine that just three years prior China was not able to make even one steel rail or one ton of quality steel products. And, three years later, China became a country which could depend on itself to make all kinds of steel products, complete sets of textile machines, various machine tools, mining equipment, and 3,000 kilowatt power generation sets. Meanwhile, domestic and international trade was also restored and saw further development. The import and export volume in 1952 doubled that of 1949, and trade with western countries also saw gradual increase.

B. The Socialist Transformation of the National Economy

In the 1940s and 1950s, nationalization of economies became a worldwide fad. Not only did socialist countries like Russia and East European countries seek to develop their economies through nationalization, but some developed countries in the West also resorted to a nationalization process, structural system adjustment, and reduction of the proportion of private ownership, as a solution to fighting the defects of the free market. In January 1940, "On New Democracy", a well-known article by Mao Ze-dong, then the leader of Chinese Communist Party, was published. In the article Mao stated that the state-owned economy of the new democratic republic under the leadership of Chinese proletariat was of a socialist nature and was the leading force of the whole national economy. Guided by the domestic and international situation, in September 1949, it was written into the Common Program of the Chinese People's Political Consultative Conference that the state shall coordinate and regulate the state-owned economy, co-operative economy, individual economy of peasants and handicrafts-men, private capitalist economy and state capitalist economy, in their spheres of operations, supply of raw materials, marketing, labor conditions, technical equipment, policies of public and general finance, etc. In this way all components of the social economy could, under the leadership of the state-owned economy, carry out division and co-ordination of labor and play their respective parts in promoting the development of the social economy as a whole. When the economic restoration was completed, the Central Committee of the Communist Party brought forth the general guidelines and tasks for socialist transition. In the transitional period, socialist ownership over production means would be realized as the single economic basis of China and its society. Meanwhile, socialist transformation of agriculture, handicraft industry, and capitalist industry and commerce would be completed. It should be made clear that China would go after socialist industrialization, with heavy industry as the emphasis and state-owned economy as the top priority whose proportion in the national economy must see constant increase.

a. The Socialist Transformation of Agriculture

Most of the national leaders of the time believed that socialist transformation of agriculture was to move agriculture toward public ownership in the forms of cooperatives and collectivization. The whole process went through three stages. Of the first stage was the development of mutual-aid teams, lasting from the founding of the People's Republic of China in 1949 to the end of 1952. The number of cooperatives formed was very limited in this stage, with only 19 agricultural producers' cooperatives available in 1950, of which 18 were elementary and 1 advanced. By the end of 1951, the number of cooperatives had increased to 130, 129 of which were elementary and 1 advanced. Mutual-aid teams operated on the principle of labor exchange, equal value exchange and collective laboring, with the ownership and management of farmland and production means remaining in the hands of team members. The second stage featured elementary cooperatives, lasting from 1953 to the first half of 1955. The reform in this stage featured land as shares and unified management, though production means were still under private ownership. Along with agricultural producers' cooperatives, supply and marketing cooperatives and credit cooperatives were founded to establish a comprehensive cooperative economic system covering production, marketing and credit. By 16 December, 1953, when the Central Committee of the Communist Party issued a Resolution of Agricultural Producers' Cooperatives, the number of agricultural Producers' Cooperatives had reached 15,000, 15 of which were advanced. In 1954, the number soared to 114,000, among which 200 were advanced cooperatives. The third stage featured advanced cooperatives, which started from July 1955. In this period, agricultural producers' cooperatives saw rapid development. A large number of elementary cooperatives were upgraded into the advanced level. Many mutual-aid teams and individual peasants were incorporated into advanced cooperatives. Most of the farmland and the other production means became under collective ownership. By the end of 1956, the number of agricultural producers' cooperatives had reached 760,000, with 220,000 elementary and 540,000 advanced. 87.8% of the national peasant households joined cooperatives. So, the socialist transformation of agriculture in terms of ownership over production means was by and large completed.

b. The Socialist Transformation of the Handicraft Industry

The socialist transformation of the handicraft industry was also conducted in the form of cooperatives, starting with supply and marketing cooperatives and consumption cooperatives, and then moving on to producers' cooperatives. From 1949 to 1952, the output value of handicraft producers' cooperatives accounted for 3. 4% of the total output value of the industry. According to some typical surveys, the labor productivity of cooperatives was at least 40% higher than that of individual handicrafts-men. The income increase of handicrafts-men after they joined the cooperatives ranged from 36% to 200% . By the end of 1954, more than 1. 21 million people had joined handicraft cooperatives, which was 4. 3 times the number of 1952. At the end of 1955, under the direction of the central leadership, the pace of handicraft industry transformation was sped up, thus dramatically promoting the development of handicraft cooperatives. By June 1956, the socialist transformation of the handicraft industry had been practically completed across the whole nation except a few remote areas. 90% of all the handicrafts-men in the nation joined cooperatives. The number of handicraft cooperative organizations reached 104, 430, and the annual output value reached RMB 10. 88 billion. The proportion of cooperatives' output value among the total output value of the industry increased from 19. 9% in 1955 to 92. 9% in 1956.

 c. The Socialist Transformation of Industry and Commerce

 In the process of economic restoration, which started right after the founding of the PRC, private industry and commerce were gradually nationalized. From 1953 to the first half of 1954, the majority of products in private industry had been turned out under the principles of "producing on state orders, unified purchase and exclusive sales", and the rest was transformed to public ownership in various forms such as wholesale purchase, consignment, and commission. In the second half of 1954, the socialist transformation of industry and commerce moved toward a higher level of joint state-private enterprises. On September 6 of the same year, the Government Administration Council issued the Provisional Regulation on State-Private Joint Industrial Enterprises, which stated the guidelines and principles of state-private joint operation and its nature, management, operation and profit distribution. It also outlined the relationship between private and public ownership and between labor and capital, etc. , in such joint operations. In 1955, the system classification of industry and commerce as well as their production and marketing modes were determined nationwide. The majority of production means had been put under state ownership and unified in terms of deployment and use. By the end of 1956, 99% of all the private industry and 82% of private commerce had realized ownership transformation; meanwhile the transformation of the other industries such as private shipping, automotive and food had also been by and large completed.

 In 1956, the proportion of socialist ownership, mainly composed of whole people's ownership, collective ownership and joint state-private ownership, reached 92.9% (see Table 1.1) of the national economy, marking the successful establishment of the socialist system based on public ownership of production means. A great reform in Chinese history, the socialist transformation promoted the productivity to a certain degree. Indeed, we cannot deny that the conversion of ownership of production means was completed within such a short time that it unavoidably left quite many loopholes, which sowed the seeds for the later downturn of the national economy.

Table 1.1   Change in Economic Structure After "Three Transformations"   Unit: %

Year	Whole People's Ownership	Collective Ownership	State-private Ownership	Total of the Three	Private Economy	Individual Economy
1952	19.1	1.5	0.7	21.3	6.9	71.8
1956	32.2	53.4	7.3	92.9	0.1	7

Source: Xiao Guoliang, Sui Fumin, Economic History of the People's Republic of China (1949 – 2010), Peking University Press, 2011, Page 91.

1.1.2   Planned Development of the Industrial Economy

Actually, the reform of the planned system started in the process of public ownership transformation. As the well-known Chinese saying goes, food is the paramount necessity of people. However, in its babyhood China was confronted with big gaps between food supply and demand. To bridge the gaps and provide raw materials for industrial construction, the government implemented the policy of state monopoly over grain purchase and marketing, and then imposed unified planning and arrangement on production means and products of the entire sector.

A. State Monopoly over Grain Purchase and Marketing Triggered by the Contradiction between Supply and Demand

In 1952, China's total grain output restored to, and even surpassed, the pre-war level. However, with the increase of urban population and the consequential increase in food consumption as well as the growing demand on agricultural materials for expanded economic construction, the contradiction between grain supply and demand was getting increasingly acute. Where private grain merchants were active, the market price of grain was usually 20% −30% above government-guided price and people became very sensitive to the fluctuation of goods price. It seemed that free market by itself was unable to stabilize goods price or meet the needs of economic construction. Therefore, in October 1953, based on a certain study, the Central Financial and Economic Commission issued a planned grain policy—the policy of state monopoly over grain purchase and marketing, which mainly consisted of the following contents. First, planned grain purchase was to be implemented. Peasants who were engaged in grain production must sell regulated types of grain to the state on quotas and at regulated prices. Second, planned grain supply was to be implemented. In urban areas, citizens were to be granted with food purchase permits with which they must present when making food purchases, while in small towns, cash crop areas and general rural areas, higher level government officials were to promulgate grain supply quantity. For grain required for the cooked food industry, food processing, hotels, trains, ships, and industry production, supply was to be provided on quotas and private purchasing was to be banned. Third, close market management was to be conducted. All sectors concerning food operation and processing, including grain shops and factories under state, local, state-private ownership, were to be under the unified leadership of the local grain authority. Private grain merchants' engagement in private grain operation was to banned. Fourth, unified national management was to be conducted. The preparation and development of all concerned grain guidelines and policies, purchasing and supply quantity, criteria and pricing, were all to be under the unified stipulation or approval of the central authority. Since then, the market gradually lost its role in resource allocation.

On October 16 and November 19, 1953, Resolution of State Monopoly over Grain Purchase and Marketing and Order to Implement Planned Purchase and Supply of Grain were issued by the Central Committee of the Communist Party and the State Council respectively. In August 1955, Provisional Regulations of State Monopoly over Rural Grain Purchase and Marketing was issued by the State Council, announcing the implementation of a quota system for rural grain production, purchase and marketing. Following it, state monopoly over purchase and marketing was also imposed on cooking oil and then sideline products. Purchase permits, such as food coupon, oil coupon, were printed and issued, and in the following 30 or more years they played an important part in people's daily lives until 1984 when the central authority abolished the state monopoly over purchase and marketing for all kinds of grains but wheat, unhusked rice, corn and soybeans in main production areas. In 1985, a contract system was initiated on grain and cotton purchase, marking the final abolition of the unified purchase and marketing system which had ruled for as long as 31 years. We can say that the policy of state monopoly on supply and marketing of agricultural products acted as the pioneer of the Chinese planned economy system.

B. Heavy Industry-Centered Industrialization Plan

As a matter of fact, it was stated in the Common Program of the Chinese People's Political Consultative Conference that in light of the backward economy and weak industry foundation, the development of heavy industry should be given top priority. After a few years of theoretical discussion and practice, at the end of 1953, The Compendium of Study and Propaganda of the General Line in the Transitional Period of the Communist Party of China was published, in which it was made clear that China must take the socialist industrialization road centering on the development of heavy industry. The strategy to develop heavy industry was determined by the domestic and international situation of the time. Abroad, after the Second World War, many newly independent nations sought to develop their heavy industry by "import substitution strategy". Besides, the outbreak of the Korean War in 1950 also drove China to put its priority on the development of the national defense industry and to lean closer to the Soviet Union. At home, China was nothing but a backward and poor agricultural nation, its situation very similar to that of the Soviet Union in 1929. For the above reasons, China was more inclined to follow the economic development mode of the Soviet Union. With heavy industry as its priority for more than a decade, the Soviet Union had successfully turned itself into an industrial nation.

This development strategy was fully reflected in the 1st Five-Year Plan period, which began in 1953 and ended in 1957 (Actually the idea of Five-Year Plans was also borrowed from the Soviet Union. For that reason, most central leaders and scholars estimated that, like what had happened in the Soviet Union, it would take China 3 Five-Year periods to complete industrialization). In this Five-Year period, state investment was mainly given to fundamental construction, especially that of industry, heavy industry in particular. For example, an amount of RMB 42.74 billion, about 55.8% of the total investment of RMB 76.64 billion, was spent on fundamental construction; besides, RMB 5.3 billion was spent on geological prospecting and prospect design. Among all the investment for fundamental construction, RMB 24.85 billion was given to industry, accounting for 58.2% of the total. And of all the investment for industrial fundamental construction, 88.88% was given to heavy industry. In this period, 694 large and medium construction projects were planned, but actually 921 projects were constructed, 156 of which were aided by the Soviet Union.

1.1.3   Planned System Featuring State Monopoly of Purchase and Marketing and of Income and Expense

A. An Introduction to Planned System

With the establishment of public ownership and government organizations adapted to planned economy, the management of national finance and foreign trade was gradually centralized; meanwhile market mechanism in labor and product markets gradually atrophied. The planned system took hold, which can be reflected in the following aspects.

First, trade circulation system. The industrial circulation was conducted in the form of cooperatives under a public ownership system. In July 1950, All China Federation of Cooperatives was founded to serve as the leading institute for all kinds of cooperatives concerning supply and marketing, consumption, credit and handicraft. In August, the Ministry of Commerce and the Ministry of Foreign Trade were established, marking the formal division of domestic and foreign trades. Domestic trade was put under the administration of the Ministry of Commerce, with unified allocation as the main commodity circulation mechanism, while foreign trade was put under the centralized control of the Ministry of Foreign Trade. In the following 2 decades, though with frequent changes, the trade circulation system basically followed the principle of "unified control of the central authority and decentralized administration at different levels".

Second, financial system. As the central bank, the People's Bank of China became a component of the Central People's Government of China, taking on the leadership and management of local banks, most commercial banks and other financial institutions, thus a centralized and unified financial management mechanism was established. The People's Bank became the only bank in China to bear the responsibility of both financial management and actual business handling. Domestically, the People's Republic of China took control of credit capital, implementing the policy of "unified deposit and loan" and officially-set interest rates. The whole banking industry was incorporated into the mandatory planned system. Externally, the People's Bank made independent and flexible adjustments on financial policies based on a fixed USD currency peg and comparison of domestic and foreign goods prices.

Third, fiscal and taxation system. After many multiple discussions and modifications, a compound taxation system, mainly composed of commodity tax, business tax and income tax, and a unified fiscal system featuring "unified income and expense" under the central authority and local management at different levels, were initiated in 1953.

Fourth, labor mobility system. Labor market remained in China, but from 1951, state-owned (or state-run) enterprises and institutions were forbidden to recruit employees from schools on their own, and graduates of colleges, universities and polytechnic schools were employed under the unified allocation. The cross-regional transferring of employees was forbidden unless approved of by government authorities. In 1953, free mobilization of labor between urban and rural areas were outlawed. As a result, the function of market as a flexible regulator was totally suppressed.

Fifth, product market. In 1953, state monopoly of unified purchase and marketing was imposed on major agricultural and sideline products. Since then, market lost its regulating function in this field. Planned distribution of production means was further expanded to larger areas.

In the 1950s, China's economic system shifted from one balancing the roles of planning and market to a planned economy system featuring administrative management. At the macro level, the national economy was put under the centralized and unified leadership of the central authority, with mandatory planned management as the main approach. At the micro level, people, finance and materials were all under the direct management of the central government while business affairs of the collective enterprises were under the direct management of local governments. The whole national economy reflected a strong mandatory and administrative nature.

B. The National Economy in Tortuous Development under Planned Economy System

It took China quite a long time to explore for itself a suitable economic development mode. It was not until the end of the 1970s when the reform and opening-up policy was implemented that the national economy went onto the road of steady development. Before that, China's economic development experienced a lot of ups and downs.

In the period from socialist ownership transformation to the implementation of the 1st Five-Year Plan, China witnessed economic restoration and then rapid development. In 1957, China's social output value reached RMB 160. 6 billion, an increase of 70. 9% compared with 1952, among which the gross output value of agriculture amounted to RMB 53. 7 billion, an increase of 24. 8% and its percentage reduced to 33. 4% compared with 1952. And the gross output value of industry amounted to RMB 70. 4 billion, more than double compared with the previous year, and its percentage increased to 43.8%. China's economy was no longer agriculture-based. In the 1ˢᵗ Five-Year Plan period, China's social output value realized an annual increase of 11.3%, with an annual increase of 10.9% in the gross output value of industry and agriculture, and an average annual increase of 8.9% in national income. The increase rate achieved in the 1ˢᵗ Five-Year Plan period ranks the highest of the 5ᵗʰ Five-Year Plan periods. Even compared with other countries of the same period, China's economic growth in this period was among the fastest. According to Maddison's calculation, from 1950 to 1973, the global GDP as a whole increased by 4.9% annually on average, among which Eastern European nations such as the Soviet Union contributed an average annual increase of 5.7%, African nations 4.5%, Latin American nations 5.2%, and Asian nations and regions (excluding Japan) 5.2%.

Unfortunately, owing to the changes of political and economic situations home and abroad, in 1958 China launched an ideological movement, and a modified overall guideline of socialist planned economy was developed, with The Great Leap Forward and People's Commune [1] as concrete approaches of economic development. At the end of 1957, The Great Leap Forward Movement was launched. Under the direction of the concept "fight against conservation, aim high and achieve greater, faster, better and more economical results in building socialism", indicators and data concerning domestic economy in various areas, from budgets to final accounts, were overstated to different degrees.

To realize the overambitious targets of industrial and agricultural development, the Central Committee stated that the whole party and nation should be mobilized to forge steel and iron and join People's Communes. In August 1958, millions of people were involved in the production of steel and iron, and one month later, the number soared to 50 million with more than 600,000 soil blast furnaces built for steel and iron forging. By the end of October, the number of people who were engaged in forging steel and iron had reached 60 million. At the peak time, as many as 90 million people were engaged in activities related to forging steel and iron, such as cutting trees, coal mining, prospecting, iron making, etc. Huge amounts of labor, materials and money was wasted. In September 1958, the number of people who were involved in

---

1　A few advanced agricultural cooperatives were combined into one People's Commune which performed all kinds of functions of local governments, including military issues, safety, trading, financing, taxation, accounting, statistical work, planning etc. One People's Commune was divided into a few big production teams each of which again was divided into a few smaller production teams. Each small production team in size equals that of a cooperative or half a village.

agriculture reduced by 38. 18 million. The ratio of agricultural laborers to industry laborers reduced from 13. 8: 1 of the previous year to 3. 5: 1. Large numbers of transportation vehicles and livestock were used for steel making, and tremendous amounts of grain and cotton was left uncollected and rotting.

In August 1958, the first People's Commune was founded and within 3 months, the campaign swept across the whole country. In November, 99% of the peasant households across the nation became members of People's Communes. The size of one People's Commune was fairly big, with about 5, 000 peasant households, 10, 000 peasants and 60, 000 *mu* farmland on average. The communes were all under centralized and unified production and operation. All the members dined in public canteens and materials were distributed on needs. In this way, an economy of scale effect was achieved to a certain degree, though very soon serious side effects showed as a result of low-efficient collective economy and compulsory system changes. In 1959, a crisis struck agriculture. Cereal yields reduced by 15% and another 10% in 1960. Urban and rural food consumption per capita reduced by 19. 5% compared with 1957, and rural food consumption per capita reduced by as much as 23. 4% .

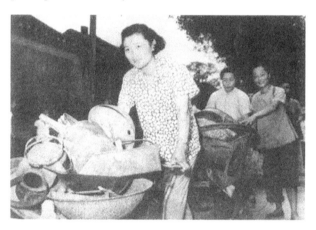

**Citizens Contributing Household Ironware during the
Steel and Iron Making Movement**

Admittedly, the Great Leap Forward and People's Commune Movements had their merits in some aspects. However, the overemphasis of the overall guideline on quick achievements was against the natural law, which unavoidably resulted in a sharp downturn of the national economy. An agricultural crisis hit China in 1959, and for the following 3 years, people lived in miserable conditions and as many as 30 million people died of unnatural causes. It was one of the greatest disasters in human history.

Having learned a hard lesson from what the wrong guideline had brought, in January 1961, at the 8th Plenary Session of the 9th Central Committee of the Communist Party of China, a guideline was passed, featuring "Adjustment, Consolidation, Supplementation, and Improvement". The Central Committee decided to carry out a comprehensive adjustment of the national economy with the following aspects as the focus. The first step was to cut down the budget for fundamental construction. In 1961 the budget was RMB 12.33 billion, a decline by 67.2% compared with the RMB 38.41 billion in 1960. And it continued to decline by 46.2% in 1962. The second step was to reduce the number of workers and urban population. The aim was to reduce urban population by a minimum of 20 million in the following 3 years; The third step was to adjust the industrial economic management system and reinforce enterprise management. A great initiative of the time targeted for economic development, it was also an element of a large-scale reform of the national enterprises. 12 trusts were founded by the Central Committee in all. The fourth step was to regulate the People's Commune Movement and reform the labor and pricing system. By 1965, the national economy saw great improvements, and people became much better off. Both industrial and agricultural productions surpassed those in 1957 with goods supply increasing and prices going stable.

The upward trend in the national economy did not last long, though. In 1966, the Political Bureau of the Central Committee of the Communist Party of China (CPC) initiated a political movement: the Cultural Revolution. In the following 10 years, under the domination of extreme leftist economic thought, system reform was constantly distorted. Although in general the economy witnessed some increase, with certain innovations in science and technology, especially in national defense where some great breakthroughs were made, the Cultural Revolution caused tremendous and countless losses in politics, economy, culture and other areas.

1.2   Transition from Planned Economy System to Market Economy System

The economic development of China in the first 30 years after its founding was full of ups and downs. Without much experience to borrow from, it had to grope its way forward like one walking in the dark. It was not until 1978 that China finally figured out the right way for its economic reform. After the Cultural Revolution, China's economic condition lagged further behind compared with developed economies. In 1979, 83.8% of the nation's population were engaged in agriculture, and agricultural laborers accounted for 84.9% of all the agricultural and industrial laborers. 0.8 billion people were engaged in agriculture with handmade farming tools. People in most regions of the country were still worrying about their daily meals and clothing. In contrast, by then all major developed countries had realized mechanization, electrification and chemicalization of agriculture. As a result, their agricultural labor productivity and commodity rates were far higher than those of China. Faced with difficult situations, most of the Chinese leaders agreed that China must re-consider its economic development strategy and approach. Besides, China must introduce the more advanced technology and management experiences from the West, meanwhile explore a development route which really suited its domestic situation. It should be noted that at the time most developed countries were also experiencing economic transformation. After years of high-speed growth, those economies entered a period of low-speed increase in the late 1970s. With a shortage of domestic markets and increasing international trade frictions, they had to look outside for market expansion and to realize industrial restructuring on a global scale. The changes in the international environment brought great opportunities. Being too wise to miss them, Chinese leaders decided to reform and opening up policy, thus successfully promoting the Chinese economy into a period of unprecedented development.

1.2.1   Reform of the Economy System

China's economic reform in the late 1970s started from agriculture, and later extended to include other sectors of the economy and macro-level policy systems. The general guideline of the reform was to exert the role of market in resource allocation, and transform the planned economy to a market economy.

A. Rural Reform: Rural Household Contract Responsibility System

In the two decades following 1958, collective production was the only mode of production organization, and it was also a system arrangement compatible with the socialist ideology of the government of the time. Although, by practicing collective production, economy of scale was realized, people's enthusiasm for production greatly decreased, which unavoidably led to low production efficiency. Between 1977 and 1978, shortly after the end of the Cultural Revolution, driven by a strong desire to get out of poverty, some peasants in Anhui and Sichuan Provinces spontaneously restored or originated different forms of a production responsibility system. With the system of "Production Contracted to Each Household" [1] initiated by some peasants of Xiaogang Village, Anhui Province, became an archetype of rural household contract responsibility system.

Following Anhui Province's lead, some other areas, including Sichuan, Guizhou, Gansu, Henan Provinces and Inner Mongolia Autonomous Region, etc., began to practice the system of "Production Contracted to Each Household" one after another. It spread to more areas and formed a very considerable scale within a very short time. In 1979, several diverse responsibility systems, such as "Work Contracted to Group", "Work Contracted to Household", "Work Contracted to Laborer", "Production Contracted to Group", and "Production Contracted to Household", coexisted in large areas of the countryside. In September 1980, Several Issues Concerning the Further Enforcement and Perfection of Agricultural Production Responsibility System was issued by the Central Committee, which justified the coexistence of different production responsibility systems based on local conditions. Household Production Contract Responsibility System became the prevailing practice nationwide and saw constant upgrades; meanwhile its main form changed from "Production Contracted to Household" to "Work Contracted to Household". [2] In 1982, Resolution on Issues concerning Accelerating Agricultural Development (draft) was passed at the 3rd Plenary Session of the 11th Central Committee of the Communist Party, marking the compulsory system transformation of the agricultural economy. The resolution stipulated that a series of policies and measures shall be issued in the following 2 or 3 years to promote economic system reform in rural areas, and an agricultural production responsibility system shall be put into practice. It is not difficult to see that the rural Household Contract Responsibility System, rather than a government invention, was a spontaneous and induced transformation which happened to be in line with the compulsory system transformation of the government.

In October 1983, The Central Committee decided to abolish People's

---

1 The common operation of "Production Contracted to Each Household" was to lease the farmland to peasants who in return delivered the regulated output to the production teams they belonged to and kept the rest for themselves. In some cases, the output beyond the regulated volume was divided between peasants and production teams.

2 The practice of "Work Contracted to Household" marks a radical change of the rural operation mode, from collective operation to household operation on leased lands. It differs from "Production Contracted to Each Household" in that it abolishes unified operation and distribution of production teams. Peasants deliver regulated taxes to the state and common reserve funds or welfare funds to the collectives as stipulated in the contract and keep the rest profits for themselves.

Communes and set up town government as the controlling political power of local rural areas, meanwhile set up Villagers Committees as rural self-governing organizations. Work Contracted to Household had become the mainstream form of Household Contract Responsibility System, marking the successful transition of agriculture from a collective economy featuring People's Communes to a household farming system based on peasants leasing land. In the process, the Household Contract Responsibility System was spread from rural collective economic organizations to state-owned farms, from agricultural production to such economic sectors as forestry, animal husbandry, sideline production and fishery.

In 1985, a new system combining Order by Contract and Purchase by Market replaced the existing grain supply and marketing policy. In the same year, control over the pricing of agricultural and sideline products, excluding that of grain and cooking oil for urban consumption, was lifted. Meanwhile, agricultural tax reform was practiced to build connection between agricultural production and market. At the beginning of 1987, the framework of a new rural economic system was basically in place and the rural economy started its transition toward specialization, commercialization and modernization.

B. Urban Reform: from Planned Allocation to Market Development

When the economic system reform was unfolded in vast rural areas, the idea of reconstructing micro incentive mechanisms was put forward for urban economic reform, which finally led to a comprehensive economic reform in 1984. The reform in cities emphasized the following two aspects. 1) to develop market entities, aiming to regulate the relationship between enterprises and the state. The objective was to set up a micro incentive mechanism. 2) to construct market, aiming to set up boundaries for government and market. The objective was to transform planned allocation of production factors into market allocation. In general, in the first decades of the urban reform, the central government made constant policy adjustments and modifications to seek the balance between power devolution and tightening. Consequently, the macro economic growth of China in this period showed obvious periodic fluctuation.

a. Reform of State-owned Enterprises

The key to regulating the relation between the state and state-owned enterprises was to give the latter certain autonomy so as to provide economic incentives for the development of enterprises. As a matter of fact, when a planned economy system still ruled the nation, the reform of state-owned enterprises was once attempted. However, it failed to solve the real problems, because it took the wrong form of delegating the administration of national enterprises to lower levels of governments, that is, to governments at provincial or lower levels. The problems remained unsolved until in the late 1970s, when a common view became prevailing among both government leaders and business people that the key to reforming state-owned enterprises is power devolution (instead of enforcing mandatory plans): so-called "Expansion of Power and Transfer of Profits". In October 1978, a pilot reform was launched in state-owned enterprises, and soon spread to other sectors such as industry, commerce, material supply, transportation, postal, telecommunication, and military industry, etc. In December 1980, the guideline featuring "Expansion of Power and Transfer of Profits" was abolished by the Central Committee and one featuring "Economic Responsibility of Enterprises" took its place. And later with the implementation of the policy of "Tax Payment Replacing Profit Delivery" in 1983, a profit distribution scheme between the state and enterprises was further regulated. Although having achieved certain results, the above reform measures indeed cause some confusion due to the lack of reforms in other relevant systems. It was not until 1984 when all kinds of economic system reforms were launched one after another that the reform of state-owned enterprises started to take a greater pace.

From 1984 to 1988, China vigorously promoted enterprise contract management responsibility and leasing systems. The vitality of enterprises involved witnessed constant increase and the profit delivered to the state rose year by year. After two contract periods (each period lasting 3 years), by 1992, almost all large and medium enterprises around the nation had adopted this or that form of contract responsibility system. The aim of practicing a contract management system was to separate enterprise ownership from management, with enterprise management who signed the contract, delivering specified amounts of profit and tax to the state. In the process, some pilot enterprises started the experiment of a shareholding system. In November 1984, as a pilot enterprise of the shareholding system, Feilo Acoustics in Shanghai issued shares to the public. Then, in July 1986, the State Council decided to reorganize the Bank of Communications and introduced the shareholding system into the financial sector. Bank of Communications became the first national joint-stock financial enterprise. From then on, Chinese enterprises gradually entered a stage of standardized, modernized operation and management.

   b. Development of Markets

   Apart from state-owned enterprises, all the other economic entities available, including individual economy, household farming, township enterprises and foreign enterprises, integrate themselves into the tide of economic reform and enjoyed rapid development. To support the economic reform, on one hand, the Chinese government conducted a thorough modification of the national fiscal and taxation system. Under the new fiscal and taxation system, over-planning was gradually eradicated. Having seen increased revenue and financial power, local authorities became more active in economic construction and took initiatives to further increase revenue and save expense. On the other hand, with the abolition of state monopoly over goods purchase and marketing, the circulation mode of production means and consumption materials were reformed to involve multiple business channels and operation patterns, and segregation among different industries and markets were broken to promote specialized division of labor. Unified allocation of materials gradually turned into commercialized operation. Various markets were opened and circulation was invigorated.

C. Planned Commodity Economy

With continuous exploration and practice, China gradually worked out a suitable development mode for the first stage of its reform and opening up practice: planned economy supplemented by market regulation. In September 1982, the concept that planned economy takes the leading role supported by market regulation was brought forth at the 12th National People's Congress of the CPC. In October 1984, Decision on Reform of Economy System was passed at the 3rd Plenary Session of the 12th Central Committee of the CPC, which was the first document officially stating that socialist economy is "planned commodity economy based on public ownership" and Chinese must "go beyond the traditional view that sets planned economy against commodity economy". This statement marked not only a great leap forward in Chinese reform theories, but also a big breakthrough in theories of economics, providing solid foundation for the transition of China's planned economy to a market economy. In 1987, at the 13th National People's Congress of the CPC, the new economic system was further explained, "planned commodity economy system of the socialist country is supposed to be an intrinsic unification of planned economy and market economy. The new mechanism of economic operation, as a whole, should be one of 'state regulating market and market guiding enterprises'. " Under the guidance of the new economic system, China's reform and opening up practice saw remarkable achievements.

1. 2. 2 Macro Economy and Industry Development under Reform

A. Rapid Increase in Economic Aggregate

In the first 10 years after China started the reform and opening up practice, the 6th Five-Year Plan was developed and implemented successfully, so was the 7th. The 6th Five-Year Plan was completed ahead of time, and the 7th, although with some setbacks, was also completed with considerable achievements. In 1978, China's Gross National Product (GNP) reached RMB 358. 8 billion and it increased to RMB 1. 58 trillion in 1989 and to RMB 1. 74 trillion in 1990. From 1979 to 1990, the GNP witnessed an average annual increase of 9. 0% . In 1978, the national revenue was RMB 301 billion and it increased to RMB 1. 31 trillion in 1989 and RMB 1. 43 trillion in 1990. From 1979 to 1990, the national revenue saw an average annual growth rate of 8. 7% . In 1978, the national fiscal revenue was RMB 112. 11 billion and it increased to RMB 324. 48 billion in 1990, an average annual growth rate of 9. 3% . In 1980, the international reserve of China was USD2. 55 billion (excluding gold reserve) while in 1989 it increased to USD17. 96 billion; by comparison, in 1989, the international reserve of India was no more than USD3. 86 billion. In 1989, China's gold reserve was 12. 67 million ounces; by comparison, that of India was 10. 45 million ounces. In terms of fundamental construction, RMB 66. 87 billion was invested for fixed assets of the units under the ownership of the whole population in 1978, and in 1990, the investment increased to RMB 292. 68 billion. By 1990, 4, 584 large projects had been completed and put into use.

Especially in the first few years of this period, China's agricultural production saw unprecedented development, with total grain yields increasing by one-third compared with that of 1978, from 300 billion kilograms to 400 billion kilograms. The gross output value of agriculture realized an increase of 68% , and farmers' average income increased by 166% . With farmers' purchasing power greatly enhanced, high-end goods, such as bicycles, sewing machines, radio sets and watches, became affordable to ordinary households.

B. Industry Restructuring and Increase in Gross Output Value

In the early stage of the reform, the restructuring of the proportions of agriculture, light and heavy industry in the economy was conducted, mainly relying on the distribution of the central government's investment. In 1978, the agricultural investment accounted for 11% of the total government investment. A resolution passed at the 3rd Plenary Session of the 11th Central Committee announced that agricultural investment would be increased to 18%, but the resolution was not put into practice, because shortly after its proposition, the innovation of the household contract responsibility system led to great increase in agricultural output. With a few years of effort made in economic restructuring and development, all the sectors of the economy developed by leaps and bounds, resulting in a rise in the proportion of agriculture and a decline in that of industry. Of industry, the share of light industry saw a rise. Compared with 1978, the share of the primary sector of the economy increased by 52. 6% in 1984, with an average annual growth rate of 7. 3%; that of the secondary sector increased by 66. 9%, with an average annual growth rate of 8. 9%. Among the secondary section, industry increased by 66%, with an average annual growth rate of 8. 8%; and the tertiary sector increased by 78. 3%, with an average annual increase of 10. 1%. In 1988, the gross agricultural output value increased to RMB 586. 5 billion, 3. 2 times more than that of 1978, which was RMB 139. 7 billion, with an average annual increase of 5. 9%. In 1978, the gross industrial output value was RMB 423. 7 billion, and in 1984 it increased to RMB 1. 82 trillion, 3. 3 times more than that of 1978, with an average annual increase of 12. 4%.

1. 2. 3   Opening Up to the Outside World

China was eager to learn advanced foreign technology and introduce foreign capitals. In 1979, the Import and Export Administration Commission of PRC and Foreign Investment Administration Commission of PRC were founded to strengthen foreign trade and economic cooperation, thus starting China's opening up to the outside world. In May 1980, in "The Instructions on Guangdong and Fujian provinces' Meeting Minutes", the Central Committee officially recognized the title of "Special Economic Zone" and decided to grant the special policy of opening up to the outside to Guangdong and Fujian provinces. In August 1980, the Central Committee designated four cities in southern China, namely Shenzhen, Zhuhai, Shantou, and Xiamen, to be special economic zones, and allowed them to practice economic systems and policies different from the rest of China. Some of the favorable policies granted to those economic special zones are: foreign-owned enterprises were allowed to operate; foreign banks and insurance companies were allowed to set up branches; import and export duties were exempted; tax rates were lower than those imposed on joint ventures in the rest of China, etc. Since then, those special economic zones have been serving as pioneers of China's economic development and growth owing to the implementation of the reform and opening up policy.

In 1984, China further opened another 14 coastal cities to overseas investment, including Dalian, Qinhuangdao, Tianjin, Yantai, Qingdao, Lianyungang, Nantong, Shanghai, Ningbo, Wenzhou, Fuzhou, Guangzhou, Zhanjiang and Beihai. In 1985, three Delta regions were opened. Areas which were opened to overseas investment were continually expanded, finally covering all the coastal cities from the north to the south. International exchange and cooperation prompted the prosperity of the domestic market and became a strong driving force of economic development. By the end of 1989, the total foreign investment in actual use of the 5 special economic regions had amounted to USD4. 1 billion, more than one-fourth of the total foreign investment in the whole country. Foreign trade export reached USD 3. 85 billion, nearly one-tenth of the total national export. Gross industrial output value reached nearly RMB 30 billion. No region of China could beat the special economic zones in the growth of economic strength.

1. 3   A Fully Open and Harmonious Nation with Market Economy in Rapid Development

By the late 1980s, China had greatly benefited from the reform and opening up practice; nevertheless, some deep-rooted problems began to emerge one after another, such as overheated investment, inflation and problems concerning the state's macro economic control, etc. Having considered the domestic and international environment of the time, the Chinese government decided to deepen the economic system reform and spare no efforts to develop the national economy. This decision ushered in a new era for China and enabled it to make outstanding contribution to the stability and growth of the world economy with high-speed growth.

1. 3. 1   Establishment of Market Economic System and Transformation of Economic Operation Mode

In 1992, ten years after the development mode of "planned commodity economy" was originally put forward, at the 14th National Congress of CPC, Chinese leaders clearly stated that the target economic mode of China was a socialist market economic system. This marked a historic leap in Chinese economic reform theory. Since then, China's reform and opening up practice has entered a great new era.

The core idea of a socialist market economic system is to exert the fundamental role of market in resource allocation under the macroeconomic control of the socialist state. This economic system matches China's socialist political system and has its own characteristics in ownership structure, allocation system, macroeconomic control and the like. In 1993, the system was written into the Constitution of the People's Republic of China. In the same year, Decision on Certain issues of Establishing Socialist Market Economy was released which gave a systematic and specific description of the objectives and basic principles of the ongoing economic system reform. At the 3rd Plenary Session of the 14th Central Committee of the CPC it was stated that to achieve the goal of economic system reform, China must stick to the guiding principle of public ownership playing the leading role and diverse economic sectors developing side by side, and must work on the following issues. a) to further transform the operation mechanism of state-owned enterprises, set up a modern enterprise system which suits the needs of a market economy and with clear ownership, explicit rights and duties, scientific management, and separation of government administration from enterprise management. b) to set up an open and unified national market system, realize the close knit relationship of urban and rural markets, link up domestic and international markets, and promote optimum resource allocation. c) to transform government functions in economic administration, set up a suitable macro control mechanism to ensure the sound development of the national economy with indirect regulation. d) to set up an income distribution system with "distribution based on work" as the main standard, meanwhile give priority to efficiency with due consideration to fairness, and encourage some people and regions to get rich first for the purpose of common prosperity. e) to set up a social security system with multiple layers and adapted to the national status of China to ensure urban and rural social security, and to promote economic development and social stability.

Later at the 15th, 16th and 18th National Congress of the CPC, the object of developing a socialist economic system was further described and confirmed, though with necessary modifications as required by the changes of situations. Guided by it, market entities came to be mature, various markets were established, systems were put under constant reform, and macro-economic control of the government became more mature and stable.

1. 3. 2   The National Economy in Sustainable and Rapid Development

Since the 1990s, China's economy has maintained rapid increase. Although overheated investment led to rising prices and then inflation, as the market economy system was gradually set up, the government established tight monetary policies and other macro-economic control measures to regulate the economy, and thus played a powerful role in solving the emerging problems. By the end of 1996, China's economy had achieved a soft landing successfully and system reform in various aspects was greatly promoted.

A. National Economy Grows Stably at High Levels

In 1992, China's GDP was RMB 2.7 trillion, and in 2002, it increased to RMB 12 trillion, and then to RMB 47 trillion in 2011. Calculated in comparable price, the average annual growth was higher than 10%. By comparison, the average annual world economic growth of the same period was no more than 3%. China has become one of the fastest-growing economies of the world, with its total government revenue increasing from RMB 348.34 billion in 1992 to RMB 10.39 trillion in 2011, and foreign currency reserve increasing from USD 19.44 billion in 1992 to USD 3.18 trillion in 2011.

B. Industrial Economy Develops Rapidly with Remarkable Success in Industry Restructuring

With strategic adjustments of the economic structure, China's industrial structure became more coordinated, with remarkable increase in quality and efficiency of economic growth. The three sectors' proportions in GDP changed from 21.8: 43.4:34.8 in 1992 to 10.0:46.3:43.2 in 2010. The proportions of employees in the three sectors were 58.5:21.7:19.8 in 1992 and 34.8:29.5:35.7 in 2011. The three sectors' contribution to GDP growth was 1.2:9.2:3.8 in 1992 and 0.4:4.8:4.1 in 2011. The proportion of the tertiary sector of the economy increased from 40.1% in 2006 to 43.3% in 2011. The tertiary sector's contribution to GDP has been continuously on the increase.

C. People's Living Standards See Constant Improvement

Per capita disposable income of urban households increased from RMB 2,026.6 in 1992 to RMB 6,859.6 in 2001, with an average annual growth rate of 8.6%, and then to RMB 21,809.8 in 2011, a year-on-year increase of 14.1%. Per capita net income of rural households increased from RMB 784 in 1992 to RMB 2,366.4 in 2001, with an average annual growth of 3.8%, and then to RMB 6,977.3 in 2011, a year-on-year increase of 17.9%. Engel's Coefficient (an economics law developed by statistician Ernst Engel) of urban households declined from 53% in 1992 to 36.3% in 2011 and that of rural households declined from 57. 6% in 1992 to 40. 4% in 2007. People's living standards improved significantly, and the number of rural people living under the poverty line decreased dramatically.

D. International Business Is Further Promoted and Deepened

Foreign economic commerce saw an unprecedented increase, with the total volume of imports and exports rising from the 6th place to the 3rd in the world and foreign currency reserve rising to the 1st place. In 2002, the total volume of imports and exports was USD 620. 77 billion in 2002 and USD 3. 64 trillion in 2011. In 2003, China ranked the 4th in the world in total volume of imports and exports, having exceeded France and Britain. And then in the following year, it surpassed Japan and won the 3rd place in the world. In 2002, the actual use of foreign direct investment was USD 52. 7 billion, and it increased to USD 116. 01 billion in 2011, an average annual increase of 12% . Since 2002, China's actual use of foreign direct investment has been among the world's Top Three.

1. 3. 3   An Important Economy Influencing World Pattern

China's reform and opening up practice has not only benefited Chinese citizens. From a global perspective, by exporting high-quality and low-priced consumption goods and daily necessities, China has contributed greatly to the substantial improvement of the living standards of people in other countries. Besides, China's reform and opening up practice helped maintain the stability of the world economy. Among many other evidences was China's outstanding performance in the East Asia financial crisis of 1997 and the world financial crisis of 2008.

A country in relative shortage of natural resources, China heavily relies on import of resources to support its economic growth. Large amounts of imports have driven the increase of resource prices, which has spurred the economic development of African countries abundant in natural resources. What's more, China's commercial intercourse with some Asian and Latin American countries has acted as a driving force for the recent economic growth of the latter. The dynamic role that the Chinese market plays in the world economy speaks for itself.

In September 2008, Lehman Brothers Holdings went bankrupt, followed by a global economic crisis. China, relying on its huge fiscal space and abundant foreign currency reserves, quickly reacted with a RMB four-trillion stimulus package, and brought its economy back on a growth trajectory in the first season of 2009. In the process China served as one of the most important driving forces for global economic recovery.

Of all the five countries which played the most important roles in driving global GDP growth in the 1980s and 1990s, China was the only country that was not a member of the G7 (Group of Seven). China's contribution to global GDP was 13. 4% that of the USA in the 1980s and 26. 7% in the 1990s. And in the first decade of the 21st century, as the largest contributor to global GDP, China's contribution surpassed that of the United States by 4% .

Case 1. 1   A Resource Allocation Mechanism Featuring State Monopoly over Purchase and Marketing: Coupons for Grain, Cloth, and Oil

Food coupons, as food purchase certificates, were first issued and circulated in China in 1955. In the following decades until 1993, urban residents had to buy food with certain coupons. On August 25, 1955, at the 17th plenary meeting of the State Council, Provisional Regulation on Printing of Food Ration Coupons in Cities and Towns was passed, and food coupons were born, as the times required. Afterwards, all kinds of ration coupons entered people's lives, one following another, including cooking oil coupons, tofu coupons, cloth coupons and the like. As required, all commodities had to be bought with ration certificates. Since then, China entered a period of coupons which would not end until nearly 40 years later. The circulation of coupons, especially food coupons, was a proof of goods shortage as a result of the long-time planned economy system.

Actually, China was not the first country to enforce coupon-based supply of commodities. . Faced with an unstable domestic situation, constant wars and commodity shortages after the October Revolution, Russia decided to enforce a planned commodity allocation. As the first commodity coupons, shoe coupons were issued in 1916. After that, various commodity coupons were printed and issued. Apart from Russia, to solve the problem of commodity shortages during the Second World War, America also issued a variety of coupons, some of which were very similar to grain coupons issued in China. By comparison, China issued the largest variety of grain coupons in the world. When the planned supply policy was enforced, all kinds of grain coupons were issued and circulated in more than 2, 500 cities, towns and counties. Besides, some large enterprises, factories, farms, schools, government authorities and institutions also issued their own grain coupons. In General, coupons circulated in China in that era could be classified into 3 types, namely, coupons for edible commodities, clothing and daily necessities. As for coupons for edible food, besides grain and oil coupons, there were those for pork, beef, mutton, chicken, duck, fish, eggs, sugar, bean products, vegetables, etc. In the category of clothing coupons, apart from cloth coupons, there were coupons for synthetic materials, cotton, singlets, vests, cloth shoes, cotton batting, etc. Among coupons for daily necessities, there were coupons for handkerchiefs, soap, tissue, washing powder, matches, rags, kerosene, coal, household appliances, bicycles, and watches, etc. Temporary and flexible coupons were also available. In a word, in that era, most commodities were under coupon-based supply. One had to purchase goods with corresponding coupons. Besides, they had to be used before the specified dates printed on them or they would lose their validity after that.

Food shortage was never a new problem for China. Instead, it had a long history. However, since the founding of the People's Republic of China, the demand for grain had been increasing dramatically, which resulted in growing contradiction between grain supply and demand. Things became even worse after 1953, when grain become a rare resource. For a while, grain shortage even developed into grain crisis. On one hand, the demand for grain was constantly rising; on the other hand, some major grain production areas were unable to deliver planned grain quantity. For a period, even major cities like Beijing and Tianjin were facing a shortage of flour supply, not to mention other cities. If left uncontrolled, the grain market would certainly have gone very chaotic, which in turn would have led to wild fluctuation of grain prices and rising payment. This would surely have affected industrial production, disturbed financial budgets, and held back economic recovery and construction. For the above reasons, the central government attached great importance to the grain issue.

Realizing that a grain crisis would badly affect people's lives, threaten the stability of the young political power, and thwart the implementation of strategies for industrialization, Chen Yun, a Chinese leader who was presiding over the nation's economic work, carried out some in-depth studies. He looked at the problems concerning grain purchase and marketing as well as what other governments had done to solve grain issues. After careful study and thought, he concluded that grain rationing was the solution. Therefore, he proposed that the Central Committee enforce compulsory purchase of grain in rural areas and grain rationing in urban areas. This was the so-called policy of "planned purchase" and "planned supply", or "state monopoly on grain purchase and marketing".

In 1953, Resolution of State Monopoly over Grain Purchase and Marketing and Order to Implement Planned Purchase and Supply of Grain were issued by the

Central Committee and the State Council respectively. Since then, state monopoly over purchase and marketing was imposed on grain circulation, and this policy was not called off until 31 years later.

Later in November of the same year, state monopoly over purchase and marketing was spread to oil circulation. In 1955, the State Administration of Grain released the first batch of national food coupons. At first, when people purchased grain with national food coupons, they would automatically get a rationed amount of cooking oil. Later, independent oil coupons were released by local grain authorities of different levels.

The circulation of grain coupons and enforcement of state monopoly over purchase and marketing policy had a positive effect on China of that era. In different periods of human history, many a nation had to deal with grain shortages. When natural disasters struck or war broke out, if governments failed to ease grain crisis with unified allocation of resources, unrest might have occurred, which would surely have threaten the political power. In the first years after the founding of the PRC, with grain demand increasing dramatically, grain shortage became an increasingly big problem. Facing this situation, the Chinese government secured direct control over agricultural products by enforcing state monopoly over grain purchase and marketing, which effectively blocked private speculation and price gouging. This measure greatly enhanced the nation's capacity of taking action and contributed to the stability of the newly-born state power.

In 1960, the whole nation entered a temporary state of "saving grain to survive the famine" to fight the famine which hit China for three years successively. There was a severe shortage of grain supply in urban areas. The quota for subsidiary food was under further reduction. What could be purchased with coupons before was not available at all. In 1961, the number of commodities which could only be purchased with coupons reached up to 156. Coupons played an essential role in people's daily lives; they were required for the purchase of almost everything including food, cigarettes, alcohol, even a packet of matches. Besides, in those days, China enforced rigid household registration management and clear separation of urban and rural households. Grain and oil coupons were only distributed to urban households monthly. That meant people from the countryside could not get any coupons if they stayed in cities. Consequently, it was impossible for peasants to take temporary jobs in cities, as they could not survive without coupons.

Owing to grain rationing, mobilization among cities became a difficult thing. There were two types of grain coupons, national and local. The former was accepted nationwide while the validity of the latter was restricted to local areas. People who traveled on business had to exchange a certain amount of national coupons in local grain stores, but before that they had to apply for a certified letter from their company or organization.

In a time of commodity shortages, the coupon system played a crucial role in securing commodity supply and thus stabilizing the society, though it did bring great inconveniences to people's daily lives. To purchase a commodity in shortage, money was not enough. Consumers had to exchange cash for the required coupons. Grain coupons, and some other coupons, became a rare thing. As a result, people began to trade them on black markets. Later, certain laws were created to outlaw black market operation of grain coupons, and coupon scalpers were imposed certain punishment according to the severity of their criminal behavior. This ranged from administrative detention, confiscation of illegal gains to being put under surveillance, reeducation-through-labor or imprisonment.

China's economic development saw a favorable turn after the 3rd Plenary Session of the 11th Central Committee. With the implementation of the reform and opening up policy, supply of goods and materials became abundant, commodity market active, and the once-strict coupon system flexible. Gradually, ration on various consumer goods was abolished. In 1983, only two types of goods, that is, grain and cooking oil remained under unified, limited supply. In 1985, the national policy of unified purchase and marketing was softened. On New Year's Day of that year, the State Council issued Ten Policies to Further Activate Rural Economy, stipulating that "unified purchasing of grain and cotton is abolished and replaced with ' Ordering by Contract' ". From then on, unified purchasing was replaced with ordering, and unified marketing was gradually abolished. People now could negotiate a price when purchasing grain, and grain coupons were no longer required. Working staff of urban grain sections no longer had to distribute grain coupons to households every month. In some large cities like Beijing, grain coupon cards were issued by the Food Bureau. When grain was purchased, the amount of grain coupons needed would be deducted from the card presented by the purchaser. With the loosening of unified purchasing and marketing policy, state-run grain stores also started to sell grain with negotiated prices. Although grain purchase and supply in this period was yet to totally rely on market mechanism, it was definitely a breakthrough from the previous grain policy by which grain was under unified pricing of the central authority.

As more and more grain coupons were stored up by households, their usage was expanded. In cities, people began to use grain coupons to trade for other commodities. It was the same in rural areas, where people showed a strong will to exchange grain for other commodities as yields of crops went up increasingly. The segregation between urban and rural areas was constantly broken. With the deepening of the reform of the market economy system, it seemed that grain coupons, a product of the planned economy, were taking on different roles. Seeing that grain coupons were no longer necessary for the new era, the government began to conduct studies on whether the circulation of grain coupons should be stopped.

The Shenzhen Special Economic Zone was the first region to abolish the coupon system. By the 1980s, the circulation and application of grain coupons had exposed many problems, which fell into two general categories. First, the price difference between grain with fixed prices and that with negotiated prices affected regular market operation, thus bringing heavy burden to government supervision and regulation. Second, the fact that the validity of most grain coupons was confined to a certain area set up barriers for talent flow and peasant migration to cities. In November 1984, the Shenzhen Municipal Committee held a meeting to discuss the issue of abolishing grain ration and grain purchase by coupons. To secure stable transition from the old to new grain policy, the municipal committee and government decided on the following procedures at the meeting: a) to increase the grain reserves of the grain sectors of the city; b) to stop the circulation of grain coupons, increase grain prices and lift restriction on grain supply. If signs of panic purchase emerged after the above policies were enforced, the government would further increase grain prices, meanwhile take countermeasures to deal with the panic. As it turned out, when the policy was implemented, the pricing mechanism and supply-demand balancing mechanism of the market played their role, and the expected turmoil didn't occur at all.

Before long, Shenzhen's experience spread to the whole nation. With the continuation of reform and opening up policy and successive good harvests of crops in rural areas, grain ration was abolished all over the country. Not only grain coupons, but all the other commodity coupons also stepped down from the stage of history. On April 1, 1993, when Notice on Speeding up the Reform in Grain Circulation System was published by the State Council, grain and oil coupons were officially abolished, and restriction on supply of grain and oil products was lifted. In the past 40 years, those coupons played an important role in people's daily lives. Having fulfilled their historical mission, they retreated into coupon collectors' collection albums. From 1994, one could hardly see any grain coupons available nationwide.

Cloth coupons were required for the purchase of cloth and cloth products as a measure to secure planned cloth supply under which purchase and sales of cloth and cloth products were under unified regulation. Beyond their original function, cloth coupons had an impact on people's spiritual lives. Those who used to live with cloth coupons would remember those days when they had to wear clothes with patches. For a time, young students even took the number of patches on clothes as a standard to judge whether one was living a plain and simple life, a lifestyle which Chinese people have always admired and honored, while people who were born later in the 1980s and 1990s would have no idea what cloth coupons were. As a coupon necessary for the purchase of cloth or cloth products, cloth coupons served as a strategic measure to ensure the planned cloth supply. Originally, cloth coupons were issued in Jiangxi and Jiangsu provinces, the major areas of cotton production. Later, the operation spread to other provinces, autonomous regions and cities. If people needed to buy cloth or cloth products in another area, they had to go to a specified place to exchange their coupons for those circulated in that area.

On September 26, 1983, "Are Cloth Coupons Still Necessary?", an internal reference, was published in Beijing Daily. Supported by large amounts of first-hand information, the author suggested the abolition of cloth coupons. By visiting and interviewing textile producers and sales departments, he was exposed to the following facts. First, cotton cloth was unsalable. Second, polyester fabric sold well. Third, the demand for cloth coupons was shrinking. Fourth, nearly every household has spare cloth coupons. Based on information collected, the writer ended his piece by citing Xi Yu jun, an economist from the Comprehensive Division, Planning Department in the Ministry of Textile Industry, "Now, the textile products are capable of meeting the low-level consumption demand of the popular masses. We have production capacity and abundant raw materials. There is no shortage in cotton textiles. It is time to abolish cloth coupons. "

On November 23, 1983, on the front page of Beijing Daily, "Ministry of Commerce Announces Temporary Waiving of Cotton and Padded Cotton Coupons to Better Meet the Needs of the Masses" was published. According to the announcement, starting from December 1, 1983, no cotton or padded cotton coupons would be required for the purchase of cotton cloth and padded cotton; besides, no cloth or padded cotton coupons would be issued in 1984. China's coupon era finally came to an end.

Grain Coupons Issued in Yanyuan County

Cloth Coupons Issued in Hubei and Shaanxi provinces

Throughout Chinese history, a life with abundant food and clothing has always been people's dream, and inadequate food and clothing would cast a shadow on one's childhood, which otherwise might be carefree. China in the 1960s and 1970s was called by present historians "the childhood of the People's Republic of China", during which shortages of living goods and materials afflicted almost all industries, regions and households. It was quite hard for Chinese housewives of that time who were well tempered by more than 70 types of coupons, food and cloth coupons in particular. From another perspective, those days of suffering has left the nation a legacy: a precious spiritual wealth which will remain in the deepest of Chinese people's hearts.

Case 1. 2　Pearl River Delta: Front-line and Pilot Zone of Economy Reform

In 1978, a major decision was made at the 3rd Plenary Session of the 11th Central Committee of the Communist Party: China will implement the reform and opening up policy. On 15 July, 1979, the Central Committee of the Communist Party of China and the State Council permitted Guangdong and Fujian provinces to implement special and flexible policies in economic affairs involving foreign countries. They also approved the establishment of tentative special export zones in Shenzhen, Zhuhai, Shantou, and Xiamen. On August 13, the State Council issued Decision on Several Questions Concerning Greater Promotion of Foreign Trade and Increase in Foreign Currency Revenue in which it was stated that China would give more power to local governments and enterprises in terms of foreign trade engagement, make efforts to increase exports, and do well in special export zone. On May 16, 1980, The Central Committee and the State Council approved of Guangdong and Fujian provinces' Meeting Minutes and renamed "special export zone" as "special economic zone". The success of special economic zones, Shenzhen in particular, provided precious experiences for further expansion of opening up areas and vigorously propelled the course of China's reform and modernization. On April 13, 1988, a resolution was passed at the 7th Session of the National people's Congress to set up Hainan special economic zone, adding Hainan province to the list of special economic zones.

Pearl River Delta is the first special economic zone in China that has broken the division of administrative regions and run on the concept of economic zones. After 28 years of reform and opening up, Pearl River Delta has become the most active and promising area of Guangdong province in commodity economy, and even of the whole nation.

Pearl River Delta Economic Zone includes seven provincial cities (namely, Guangzhou, Shenzhen, Zhuhai, Dongguan, Zhongshan, Foshan, and Jiangmen), the downtown area and three counties (Huiyang, Huidong, and Boluo) of Huizhou City, and two districts (Duanzhou and Dinghu) and two counties (Sihui and Gaoyao) of Zhaoqing City, with a total area of 41, 600 square kilometers and a population of over 22. 62 million. Since the implementation of the reform and opening up policy, this economic zone has been regarded as a sample zone because of its extensive opening to the outside world and rapid growth in economy and household income.

The population of Pearl River Delta Economic Zone accounts for nearly

30% of the total population of Guangdong province. By contrast, in terms of major economic indicators, this zone's contribution to Guangdong province's economic development accounts for about 2 to 3 times as much as its percentage of population. It is not only the most powerful and developed area of the province, but also one of the best performing areas in the whole nation. With only 1. 82% of the nation's population, this region contributed 11. 09% of the nation's added value of the tertiary sector of the economy, 34. 01% of the nation's total foreign trade export, and 21. 13% of the nation's total foreign investment in actual use. There is no denying that Pearl River Delta is one of the few Chinese regions which enjoy the highest degree of opening to the outside world. It is reported that the GDP of this economic zone in 2005 was RMB 1. 81 trillion, an increase of RMB 273 billion from the previous year. Due to macroeconomic regulation, in 2005, the economic growth in this region slowed to 15. 8% , yet still higher than 10. 2% —the national average.

For quite a long time, the comprehensive economic strength of the Pearl River Delta Region has ranked very high among all the regions in Guangdong province, and even in the whole nation. With a development mode featuring "rapid realization of industrialization with export-oriented economy", Pearl River Delta has seen great growth. What's more, it has contributed to China a new mode of industrialization with Chinese characteristics applicable to coastal regions. Thanks to it, the industrial structure of the region was able to achieve sound and fast transformation from agriculture-oriented to the secondary and tertiary industry-focused, and thus made remarkable contributions to China's economic growth and enhancement of the country's overall strength.

With nearly 30 years' rapid development, now Pearl River Delta has become one of the largest manufacturing bases in China. Among all the sectors of the economy, hi-tech manufacturing industries are developing especially fast. Take the electronic information technology (IT) industry as an example, its output value accounts for nearly 96. 8% of Guangdong province's total. Both the output value of electronic and communication equipment manufacturing and that of electric machinery and equipment manufacturing rank first in the nation, accounting for 32. 1% and 25. 1% of the nation's total respectively. The output of IT products and household appliances each takes up more than 19% of the nation's total. A modernized IT enterprise group and major household appliance enterprise group are taking shape. Presently, Pearl River Delta has formed three distinctive divisions of industry specialization.

The first, is so-called "the corridor of Guangdong's electronic information industry"—the largest electronic communication manufacturing base in China, concentrated on the east shore of Pearl River Delta, including Dongguan, Shenzhen and Huizhou. Of the three cities, Huizhou is not only one of the most important color TV set manufacturing bases, with a number of color TV brands (TCL, for example) well known home and abroad, but also an international high-level electrical product base which boasts two-thirds of international market share, with such brands as Qisheng and International Electrical. Besides, it is also an important circuit board manufacturing base of Asia.

The second, is an industry belt centered in Zhuhai and Zhongshan on the west shore of Pearl River Delta, which specializes in the production of household durables and hardware products. For example, Zhongshan City is well known for its development mode of "one town, one product", the northern area of which specializes in small domestic appliances and hardware products, the middle area in apparel and furniture industry, the northwestern area in lighting processing, and the southern area in export-oriented processing.

The third, is the industry belt of electrical machinery, textile and building materials centered in the cities in the middle part of the region, including Guangzhou, Foshan and Zhaoqing. Once the host city of Peugeot cars and ethylene projects, Guangzhou City boasts a large number of well-known brands, such as Guangri Elevator, Foshan Lighting, and Rifeng Piping Systems, etc.

It is evident that Pearl River Delta is becoming a world-class manufacturing base of both traditional and modern hi-tech products.

However, over the course of its development, Pearl River Delta has had to face certain problems. Presently, one of the major problems facing this region is the harmful competition among cities of similar administrative status and economic strength. Local sectionalism and utilitarianism grows very rapidly in an environment where each city is busy pursuing its own development goals and ignoring others. As a result, the economic ties between different cities of the region may become more and more loose, which may possibly lead to the emerging of an isolated "small yet all-inclusive" economy system.

According to the general rule of economic development, a regional economic development strategy tends to put the priority on the construction of central cities whose development will in turn drive that of the surrounding areas. According to this strategy, Pearl River Delta should make efforts to exert the driving role of the central cities by establishing the leading status of Guangzhou and Shenzhen, and meanwhile further integrate all kinds of resources available in the region. Besides, it should exert the role of government as a micro guide and market regulator, and take better advantage of favorable policies and law of value to gradually realize resource sharing within the region, optimize resource allocation, and improve the overall competitiveness of the region as a whole.

What's more, the radiation effects of Pearl River Delta as a hi-tech industry center is not yet in full force. Each area is just like a silo, isolated from one another, which is to the disadvantage of industry upgrades. So, experts call for the region to develop its own core technology and products, improve the ability of independent innovation and strategic industry restructuring, develop independent intellectual property rights, establish superior supporting industry systems, and form competitive industry chain and clusters. Only by taking such measures can the competitiveness of Pearl River Delta in manufacturing be enhanced in a real sense.

To sum up, the economic and social development of Pearl River Delta Economic Zone has shown the following features.

First, its economy has seen sustainable and rapid growth thanks to the implementation of the reform and opening up policy. From 1980 to 1996, the region's GDP had achieved an average annual growth rate of 17.8%, not only higher than the provincial average (14.5%) and the national average (9.7%), but also higher than the average growth rate of the Four Asian Tigers in the takeoff stage of their economic development[1]. The GDP of the region shot up from USD 8 billion in 1980 to USD 766.99 billion in 2012.

Second, its economy is mainly export-oriented. Making full use of its regional advantage to tap into resources of Hong Kong, Macao and of overseas compatriots, guided by the international market, and based on the domestic market, Pearl River Delta has succeeded in driving its export-oriented economy to achieve great development. In 1994, the total export trade of the region was up to USD 38.46 billion, 76.6% of Guangdong province's total, and foreign investment in actual use was USD 8.80 billion, accounting for 68% and 24% of Guangdong province and the nation's total respectively.

Third, the industry structure has undergone constant optimization. The industry restructuring was conducted from the following three aspects. a) to join the global industrial chain, to achieve independent innovation and then to reach the high end of the global industrial chain. b) to strengthen regional cooperation with Hong Kong, Macao and others to promote the integration of modern service industry and manufacturing industry. c) to transform the economy from extensive to intensive, and develop industry clusters for cyclic economy. In the 21st century, Pearl River Delta has transformed itself from a traditional agricultural

---

1   Source: http://www.ttshopping.net/article/82/238/show/755068884226.html

economy to an advanced manufacturing center, and successfully developed an economic mode featuring optimized industry structure and the dominant role of the secondary and tertiary sectors of the economy. The proportion of the primary, secondary and tertiary sectors of the Pearl River Delta's economy in its GDP changed from 25. 8 : 45. 5 : 28. 9 in 1980 to 2. 1 : 49. 3 : 48. 6 in 2010. Generally speaking, the region has practically accomplished the transformation from traditional agriculture to industrialization and then to industrial diversification.

Fourth, balanced development of urban and rural areas is realized. Since the reform and opening up practice, with industry restructuring, the region has basically formed a sound pattern of agricultural industrialization. With urbanization accelerating, a management and production mode featuring marketization, socialization and intensification is taking shape, which will further promote the balanced and coordinated development of urban and rural areas. At the end of 1970s, there were no more than a few dozens in the region; by contrast, the number increased to 200 in the mid − 80s, and to 406 in 1992, 597 in 1994. Within 15 years, the number of towns in the region increased by nearly 10 times. In 1994, the non-agricultural population of the region accounted for 45. 2% of the region's total, 16% higher than that of the average in Guangdong province. By contrast, now there is a town every 65. 13 square meters. [1] In the process of urban-rural integration, Pearl River Delta has formed a very distinctive economic integration circle.

Fifth, the flow of such essential production factors as labor force is getting healthier. The Pearl River Delta Region is the largest gathering place of external workers in China. In the early 21st century, millions of external workers were employed in the region and they formed a very large, unique group. Under the market economy system, the free flow of labor force enabled this region to realize optimal allocation of human resources, thus offering strong technical support for the sound development of its economy.

Case 1. 3   Lenovo: Pioneer of China's State-Owned Enterprise Reform

Lenovo Group Ltd. is a multinational innovative technology company made up of the original Lenovo business and PC business of IBM. In 2012, Lenovo ranked 370 on the Fortune Global 500 list. As a leading brand in the global

---

1   Source: http://news. iqilu. com/shandong/hsj/news/2010/0319/203676. shtml

personal computer market, Lenovo develops, manufactures, and sells technical products which are reliable, safe and easy to use as well as professional quality services, helping its global clients and partners achieve success. The major Lenovo products include desktops, servers, laptops, printers, palmtops, main-boards, cellular phones, etc. Since 1996, Lenovo has ranked first place in computer sales to the domestic market. In recent years, it has seen even more rapid development. Since 2011, it has ranked number 2 in computer sales on the global market. In January 2011, Lenovo formed a joint venture with NEC, Japan's number 1 PC company, reflecting its great aspiration of re-shaping the notebook computer industry.

Having grown out of the New Technology Development Company of the Institute of Computing Technology, Chinese Academy of Science, Lenovo was originally an enterprise under the ownership of the whole population. In 1984, with the deepening of the reform in scientific and technical systems, private scientific and technological enterprises emerged one after another in China. It was then that the Chinese Academy of Science initiated the operation mechanism of "one academy, two systems". The New Technology Development Company was founded in November 1984, when Zeng Mao-chao, then the head of Institute of Computing Technology, called a meeting and put forward the reform plan in front of all the important professionals of the institute featuring "attack with two fists". One of the "fists" was to delegate a few scientific and technical personnel to form a team which was to operate on a presidential responsibility system with autonomy in operation, personnel and financing. The team would get a loan of RMB 200,000 from the institute as initial capital. Among the team members was Liu Chuan-zhi, the paramount leader of Lenovo. Zeng Mao-chao expected that the team would act as a pioneer and break a new path for scientific and technical development of the institute.

So, the New Technology Development Company attached to the Institute of Computing Technology of Chinese Academy of Sciences, was founded, with an aim to develop, produce and sell high-tech computer products. In the beginning, the company had nothing but a loan of RMB 200,000, 2 rooms and 11 professional staff. But at any rate, its founding marked the start of a new company operating on the principle of "self-financing, free combination, independent management and responsibility". Fortunately, the hard work of the staff paid off. The company's sales of computer parts and computer sets reached RMB 3 million in 1985, RMB 18 million in 1986, RMB 73 million in 1987, RMB 134 million in 1988, RMB 220 million in 1989, RMB 600 million in 1990, and RMB 1 billion in 1991. Of the total sales, that of computer products Lenovo developed independently accounted for 50%, and adding that of products Lenovo redeveloped and co-developed, it accounted for 95% of the total sales. From 1985 to 1991, the profit and tax generated by Lenovo had reached RMB 83 million, of which 10.66 million was turned over to the Institute of Computing Technology.

For Lenovo, the practice of presidential responsibility was epoch-making. As a state-owned enterprise by nature, most of Lenovo's profits belonged to the state, yet its operation mechanism was based on the above autonomous principles which reflected clearly-determined rights and responsibilities. The company enjoyed large freedom in operation and its staff were "quasi-owners" of the company. This was a very innovative act and a practice ahead of its time, proof of the open-mindedness of the Chinese Academy of Sciences. The advanced enterprise system enabled the pioneers of Lenovo to play their talents to the fullest so that they could successfully lead the company to a higher and higher level. Under their leadership, Lenovo competed freely with other enterprises as an equal entity on the market and achieved constant development.

Everything has two sides. On one hand, Lenovo was blessed with excellent opportunities; on the other hand, Lenovo's development was unable to get rid of the limitations of the times. As the reform of state-owned enterprises in China was still under way and far from complete, it was inevitable that certain problems would arise in the process of Lenovo's development. As one important segment in the process of establishing the market economy system, the state-owned enterprise reform showed its own defects. Especially in the early stage, operation mechanism reform was not radical enough, which caused two major problems. First, the lack of effective incentive mechanisms failed to motivate enterprise leaders and employees who were supposed to provide a key momentum for enterprise re-invigoration. Second, to pursue their own benefits, enterprise leaders with power in hand made a large number of operation decisions focusing only on short-term profits.

Though confined to the limited system, Lenovo still saw rapid development. The first generation of its leaders, a group of outstanding engineers and entrepreneurs headed by Liu Chuan-zhi, should take much of the credit. They prepared the company's development plan, set up a rigorous self-discipline mechanism as well as standardized management, and injected integrity into the company culture. Their work paved the way for the smooth transformation of the company into a joint stock enterprise where multiple economic elements coexisted. Since the very beginning, Lenovo had determined to abolish the dominating "Big Pot System" (getting an equal share of things regardless of the work done) and implement a presidential responsibility system: As the legal representative of the enterprise, the president was accountable for possible problems. Meanwhile, Lenovo took concrete measures to conduct necessary supervision and restriction on the staff. As stipulated, the profit was distributed among different sectors by the ratio of 5: 3: 2, that is, 50% of the profit would be delivered to the state; 30% put into an enterprise welfare fund, and 20% distributed among the staff as bonus. When the bonus was distributed, as staff at the highest level, the president and vice president enjoyed the best offer but had no right to use the surplus value. The president was under the constraint of the Board of Directors. Leaders at different levels were all subjected to employment and job responsibility systems. Payment was not fixed for them. If they performed well, they would get timely award, while if they performed poorly or broke rules, they could be fired at any time. Under this system, everybody in the enterprise had a strong sense of urgency and crisis. As the staff said, "Lenovo was like a big ship on whose mast was hanging a war flag under which people who were willing to fight for the common cause gather, standing together through storm and stress, and sharing weal and woe".

From 1984 to 1988, Lenovo developed 153 pieces of computer software and hardware, of which 26 pieces achieved fairly large economic benefits. The most outstanding software of all was the hit product—Legend Chinese Character Input System, which produced huge economic and social benefits with total sales amounting to 15, 000 sets and a production value RMB 45 million (excluding its byproducts). This system won a number of awards, including the First Prize of Beijing Chinese Character System Competition, Application Support Award granted by Electric Vibrator Office of the State Council, the First Prize in Technological Advance awarded by Chinese Academy of Sciences, and the First Prize of State Technological Advance Award. Lenovo is the first enterprise in Zhongguancun Science Park that has won the highest state award with its high-tech product.

From 1988 to 1994, Lenovo witnessed a stage of high-speed development. In April 1988, Beijing Legend Company, China Technology Transfer Company and Hong Kong Daoyuan Company co-founded Hong Kong Legend Ltd, whose revenue reached USD 11. 74 million in the first 9 months after its founding, its net profit three times as much as the total investment of the three founders.

The creation of Hong Kong Legend Ltd. was only the first step taken by Lenovo under its overseas expansion strategy. It helped Lenovo successfully expand its business onto the overseas market and accumulate large amounts of capital. The second step was to set up a multi-national corporation embracing a R & D Center, production base and a global sales network. The third step was to realize economy of scale. In May 1988, Lenovo released its first job advertisement seeking employees among the public. The ad was placed on the front page of the China Youth News. A group of young and promising graduates and postgraduates answered the call and brought their vitality to Lenovo. They grew together with Lenovo and later became its backbone force. Yang Yuan-qing and Guo Wei were among this group.

In the early 1990s, China's computer market entered a stage of rapid development. The market demand for computers was breaking one million. To meet market needs and make profit from it, one after another domestic computer manufacturers began to assemble all kinds of microcomputers; meanwhile foreign manufacturers also realized the great potential in China. To get a market share, they spared no effort to promote computers of various brands to China. Facing the new opportunities, having conducted a thorough analysis of the market trend and Lenovo's capability in technology, talents and capital, and taken into consideration government's protective policy for domestic computer industry, Lenovo's entrepreneurs brought forth the vision of creating and developing Lenovo's self-owned computer brand for the domestic market. It was then that Lenovo officially started its competition with other world-famous computer manufacturers in the Chinese market.

In 1990, Lenovo Group, engaged in an overseas-domestic complementary operation, brought to market Legend 286—its own brand of computer. Since then, Lenovo has closely followed market changes and the development tendency of computer technology, and kept on improving and developing its own products. In 1991, half a year after Intel launched 486 chip, Lenovo successfully produced the first 486 computer in China. In 1993, three months after the Pentium chip was invented, Lenovo produced the first Chinese Pentium computer (586). On November 2, 1995, the first Pentium computer (686) based on Pentium Processor was launched in the United States by Intel, and just one day later Lenovo released the same type of product. This was strong proof that Lenovo Group had nearly, if not actually, possessed world-class computer technology.

The reform of China's state-owned enterprises was evolutionary, starting with the reform of operation mechanisms followed by system reform in other aspects. With the perfection of the market economy system, people became more concerned about the income distribution system as it was closely related to their own interests. Thus, it had become an important issue for Lenovo Group to reconcile the contradiction between the interests of the enterprise and those of individual employees. In 1994, an agreement between the Chinese Academy of

Sciences and Lenovo management was reached outlining that Lenovo's Shareholding Employee Committee had the right to divide 35% of enterprise dividend. Up to that point, Lenovo's entrepreneurs had basically realized the consistency of responsibility, power and benefits. The idea of redistributing 35% of enterprise dividend was not at all a new invention, but in the Chinese business environment of that time, it indeed was a pioneering initiative and a breakthrough from traditional distribution patterns, as it effectively aligned individual interests with enterprise development. This new distribution mode formed a sound incentive mechanism and thus was effective in securing the long-term stable growth of the enterprise. In brief, the reform in distribution system was significant to Lenovo's operation and development in two aspects. First, as it clearly reflected the different contributions of entrepreneurs, management and other employees, it helped to optimize the human resources structure. Retired staff or the newly employed, everybody's interests heavily relied on the development of the enterprise. As a result, the elderly leaders would be more than willing to promote and support promising younger employees to leadership. Once granted dividend rights, young staff would work harder and be more courageous to make innovations. Second, for a high-tech enterprise like Lenovo, the reform in the distribution system contributed to innovation and perfection of its enterprise system. As a major shareholder of Lenovo, the Chinese Academy of Sciences had given full support to its reform, promoting Lenovo to develop a system of "operating independently, assuming sole responsibility for its profits and losses, and seeking self-development and self-discipline. "

In March 2000, Lenovo's reform proposal about a property rights incentive system was approved by both the Ministry of Finance and the Ministry of Science and Technology. According to the proposal, Lenovo would change from a holding company to one of limited liability, and the 35% of dividend rights was to be converted to share ownership. Lenovo walked the first step toward a joint-stock enterprise. The Chinese Academy of Sciences and the Shareholding Employee Committee of Lenovo Group Holding Co. Ltd became the two major shareholders. The latter bought 35% of Lenovo's shares with the 35% dividends. Since then, Lenovo has become a company of limited liability, with systems in property rights, operation and financing all improved. This was an important milestone in Lenovo Group's development. The reform in the property rights system fit into the development trend of a modern enterprise system and the new system met the needs of high-tech enterprises, especially the needs of listed companies. In terms of distribution pattern, Lenovo offered stock options to its staff, making it possible for the latter to share the results of enterprise growth, thus motivating them to work hard and identify with the enterprise. This system complied with Lenovo's company culture and values—integrating individual pursuit into the long-term development goals of the company.

On September 8, 2009, China Ocean-wide Holding Group became the third major shareholder of Lenovo Holding Ltd. , having acquired 29% Lenovo's shares, which marked another significant step taken in the reform of Lenovo's property rights system. Having developed more than ten years in business and having experienced three major property rights reforms, Lenovo established a modern enterprise system featuring clearly defined property rights, duties and responsibilities, separation of government administration from enterprise management, and scientific management. Imagine when it was firstly founded, Lenovo had no more than RMB 200,000, and now it has developed into a large-scale enterprise group with up to RMB 8 billion in assets and annual sales revenue of RMB 20 billion. We can largely attribute its rapid development to the success of the property rights system reform. Lenovo's success could provide very important and valuable references to most of the Chinese state-owned enterprises under reform as well as other struggling high-tech and private enterprises to gain a foot in the tide of market economy.

In April 2003, Lenovo Group, in Beijing, officially announced its new global logo "Lenovo", which would replace the original logo "Legend". Lenovo became the first Chinese company to set up a global partnership with the International Olympic Committee. In May 2005, Lenovo completed the acquisition of IBM's personal computer division, marking a new stage of Lenovo's development.

Presently, Lenovo Group has two headquarters, one in Beijing, and the other in New York, with the two operation centers located in Beijing, China and Raleigh, North Carolina, USA. The new Lenovo's sales network covers the whole world through its own sales agencies, partners and coalition with IBM, and with 27,000 employees scattered in different parts of the world. Its R & D centers are stationed in China's Beijing, Shenzhen, Xiamen, Chengdu and Shanghai, Japan's Tokyo, and Raleigh, North Carolina, USA. With PC manufacturing bases in China's Beijing, Shanghai, Chengdu, Huiyang and Shenzhen, India's Pondicherry and Mexico's Monterrey, Lenovo has adopted global contract manufacturing and original equipment manufacturing (OEM) modes.

In 2008, for the first time Lenovo entered Fortune magazine's Top 500 list, and ranked 499 of all the top 500 enterprises. In 2012 for the second time, Lenovo entered the list, ranking 370, with a total annual revenue of USD 29.57 billion and a profit of USD 0.47 billion.

Questions for discussion:

1. Why did China decide to take on the road of industrialization of heavy industry in the 1950s?

2. Why did China implement a planned economy system?

3. Why did China transform the planned economy to a market economy?

4. How do you comment on China's economic system reform?

5. What impact has the development of China's market economy had on other countries?

Ever since the reform and opening up, China's economy has kept a rapid growth for over 30 years in succession, which is a shocking event to the world. What effective polices and measures have been taken by the Chinese government that have made a backward semi-colonial and semi-feudal country the world's factory? What on earth is the magic weapon that enables China to walk out of the bottleneck in the early years of its economic development, to promote the modernization of its agriculture, manufacturing and service industries, and to make progress in both production efficiency and economic growth? What useful experience and lessons can China offer to other developing countries? These questions are possibly the most significant to research into the development of China's industrial economy.

Chapter 2

The Development of China's Industrial Economy

2. 1　Agriculture: The Food Problem for 1. 4 Billion People

2. 1. 1　China's Reform Initiated by Food Shortage in Rural Areas

As the largest developing country with a population of 1. 4 billion, how to meet the needs of the people's daily essentials has always been a thorny problem besetting the Chinese government. A crucial solution to this problem is to develop agriculture, to stimulate initiatives of the rural people and to promote their production efficiency. This policy has been firmly implemented ever since the founding of PRC, especially since the reform and opening up that started 30 years ago.

With farmlands allocated to the peasants (the land reform in rural areas) in the early days of New China, the Chinese peasants got the lands that had been unavailable to them during the previous 2000 years of feudal society. For the first time, there was no need for them to give their harvest to the landlords without any compensation, and, as a result, their initiative in labor was greatly inspired. This was not only helpful to the recovery and development of China's economy, but also an important accumulation of experience for the development of industry thereafter.

In the 1950s, the Chinese government launched a land collectivization campaign with an idea of "running into communism", turning from the home ownership of farmland pursued in the land reform into a collective ownership so that a unified management was achieved. And during the movements of "Great Leap Forward" and "People's Commune" from 1958 to 1960, the agricultural production cooperatives were organized further into the people's communes, with all the rural lands owned by a new collective — the people's commune. The peasants worked together on the collectively-owned lands and shared the values they created with their labor. As this land reform was based on a traditional idea of egalitarianism, it totally deprived the peasants of their rights to own, manage and use the land for profits. The system of "distribution according to need" was carried out blindly without an overwhelming abundance of material wealth. As a result, it turned out to be a "raising sluggard" system, which, in turn, led to a sharp drop in China's agricultural production efficiency. By the end of the 1970s, the problem of feeding the family, or the problem of survival, had become an urgent one to be solved for the peasants in many of China's rural areas.

Just with the intention of improving production efficiency, numerous Chinese peasants began to consider a new operation mechanism. This contributed to a great bottom-up reform — the Household Contract System of Responsibility Linking Remuneration to Output (simplified as Household Responsibility System). In 1978, 18 households in Xiaogang Village of Fengyang County, Anhui province, discussed and signed a simple guarantee bond of no more than 100 Chinese characters. They decided to secretly distribute the collectively-owned land to individual households so that they could enjoy the rights of both ownership and management. The labor initiatives of the peasants were stimulated once again. They had a good harvest in the same year, with an output four-to-five times that of previous years. Such an act seemed to have violated the government policy of that time, but it turned out to be a great success and started to be well known by the public.

In 1980, Deng Xiao-ping, one of the top Chinese leaders then, made a public and positive assessment of the reform in Xiaogang Village. This meant that the spontaneous reform of these peasants began to be accepted by the government, and a nationwide promotion of their experience was underway. *The Minutes of the National Rural Work Conference*, transmitted by the Party Central Committee, explicitly put the measures of contracting with each household for production quotas initiated by Xiaogang Village under the Household Responsibility System in China's socialist collective economy. In 1983, the Party Central Committee made it clear that the Household Responsibility System was a great pioneering undertaking of the Chinese peasants under the leadership of the Party Central Committee and a new development of Marxist agricultural cooperation in China. The revision of the *Constitution of the People's Republic of China* in 1982 and *The PRC Law on Land Management* passed in 1986 institutionally specified the division of land ownership and declared that Household Responsibility System merely separates land ownership from the right of land management. It didn't change the nature of collective ownership of China's rural lands. In this way, the legitimacy of the Household Responsibility System was defined by law to grant the Chinese peasants the right to manage the land and to share in the profits, so that the peasants' initiative in labor was stimulated.

In 1991, the 8th Plenary Session of the 13th Party Central Committee passed *The Decision of the Central Committee of CPC on Further Strengthening Agriculture and Rural Work*. The Decision put forward the idea that the Responsibility System, chiefly the Household Responsibility System, and the structure of unified and decentralized management should be made a basic system for a long period of time and should be constantly enriched and improved.

The Household Responsibility System, which originated from an attempt of the Chinese peasants to solve their food problem, opened the door to reform in China. From the popularization of the Household Responsibility System in the rural areas to the reform of state-owned enterprises, in which the authority of ownership and management was separated in the same way, the curtain of a vigorous reform went up. This was also an important factor for the revival and take-off of China's economy.

Who would have thought of such a thing, that some poor Chinese peasants would have awakened China — the Orient Lion as Napoleon called it. The resigned choice became the prelude to a grand reform of China's economic system, which is a true portraiture of the butterfly effect in the eyes of many foreign friends who know about China's economy.

2. 1. 2   Modernized Chinese Agriculture

As a traditional agricultural country, China's 5,000 years of traditional civilization was created by the development of agriculture and agricultural technology. The invention of stone axes and stone spades improved the efficiency of land cultivation, propelled the collaboration inside clans, enabled the ancient Chinese to live in groups, and thus contributed to the formation of different states as well as Chinese civilization. The cattle plough invented during the Spring and Autumn period, the animal-drawn seed plough in the Han Dynasty, and the curved-shaft plough in the Tang Dynasty became a symbol of innovation in cultivation methods and production tools in ancient China. So it was the advances in agricultural technology that promoted the development of grain production in China and gave birth to traditional Chinese civilization.

In the early days of New China, agricultural production was in an extremely weak position due to the prolonged wars and the squeeze of imported grains. It was the land reform of the government that stimulated the peasants' initiative of labor, which enabled China's agricultural production to recover and develop within a very short period of time. By the mid −1950s, China was basically self-sufficient in agriculture.

Chinese leaders showed great concern over agricultural technology and development. As early as 1958, Mao Ze-dong drew up eight measures to improve agricultural production on the basis of people's practical experience and scientific research. This was the famous *Eight-Character Charter for Agriculture,* the main contents of which were: soil (deep ploughing, soil improvement, a general survey of soil and land planning), fertilizers (rational application of fertilizers), water (water conservancy development and reasonable use of water), seed (popularizing improved seed strains), close planting (rational close planting), protection (plant protection, prevention and control of plant diseases and elimination of pests), management (field management) and implements of production (improvement of farm tools). This *Eight-Character Charter* was included in the *Decision On the Plan for the National Economy in 1959* formulated by the 6th Plenary Session of the 8th Party Central Committee. It was the guiding ideology for the scientific development of China's agriculture for a very long period of time.

After the reform and opening up, the household responsibility system profoundly stimulated the labor initiative of the rural people and improved China's agricultural output. And at the same time, the Chinese Government, under the guidance of the slogan "science and technology is the primary productive force", began to promote the innovation and diffusion of agricultural science and technology in rural areas, which improved the contribution of science and technology to the development of agriculture.

Since the 1980s, rural technology service stations were universally set up in China's rural areas, with specially-trained personnel to impart knowledge of agricultural science and technology to the rural people, to provide them with such agricultural materials like seeds and fertilizers, and to instruct them in the techniques of scientific breeding, crop grafting and greenhouses planting. This shows that China has shifted from traditional agricultural production to technical agriculture.

The development of hybrid rice is an epitome of China's agricultural science and technology. In the Chinese diet, rice is much more important than wheat. However, at the traditional level of agricultural technology, the cultivation of rice was easily affected by soil, climate and plant diseases and insect pests. With an annual yield of about 300kg per mu, it was difficult to satisfy the food demands of the whole nation, which led to periodic famine when major natural disasters occurred. As early as the 1960s, Yuan Long-ping, a Chinese agricultural scientist, began his research on his Super Rice in the hope of improving rice production and its disease-pest resistant ability. In 1973, he successfully cultivated the long-grained non-glutinous hybrid rice "Three Lines" after a long period of cultivation, with the average yield increasing by over 20%. In the winter of 1975, the State Council made a decision on the rapid expansion of trial planting and vigorous promotion of hybrid rice. Plenty of manpower, material and financial resources were invested to propagate seeds for three generations a year and to spread them at the fastest speed. The next year, the designated demonstration area reached 2.08 million mu and the new rice began to be put into production all over the country. By 1998, the acreage under hybrid rice was 194 million mu, accounting for 39.6% of the country's total rice area.

Yuan Longping and His Hybrid Rice

Later in 1995, Yuan Long-ping cultivated bilinear hybrid rice with PTGMS rice as the basic material. In 2000, he developed and promoted his super hybrid rice. And by 2003, more than half of the sown area of rice in mainland China was Yuan's hybrid rice, with 20% of the rice in the world produced using Yuan's hybridization technique. In 2007, rice yield in mainland China was 500 million tons, with its hybrid rice grown on a trial basis in Central Asia, Southeast Asia, North America and South America, and its rice hybridization technique widely applied the world over. On September 19, 2011, an inspection and approval team from the Chinese Ministry of Agriculture announced that the yield of the 100 mu experimental super-hybrid rice (Y dual superiority No. 2) field averaged 926.6 kg per mu, creating a peak record of rice yield over a large area. And Yuan Long-ping, as "Father of Hybrid Rice in China", has been written into the annals of history and has become an iconic figure of agricultural science and technology.

In 1989, Jiang Ze-min put forward a slogan that "promoting scientific and technological progress is the historic mission of both the Party and the people", stressing that we should vigorously develop agriculture by relying on the progress of science and technology. All regions in the country should firmly grasp the link of sci-tech progress, and strive to raise agricultural productivity, to increase output per unit area and to make effective use of the resources on the basis of their respective levels of economic and cultural development, their natural conditions and farming characteristics. On the one hand, we should energize the popularization and application of advanced applicable technology so as to have returns of scale as soon as possible. On the other hand, we should give priority to the research and development of key sci-tech projects and guarantee the staying power of agricultural and rural economic development. The focus of agricultural technology should be shifted to the introduction, demonstration and popularization of advanced applicable technology, with multiform service organizations established and strengthened, and with rural scientific and technical teams further stabilized and expanded. We should explore new sources of funds and increase our input in science and technology, in order to push rural production forward towards moderately large-scale management, specialization and socialization and to guide the rural people onto a path of achieving common prosperity through science and technology.

In 1996, Jiang Ze-min further put forward a slogan of "undertaking a new revolution in agricultural science and technology". In response to the call of the state leader, the Chinese Government promulgated *A Program for the Development of Agricultural Science and Technology (2001 – 2010)*, which clearly proposed that we should promote a new agricultural sci-tech revolution and achieve the great leap from traditional agriculture to modern agriculture. And on the basis of the general trend of the industrialization of agriculture, the urbanization of rural areas and the knowledge of rural people, it introduced four shifts in agricultural science and technology. Firstly, we should shift from mainly seeking quantity to seeking quality and beneficial results. Secondly, we should shift from service for agricultural production to service for the harmonious development of production, processing and ecology. Thirdly, we should shift from giving first place to resources techniques exploitation to the combination of resources exploitation and market development. And fourthly, we should shift from being domestic-market oriented to being domestic-and international-market oriented.

Since the beginning of the new century, the Chinese government has shown consistent concern over agricultural science and technology. Problems related to agriculture and rural areas have been occupying the leading position for a long time in the programmatic and guiding No. 1 Document that determines the work of the state at the beginning of each year. From 2004 to 2012, the topic of the No. 1 Document had been "rural areas, rural people and agriculture" for nine years in succession. On January 1, 2012, the Chinese government published a No. 1 Document titled *Opinions on Accelerating Agricultural Technological Innovation and Continuously Improving the Ability to Ensure Adequate Supply of Agricultural Products*. The document is divided into 6 parts and 23 items, including: to increase the momentum of input and work so as to continuously promote the steady development of agriculture; to guide the construction of modern agriculture relying on technological innovations; to improve the ability to promote agricultural technology and greatly develop socialized service in agriculture; to strengthen educational training in science and technology and to cultivate a new talent team in agriculture; to improve on facilities and equipment and constantly consolidate the material foundation of agricultural development; to raise the efficiency of market circulation so as to ensure a stable and balanced supply of agricultural products. The document pointed out clearly the direction for the future development of agricultural science and technology.

Benefited from the progress in agricultural science and technology, China has broken away from the traditional mode of agriculture that depends on physical labor and animal power and has turned to one depending on the development of agricultural science and technology. And it has gradually realized agricultural modernization and technicalization by way of developing biological agriculture, three-dimensional agriculture and ecological agriculture. In this way, China feeds one fourth of the world population with merely 9% of the world's cultivated land. The advance of science and technology has become a fundamental guarantee to China's agricultural development.

2. 1. 3　The Problem of the Rural People Is the Problem of China

For a country with a population of 1. 4 billion, the solution to the survival and development of the 800 million rural people, who account for the vast majority of the Chinese population, means the basic solution to the same problem for all Chinese people. In a sense, the key to the problem of China is the problem of the rural people.

In the long-term agricultural society, the peasants were usually tied to the land on which they worked, engaged simply in crop production and processing. It is this binding relationship between the peasants and the land that has limited the field of vision of the vast numbers of peasants and has restricted their development space. After the founding of PRC, the policy of allocating croplands to peasants had indeed satisfied their desire for land and stimulated their initiative in labor. However, this policy inevitably brought about a closer connection between the peasants and the land they owned.

The household-responsibility system has established a new relationship between the peasants and the land. The state or the collective owns the land, while the peasants have gotten the right to independently manage the production on the land and to own the earnings of the production. Moreover, the development of a socialist market economy, especially the liberalization of land circulation and transaction, has broken the adhering relationship between the peasants and the land, thus a new peasant form has come into being.

In the early days of PRC, due to the limited land resources and the large population, agricultural production was usually undertaken through traditionally simple agricultural movement. Large-scale agricultural production with farm machinery and western mode of agricultural management could never be realized in China. During the people's commune movement in the 1960s, the Chinese government simply nationalized the land that had been distributed to the peasants and arranged, by way of administrative order, for the peasants to work on collective land and to use collective farm machinery and big livestock. As it didn't clearly define the right for the peasants to make profits from their own labor, this measure became an unrealizable equalitarianism, which was doomed to failure.

Under the household-responsibility system, the peasants regained the rights to use the land for profits, which also enabled some well-off peasants to obtain the rights to use more land for profits by way of land transaction or land leasing. Therefore, both the return of economy of scale and the utilization rate of farm machinery in agricultural production were promoted. In some areas with rich land resources, like Northeast China and Xinjiang Uygur Autonomous Region, large tractors and combine harvesters were popularized in agricultural production long ago.

However, while promoting the mechanization and modernization in agriculture, the liberalization of land transaction brought about a new group of people in the rural areas — peasants who lost their land. In a traditional sense, the concept of peasants is closely related to land and agricultural production. However, if the peasants who were long engaged in agricultural production choose to sell their land, as was needed for rural development and agricultural production, it will lead to them becoming landless or their family's per capita share of cultivated land reduced to less than 0.3 mu. This means they can no longer raise their family by means of agricultural production. So they have to seek new ways of living, being forced to become industrial workers needed for China's industrialization.

Together with the progress of China's industrialization, migrant workers have become a group that cannot be ignored in East China where the economy is relatively developed. The so-called migrant workers are the peasants who are no longer needed in the course of agricultural modernization. As modern agricultural production no longer needs enormous laborers, more and more peasants are emancipated from the land. They choose to be engaged in manufacturing and processing work where the processing industry is relatively developed, either for higher income or because they have lost the land on which they relied for existence.

However, in modern China or in Euro-American countries at their initial stages of economic development, the quality of the peasants, due to the limitations of their own modes of production, is generally lower than ordinary citizens. This not only restricts the production efficiency of agriculture, but also greatly restrains the peasants from changing to other industries. In the course of China's industrialization, peasants, as a major labor resource, could only take on some simple processing work instead of professional or technical work as a result of their lower educational, technical and cultural levels. Inevitably, the status of peasants have become a weak point of China's labor forces, which, in turn, has compelled the Chinese government to make more effort to promote the quality of the peasants.

Back in the early days of the PRC, our government passed *An Instruction for the Sparetime Education of the Peasants*, and carried out peasant's educational work in rural areas, aiming mainly at wiping out illiteracy. In September 1979, *A Resolution on Problems in Accelerating the Development of Agriculture* was issued to improve the scientific and cultural quality of the peasants, especially the young. In

1982, the Ministry of Education issued *An Interim Measure of Running Peasants Technical Schools at County Level*, which explicitly defined the management methods of agricultural training schools to foster basic-level cadres and agricultural technicians for rural areas. On the basis of these measures, China made great achievements in peasants' education. By 2008, China had 3 colleges for the peasants, with 1, 000 undergraduate students; 221 specialized secondary schools for the peasants, with 92, 056 students; 379, 000 peasant technical training schools, with 57. 526 million students; 2, 304 peasant middle schools, with 365, 000 students; and 105, 000 peasant primary schools, with 4. 597 million students. These schools have made important contributions to the promotion of the quality of the rural people.

In any country, agriculture is a crucial sector that decides its economic security. For China, a country with a population of 1. 4 billion, to be self-sufficient in agricultural production is also an indispensable assurance for a long-term and steady economic development. So, many measures have been taken by the Chinese government to increase the income of the rural people and to relieve their burdens.

In 1996, the Chinese government issued a document named *A Decision of the Central Committee of CPC and the State Council to Really Relieve the Burdens on the Rural people*, which pointed out that "the heavy burdens on the rural people have become a prominent problem affecting rural reform, development and stability". The decision also put forward 13 specific measures to relieve the heavy burdens of the rural people, among which were: a) the policy of agricultural tax will be kept stable and unchanged; b) the policy will be kept stable and unchanged that fees deducted from the total income at the village level and fees planned as a whole at the township level are no more than 5% of the peasants' net income per capita in the previous year; c) the system will be kept stable and unchanged that the rural people should take part in unpaid labor and accumulated labor; d) forbidding any activities for reaching a set standard with money or materials or labor paid by the peasants; e) forbidding any form of funding-raising activities in rural areas that are beyond legal rules; f) forbidding any arbitrarily collected fees or unreasonable price increases and unjust fines.

In 1998, *Notice about Earnestly Reducing the Burdens on the Rural People* introduced 9 regulations: a) strictly controlling the fees deducted or planned as a whole; b) resolutely putting an end to the arbitrarily collected fees, indiscriminate collection of funds, unjust fines as well as all kinds of apportions; c) strictly strengthening the management of the unpaid labor done by the peasants; d) strictly executing the national agricultural tax policy; e) forbidding the act of deducting taxes when purchasing the peasants' grains; f) prohibiting the act of compelling the peasants to loan in order to pay taxes; g) earnestly reducing unproductive expenditures at the township or village levels; h) strictly investigating and prosecuting any actions to increase the peasants' burdens in violation of the law and discipline; i) further strengthening the leadership of the work to reduce the burdens of the rural people.

In 2001, *Notice on Reducing the Burdens on Rural People* was issued by the General Office of the State Council. In 2006, *An Opinion on the Present Work on Reducing the Rural People's Burden* was published. And, in 2012, *An Opinion on Further Reducing the Rural People's Burden was* published by General Office of the State Council. All these documents manifested that the Chinese government pays close attention to reducing rural people's burdens. In 2011, the percentage of the per capita fees directly paid by the rural residents in their per capita net income was 43 percent lower compared with that of 2005. With the beneficial-to-peasant policies continuously strengthened, the rural people got more and more items, and larger and larger sums, of subsidies in agricultural production, compulsory education, health care and social security. Thus, a new pattern was gradually formed: "the rural people grow crops with subsidies; their children go to school without tuition; their medical expenses can be reimbursed; hardship grants are given to the poor; and pension is given to the old".

On Dec, 29, 2005 *A Decision of the NPC Standing Committee to Abolish 'The Agricultural Tax Regulations of the People's Republic of China'* was passed at the 19th Session of the Standing Committee of the 10th NPC. The decisions declared that from January 1, 2006 agricultural tax would be eliminated in China, marking that the agriculture tax, which had been imposed for more than 2000 years, had now become history.

It is with the policy support of the Chinese government that the burdens of the rural people have been continuously reduced and their lives greatly improved. Now they have ridded themselves of the tragic fate of being oppressed and exploited and gotten on to a road of material wealth.

2. 1. 4   To Modernize New Rural Area

In the development of China's modern economy, the binary urban-rural development is a relatively prominent issue. Although, compared with the situation before 1949, there has been a great improvement in rural infrastructure. However, increase in the income of the rural people still lags behind the process of China's urbanization and the income growth of other citizens. Moreover, regional disparity and inequalities of income distribution have been enlarged, and Gini coefficient has gone up. So, to reduce the disparity of regional development and the inequality of income distribution has become an urgent problem faced by the Chinese government.

During the take-off of China's economy, what attracts the most attention is the springing up of metropolises like Beijing and Shanghai. With the economic prosperity of these cities, their space expands continuously to surrounding areas. Take Beijing as an example. When people talked about Beijing at the beginning of the reform, they just meant the area within the three ring-roads. Nevertheless, it is unbelievable that the expansion of the city is just like ripples created by a pebble thrown into the water, spreading out ring by ring. Now, the fifth and sixth rings, as well as the seventh ring that had been planned as early as 1993, have enlarged Beijing's area nearly ten times. As a result, many of the suburban areas are now incorporated into the urban districts.

For the rural people living in zones joining the town and the country, the expropriation of their lands is inevitable. In accordance with the collective land ownership system, the lands are owned by the state, while the rural people only have the right to use the land for profit. This provides a system guarantee for the government to expropriate their land. Therefore, in many places the lands of the rural people were taken over by the government at prices lower than those on the market, making forced expropriations by abusing its right of ownership and coercive force. Very often, these may result in disputes concerning land expropriation and resettlement.

With their lands being expropriated, the rural people will have no lands on which they labor. As there is not a sound social security system, it is easy for them to fall into a difficult situation. To make a living, they have to leave home for the urban area, which, on the one hand, provides an increased labor force for the city, and, on the other hand, brings about factors of instability.

At the same time, the surrounding rural areas are constantly contracting in the process of urbanization and the expansion of cities, which leads to a continued shrinkage of China's farmland. In 1996, China's cultivated area was 1. 951 billion mu, which seemed to be a large number. However, the cultivated area per capita was quite limited based on the population of 1. 4 billion people. Even so, with the expropriation of rural land, the cultivated area is still reducing at a faster pace. In 2006, the third edition of *An Outline of the Overall Plan for the Utilization of Land in China (2006 – 2020)* was published by the State Council, which sets forth 6 obligatory targets and 9 anticipated targets for the goal and task of land utilization in the following 15 years. It sets an explicit red-line task of keeping

China's farmland at 1. 818 billion *mu* and 1. 805 billion *mu* by the years of 2010 and 2020 respectively, ensuring the basic number of 1. 560 billion *mu* of farmland remain unchanged and with some improvement in quality. This has also set higher demands on China's urbanization and rural development.

As suggested in the basic Western theory of regional economy, in the process of urbanization, the development of a city center will absorb a great amount of production resources from the surrounding regions. As a result, the capacity of economic development in these regions will be restricted. In the process of China's urbanization, this so-called polarization effect is especially obvious. The development of some big cities in East China tends to benefit from the influx of rural workers from other places, which provides sufficient cheap labor for the local manufacturing and service industries. The drain of resources from backward regions to advanced cities strengthens the dominant position of cities, which results in an increasing economic gap between them. For the rural areas, the drain of surplus manpower, especially those with high quality or skills, will further decrease their employment opportunity and development space. In this way, a path-dependent tendency is formed, giving rise to an unfavorable position for the rural areas in their long-term competition with the cities.

Benefiting from the low unemployment rate brought about by the drain of manpower, the pressure of employment in the rural areas was reduced. Certainly the trickle-down effect formed in the construction of a rational division system between the rural areas and the cities will play a positive role in the development of rural areas. However, as far as China's urbanization is concerned, its trickle-down effect is far less than its polarization effect, leading to the continued enlargement of the urban-rural disparity.

Having realized the side effects of the continuous expansion of urban-rural disparity for the development of rural economy, the 5th Plenary Session of the 16th Party Central Committee passed, in October, 2005, *A Proposal on the Outline of the 11th Five-Year Plan*, which introduced a request of "developed production, affluent life, civilized rural atmosphere, clean and tidy village environment and democratic management" so as to promote the construction of new socialist rural areas.

However, a definite template in the construction of new socialist rural areas is not in existence. In China, there are more than 3. 2 million villages, whose natural conditions, economic development and habits and customs vary greatly from place to place. Even in the same city, the development situations of varying villages can be totally different from each other. So, it is necessary for the Chinese government to adjust measures to local conditions with consistent innovation and improvement, and renovate villages based on their existing conditions.

The most important task in developing new socialist rural areas is to promote economic development in those regions. For any village, the construction of new houses is merely an external presentation of its economic development. Without an advanced village economy, the construction of new rural areas is rootless because it lacks sufficient construction funds. Therefore, based on promoting the economic development of villages, local governments strive to develop village economy with its own features, and to boost the income of the rural people in order to lay a solid foundation for developing new socialist rural areas.

In the development of new socialist rural areas, infrastructural construction has become a key point. At present, the urban-rural disparity is manifested not only in their different production modes and lifestyles, but also, to a large extent, in the inconvenience of life due to the lack of infrastructural construction in rural areas. Local governments tend to place more stress on such infrastructural construction as roads, hydropower and bridges, while at the same time, building libraries, cultural centers, recreation and sports centers and fitness sites. In this way, more guarantee is provided for a more fulfilling life for the rural people.

Ecological and environmental protection has also become two key factors for the construction of new rural areas. By adopting various economically rewarding policies, the Chinese government has actively developed clean energy techniques such as biogas, straw gasification, small hydropower, solar energy and wind power generation. Further biogas pits may become a driving force for the improvement of hog pens, toilets and kitchens, making sustainable and circular development a central point for the whole rural construction. This not only promotes the rural infrastructural construction, but also reduces the waste of resources and improves the environment.

The reason we call it the construction of "new" rural areas is that different regions adjust measures to their local conditions and create new villages with local features. For instance, villages with many classical buildings may make the most of their classical style and create tourism towns; villages with well-known special products can build specialty towns; villages with families specializing in breeding may give full play to collective breeding and planting; suburbs of a city can provide leisure travel and farmhouse tours for those who live in the downtown areas. In this way, they can create their own superior brands and boost the development of the rural economy.

For the vast number of rural people, the construction of new rural areas is an important work that may bring them wealth and happiness. While for the

Chinese government, it's an important task to narrow the urban-rural disparity and to bring about a coordinated development for China's economy. Therefore, in the Chinese Government's agricultural development program, the construction of new rural areas has become the core for the regional development of many rural areas.

2. 2   Manufacturing Industry: Factory of the World

2. 2. 1   The Establishment and Development of China's Industrial System

Before the founding of PRC, industrial capital for textile, machinery and food emerged gradually in big cities like Shanghai, Beijing and Tianjin. However, under the multiple oppressions of foreign capital as well as domestic feudal forces and bureaucratic capital, the foundation of China's industry was still rather shaky, with low production capacity and technique level. In the early years of PRC, the industrial capital that had suffered from long-term wars was on the verge of collapse.

By expropriating bureaucratic capital represented by the four large families Jiang, Song, Kong and Chen, regulating foreign capital enterprises in China and retrieving national industry capital, China gradually built up its own industries and established the early system of state-owned capital. And by promoting democratic reform and production reform in the state-owned enterprises, the workers and staff became masters of the enterprises. They made great contributions to the recovery of China's economy through labor contest and improvement of machinery, equipment and operation methods.

Due to the sudden outbreak of the Korean War, the Chinese government then strengthened the development of and support to heavy industry, especially the military industry. From 1949 to 1952, China emphatically transformed the heavy industries based on the original bureaucratic capital, and established 330 new enterprises, 4% of which were large and medium-sized enterprises. By 1952, the total output value of China's industrial production had reached RMB 34. 33 billion, with an annual growth rate of 4. 8% . The ratio of industrial production to the total output value of industry and agriculture had increased from 30% in 1949 to 41. 5% in 1952. In the gross value of industrial output, the ratio of heavy industry had risen from 26. 4% to 35. 5% .

Similar to the experience of the Soviet Union, China also chose the strategy of giving priority to heavy industry in the process of industrialization. In 1952, Mao Ze-dong pointed out that "the speed of industrialization depends first of all on the development of heavy industry. Therefore, large-scale construction should be focused on the development of heavy industry". Later, in the *Report on the Major Domestic Situations in China in the Past Three Years*, Zhou En-lai said that "the central link for the five major constructions is heavy industry, especially iron and steel, coal, electricity, oil, machine building, airplanes, tanks, tractors, shipping, vehicle manufacturing, military industry, nonferrous metals and basic chemicals.

In 1953, in an article titled *Mobilizing All Available Forces to Build Our Country into a Great Socialist Country — An Outline for the Study and Publicity of the Party's General Line in the Transitional Period*, Mao Ze-dong set out explicitly that, in a considerably long period of time, China would gradually accomplish industrialization and make a socialist transformation of agriculture, handicraft industry and capitalist industrial and commercial enterprises. At this stage, China had basically decided on a road of socialist industrialization characterized by giving priority to heavy industry.

In order to reach the target of "socialist industrialization", most of the infrastructural funds in the 1st Five-Year Plan, which began in 1952, were oriented to basic industrial construction. In the RMB 42.74 billion basic construction funds for all departments, the infrastructural funds for industrial departments were RMB 24.85 billion, accounting for 58.2% of the total. And in the funds for industry, those for heavy industry accounted for 88.8%, while those for light industry, merely 11.2%. With the construction of such large-scale heavy-industry projects as Changchun Auto Plant, Shenyang No.1 Plant of Machine Tools and Luoyang Tractor Plant, an integral industrial system was initially formed in China.

Evidently, merely relying on the market, it was very difficult for China, a poor and backward country, to establish a large and complete industrial system in a short time. The early-stage policy framework of the Chinese government to vigorously develop socialist industry by focusing on heavy industry not only played a great role in pooling our national resources to develop a heavy industry that was more significant to our national economy, but also was very helpful for accelerating China's industrial construction. However, after the twists and turns of the Cultural Revolution, China's industrial system remained imbalanced up to the year 1978.

During the 30 years from 1949 to 1979, China's heavy industry and light industry increased by 98 times and 22 times respectively, while agriculture increased merely by 2.7 times. Obviously, the whole industrial structure reflected that heavy industry was too heavy, while agriculture lagged behind. However, agriculture was a supplier of many raw materials and intermediate products for the development of industry. The lagging-behind development of agriculture and raw-material industry, in return, had led to a low production efficiency and imbalanced development of China's industry. Thus, taking a new path for our industrial development and adjusting the structure of China's industrial system then became an urgent problem to be solved.

Facing such a difficult economic situation, the 3rd Plenary Session of the 11th Party Central Committee (1978) put forward a plan to readjust our national economy so as to solve the long-standing economic imbalance, and to give priority to the development of agriculture. Only by consolidating agriculture, the basis of our national economy, could we guarantee the rapid development of the whole national economy. This also showed that, for the first time, the Chinese government had shifted its focus of work from heavy industry to agriculture.

With the promotion of the family responsibility system in the rural areas and the reform to enlarge the decision-making power of state-owned enterprises, a reform of China's economic system was in full swing in the 1980s. At the same time, with the progress of opening up, foreign-owned enterprises sprung up like mushrooms in China, which played an important supplementary role in China's industrial production at that time.

The smooth fulfillment of the 6th Five-Year Plan from 1979 to 1984 also promoted the optimization of China's industry structure. The total agricultural output value had increased by 55.4% in 1984, compared with that of 1978. With an annual growth rate of 7.6%, it was the fastest growing period since the founding of New China. Meanwhile, light industries such as cotton cloth and chemical fibers developed by leaps and bounds, and such household electric appliances as electric fans, television sets and refrigerators began to come into ordinary Chinese homes. But the proportion of heavy industry such as machinery and chemical engineering declined slightly.

The reform in the economic system further propelled the reform in the price mechanism. The Chinese government no longer practiced an overall control over the prices of all commodities as it had done before under the traditional planned economy. Instead, by introducing a double-track pricing system, it vigorously developed commodity circulation and promoted the functions of price mechanism in the allocation of resources. The result is that, while promoting the development of a socialist market economy, it also triggered an overall price increase in 1988.

In the face of serious inflation and market turmoil, the 5th Plenary Session of the 13th Party Central Committee adopted, in 1989, A Decision on Further

Improving the Economic Environment to Rectify the Economic Order and Deepening the Reform. The government began to comprehensively adjust industrial structures and to increase input in relatively weak infrastructural industries such as agriculture, energy and transportation, so as to make sure of the steady growth of grain, cotton and other agricultural products, and to curb the continued running-up of prices.

Through the reform of the economic system, the improvement of the economic environment and the rectification of the economic order, China gradually got rid of the abnormal development pattern in the early years of New China, which was dominated by heavy industry. Its economy kept a momentum of long-term and rapid development and the structure of its national economy was continuously optimized. This laid an important foundation for the take-off of China's economy after the comprehensive reform and opening up in the 1990's.

2. 2. 2　China's Manufacturing Industry in the Reform and Opening up

In the early period of its industrial development, China chose a road that was similar to that of the Soviet Union. Taking advantage of the state-planned economy that could make a planned allocation of the resources of the whole nation, China concentrated its resources on heavy industry, which had an external influence on the national economy, in order to stimulate the nation's industrialization. However, it was obvious that, in this process, the demands of government funds by light industry, which supplied products for people's livelihood, as well as those by agriculture would be curbed. During a very long period of time before the end of the "Cultural Revolution", China adopted a practice of "agriculture nurturing industry, and light industry nurturing heavy industry", with agriculture and light industry being squeezed. Although this practice accelerated China's industrialization at the beginning, it easily resulted in a serious imbalance of industrial structure, which, in turn, led to serious social contradictions. The collapse of the Soviet Union in the 1990s was derived from the intensification of these contradictions. The Chinese government had insight into this situation, so it adjusted the imbalance of the domestic economic structure and gradually solved the contradictions with market-oriented reform and opening up to the outside world.

Based on the concepts of China's top leaders in the early years of New China, the state, as a socialist country, must vigorously develop the state-owned economy. Other economic sectors that did not comply with the socialist economic nature should not be allowed to exist. Just based on this consideration, the Chinese government regained the bureaucratic − capital and foreign-capital enterprises in China by way of confiscation or expropriation, and retook the national capital enterprises by way of redemption. So, in the early days after the "Cultural Revolution", China had formed an economic pattern that was dominated by state − owned enterprises. As the ownership of the enterprises belonged to the state, and the senior managers of the enterprises, who were responsible for management only, were appointed by the government, all the profits were turned over to the state. As such, the managers were empowered only to manage, without ownership or the right to make profits. Under such a distorted mechanism of agency by agreement, the operational efficiency of China's state − owned enterprises was extremely low, which, in turn, seriously affected their competitive edge on the international market.

In 1984, the 3rd Plenary Session of the 12th Party Central Committee put in place for the first time the strategic thinking of invigorating state-owned enterprises and fostering the development of the market through the reform of the economic system. Since then, the reform of the contract responsibility system and shareholding system was gradually popularized in many state-owned enterprises. And on the other hand, the existence of individual economy, and the rationality of collective economy and foreign capital economy were recognized by the government. In 1987, the report of the 13th National Congress of CPC pointed out that "at present, the development of economic sectors other than the state-owned sector is not enough rather than too much. We should encourage the development of urban-rural cooperative economy, individual economy and private economy. " By the end of 1988, the number of registered individual businesses in urban and rural areas had increased to 14. 55 million, that of employed people had increased from 0. 31 million in 1979 to 23. 049 million, and that of private enterprises, over 0. 2 million.

After years of reform and opening up, China maintained an economic growth rate of over 8% for a long period of time, creating a Chinese miracle in the world's economic development. [1] The reality broke the prediction of the late Chinese leaders for a socialist economy. And the CPC and the Chinese government have gradually enriched and improved, in the rapid economic development, their own theory of a socialist economy.

---

[1]   As a matter of fact, China's annual economic growth rate since 1978 has been over 8% for more than 30 years. This is the first time for a big country in the world to maintain economic growth for such a long time. China's economic development has also become a real miracle in the post-war global economic development.

In 1982, the 12th National Congress of CPC put forward a development principle of "relying mainly on planned economy, with market regulation being a subsidiary". This redefined the relation between the plan and the market, thus reversing the traditional concept that looked on socialism and the market economy as opposite to each other, breaking the traditional pattern dominated by the planned economy, and providing guidance for the development of the market economy, and for price reform as well as the operating mechanism of enterprises. In 1992, the 14th National Congress of CPC summarized Deng Xiao-ping's theory of building socialism with Chinese characteristics. It created a basic ideology of combining the fundamental principles of Marxism with China's specific practice and building socialism with Chinese characteristics, and made clear the reform objective of building a socialist market economy system. And in 1993, the 8th National People's Congress incorporated "the state implements socialist market economy" into the Constitution. By then, China's economic development and market-oriented reform had a systematic guarantee.

In the early days of New China, due to its strained relations with the two superpowers — the United States and the Soviet Union, China was forced to adopt a development path of independence and self-reliance. Although, by the end of the Cultural Revolution, China had established an initially complete industrial system after 30 years' of striving, there were still many problems in the industrial structure and industrial foundation of the whole country, with obvious gaps existing between its industrial development and work efficiency and those of the developed countries in the West.

It was since the end of the "Cultural Revolution" that the second generation of Chinese leaders, with Deng Xiao-ping as the core, started, for the first time, to have the world in view, to really understand the development of all countries, to face up to the gap between China and other countries, and to make an effort to narrow the gap with the developed countries in the West. Internationally, Margaret Thatcher was elected British Prime Minister in 1979, and Ronald Reagan was elected American President in 1980. Both of them chose a relatively open policy: economic liberalism. Therefore, openness and freedom became the main themes of the world then.

In such a historical background, it was inevitable that the Chinese leaders then should choose to "go out and welcome in" and to promote the cooperation with other countries by developing international trade. In 1980, Shenzhen, Zhuhai, Shantou and Xiamen were defined as Special Economic Zones, marking a new chapter for China's opening up.

According to the traditional theory of advantage comparison, the abundant cheap labor is a key factor for China, a developing country with a population of 1.4 billion people, to win in international competition. Therefore, at the beginning of reform and opening up, China's processing and manufacturing industry developed most rapidly. Taking advantage of the abundant cheap labor, a large number of labor-intensive processing and manufacturing enterprises rose rapidly in China's southeastern coastal provinces like Guangdong, Fujian, Zhejiang and Jiangsu. Light industries, including textile, clothing, household appliances and toys, made remarkable progress.

In 2001, after years of tough negotiations, China formally joined the World Trade Organization (WTO). Since then, China really integrated into the world. With the participation of a big country — China, international trade and global division of labor become more complete.

Having experienced the shock of two financial crises: the Asian financial crisis in 1997 and the sub-prime mortgage crisis in 2008, China's foreign trade was seriously affected for a time. However, as a most important processing country and the world's factory, export has always been a major propelling force for China's economic development. Overseas markets and foreign capital enterprises play a more important role in China's economic development.

2.2.3　From "Made in China" to "Invented in China"

For many foreign investors, China is not only the world's processing factory with abundant cheap labor resources, but also a huge market with 1.4 billion consumers. So, almost all of the Fortune 500 companies have successively come to China since the reform and opening up. Choosing China, they get an opportunity to increase their business achievements.

Of course, the biggest advantage of attracting many foreign investors to China is its abundant cheap labor resources. Therefore, at the beginning of opening up, the foreign capital enterprises coming to China were mainly in the fields of processing and manufacturing that needed a large number of cheap labor, especially in light industries such as textiles, toys, electrical appliances, etc. After coming to China, these enterprises gradually discovered that, as China was still in the development stage, their own advantage was in brands, research and development, and marketing, while that of China depended on low processing cost, which was precisely in line with the rule of Smiling Curve. Hence, in the process of actual investment, Original Design Manufacturer (ODM), which can make full use of the advantages of both sides, is a common mode of cooperation with due division of labor in China's manufacturing enterprises. Foreign businessmen tend to provide technology and design, even some intermediate products and raw materials, while Chinese enterprises make use of the abundant cheap labor to process or assemble according to the designs provided by the foreign party. In this process, due to their holding the core technology and brands, foreign capital enterprises usually have the upper hand in competition, while China is in an unfavorable position as it is facing the competitive pressure from Southeast Asian and South Asian countries that also have abundant cheap labor resources. With their advantages in technology and brands, foreign capital enterprises can have an overwhelming superiority in the value chain of products and make maximum profits. In contrast, Chinese enterprises can only get the meager processing profits. To some extent, this restrains the Chinese manufacturing enterprises in terms of their international competitiveness.

In fact, with the prominence of the Chinese value, the advantages of China's cheap labor resources and markets gradually become salient. Processing trade has long been a major form of China's economic cooperation with foreign countries. The share of processing trade has always been half in China's current foreign trade, which is an important source of China's huge trade surplus.

In the coastal provinces of Southeast China, the rise of a more extreme form of processing trade, called foundry business, played a great role in the development of China's foreign trade. In this form of trade, foreign capital enterprises provide techniques, designs, as well as raw materials and spare parts, while Chinese joint ventures make some simple processing or assembly of the raw materials according to the requirement of the foreign enterprises. All products will not stay in China, but will be re-exported to overseas markets in accordance with the needs of the foreign enterprises. Throughout the production process, Chinese enterprises, as the supplier of foundry service, only undertake a small amount of production and assembly work, so they can only get extremely meager processing profits. Especially when the overseas markets are hit by a financial crisis and fall into a recession, foreign enterprises will try their best to squeeze the processing profits, which will lead to the employees' relatively adverse working environment, deficient safety and security guarantee and subpar salaries and welfare. As a result, the so-called "sweat shops" come into existence, leading to disputes in the joint venture process, even becoming the excuse for overseas human-rights groups to accuse China of abusing human rights. In fact, the root is that Chinese enterprises are unable to seize the high-end position in the global value chain, which results in their lack of adequate discourse power and deficient profit margins. It is an inevitable phase for backward developing countries to participate in international labor division.

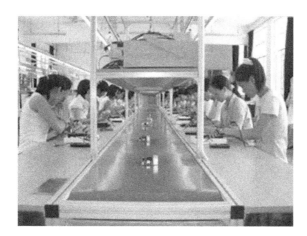

An Assembly Line in a Chinese Factory

Although the processing trade can only guarantee the integration of China's manufacturing industry with the world market at a low level, this is, however, a basis for China's manufacturing industry to take off. By undertaking a large amount of overseas processing orders and introducing foreign equipment and technology, small and medium-sized private manufacturing enterprises in the coastal provinces of Southeast China got an unprecedented opportunity for development. Through this long-term processing trade, these private entrepreneurs have gotten to know the overseas market, accumulated a wealth of experience in the development of manufacturing, gradually cultivated their own research and development capabilities and established their own brands. On this basis, China's national manufacturing industry has made overwhelming progress.

In the current Chinese processing trade, the operation mode of processing production purely with foreign techniques and equipment accounts for a large share. But, a novel mode of processing trade, ODM, attracts overseas manufacturers more. These overseas enterprises only need to provide basic requirements on the product's function and style, while the Chinese manufacturing enterprises can take advantage of their own research and development capabilities to develop and design products that are up to the standard of the foreign enterprises. In this process, the manufacturers are not only responsible for the manufacturing, but also for part of the designing. The higher the requirements, the higher the profits they can share. And this has enabled China's manufacturing industry to evolve toward the high-end position in the global value chain and to improve its reputation in the world.

As the largest developing country in the world, China's consumption and production are still at a lower level. This leads to a situation that China's manufacturing industry tends to do imitation and integration in designing, with a lower proportion of originality and functional innovation. Besides, due to a higher sensitivity of the market to prices, and a greater elasticity of price demand, China's manufacturing products often become synonymous with "cheap and low-quality". This means that the development of China's manufacturing industry still has a long way to go.

With the consistent development of China's manufacturing industry, its research and development capabilities and technical level have kept improving. Since 2000, along with China's economic development and the appreciation of RMB in exchange rate, more and more Chinese enterprises have strengthened their exchange with advanced enterprises and introduced more advanced technology and management experience by way of transnational mergers and acquisitions, hoping to narrow the gap between China's manufacturing industry and advanced western manufacturing industries, and to help China realize its dream of surpassing the United States and Europe. The world has witnessed China's manufacturing industry outstripping all countries through a series of great transnational mergers and acquisitions, such as Lenovo's acquisition of the computer giant IBM's PC business, Geely's acquisition of Volvo.

2. 3 Service Industry: A Perfect Embodiment of Industrial Modernization and Urbanization

2. 3. 1 Changes in the Concept of Service

During a long period of time after the founding of PRC, Chinese leaders followed the traditional Marxist economic thought. They considered production labor as work that produced tangible products in industrial or agricultural productions, but deemed such service sectors like commercial circulation and finance that provided social services as sectors of unproductive labor. Thus, in the long-term economic development, more attention was paid to industry and agriculture, especially the heavy or chemical industries that had obvious external effects on our national economy, while service industries like commercial circulation were neglected for a long time as dregs of capitalism. Particularly under the traditional planned economy system, the distribution and circulation of commodities were implemented through executive orders from the government. The circulation and finance industries were dominated by a few state-owned enterprises, with decisions made on the basis of the needs of the government, but not the needs of the market, which led to the low product-distribution efficiency in China at the beginning of reform and opening up. This kind of low efficiency was also widespread in the Soviet Union before its disintegration. To some extent, it reflects the drawbacks of the planned economy.

Even in the early years of the reform and opening up, many transactions in private that could promote the circulation of commodities were still regarded as a kind of crime — speculation, which was severely punished by the legal branches. By the mid and late 1980s, although the number of self-employed laborers in commercial circulation kept increasing, they were still discriminated against. It was not until the 13th National Congress of CPC in 1987 clarified that individual and private economies were a beneficial supplement to the socialist market economy that service industries like commercial circulation developed in real terms.

In fact, after the reform and opening up, the Chinese leaders, who had the whole world in vision, began to face up to the rules in the development of the western economy as well as in the evolution of every country's industrial structures. They realized for the first time that, with the growth of the western economy, the service industry, rather than the manufacturing industry to which they always paid close attention, became the center of the national economy in those developed countries, and that people who were employed in service industry became the major source of social employment. In the developed Euro-American countries, the proportion of service industry is more than 70%, or even more, in the national economy. Even in other developing countries, the proportion of service industry is about 50%. But in the early years of China's reform and opening up, the manufacturing industry still occupied a dominant position in our national economy. The proportion of the service industry was merely over 20%, not only far below the world's average, but also below that of other developing countries.

At the beginning of the reform and opening up, due to the fact that China was still pursuing the traditional system of a planned economy, almost all the production materials and consumption resources were produced by state-owned enterprises, and were purchased and sold by the government. There was no need for the enterprises to take into consideration the type and scale of market demands, since all the products were uniformly distributed by the government. On the other hand, in an era of goods scarcity, neither agricultural nor manufacturing goods could meet people's demands for consumption. The government had to control the gap between social demands and social production by way of administrative allocation and coupon-based supply. With the deepening of the reform and opening up, coupon-based supply and planned commodity allocation couldn't satisfy the desire of the Chinese people to improve their living standard. And the development of the service industry had become a prevailing trend.

In 1981, Deng Xiao-ping proposed for the first time in *The Decision on Some Historical Problems of CPC Ever Since the Founding of* PRC that we should implement a planned economy based on public ownership, and at the same time, bring into play the regulating function of the market and greatly develop socialist commodity production and exchange. The report, delivered at the 12th National Congress of CPC in 1982, clarified again the basic principle of "relying mainly on planned economy, with market regulation being subsidiary. " This shows that a consensus had been achieved in the Chinese government to encourage the development of commodity markets and to develop the commercial service industry.

It is under the guidance of the idea to establish and develop socialist commodity exchange that the Chinese government has gradually liberalized the control of prices. Except such important materials as fuel, raw materials, machinery and electronic products, the supply of other products has all been liberalized. China has transferred the original operation mode of unified allocation of resources to a commercial one by actively developing stores for production means, or for synthetic transaction. While developing the main channels of state-owned commerce and supply and marketing cooperatives, it actively brought the roles of the collective and individual commerce into play. In 1982, the General Supply and Marketing Cooperative, the Ministry of Grain and the Ministry of Commerce were merged into a unified Ministry of Commerce in charge of domestic trade, which boosted the development of China's commerce.

In 1984, the 3rd Plenary Session of the 12th Party Central Committee passed *A Decision on the Reform of the Economic System,* which pointed out, for the first time, that the socialist economy was a planned commodity economy based on public ownership, and tried to break the traditional idea that a planned economy was in opposition to a commodity economy. The theory of developing a planned commodity economy had become the basic guiding ideology of China's reform and opening up.

In March, 1985, the State Council approved *A Report on Establishing Statistics of Tertiary Industry* made by the National Bureau of Statistics, which truly defined the basic sphere of the tertiary industry, or service sector as we now call it. In this report, China's industrial structure was classified for the first time into three different industries: primary, secondary and tertiary. The primary industry is dominated by agriculture, including forestry, animal husbandry and fishery. The secondary industry is based on industry, including mining, manufacturing and construction. The tertiary industry consists of all other industries except the primary and secondary ones, including mainly the circulation and service sectors, which is further classified into four levels. At the first level is the circulation department, including transportation, post and telecommunications, commercial catering, as well as material supply, marketing and storing. At the second level are the production and livelihood service departments, including financial and insurance service, geological prospecting, real estate, public utilities, resident services, tourism, information consultation and all kinds of technical services. At the third level are service sectors for improving the scientific and cultural levels and residents' consciousness, including education, culture, radio, television, scientific research, public health, sports and social welfare. At the fourth level are service departments for the public needs of the society, including the state organs, party and government bodies, social organizations and the army and police. What is worth noticing is that the classification of tertiary industry into four sectors is basically similar to the internationally popular "four-sector classification of the service industry" developed by Browning and Singerman, who classified it into mobile, producer, consumer and social services. Among them, the second class of service industry concerning production and livelihood almost covers all the producer service industry, which is the first definition of service industry really made by our government and its initial understanding of a producer service industry.

In Sept, 1997, the concept of modern service industry was proposed in the report of the 15th National Congress of CPC. This meant truly that the understanding of our government about the status of the service industry in the modern economy had reached a new level, and that the service industry had become an important part in China's economic development. What's more, this concept also pointed out the direction for the development of the service industry in our country.

The Proposal of the Party Central Committee to Formulate the 10th Five-Year Plan made at the 5th Plenary Session of the 15th Party Central Committee pointed out clearly that, in the period of the 10th Five-Year Plan, "we'll develop modern service industry, reorganize and transform traditional service industry, and significantly increase the proportion of added value of service industry in the GDP, as well as the proportion of service industry employees to those of the whole society". The proposal also made a specific plan for the development of the modern service industry, that is, "In modern service industry, service standard and technical content should be improved. We'll vigorously develop service industries in the fields of information, finance, accountancy, consultation and law, so that the overall standard of the service sector will be promoted. Traditional service industries will be transformed with modern operation modes and service techniques, with great importance attached to the development of commercial circulation, transportation and municipal services, to the pursuit of such organizational forms and service modes as chain-store operation, logistics? distribution, multimodal transportation and online sale, and to the improvement of service quality and operational benefits. " From then on, development of service industry had become an aspect that could not be ignored in the development plan of the Chinese government. And the role of the modern service industry in China's modern economy was promoted to an unprecedented position.

The report of the 16th National Congress of CPC put forward a principle of "informationization stimulating industrialization and industrialization promoting informationization", so as to explore a new way of industrialization with high technical contents, good economic benefits, low resource consumption, little environmental pollution and full play of human resource superiority. This shows that the Chinese government has realized the important role that the producer service industry plays in boosting industrialization and informationization. It is also an indication of our deepened understanding of the producer service industry.

In the 11th Five-Year Plan, the expansion of production service was clearly regarded as an important way to facilitate the development of the service industry. The plan advanced some major measures to boost the producer service industry, such as giving priority to transportation, vigorously developing modern logistics, orderly developing financial service, actively developing information service, and standardizing commercial service.

In 2007, based on the overall direction and fundamental train of thoughts defined in the 11th Five-Year Plan for the development of the service industry, the State Council issued a document named *Suggestions on Accelerating the Development of Service Industry*. The document further underscored the significance of developing the service industry, specified its overall requirements and major objectives, and especially emphasized that " we should develop production industry and promote the integration and interactive development of modern manufacturing industry and service industry". Moreover, it put forward the train of thought for the development of the producer service industry, that is, to deepen the division of labor based on specialization, to boost business outsourcing, and to strengthen the core competitive power, which decided on a relatively complete path of reasoning for the future development of China's service industry.

Since the founding of PRC, it has taken quite a long period of time for the Chinese government to recognize the producer service industry. It moved from ignoring the role and status of the service industry in our national economy to emphasizing the development of the modern service industry in the report of the 15th National Congress of CPC, and then to clarifying the development of the producer industry in the 11th Five-Year Plan. With the status of the service industry, especially the producer service industry, becoming increasingly prominent in our modern economy, China will further clarify in detail the strategic position of the producer service industry in our modern economic system, refine its development concepts, and achieve a more rapid and sound development of the producer service industry by using strategic industrial policies.

2. 3. 2 The Development of Service Industry and China's Urbanization

According to the general rules of economics, urbanization arises from centralized population of employment and public services that are caused by the regional concentration of industries. At the beginning of reform and opening up, the development of China's economy centered on the manufacturing industry. So, the process of China's urbanization benefited from manufacturing enterprises, especially large-scaled ones that concentrated in a certain region. For example, Daqing in Heilongjiang and Shiyan in Hubei are cities that arose respectively from the Daqing? Oilfield and the Second Automobile Works. It can be said that, without these large and medium-sized enterprises, there would not be these corresponding cities.

However, with the overall development and more detailed classification of China's manufacturing industry, as well as the clearer cooperation with due division of labor after the reform and opening up, the modern manufacturing industry no longer existed independently merely by relying on a certain large or medium-sized enterprise as it did 30 years ago. Before the reform, China's enterprises strived for "large and all-inclusive" and "small but all-inclusive". As there wasn't a stable and reliable commodity market, it was very difficult for them to get from the market all the products and services they needed for their own development. An enterprise not only undertook independently the whole process of the value chain, including the purchase, processing and fine processing of raw materials, as well as the production, assembling and sale of products, but also performed some additional functions like providing the staff with meals, medical care, education, entertainment, etc. Under such traditional mechanism, a large state-owned enterprise was often a small society, or a small community, or even just like a city.

Under the system of planned economy, an enterprise undertook independently the functions of community service. Such an operation pattern certainly would result in ambiguous division of labor and low efficiency. These community service functions, while serving the employees of the enterprise, would bring great operational pressure to the enterprise, sometimes leading to collapse. Taking on too many social functions became an important cause for the low efficiency of state-owned enterprises under the system of planned economy.

The reform and opening up has helped many state-owned enterprises decompose excessive and unnecessary social functions. And the constant perfection of social service enables the employees to get from the society more social services at lower cost. Therefore, the marketization of social service has become an important factor in perfecting the functions of the cities and in boosting the development of China's urbanization.

With the gradual development of China's reform and opening up, such traditional social services undertaken by state-owned enterprises like medical care, education and caring for the old have gradually gone in the direction of marketization. Under the system of planned economy, once a person became an employee of a state-owned enterprise, he/she would almost never change his/her job. He/she would work there all his/her life. Sometimes even generations of the family would do similar jobs in the same enterprise. They wouldn't worry about unemployment, nor would they worry about their own health, their children's education and their being taken care of in old age. These service functions had all been shifted by the state onto the enterprises. In such a society, becoming an employee of a state-owned enterprise would mean that you have gotten an iron rice bowl — having a secure job, and lifetime insurance. Under such an operation mechanism, an enterprise, on the one hand, didn't have to arouse the employees' enthusiasm for work, and with no pressure and impetus, the efficiency of the employees couldn't be ensured. On the other hand, once an enterprise had given employment to a person, it had to undertake all the service functions for the employee during his/her lifetime. Therefore, the economic pressure on an enterprise was very great, which limited not only the growth of its business performance, but also the continuous expansion of the enterprise.

Under a system where the enterprises undertook the functions of social service, whether it be a hospital, a school or a restaurant, they were all subordinating branches of an enterprise. What they were facing were the staff of the same enterprise or of the same system. Therefore, what they were concerned about was merely to meet the service needs related to the staff, but not to make profits. In this way, there was basically no need for these service organizations to assess their benefits and costs, let alone to worry about the source of customers. So, there was almost no service institution ever caring about the satisfaction of the customers and the quality of its service. Following such an operational pattern, China's service industry could develop only at a low level.

However, the reform and opening up stripped the enterprises of their functions to act as a society. What the enterprises undertook was merely the relevant manufacturing function, for all other service functions could be obtained from the market. Under this mechanism, service enterprises independently became the main part of the market for the first time. They had to meet certain service needs of the customers by providing services to the market, and, in this way, make maximum profits. In the fierce market competition, if a service enterprise wanted to have as many customers as possible, it had to constantly improve the quality of its service, and do its best to make the customers satisfied. Only in this way could we boost true development of China's service industry.

With the thriving of China's economy, many service enterprises, such as business and trade circulation, health care, education and finance sprung up in areas where enterprises and population assembled. It is no longer the concentration of enterprises or population around one or some manufacturing industries, but the coordination among different industries, especially comprehensive industries, aiming at improving the development of the manufacturing industry and the quality of people's livelihood by way of a service industry, which further accelerated the urbanization process in China. To some extent, China's urbanization was manifested as the concentration and leading development of a service industry.

Of course, the marketization of such service functions as medical care and education has brought about some social problems while it has comprehensively promoted the standard of China's service industry. Under the system of a planned economy, hospitals and schools were component parts of an enterprise, mostly performing the function of market service, but ignoring their economic function. After the market-oriented reform, almost all hospitals and schools were pushed into the market, with their aim of operation turning to pursuing maximum profits just like other enterprises.

However, compared with the manufacturing industry that produces goods only, both medical care and education have more external influence on the economy. They bring about more social benefits than economic profits. In this case, if we simply push these social service functions to the market by way of marketization and assess their operation efficiency merely based on the profits they make, it will certainly lead to imbalanced resource allocation. Especially, in a populous country like China, where both income distribution gap and regional gap are obvious, the allocation of health care, education and other services simply based on economic profits will surely give rise to the Matthew Effect: the rich can enjoy better health care and educational services, while the poor cannot get even the basic health care and education. In recent years, "unaffordable medical treatment" and "unaffordable schooling", as two hard nuts to crack in the marketization of China's service industry, have aroused the concern of the Chinese government.

Since the coming of the new century, China's service industry has been further developed with the growth of the information technology revolution and knowledge-based economy. More and more employees in the service industry have begun to transform traditional that field with new techniques, business styles and service modes. They have created market needs, guided social consumption and provided the society with high value-added, high-level and knowledge-based production services and life services. More and more service industries have been separated from the traditional primary and secondary industries, or have emerged with detailed social division of labor.

The service industry not only can promote industrial integration and upgrade the level of other industries, but also can become an important driving force in the development of China's regional and urban economy. Indeed, the assemblage of service industries has become a great impetus to China's urbanization.

2.3.3 Service Industry and the Optimization of China's Industrial Structure

During quite a long period of time after the founding of PRC, the development of China's industrial framework had always centered on the manufacturing industry represented by heavy or chemical industries. Agricultural and service industries were merely auxiliary ones that provided relevant services for the manufacturing industry. For the Chinese people who were just liberated from the long-standing wars, such a strategic choice did have the effect of concentrating resources to deal with major problems. By first developing heavy or chemical industry that provided capital goods and raw materials for the national economy, China had indeed restored its economy and established a relatively complete industry structure in a short period of time. However, by the end of the "Cultural Revolution", this abnormal industrial structure had become an obstacle that hindered the development of China's economy. Thus, the Chinese government was forced to further optimize China's industrial structure, improve the level of its industries and realize the take-off of its economy by means of reform and opening up.

In China's pre-reform plans for economic development, the manufacturing industry was regarded as a major driving force, so more resources were put into heavy or chemical industries like automobile, petrochemical and machinery industries, and traditionally superior industries like household appliances and textiles. It was hoped that, with the leading development of these superior industries, China could greatly develop the export of finished goods, build the brand image of "Made in China", and improve the international competitiveness of China's manufacturing industry as well as its economy.

Nonetheless, due to the long-term focus on the use of cheap labor, China's manufacturing industry has always competed in the low-end manufacturing fields. In some international markets, "Made in China" has even become synonymous with cheap and low quality. The rapid development of the manufacturing industry didn't synchronously enhance China's competitiveness as we had assumed. Moreover, in modern economic society, production service links such as research and development, and marketing, have already replaced the traditional processing and manufacturing links and become most profitable. China's strategic choice of the long-term focus on manufacturing, and even the building of a world factory, on the contrary, has led to a continuous profit reduction of China's export goods.

Nowadays, with the rapid development of a modern economy, the penetration and integration between different industries are continuously strengthened. Modern industries have already broken away from the clear boundary between the existing industries, paying more attention to the coordinated development of different industries. The lagging-behind development of any industry can seriously affect the coordination of the whole industrial system, while the rise of production services has undeniably proven this historical trend.

Although from the prospect of industrial belonging, production service still belongs to the service industry, it has countless ties with the development of a manufacturing industry. In many cases, production service can even become a weak point in the development of a manufacturing industry within a country or a region. As a result of the failure of production service to achieve a coordinated development, the manufacturing industry is confronted with difficulties, with its development being restricted.

As for a modern manufacturing industry, without a developed financial system, some related financial services such as financing, trust, security, insurance and exchange can't keep pace with the development of an enterprise, which will certainly be like a river without sources, a tree without roots, lacking a long-term motive force.

Today, with the rapid development of the global economy, every manufacturing enterprise is no longer confined to a certain specific region: developing in isolation for local customers. Instead, in the global market, they will face up to fierce competition from both domestic and international rivals and conduct business for customers all over the world. And this also requires them to have a global perspective in financing, business processing and asset management. However, it is very difficult for any enterprise to finish such an arduous task simply by relying on its own capacity. And, even if these tasks can be accomplished, the input cost will be huge. Therefore, specialized and high-level financial institutions are needed to provide an enterprise with financial services such as financing, securities, trust, wealth management, leasing, guarantees and Internet commercial banks, to optimize the capital portfolio of the enterprise, reduce its operational risk and improve its international competitiveness.

If we take the national economy as the body of a human being, modern logistics is just like the circulation of blood. Without a strong logistics industry, it is impossible to realize either the efficient transportation of materials among different regions within a country, the cooperation of its regional economy, the construction of industrial systems, the pursuit of global markets, and the foreign investment of an enterprise.

In the early development of China's economy, the notion of modern logistics did not exist. We simply took it as physical labor with low technical requirements, like transportation, storage or portage of goods. However, with the development of the modern economy, logistics has long been an important part of modern supply-chain management. By virtue of modern information technology and equipment, it has developed into a rationalized service pattern as well as an advanced service process, which can ensure the accurate, timely, safe and door-to-door delivery of goods from supplier to receiver, with both quality and quantity guaranteed. Evidently, logistics is no longer purely physical labor, but one that demands the organic combination of the knowledge of modern supply chain management, the latest information technology, and modern service concept. Only when an efficient operation of logistics is realized, can our economy be activated in the future.

Tianjin Port with Vigorous Development

Traditional manufacturing industry more often pursues development within itself. It means that, in order to gain greater economic profit, a manufacturing enterprise will take advantage of all its resources and improve the efficiency of its utilization. Modern manufacturing industry, however, has long smashed the fetters of its traditional predecessor. It tries to make full use of the resources of the whole society on a broader market, to realize the division of labor based on industries as well as a coordination of development in or among industries, and to create greater benefits for both the enterprise and the society.

Based on the development idea of a traditional manufacturing industry, an enterprise is usually in pursuit of a large-and-all-inclusive mode of development, which means that all links in the production and management should be fulfilled within the enterprise itself. Nevertheless, with the increasing complexity of a modern economic system, the operation of modern industry has become more and more complex, with a much higher level of specialization being required. No matter how large an enterprise is, it cannot solve all problems independently, while the rising of production service has cracked this hard nut for modern enterprises.

Originally, such high-tech services as research and development, designing and information service must all be put in line with the operation of an enterprise. However, these services are usually carried out by more professional personnel, with closer information exchange and larger scale of research and development investment. Thus, for many small or medium-sized enterprises, it seems impossible for them to have these functions realized, while a lack of these functions will have an impact on the development of these enterprises. Consequently, for such related work, they have to employ staff of undesirable quality and invest less in research and development, which will inevitably affect the input cost of related sources.

On the other hand, some professional commercial functions, such as accounting, auditing, tax administration, production management, marketing and market research, are also in need of high-level professionals. But the investment in these areas is usually limited by the small size of an enterprise, which, in turn, will affect the realization of these functions.

Thanks to the development of production services, such high-tech and professional commercial services as mentioned above can be outsourced to related professional institutions. Thus, an enterprise can concentrate its own resources on its superior core links and entrust the auxiliary functions in which they don't have an advantage to professional production services. In this way, an enterprise can improve the efficiency of utilizing its own resources and accelerate the growth of profits while getting professional and efficient services in related areas.

With the development of modern science and technology, industrial division becomes more specialized. Even within the same industrial sector, due to their different-degree application of science and technology and their different-proportion allocation of economic resources, there is an obvious difference in the social division of labor, and the difference in the content and requirement of the division is more and more evident. That the advancement of science and technology will boost the specialization of the social division of labor has become a natural trend in the development of a modern economy. And the development of service industry provides a guarantee for this trend.

In the development of the traditional manufacturing industry, an enterprise could improve its production efficiency and gain economic returns brought about by the division of labor merely through allocating its personnel and resources on the basis of different production links and realizing the division of labor based on personnel within the enterprise itself. However, in the progress of the modern manufacturing industry, the emergence and expansion of production service have extended the social division of labor within a manufacturing enterprise to a broader external market. By way of outsourcing, an enterprise can transfer a certain link of production to the external market. It can gain maximum economic returns brought about by specialized division of labor merely by concentrating its resources on the operation and production in its superior areas.

In fact, with the progress of modern science and technology, more and more human capital and technology have been applied to the manufacturing process in the development of China's modern manufacturing industry. This not only leads to the specialization of production processes, but also makes it a necessity to refine the division of labor. No enterprise can fulfill the production links all by itself as traditional manufacturing enterprises did. Under modern industrial system, it is almost impossible for a single enterprise to have professional allocation of staff and high-quality service supply in all its producing links. Some service items, such as banking, logistics, production management, accounting and finance, can be completely separated from the enterprise. This has helped the making of the production service industry.

After China's accession to the WTO, a tighter business connection has been formed between China's enterprises and the world market. A great number of foreign enterprises have come to China, especially banking institutions represented by Citibank and Goldman Sachs, logistics enterprises represented by Federal Express and DHL Express, and accounting service enterprises represented by Deloitte and Price Waterhouse Coopers (PWC). While winning great market share in China, they have also helped to upgrade the overall level of China's production service. Benefited from the diffusion of knowledge and the flow of staff, more and more Chinese production service enterprises have gained more advanced operation and management experience in their competition with multinational companies, which contributes to the upgrading of the overall level of China's production service.

More importantly, in the development of China's industry, production service tends to be a link that most depends on professional knowledge and technical capital, and also a link that can increase the additional industrial value. In the initial stage of processing trade, most of China's manufacturing enterprises merely occupied the processing and assembling position of the international value chain. The complicity and technical capacity of their production were strikingly low, which greatly constrained the level of China's industrial structure. To some extent, the backwardness of the service industry was a weak point in China's economic development. Therefore, vigorously developing a modern service industry and giving full play to its support for the first and second industries will be of great significance in adjusting China's industrial structure and transforming the pattern of its economic growth.

Having this point in mind, the Chinese government strives to develop production service so as to improve the country's industrial structure and to transform the pattern of its economic growth, thus strengthening the competitiveness of China's industry in the global market. In 2007, *Some Opinions on Speeding Up the Development of Service Industry* was approved by the State Council. And the 12th Five-Year Plan published in 2011 clearly put forward the idea of "deepening the professional division of labor, accelerating the innovation of service products and service modes, promoting the fusion of production service and advanced manufacturing industry, and speeding up the development of production service". This idea will be fully carried out in the strategic choice for our future economic growth, which will promote the constant optimization of our industrial structure in the future. Meanwhile, giving priority to the vigorous development of production service also shows that the Chinese government has attached great importance to the role production service plays in upgrading our future industries.

In the future, the production service industry, rather than the traditional manufacturing industry, will become the forward position where economic development is closely related to knowledge innovation. Meanwhile, the manufacturing industry, especially the production link, will become the area where knowledge and technical skills are least demanded and where least economic returns are gained. This means that the most important sphere for China to achieve a sustainable development and to transform the pattern of its economic growth is right in production services. So, to promote the development of production services by means of powerful policies will be an inevitable choice for sustainable development in China.

Case 2. 1   Huaxi Village: A Model of the New Rural Areas

For those foreign friends who have been to China, the rural economy is synonymous with low and shabby houses, poor and unenlightened villagers as well as traditional mode of farming. Compared with the cities, China's rural area is a seamy side of the Chinese economy: impoverished, unenlightened and ignorant. However, there is a village in China whose economic development is better than that of ordinary cities. The wealth that its villagers possess rivals that of the middle class in developed western countries. The construction of the village is so magnificent that it seems to be a gorgeous park. Perhaps many foreigners may doubt there is such a prosperous village in China. But in fact, this prosperous village does exist. It is the Huaxi Village, known as the "First Village in China".

Since ancient times, Jiangsu province has been famous as a prosperous land teeming with fish and rice. Especially the region in the south of Jiangsu, benefiting from the economic influence of Shanghai, has gained economic prosperity from early days. As early as the beginning of New China, a large number of national capitalists, represented by Rong Zong-jing and Rong De-sheng, emerged in Wuxi, a city of Jiangsu province. Accordingly, the original manufacturing industries such as flour, spinning and silk reeling began to take shape, which made Wuxi the industrial base of China at that time. It is on this fertile land where China's early industry and commerce occurred that Huaxi Village has become prosperous and accomplished the fame of "First Village in China", relying on the development of collective enterprises and on manufacturing.

Situated in Jiangyin, Jiangsu, Huaxi Village used to be an ordinary village unknown to the public, but it became famous because of its extraordinary path to development.

After the "Cultural Revolution", the household responsibility system became very popular in the rural areas of China. Land was distributed to the peasants so that they had the freedom of how to use it and could enjoy the harvest from the land. However, as Huaxi Village is situated in the most populous Jiangsu province, its cultivated area was limited. If the land were allocated to all the villagers, each household would have a very small piece of land to cultivate. Obviously, this would restrict the peasants' capacity of cultivation and production, and would result in a great waste of labor resources. To address this potential problem, Wu Ren-bao, the party branch secretary of Huaxi Production Brigade, came up with a bold idea: to adjust the industrial structure of Huaxi Village in accordance with its special conditions instead of simply imitating the household responsibility system. That is, the total 600 *mu* of farmland in Huaxi Village was contracted to 30 expert crop growers, who were responsible for the cultivation of the whole village, with the rest of the laborers transferred to industry. The villagers committee actively organized a village-run collective economy, arranging for the villagers to work in the village-run enterprises. This was, no doubt, a bold practice in China when the reform and opening up was just underway.

Although China was in great need of manufactured goods at the beginning of the reform and opening up, no one dared to establish manufacturing enterprises at that time. It was under this circumstance that Huaxi Village got a great opportunity. Its village-run enterprises were operated very well and the income of the villagers working there were higher than what they would have received doing crop cultivation. In the mid − 1980s, when the villagers became increasingly wealthy, Wu Ren-bao called on them to become shareholders of the collective economy, which not only solved the capital problems of enterprises, but also guaranteed a more stable source of income for the villagers.

In 1994, Huaxi Company Group was established. With a variety of industries like steelmaking, pipe welding, spinning and clothing and over 10,000 staff members, it became a business model of collective economy in southern Jiangsu province. In 1999, Huaxi Village A-share, the first stock named after a village, was listed on China's Shenzhen Stock Exchange, a symbolic event in the development of Huaxi Village.

It is by virtue of the reform and opening up that Huaxi Village got onto a fast track of development. At the beginning of the reform and opening up, its gross output value of industry and agriculture amounted to RMB 13.49 million. Its economic aggregate was over RMB 10 billion in 2003. In 2004, the annual salary of a Huaxi villager was RMB 122.6 thousand, far more than the RMB 2936 per capita net income of peasants nationwide, and the RMB 9,422 per capita disposable income of urban residents. As we can see, the income of Huaxi villagers was 41.76 times that of the peasants and 13.01 times that of urban residents. Nowadays, Huaxi Village is known far and wide as "First Village in China", where all villagers live in affluence, with every household owning cars and villas.

The Famous "First Village in China"

Seeing the success of Huaxi Village, people everywhere of the country came to investigate and learn from its experience: daring to be the first, struggling bravely to achieve common prosperity. Besides, neighboring villages wished to join in Huaxi Village and to share its experience. So, in June 2001 three administrative villages nearby were incorporated into Huaxi Village, forming Huaxi Village One. Thereafter, over 20 administrative villages joined Huaxi in succession. By 2011, the area of Huaxi Village was more than 35 square km and its population increased from about 2,000 to 35,000. The original 20 villages were divided into 13 regions, in accordance with the number sequence, named respectively as Huaxi Village One, Huaxi Village Two, up to Huaxi Village Thirteen.

As a famous representative of the construction of new socialist rural areas, Huaxi's success represents the direction of China's modern rural area construction.

And its experience tells the world that the numerous Chinese peasants in the vast rural areas are able to achieve common prosperity under the socialist economic system. This is also a concentrated incarnation of the superiority of the socialist system.

To a great extent, Huaxi Village's experience is embodied in its unified operation system. As early as the 1960s when most rural areas in China were following the accounting mode: three-level ownership (commune, production brigade and production team), with production team as the basic accounting unit, Huaxi had adopted a unified accounting method with production brigade as the basic accounting unit. Through centralizing the decision-making power in management and optimizing assessment objectives, Huaxi became a typical example in the rural areas of southern Jiangsu.

When the reform and opening up was formally carried out, the rural areas throughout the country began to implement the household responsibility system, to distribute such production means as land to each household, and to turn collective decision-making into individual or household responsibility. However, Huaxi Village didn't follow the trend. Instead of carrying out the household responsibility system, it stuck to its usual way of unified brigade accounting regardless of the pressure. Thanks to Wu Ren-bao's insight and boldness, Huaxi Village dared to be the first to take an unusual road and became the first to enjoy the benefits brought about by mechanism innovation.

Due to its long-term unified decision-making, the Party committee of Huaxi Village created a special management and operation system. In regard to accumulation and distribution, they stuck to the following principle: less distribution, more accumulation; drawing less cash but investing more. Under this principle, every worker of the village-run enterprises only drew 30% of his/ her monthly wage, with the remaining 70% kept in enterprises as current capital and paid off in one lump sum at the end of the year. Bonuses were usually three times that of the wage, but was invested as share capital, thus the next year the workers could gain profits from these shares. As to the over-fulfilled profits, it was divided into two parts, with 20% turned over to the village and 80% given to the enterprises. As to the retained part of over-fulfilled profits, 70% was used as awards (10% for the factory director, 30% for the managers and 30% for the staff respectively) and the other 30% was used as accumulation capital for enterprises. The personal bonus of the contractors was kept as equity in the enterprises, functioning as the security fund for risks. Such a distribution system seemed unsatisfactory, even somewhat domineering, but it ensured the scarce source of capital in the long-term development of the village-run enterprises.

Since 2001, with more and more villages voluntarily joining Huaxi, the Huaxi people have created another management mode: "one separation and five unifications". On the one hand, the enterprises have to be separated from the village. After the merging, the original village was still self-governed, with its villagers committee elected by the original villagers. On the other hand, not only the old Huaxi Village, but also the newly-joined ones, had to implement a unified management under the unified decision-making system, which was manifested in 5 aspects: 1) The economy was managed uniformly by Huaxi Village; 2) The laborers were arranged uniformly under the same condition; 3) The welfare was handed out uniformly by Huaxi Village; 4) The planning and construction of each village was carried out uniformly by Huaxi Village; and 5) Everything was under uniform leadership of Huaxi's Party committee. With this decision-making and management system, the decision-making power of the enterprises and the new villages was guaranteed. And what's more, full play was given to the advantage of unified planning and management, which was an important guarantee for the economic development of Huaxi Village.

Nowadays, Huaxi Village is not merely an ordinary village, but has become an example of China's new rural areas and an important tourist attraction in the new rural areas south of the Yangtze River. The soaring Huaxi Building with a height of 328 meters, the beautiful scenery people can feast their eyes on from a helicopter, as well as the solid gold bull sculpture which weighs one ton, are all a demonstration of the prosperity of the Huaxi villagers and the happy life of the new generation of Chinese farmers.

Case 2. 2   Jinjiang: The City of Sports Shoes in China

Since the reform and opening up, China's manufacturing industry has gone through the development path from ODM processing for foreign companies to indigenous innovation and self-owned brands. The development of the sports shoes industry in Jinjiang, Fujian province, has become a microcosm of the great transition from "Made in China" to "Created by China".

Jinjiang used to be a small town on the southeast coast of Fujian province. For a long period of time, many residents in Jinjiang chose to migrate to other places due to the hard life there. Jinjiang, therefore, has been known as a place where "nine in ten households live overseas", thus becoming a famous "hometown of overseas Chinese".

After the reform and opening up, the old hometown of overseas Chinese radiated new vitality. Besides its traditional industries like planting, fishing and aquatic farming, it established joint ventures and vigorously developed manufacturing by introducing investment from overseas Chinese. In the 1980s and 1990s, a modern manufacturing system was created in Jinjiang, mainly represented by footwear, garments and ceramics, with a preliminary development of manufacturing industry being realized.

Since the beginning of the reform and opening up, shoemaking has been a leading industry in the industrial structure of Jinjiang, which plays a very important role in the development of the local economy. At first, of course, Jinjiang attracted foreign investment mainly through its low labor costs. The same was true in other Chinese cities, and this became the primary production source in the development of their manufacturing industry.

However, at that time, as the consumption ability and level of the Chinese market greatly restricted the demands for manufactured goods, the technological level of Jinjiang's shoemaking industry was rather low. Shoes were manufactured with relatively traditional "half-mechanized and half-manual" techniques, which benefited much from the financial support of overseas Chinese. Such a production mode, though relatively inefficient and of low-quality, met the needs of the early economic development of Jinjiang, and also conformed to China's consumption level then.

After the 1980s and 1990s, with the gradual maturity of Jinjiang's sports shoes industry, some world-famous brands like Nike and Adidas entered China and chose Jinjiang as an ideal place to establish ODM enterprises as it had a solid foundation of shoemaking. In fact, since the end of the last century, world-famous sneakers manufacturers, represented by Nike, have turned to "asset-light mode of operation". That is, they control the designing and marketing of the products and transfer such high human-resource-utilization links like processing and manufacturing to China and other countries and regions with lower human-resource cost. This outsourcing production mode had a very obvious effect on the rise of the manufacturing industry in China and Southeast Asia.

During the ODM phase, in order to guarantee the quality of their products and maintain their own brand images, foreign manufacturers such as Nike would inevitably introduce advanced shoe-making equipment to the ODM factories and conduct detailed training. Therefore, the ODM factories in Jinjiang gradually mastered the advanced shoemaking techniques and improved their own management capacities. However, in the ODM mode , Chinese factories get very little labor remuneration. Most of the profits from the sales of the products go to foreign manufacturers who own the brands and techniques. For example, a pair of

Nike at that time retailed at USD100 in America, but its material expense was merely USD 15. 67, and the factory price in China was merely USD 24. 71, including a direct labor cost of USD 2. 58, a management cost of USD 4. 56 and a profit of about USD 1. 9 for the factory. When this pair of shoes with a factory price of USD 24. 7 was shipped to the United States, Nike Company set the wholesale price at USD 52. 03. And when it reached consumers, its price was as high as USD 100. Such a cruel phenomenon taught a lesson to the sports shoes enterprises in Jinjiang—that they should have their own techniques and brands.

Since the 1990s, shoe-making enterprises in Jinjiang, represented by Anta and Peak, have been attempting to create their own brands with their experience and techniques accumulated in doing ODM for famous shoe-making enterprises. In this way, they have turned from earning a meager ODM profit into developing self-reliant techniques and products as well as self – owned brands.

The transition of Jinjiang's shoe-making enterprises didn't go smoothly at the beginning due to their gap in brand and techniques. But the innovative strategies adopted by two well-known enterprises set up an example for other enterprises to imitate. To some extent, celebrity endorsements and market segmentation have become the magic weapon for Jinjiang's shoe-making enterprises to compete in the international market today.

In 1999, a shoe-making enterprise named Anta was in trouble with its production and management. The boss of the enterprise, Ding Zhi-zhong, got in touch with Kong Ling-hui, one of China's table tennis stars, and invited him to be the spokesman for his sneakers. Though Anta's capitalwas rather tight then, Ding Zhi-zhong resolutely decided to take the last shot with with a fee of RMB 800, 000. As you know, RMB 800, 000 as an endorsement fee was no doubt an astronomical figure in China's sports circle then. Along with Kong Ling-hui's words "I choose, I like", the Anta brand quickly became popular all over China, with sales of its product increasing rapidly. And the enterprise not only got out of the dilemma of bankruptcy, but also became the leading shoe-making enterprise in Jinjiang. Since then, more and more shoe-making enterprises in Jinjiang began to choose more stars in sports, literature and arts as their product spokespersons. By now, there was as many as 44 advertisements for Jinjiang sports shoes on the CCTV sports channel, which meant that consumers saw Jinjiang sports-shoe ads played at set intervals every few minutes. Their spokespersons ranged from NBA super stars to Olympic champions, to singers and anchormen. Such celebrity effect has helped more and more people recognize Jinjiang's shoe-making enterprises as well as the Chinese brands of sports shoes.

The manufacture and sales of Chinese sneakers at an early stage adopted an extensive management pattern, without obvious differences between different products in terms of product type and technical characteristics. This kind of management pattern was OK in the early development of Chinese sneakers market. However, with the expansion of China's sneakers industry and the maturity of the sports-shoes market, gone are the days when one product fits every customer. If shoe enterprises in Jinjiang didn't win the trust of consumers in terms of product differentiation, it would be impossible for Jinjiang to become "the city of sports shoes" today. Just at the end of the last century, Xu Jing-nan, the boss of a shoe enterprise in Jinjiang who loved basketball, began to specialize in manufacturing basketball shoes. This enterprise, called Peak, has successively invited nearly 10 NBA basketball stars to advertise its products. Suddenly, the media was filled with the news of NBA stars wearing Chinese sports shoes to play basketball, and Peak almost became a synonym for basketball shoes. Nowadays, the classification of products based on their functional differences has become a common choice of shoe enterprises in Jinjiang, such as football, basketball and jogging shoes. More and more customers tend to choose shoes that are most suitable for the sport they love, which also has promoted the development of Jinjiang's shoe-making enterprises.

Today, more and more sneakers enterprises like Anta, Peak, 361°, Jordan and Deerway have established their brand influence in China's sports shoes market. And by sponsoring the Iraq football team, the Spanish basketball team, the Premier League and Spanish Primera Liga, a growing number of Jinjiang's brands are trying to exploit the international sneakers market. Perhaps in the near future, the small city of Jinjiang can produce world famous sports-shoe brands alongside Nike and Adidas.

In fact, like many other Chinese manufacturing enterprises, Jinjiang's shoe-making enterprises gradually created their own brands by absorbing foreign investment, introducing foreign technologies, and then by application and imitation. Maybe in the early days of development, imitation and learning were the key factors of their success, but imitation can never make a manufacturing giant. Only by choosing creation and challenges, can they create true world-famous brands. The sports shoes enterprises in Jinjiang have just taken a growth path from imitation to innovation, and from "Made in China" to "Invented in China". Their success is also an epitome of the development of China's manufacturing industry.

Case 2. 3   GOME: A Retail Giant Rising from a Street Shop

In China's retail market of home appliances, GOME has always been a leading enterprise. The fight between GOME and Suning constitutes the meeting of two heroes in China's home appliance retailing. Therefore, the development as well as the rise and fall of GOME has also become the symbol of the whole of China's home appliance retail industry.

In 1986, Huang Guang-yu came to Beijing, at the age of 17, to fight for his future with his brother, Huang Jun-qin. In addition to the RMB 30, 000 borrowed from relatives and friends, all he had was his hopes for the future. Without skills and capital, Huang Guang-yu chose retail business like many other individuals going into business, hoping to make some hard-earned money by speculating in goods. At first, he chose clothing retail, but the business had always been rather depressed. On January 1, 1987, Huang Guang-yu turned to selling electric appliances, thus the shop sign was changed from the early GOME clothing store to GOME electric appliance store. However, even Huang Guang-yu himself couldn't have thought that such a small shop of less than 100 square meters would develop into a flagship brand and leader of China's retail industry of home appliances.

GOME Electric Appliances

The key to Huang Guang-yu's success was his unique insight. Just as he had thought, the Chinese who became rich soon after the reform and opening up would inevitably have a strong demand for household appliances, which was bound to bring about great opportunities to the retail market of household appliances. Maybe it was also beyond his imagination that the household appliances that were still in short supply in the 1980s would soon enter every ordinary Chinese home.

At the beginning of the reform and opening up, due to the lack of domestic manufacturers and advanced technology of household appliances, only very rich families could buy household appliances like color TV sets and refrigerators from abroad through social relations. As the supply of household appliances was very limited, even if a store was able to get them, only those with coupons were qualified to buy a color TV set or a refrigerator. Without a coupon, even those with money could not get household appliances from the market. In other words, there was no household appliance retail market in China in a real sense during that period. Because household appliances were both scarce and precious, there was no need for a professional household appliance retail enterprise.

However, no one had imagined that China's appliances industry could achieve a leap-forward development from scratch within a few years, benefiting from introducing a large number of appliance production lines from abroad. Almost half of China's provinces and cities deemed household appliances as the core industry in the local economic development and actively introduced the most advanced production lines. By the 1990s, China had become the world's largest manufacturer of household appliances.

The continuous increase in the supply of household appliances gave a golden opportunity of development to Huang's GOME store. As the supply of goods was adequate and the market demands were strong, Huang's business began to boom. In just a few years, Huang Guang-yu opened several branch stores in Beijing and implemented chain operation under his leadership. All the stores, old or new, were called "GOME" and had unified brand and management, saturating the Beijing market. Nearly every Beijing citizen knew that merchandise in GOME was cheap and adequate. Whenever they wanted to purchase household appliances, GOME was their best choice. Obviously, Huang Guang-yu won his reputation in the household appliance retail industry in Beijing.

In 1999, Huang finally chose to open a store in Tianjin and made an instantaneous hit, creating a legend in the household appliance retail industry. From then on, GOME marched onto a path of rapid development through expansion to the whole nation. In just two years' time, GOME set up 49 regular chain stores and 33 franchised outlets in 12 cities. According to the 2002 ranking list of China's chain enterprises (released by China Association of Chain Operation in 2003), GOME, with annual sales of RMB 10.896 billion, ranked No. 4 among China chain enterprises and No. 1 in the household appliance retail industry. And in 2003, Huang's individual worth reached RMB 1.8 billion, ranking 27th in the Hurun Fortune List.

2004 was an important year for the development of GOME. As a private entrepreneur, Huang was eager to raise more money, by listing and financing, for the development of GOME. However, the listing process of China's Shenzhen Stock Exchange was relatively complicated, so Huang chose to go public through buying a shell in Hong Kong Securities Market where the listing process was more flexible and simple. In fact, to prepare for this asset operation, Huang founded Pengrun Investment Co. Ltd. early in 1999. And in 2004, Huang first injected the high quality assets of 94 GOME stores in 22 cities into Pengrun and then realized the listing of GOME in Hong Kong through the shell. As a result, Huang became China's richest man with assets of RMB 10. 5 billion.

The success of GOME can be attributed to three magic weapons: chain operation, price war and service innovation. When GOME was founded, chain operation was a new thing in China, but Huang had seen the advantages of chain operation mode long before. While setting up stores and expanding business, he decided on the rules and regulations of GOME chain operation by formulating the *GOME Management Manual* in 1998, laying a solid foundation for GOME to get into markets all over the country. And since then, the *GOME Management Manual* had gone through several revisions. In addition, he also combined the management rules and regulations as well as successful experience of other chain enterprises at home and abroad with GOME's experiments for many years, summarizing a set of management patterns suitable for GOME's development.

In China's household appliance retail market, GOME has always been regarded as a price butcher, because it provoked price wars again and again. By lowering the profits as reward to the customers and adopting the strategy of "small profit but quick turnover", GOME has established the market image of lowest price. In 2000, when numerous Chinese color TV manufacturers hoped to jointly maintain a high price in the color TV industry by establishing a price alliance, it was GOME that initiated the color TV price war, directly routing the attempt of the alliance to monopolize prices. In recent 10 years, it was GOME again that squeezed out the price bubbles in China's household appliance retail industry through the price wars against Suning and Jingdong, keeping the price of Chinese household appliances always at a reasonable level.

During its development, GOME kept improving customers' satisfaction through service innovations time and again, from the early "return if not satisfied", "mysterious-shopper in action" to "deposit for the protection of customers' rights", "compensation in advance" and "rainbow service" (a service alliance formed together with household appliances giants like Haier, Hisense and Kelong), which guaranteed GOME's market leadership.

In 2008, GOME suffered an unprecedented crisis. Huang Guang-yu, the founder of GOME and also chairman of the board, was arrested by the public security organ for charges of illegal business dealing, insider trading and unit bribery. Later he was sentenced to 14 years in jail with a fine of RMB 600 million. As Huang had always been regarded as the ideological prop and symbol of GOME, his imprisonment put GOME's business in a tight spot and also gave more market opportunities to its biggest rival, Suning. Especially in 2012, the battle for the control of GOME between Chen Xiao, the then chairman of the board, and Huang's family members revealed the chaotic situation in GOME's leadership and management in the post—Huang Guang-yu era.

After the battle for stock ownership, GOME may have lost its aggressive and strong position in the market during the Huang Guang-yu era, and has maintained a low profile when confronted with the successive challenges of Suning and Jingdong. However, as soon as online sales of home appliances became the new trend of the market, GOME bought out Kubah net, a website for the sales of home appliances, and formed a GOME online shopping mall. Without being noticed, GOME had become an important force in China's online sales of home appliances.

As a matter of fact, the development of GOME is an epitome of many Chinese private enterprises. Benefiting from the favorable opportunities created by China's reform and opening up and the bold decisions and scientific management of managers, many private enterprises have grown rapidly, or are in rapid growth. Their progress is guaranteed not only by such factors as situation, environment and leadership, but also by other opportunities. However, these non-state-run enterprises growing up during this period will be faced with either the bottleneck of leaders' personal capacity or the risks of some illegal operations during their development, bringing about much uncertainty to their growth. Fortunately, with the application of a modern enterprise system in China, more and more Chinese enterprises have rid themselves of "the rule of men" and turned to "the rule of law". Only if an enterprise has surpassed its leaders or founders, like GOME, can it be a promising one worthy of our expectations.

Questions for discussion:

1. Why did China's reform start from the rural areas?
2. What is the relationship between urbanization and the development of new rural areas?
3. Think over the reasons why China chose processing trade at the beginning of the reform and opening up, from the perspective of the international division of labor.

Regional economy is an inevitable issue to be dealt with in the development of any large country's economy. In China, different regions, the inland or the coastal areas, the east, the central, or the west, or even the present regional plates, have developed differently under specific historical backgrounds and in different periods of time, taking advantage of their own natural, geographic and humanistic resources. Their regional economies have experienced the evolution of strategies, structures, and policies in the course of transformation of the economic system and economic growth mode as well as the increasing involvement in global competition.

Chapter 3

The Strategy and Policy Evolution of China's Regional Economy

Since the founding of the People's Republic of China in 1949, the development of China's regional economy has gone through three major stages: the balanced development stage(1949 – 1978) before Reform and Opening up, the non-equilibrium development stage(1978 – 1999) from Reform and Opening up to the end of the 20th century, and the coordinated development stage(2000 – 2014) in the new century. Different regional development strategies have been implemented for each stage, and the government's economic policies have been changing and improving as well.

3. 1 Balanced Development of Regional Economy in the Period of Planned Economy

3. 1. 1 The Zero Foundation of Regional Economy

When the PRC was founded, industrial productivity and resources were extremely unevenly distributed, and the centers of industry were disjointed with places of raw materials and consumption. Large cities on the east coast were the center of China's regional economy. Although the east coastal area covers less than 12% of the whole county's land area, it accumulated over 70% of the modern industrial enterprises, especially three cities/provinces, Tianjin, Liaoning, and Shanghai, which contributed more than 55% of the total Gross Industrial Output Value of the entire coastal areas. In contrast, the vast western area, which occupies 68% of the territory, was still a barren land in industry. Besides, the east coast was facing the threat of a war under the international political environment of that time. As a result, considering the overall national economy, the transfer of economic center from east coast to the inland was imperative.

3. 1. 2   A New Start: Proposal and Implementation of Balanced Development Strategy

The main principle and pattern for socialism productivity distribution, which was elaborated by Marx, Engels, Lenin and others and was adopted by the Soviet Union, is a kind of balanced allocation throughout the country. Guided by this theory and aiming to counterpoise the regional productivity and enforce national defense security, the Chinese government decided to change the unbalanced economic layout and develop industry in the inland. A Balanced Development Strategy was implemented through regional policy preferences, industry structure, investment in key areas, etc.

From 1949 to 1978, the period of planned economy, the central government enforced economic policies by two means under the Balanced Development Strategy. One was to subsidize the West by fiscal revenue allocation and impose a higher ratio of fiscal revenue transfer to the central government on the east coastal provinces. The other was to give the inland priority in national infrastructure investment and layout through mandatory planning. Two massive developments of industry in the western area were conducted during the 1st Five-Year Plan [1] and the Third Front Construction afterward. Following is a brief review of the progress of China's regional economy policies in the planned economy period(see Table 3. 1).

---

[1]   1953-1957.

Table 3.1   The Implementation and Development Status of China's Regional Economy Policies from 1949 to 1978

Period	Policies	Development Status
1949	The east coastal area produced 77% of the national industrial output, while the slowly developing west area only accounted for 6%.	The imbalance of regional economic development posed a serious challenge for PRC
Economic Recovery 1950 – 1952	Recovering and constructing the coastal industrial bases in Shanghai, Liaoning, et al; transferring part of coastal industrial enterprises to the Northeast, Northwest, North China, and East China.	Industry in central and western areas began to be developed, where the industrial output increased by 1.5 times.
1ˢᵗ Five-Year Plan (1953 – 1957)	Concentrating on Southwest and Northwest, enforcing the construction of the northeast industrial base(Anshan Steel as the center), the central industrial base(Wuhan Steel as the center), and the north industrial base (Baotou Steel as the center). 68% of the national large-scale industrial construction projects were located in the inland. 46.8% of the basic construction funds were invested in the central and west areas and 36.9% in coastal areas.	A series of industrial bases were built in the central and west areas, where the industrial outputs reached 34.1% of the country with an average annual growth of 20.5%. Over the same period the growth was 16.8% in coastal areas.
2ⁿᵈ Five-Year Plan (1958 – 1962)	Continuing to develop the basic projects like Wuhan Steel, and Baotou Steel; constructing steel, nonferrous metals and other large projects in Southwest and Northwest, and large hydro-power plant in Sanmenxia surrounding areas along the Yellow River; developing oil, nonferrous metals and other industry in Xinjiang.	The industry of central and west areas transformed into heavy industry.
Economic Adjustment Period (1963 – 1965)	Focusing on the development of heavy industries in North China and Northeast China. Steel industry investment was transferred to central and west areas in Panzhihua, Chengdu, Xining, Shaanxi and Guizhou. Coal industry was established in Northwest, Southwest, and East China; machinery industry bases were in central and inland areas.	The central and west areas had 58.3% of the total basic projects construction. The investments in central and west areas were 1.67 times than those in eastern areas.
3ʳᵈ Five-Year Plan (1965 – 1970) and 4ᵗʰ Five-Year Plan (1971 – 1975)	Constructing Third Front primarily in the Southwest during the 3ʳᵈ Five-Year Plan, and transferring to West Henan, West Hubei, and West Hunan in the 4ᵗʰ Five-Year Plan. Putting efforts to build the Great Southwest, dividing the country into ten Economic Coordination Zones.	A series of distinctive, independent, and highly cooperated industrial systems came into being around the construction of Third Front.

Source: Li Zi-ru, Wen Xian-ming and He Zheng-chu. Economic development from balanced to imbalanced. *The National Conditions and Strength of China*, 2002. 5.

The two to three years after 1949 was an economic recovery period with development focusing on the industrial bases in Northeast China, during which a series of key programs on coal, electricity, aluminum smelting, machinery, etc. , were launched. The 1st Five-Year Plan brought out the guideline of "planned and balanced arrangement of industry in the country" and indicated that "industrial productivity should be distributed properly throughout the country so as to make industry close to the places of raw materials, fuel and consumption, to meet the needs of national defense, to change the current situations, and to develop the economically backward regions. " Therefore, the government put infrastructure investments and heavy industry layouts primarily in the northeastern and inland provinces, concentrating on constructing major industrial bases including Wuhan, Baotou, Lanzhou, Xi'an, Taiyuan, Zhengzhou, Luoyang, and Chengdu.

The primary deployment for the 2nd Five-Year Plan [1] was "to actively and fully utilize and appropriately develop the existing industries in coastal areas along with the massive industrial development in inland area". However, the vision was interrupted by the Great Leap Forward, a national campaign taking place in 1958, when the whole country was divided into numerous communes, each commune pursuing its own massive industrialization without considering resource conditions and feasibility. Projects of different scales emerged everywhere. The movement was not successful. In order to reverse the situation, the government began to readjust the national economic layout from 1963 to 1965, according to the principle of "adjustment, consolidation, enrichment and improvement". Many local small and medium-sized enterprises were shut down and some improperly deployed programs were terminated. The overall regional development priority was given to the heavy industry in East China, and the inland industry continued to be strengthened.

In 1964, the United States' engagement in the Vietnam War and the tension between China and the Soviet Union prompted the central government to estimate a strong possibility of an increasingly serious international situation and the threat of war. The significant strategy of Third Front Construction [2], aiming

---

[1]   1958–1962.

[2]   The Third Front Construction was based on national industrial distribution classified by first front, second front, and third front. As the strategic rear of the country, the third front was mainly the remote mountainous areas in the inland, including the western provinces of Sichuan and Guizhou, most parts of Yunnan, Shaanxi, and Gansu, western Qinghai, as well as western Henan, western Hubei, western Hunan, southern Shanxi in the central region, west Hebei, northern Guangdong, northwestern Guangxi in the eastern region. The construction of third front was mainly through the support of costal industrial enterprises, or even the transfer of these enterprises to local areas. The first front referred to the coastal provinces in the southeast, and the frontlines in the western frontiers.

to make preparation for war, was proposed. In April 1965, the central government issued the *Instructions on Strengthening Preparation for War*, calling for an instant concentration on building national and provincial strategic rears.

During the 3rd Five-Year Plan period, the national investment was focused on the construction of the Third Front areas in the Southwest of China far from the coast and the north, including provinces like Sichuan, Guizhou, etc. And the primary industries to develop were those supporting national defense, including the railway, steel, power, and chemical industries. In the 4th Five-Year Plan, the main construction of the Third Front was moved to West Henan, West Hubei, and West Hunan, the so called "Three Wests", to develop the Great Southwest, and the priority was put on the development of small coal mines, small steel plants, fertilizer, cement, machinery, etc., the local industries that could serve agriculture. During this period, a series of distinctive, independent, and highly cooperated industrial systems came into being. The whole country was divided into ten Economic Coordination Zones, including Southwest China, Northwest China, Central China, South China, East China, North China, Northeast China, Shandong, Fujian, Jiangxi, and Xinjiang.

3.1.3　Effects: Reversing the Imbalanced Productivity Layout

In nearly 30 years after the founding of PRC, the balanced regional economic development strategy expanded the space for productivity development, especially the policy of large-scale investment tilt, and effectively promoted the economic and social development of the inland areas. A heavy industry-oriented industrial production system was basically established. The economic gap between the inland and the east coast was narrowed. Generally speaking, from the 1950s to the middle of the 1970s, the inland areas were given bigger basic construction investment than the coastal areas and the accumulated investment ratio was approximately 1: 0.74 as shown in Table 3.2. The regional economic policies in the period of planned economy contributed a lot to the balanced allocation of productivity in the country, which was presented as the west moving of major projects in the 1st Five-Year Plan and the massive construction of the Third Front. Three-fourths of the 156 major projects were aided by the Soviet Union and two-thirds of the total investment were put into the inland. Of the 694 large-scale basic construction projects (with an investment of more than RMB 10 million), 68% were distributed in the inland. Meanwhile, 66.8% of the investment in infrastructure during the Third Front construction was allocated to the inland.

Table 3. 2   Proportion of Basic Construction Investment on Coastal and Inland Areas
from 1st Five-Year Plan to 4th Five-Year Plan Period

Region	1st Five-Year Plan (1953−1957)	2nd Five-Year Plan (1958−1962)	1963−1965	3rd Five-Year Plan (1966−1970)	4th Five-Year Plan (1971−1975)
Coastal	36. 9	38. 4	34. 9	26. 9	35. 5
Inland	46. 8	56. 0	58. 3	64. 7	54. 4
Coastal∕ Inland	0. 79	0. 69	0. 6	0. 42	0. 65

The purchase of motor vehicles, ships, aircrafts and other national unified investment were not classified
into any region, therefore, the sum of coastal and inland proportions is less than 100% .

Source: Department of National Economy Statistics, National Bureau of Statistics. *Compilation of
China's Statistics in 50 Years.* China Statistics Press. 1999.

The preferential policies for the inland areas promoted the fast development
of the once blank areas. The strategic objective of balanced development of the
regional economy was basically realized. The proportion of industry in the inland
areas increased substantially, and a number of industrial bases of considerable size
and strength were established, which played a positive role in enhancing the
utilization of the abundant resources in the west, accelerating the economic
development in the coastal areas and improving the overall strength of China's
economy. The steel industrial bases in central and western regions, new heavy
machinery industrial bases in central regions, and a batch of new bases of steel,
nonferrous metals, petroleum, large hydropower in the Southwest, Northwest,
Sanmenxia city and other regions were established during this period. A number
of textile industrial centers were developed in Beijing, Shijiazhuang, Handan,
Xi'an and Xianyang. In addition, railways of the Chengdu-Chongqing, Baoji-
Chengdu, Tianshui-Lanzhou, Lanzhou-Xinjiang, and highways of Qinghai-
Tibet as well as Sichuang-Tibet were constructed. The industrial bases built in
Lanzhou, Xi'an, Chengdu, Luoyang, Wuhan, Taiyuan, Baotou and other
major cities were gradually formed, and a group of enterprises were established in
Third Front regions of West Henan, West Hubei and West Hunan.

The imbalanced productivity layout was amended after the recovery and
construction of the national economy during the planned economy period. From
1953 to 1978, China invested RMB 341. 77 billion in the inland, which
accounted for 60. 5% of total investment in the country and 54. 9% of the
national basic construction funds. The ratio of the coastal areas' industrial output
to that of the inland dropped from 7: 3 to 6: 4. The rapid development of
productivity in central and western regions laid a solid foundation for further
development.

3.1.4　Defect: Development at the Expense of Efficiency

The balanced regional economic development strategy formed an equality throughout the country; however, at the expense of efficiency. Without considering the characteristics of the natural environment, economic foundation, geographical conditions and human resources in different regions, the strategy promoted a distribution of industry everywhere in the country, neglecting the economics of scale and agglomeration, which are the basic development laws. The artificial balanced industrial production distribution led to a low overall economic efficiency, and return on the investment was generally low. As shown in Table 3.3, despite the investment preferences towards the inland areas, the coastal areas still had a larger industrial output. In 1978, the proportion of coastal industrial output only decreased by 1.6% compared with 1952, while the proportion of the inland over the same period increased by 8.9%. The proportion of coastal GDP was also higher than that of inland. By 1978, the coastal GDP proportion even increased by 1.8%, while that of inland decreased by 1.8%. The policy preferences neither brought satisfying economic efficiency to the inland nor narrowed the development gap between the inland and coastal areas(see Table 3.3).

Table 3.3　Comparison of Major Economic Indexes between Coastal and Inland Areas in 1952 and 1978

		Region	
		Coastal(11 Provinces)	Inland(18 Provinces)
Percentage of Industrial Output Value	1952	61.7	31.0
	1978	60.1	39.9
Change in Percentage Points		−1.6	+8.9
Percentage of National GDP	1952	50.7	49.3
	1978	52.5	47.5
Change in Percentage Points		+1.8	−1.8

Note: The statistics of 1952 did not include the data of Guangdong, Jiangxi and Tibet.

Source: Department of National Economy Statistics, National Bureau of Statistics. *Compilation of China's Statistics in 50 Years*. China Statistics Press. 1999.

After nearly 30 years of investment and construction tilt towards the inland, the balanced regional economic development strategy under the planned economy did not fundamentally achieve its strategic objectives. Although the proportion of investment was reduced, the economy in coastal areas managed to develop rapidly due to their advantages in environmental conditions, industrial foundation and human resources. From another perspective, the strategy, pursuing the balanced development between the coast and the inland, was implemented for a closed economy, and therefore emphasizing the development and cycle of the domestic economy. The role of the international market in balancing the regional and inter-industry development was comparatively neglected. The neglect was kind of inevitable in the specific conditions, but as the external political and economic conditions had changed, the continuous implementation of the balanced regional economic policies would no longer help China's opening up and economic development. Therefore, the strategy had to be changed.

3. 2   Non-Equilibrium Development of Regional Economy in the Period of Reform and Opening up

3. 2. 1   Breaking up the Stagnant Planned Economy

In 1978, the Third Plenary Session of the 11th Central Committee of the CPC started a new chapter of Reform and Opening up for China. The regional economic development thus entered a new era.

Firstly, the regional economic development was re-established under the guiding ideology of the "common prosperity" and the "two overall situations" first proposed by Deng Xiao-ping. At the central working meeting held on December 13, 1978, Deng Xiao-ping made the speech *Emancipate the Mind, Seek Truth from Facts and Unite as One in Looking to the Future*, arguing that "I think our economic policies should allow part of the regions, enterprises, workers, and peasants to earn more and live better sooner than the others, through their hard working…they will set examples for other regions and units, who will learn from them … thus helping the people of all our nationalities to get prosperous comparatively sooner. " In March 1983, he proposed " making use of the comparative advantage, avoiding weak points and acknowledging the imbalance. " In September 1988, he suggested that the government should "accelerate the opening up of coastal areas, making this vast zone with a population of 200 million quickly develop first, so as to drive a better development of the inland. It was a matter regarding the overall situation; the inland should show consideration for the overall situation. "

Secondly, the regional developing theories and experience in other countries, especially Hirschman's theory of non-equilibrium growth and

Perroux's growth pole theory, provided strong theoretical supports for China. The non-equilibrium growth theory emphasizes that economic growth is unbalanced, and the developing countries should concentrate the limited resources and capital on several major sectors, especially the sectors with strong correlation and resources allocation effects. Areas with better conditions should be developed first, through the transfer of elements and industries from high-gradient regions to low-gradient areas, promoting the development of backward areas.

Lastly, international situations had changed significantly; peace and development had become the dominant trend in international relations. China's relations with the United States, Japan, the Soviet Union and neighboring countries continued to be improved, which created conditions to concentrate on the development of the domestic economy.

Based on the experiences and lessons learned from regional economic development after 1949, China made a great adjustment in its regional economic policies. A balanced regional economic development strategy was discarded to avoid sacrificing the efficiency, creating an efficiency-oriented non-equilibrium strategy. Regional economic development began to be planned according to various aspects such as geographic advantages, resource advantages and technical advantages, rather than the previous artificial manipulation of industrial layout. Reform and opening up was implemented in the eastern areas first, aiming to drive the economy in other regions and finally realizing prosperity throughout the country.

3. 2. 2 Efficiency-Oriented Non-Equilibrium Regional Economic Development Strategy

From 1978 to 1991, affected by Hirschman's non-equilibrium growth theory, the central government made investment and industrial distribution preferential to the coastal areas, which had better resources and economic foundations. The disadvantaged areas and ethnic minority regions were subsidized by the central government. The economic policies supporting the coastal areas mainly included three aspects: investment tilt, attempt to open to the outside world, and attempt to create system reform and various preferential policies.

A. Transfer of Investment Priority to the East Coastal Areas

Under the preferential strategy for the east coast, the investment proportion in these areas continued to increase. The 6th Five-Year Plan proposed "to make active use of the existing economic foundations in the coastal region and give full play to their strengths to further drive the development of inland areas". As shown in Table 3. 4, the proportion of basic construction investment in coastal areas was for the first time higher than the inland areas by 1. 2% . The coastal areas became the main target for China's regional investment and the pioneer of development. During the 6th Five-Year Plan period, the construction of textile bases was strengthened in 20 major cities, including Shanghai, Beijing, Tianjin and Dalian, and technological transformation was completed in these cities as well. During the 7th Five-Year Plan period, the coastal proportion of basic construction investment increased from 47. 7% to 50. 9% , and the proportion of the inland decreased from 46. 5% to 40. 1% . The investment ratio between coastal and inland areas became 1. 03 : 1, compared with 1. 27 : 1 in the previous period.

Table 3. 4   Proportions of Investment from 5th −7th Five Year Plans Period(%)

Region	the 5th Five Year Plan (1976−1980)	the 6th Five Year Plan (1981−1985)	the 7th Five Year Plan (1986−1990)
Coastal	42. 2	47. 7	50. 9
Inland	50. 0	46. 5	40. 1
Coastal/Inland	0. 84	1. 03	1. 27

The purchase of motor vehicles, ships, aircrafts and other national unified investments were not classified into any region, therefore, the sum of coastal and inland proportions was less than 100% .

Source: Department of National Economy Statistics, National Bureau of Statistics. *Compilation of China's Statistics in 50 Years*. China Statistics Press. 1999.

B. First Opening to the Outside World

The pace of opening to the outside was accelerated in this period. The east coastal areas were the first opening up regions, which were given various preferential policies. From 1978 to 1990, China made up "the economic strategy of primarily opening the coastal areas and gradually opening the inland areas". The opening was started from establishing special economic zones(SEZs) in east coastal areas. The CPC Central Committee and the State Council decided to adopt special policies and flexible measures for foreign economic activities in Guangdong and Fujian. Since 1980, four SEZs have been established in Shenzhen, Zhuhai, Shantou in Guangdong province, and Xiamen in Fujian province. In 1988, the island of Hainan was founded as a province and designated as the biggest SEZ in China. China created a beginning for socialist countries to establish SEZs. Recognized as a landmark milestone in China's opening history, these SEZs functioned as laboratories for economic system reform and windows for opening to the outside. Based on the experiences gained from SEZs, China went on to designate open coastal cities and coastal economic and technology development zones. In April 1984, the State Council further opened 14 coastal cities to overseas investment: Tianjin, Shanghai, Dalian, Qinhuangdao, Qingdao, Yantai, Lianyungang, Nantong, Ningbo, Wenzhou, Fuzhou, Guangzhou, Zhanjiang and Beihai. Besides, 12 economic and technology development zones were established in Dalian, Qinghuandao and other cities, adopting similar policies as the SEZs. In February 1985, 61 cities and counties of the Pearl River Delta, Yangtze River Delta, and Xiamen-Zhangzhou-Quanzhou Triangle Area(in South Fujian) were designated as coastal economic development zones, where the urban areas of the cities and counties and the permitted industrial satellite towns could implement the policies of open coastal cities. In 1988, the Shandong Peninsula and Liaodong Peninsula were designated as open economic zones, and Taiwanese investment zones were established in Fujian. In 1990, the development and opening of Shanghai Pudong New Area was approved, which was entitled to certain preferential policies of SEZs.

C. First System Reform

From 1979 to 1987, the foreign trade system reform focused on changing the highly concentrated operating system and the single management system of mandatory plans, in order to decentralize the foreign trade rights. After that, There was an overall advancement of foreign trade system reform from 1988 to 1990. Aiming to boost the energy of enterprises, the foreign trade system reform in the east coastal areas included the implementation of the contract responsibility system to replace the original target control by using foreign exchange. The system of planned foreign trade was further reformed and a pilot experiment of self-financing was done in enterprises of light industry, crafts and apparel. Taking the areas along the east coast as the national strategic center of regional economic development, the government adopted the foreign trade strategy to make township and village enterprises the engine, and put two ends of production (material purchasing and goods sale) into the international market to promote a large-volume of import and export in order to speed up the development of east coastal areas in the world economic cycle(see Table 3. 5). In addition, various incentives in finance, taxation, credit and investment were given to the eastern areas, such as deducting the tax, expanding the local autonomy of investment, establishing and opening financial markets.

Table 3.5　Major Steps of East Coastal Areas' Development as Economic Focus

Main Strategy	Period	Specific Measures
First opening the east coastal areas to the outside world	1980	First four SEZs were established in Shenzhen, Zhuhai, Shantou, and Xiamen.
	1984	The State Council designated 14 open coastal cities.
	1985	The island of Hainan was founded as a province and designated as the biggest SEZ in China.
	1990	The development and opening strategy for Shanghai Pudong New Area was proposed. Bonded areas were established in Tianjin, Shanghai, Guangzhou, and Jiangsu, etc.
Basic construction investment tilt to the east coastal areas	1981–1989	The east coastal areas were given basic construction investment of RMB 357 billion, which accounted for 50.1% of the national investment. The central and west areas got 34.4% of the total investment.
First foreign trade system reform and preferential policies	1988	Foreign trade system reform was first implemented.
	1988	Various incentives in finance, taxation, credit, and investment were given to the eastern areas, such as tax deduction, expanding the local autonomy of investment, establishing and opening financial markets.

D.　Effect of the Efficiency-Oriented Non-Equilibrium Strategy

The positive effect of the efficiency-oriented non-equilibrium strategy was primarily reflected in what people said, "a peacock flying to the southeast", the name of an ancient opera, describing the concentration of production factors in the southeast coastal areas. The coastal areas were granted the priority developing opportunity under reform and opening up and the non-equilibrium strategy. From 1986 to 1989, the coastal provinces got the largest proportions of national investment. Meanwhile, under the guidance of the export-oriented strategy and tax preferential policies, the southeast coastal areas attracted a lot of foreign direct investment. As domestic and foreign capital flooded into the coastal areas, the region became the best place for emerging industries. The east coastal areas became the fastest developing region in China as well as the most dynamic, which not only pushed China's internal reform and opening to the outside world, but also maximized the overall efficiency of the national economy. In 1984, the 14 open coastal cities, with only 7.7% of the national population, produced 23.1% of the industrial output, and industrial output per capita was three times that of the national average. From 1985 to 1990, national exports increased by 1.1 times, while the eastern areas increased by 2.5 times. The eastern areas' proportion of national export increased from 74.2% to 80.8% from 1985 to

1990, during which the use of foreign funds increased by 2.2 times, growing from USD 1.75 billion to USD 3.89 billion. In addition, the pioneering development of the eastern areas resulted in a strong radiation, expanding and promoting effect, which supported the development of the central and western areas to a certain extent, promoting the formation of three major economic regions, namely, the eastern, central and western regions. Compared with 1985, the economic growth rate in 1990 exceeded 100% in all three regions, of which the western region had the highest rate, up to 122.5%. From 1978 to 1992, the annual average growth rate of national income per capita reached 8.28%, 6.73% and 7.1% respectively in those three regions, compared with 4.63%, 2.92%, and 3.53% from 1952 to 1978.

However, the non-equilibrium economic development strategy also resulted in some negative effects. Firstly, the regional economic development gap was widened. The fast development in the eastern areas attracted a lot of factors of production from the central and western areas, where the development impetus was weakened. Equality was comparatively neglected in pursuing efficiency. Secondly, the eastern provinces, contesting for the central government's preferential policies, on which economic development mainly relied, and domestic and foreign investment, tended to have unhealthy competition which led to economic blockade. The similar industrial structure also increased the unhealthy competition. Blind pursuit of economic growth also caused energy shortages, environmental pollution and other conflicts and problems.

In conclusion, the non-equilibrium strategy and policies accelerated the transfer of China's economic development focus to the east coastal areas, whose rapid development substantially increased the national strength. On the other hand, the strategy also caused greater gaps among three major regions.

3.2.3　Non-Equilibrium Regional Economic Development Strategy Focusing on Efficiency and Equality

A.　Regional Economic Strategy Started to Consider Equality

As the economic development gap between the three major economic zones continued to expand, and the inadequate supply of energy and raw materials resources created an urgent need to accelerate the development of the central and west regions, the regional economic development strategy in China had to consider the equality of economic development while maintaining the efficiency of economic growth. In 1990, the 8th Five-Year Plan first requested a rational division and coordinated development of regional economy. The 9th Five-Year

Plan proposed "coordinated development of regional economy, and gradually narrowing the regional economic gap", and made it a major principle to guide the economic and social development in the coming 15 years. In 1997, the report to the 15th National Congress of the CPC emphasized the importance of "gradually narrowing the regional development gap in various ways" and "promoting the rational distribution and coordinated development of regional economy. "

In the 1990s, China began to adjust its regional economic strategy, implementing preferential policies for certain regions and industries to promote the development of the backward central and western regions, while maintaining the advantages of the east coastal regions. To keep the advantage of the eastern areas, 15 bonded areas were established in Shanghai Waigaoqiao, Tianjin Port, Shenzhen Futian, etc. The coastal economic open zones were further opened, and much more economic and technological development zones were established. The promotion of central and western economic development also started from opening to the outside. A number of cities along the borders, rivers and railway lines were opened. In 1992, 13 border cities and capitals of inland provinces as well as autonomous regions were opened, including Heihe, Suifenhe, Manzhouli, Huichun, Erenhot, Yining, Tacheng, Bole, Wanding, Ruili, Hekou, and Dongxing. In August 1994, the government established the Three-Gorges Economic Open Zone, opening the cities of Yichang, Wanxian, Fuling, Yueyang and Wuhu along the Yangtze River. Afterwards, a number of cities along railway lines were opened, including Lianyungang, Xuzhou, Zhengzhou, Xi'an, Lanzhou, Urumqi, Alashankou, etc. By then, a diversified pattern of opening integrating border, river, and railways areas had been formed in central and west China. In addition, the opening of the central and western regions was also expanded by encouraging the foreign invested enterprises in eastern regions to invest in central and western areas. A number of national economic and technological development zones were established, and the approval authority for foreign investment was increased in the inland. A multi-level, multi-channel and comprehensive opening pattern was formed in China

During the 9th Five-Year Plan period, the government, aiming to narrow the economic development gap between the eastern regions and the central and western regions, took the following six specific measures: 1) giving priority to distributing the resources exploitation and infrastructure construction projects in the central and western regions; 2) increasing the financial support for the central and western regions through central government's financial transfer payment system; 3) enhancing the self-developing ability of the central and western regions by adjusting the prices of resource products; 4) providing more support to poverty-stricken areas and supporting economic development in minority areas; 5) accelerating reforms to attract more foreign investment; 6) strengthening the economic and technological cooperation between eastern regions and central and western regions; encouraging more professional human resources to move to the central and western regions. Under the stimulus of these policies, the economy in these regions witnessed quite a rapid growth. In 1996, the economic growth rate in the central and western regions had approached the East, and the investment growth rate had surpassed the East.

B. Adjustment of Regional Economic Policies Failed to Narrow Development Gap

Although the national policy had been adjusted, the gap of economic development between the East and the West was not narrowed. The polarization effect in the market economy was obviously shown in the better and faster growth of the eastern region compared with the central and western regions, and all kinds of resources, production factors, and human resources kept assembling in the East. The center of the national economy was still in the East. Although the economic development in eastern, central and western regions all gained fast growth, the growth rate gap was still very obvious. The East got the highest rate, while the West had the lowest. As is shown in Table 3.6, in terms of both the proportions of GDP and GDP per capita, the regional gaps widened quickly. The proportion of GDP in eastern regions had continued to expand by 1995, while the proportion of central and western regions kept shrinking. The gap of GDP per capita was even greater. In 1995, the eastern GDP per capita was 1.42 times that of the national level, 1.68 times of the central, and 2.37 times of the west (see Table 3.6).

Table 3.6   The development Gap between the Three Major Economic Regions

	GDP						GDP per capita					
	1985		1990		1995		1985		1990		1995	
	Billion RMB	%	Billion RMB	%	Billion RMB	%	Billion RMB	%	Billion RMB	%	Billion RMB	%
Whole Nation	896.44	100	1854.79	100	5847.81	100	84.69	100	162.23	100	485.40	100
East	457.68	51.1	998.58	53.8	3384.20	57.9	106.38	125.6	212.63	131.7	688.23	141.8
Central	267.54	29.8	547.92	29.5	1590.75	27.2	71.42	84.3	134.57	82.9	370.46	76.3
West	120.76	13.5	268.64	14.5	711.12	12.2	56.83	67.1	116.17	71.6	290.20	59.8

Note: The disposable income per capita of urban residents in western regions does not include data from on Tibet.

Source: National Bureau of Statistics. *China Statistical Yearbook 1996*. Beijing, China Statistics Press. 1996.

The development gaps between the three regions could also be seen through their industrialization and urbanization. The rate of industrialization in the East rose from 40. 3% in 1990 to 42. 9% in 1995, reaching the middle level of industrialization. The rates in central and western regions increased substantially in the first half of the 1990s; however, the rates were 3. 8% and 8. 3% lower than the East respectively. There were altogether 640 cities in China in 1995, of which 75 were large and medium-sized with a population of over 0. 5 million. Of all the cities, 290 (45. 3%) were located in the East with 38 (50. 7%) of them being large and medium-sized cities; 234 cities were in the central regions with 29 of them being large and medium sized. The West had 116 cities with only 8 large and medium-sized cities. Moreover, the unbalanced developments led to a lot of problems, such as fighting for resources among local governments, inter-regional barriers, unfair competition, distorted industrial layout, unbalanced social identity (see Table 3. 7) . These problems hindered the economic development and market growth and at the same time seriously disturbed the order of the regional economy.

Table 3. 7   Problems Caused by Unbalanced Development

Major Problems	Main Manifestation
Unbalanced flow and accumulation of resources under market mechanism	Under the market mechanism, economic factors naturally flew to the regional economy that had a higher level of preferential conditions, which led to the accumulation of superior economic resources and serious unbalanced regional development in the country.
Unequal competitions	Unequal competitions was common among different regions, different areas within a region, and sectors of different forms of ownership.
Distorted industrial distribution	The developed regions had advantages in developing whatever industry, and therefore enterprises kept coming in, whereas it was difficult for backward provinces to make use of their human and natural resources to develop industries. The developed regions were over-invested, while the backward regions were lacking in investment. National industrial distribution was distorted. Enterprises tended to be smaller and too much scattered. Investors led by local government were enthusiastic for developing and processing high-profit products. As a result, regional specialization was weak, and a lot of scarce resources were wasted.
Regional gap widened	The economic development gap between the eastern region and central and western regions kept widening. The economic aggregate and GDP per capita of central and western regions had a big gap with the eastern region and average national level.

Cont.

Major Problems	Main Manifestation
Unbalanced social identity	The concept of imbalance had permeated into every class, sector, and region and brought out a multi-level unbalanced layout, which finally caused identity crisis. Social anomie caused by unbalanced economic development inevitably led to tremendous pressure on political order. Regional frictions increasingly intensified the blockade. Local governments use various means to build numerous trade barriers and set up blockade for movement of local resources, technology, personnel and goods. Administrative power was used to intervene in the export of local raw materials, capital and personnel and the import of goods, which seriously hindered the development of the economy and market and destroyed regional economic orders.

3. 3   Coordinated Development of Regional Economy in the Period of Comprehensive Development

Since 1999, considering the disadvantages of the non-equilibrium strategy, the central government began to think about adopting a coordinated regional development strategy. While focusing on comprehensive development of the regional economy, the strategy also included expanding domestic demand, ecological protection and other important topics into its scope. Along with the leading development of eastern areas, the central government brought forward the Western Development Strategy, The Strategy of Revitalizing Old Industrial Bases in Northeastern China and Rise of Central China Plan. By then, China had formed a "four-wheel-drive"[1] pattern of regional development. The four major economic regions, geographically distinctive and given clear development tasks and goals, would become the bases for developing the regional economy and building harmonious socialist society. China thus entered a new stage of regional development.

3. 3. 1   The Overall Implementation of Coordinated Regional Development Strategy

In the vast territory of China, the levels of economic and social development were uneven in different regions due to the disparities in natural conditions, resources and industrial foundation. A country with only some prosperous areas is

---

1   The "four-wheel-drive" means the development distribution pattern that consists of four priority development zones of the west, the northeast, the central, and the east.

not really prosperous. Coordinated development concerns not a certain region but the whole country. The central government attached great importance to the promotion of coordinated development and took a series of actions. As the strategies for eastern leading development, western development, northeastern vitalization and central rise were implemented, a number of regional planning and policies were approved, and the strategy of coordinated development became an important part of national economic strategy. In this new pattern, the eastern, central and western regions could interact, complement and support each other, and develop together. In 2007, the western economic growth rate surpassed the eastern for the first time. After that, the economic growth rates of the central, western, and northeastern regions were higher than the eastern regions for four consecutive years from 2008 to 2011.

A. The Strategy for the Eastern Region's Leading Development

China's eastern region includes ten east coastal provinces and cities, namely, Beijing, Tianjin, Hebei, Shandong, Jiangsu, Shanghai, Zhejiang, Fujian, Guangdong and Hainan. With an area less than 10% of the country(916,000 square kilometers), it has 38% of the national population(about 510.63 million in 2011). The region is marked by rich human resources, sophisticated industrial systems, and high levels of modernization and opening.

Having gained advantages in the beginning of the Reform and Opening up, the eastern region should strive to take the lead in realizing modernization under the new strategy of coordinated development. Therefore, "four taking-the-lead objectives" were set for the eastern region. Firstly, taking the lead to improve its self-dependent innovation capacity. Secondly, taking the lead to realize the optimization of economic structure and the transformation of growth patterns. Thirdly, taking the lead to improve the socialist market economy system. Fourthly, taking the lead to help the central and western regions in their economic development. With the implementation of east leading development strategy and marked by the rise of the Pearl River Delta(PRD), Yangtze River Delta (YRD) and the Bohai Economic Rim (BER), regional economic integration has become increasingly significant in the east region. PRD, YRD and BER have accelerated the integration of regional development in recent years, and their stimulation effects to the surrounding areas are getting stronger.

The *Framework for Development and Reform Planning for the Pearl River Delta Region(2008 – 2020)* was announced in January 2009. According to the framework, the PRD is composed of nine major cities in Guangdong province, namely, Guangzhou, Shenzhen, Zhuhai, Foshan, Jiangmen, Dongguan, Zhongshan,

Huizhou and Zhaoqing, which will be developed from a pilot region into a world-class base for manufacturing and service industries, and an important national economic center. The *Framework Agreement on Hong Kong-Guangdong Cooperation* signed in 2010 marked a big step for PRD's economic integration forward into Pan-Pearl River Delta. In 2011, the Greenway Network of PRD, with a total length of 2, 372 kilometers, was finished, realizing the fast connection of the nine major cities. With additional branch ways, the network also links major tourism destinations and scenic spots. Five regional integration plans for infrastructure, industrial distribution, public service, urban and rural planning and environmental protection have been carried out in PRD. Regional economy and social development have made a breakthrough and comprehensive strength increased substantially. The total GDP of PRD reached RMB 4. 37 trillion in 2011, with a growth of 9. 9% compared with 2010, and the GDP per capita reached RMB 77, 637.

The *Regional Plan for Yangtze River Delta* was officially approved in May 2010, aiming to turn the YRD region into an important international gateway to the Asia-Pacific region, the world's major modern service industry and advanced manufacturing center, and a city agglomeration with strong international competitiveness. The plan also proposed to develop YRD into a well-off society by 2015, and strive to realize modernization by 2020. In order to achieve regional integration, the Yangtze River Delta constructed a regional rapid transit network to shorten the distance between cities and build a "one hour commute", "three-hour economic circle", and gradually realize the "one-city effect". Inter-city highways of Shanghai-Ningbo, Shanghai-Hangzhou and Shanghai-Hangzhou-Ningbo were constructed to link the major cities in the YRD region. By 2011, the GDP of YRD reached RMB 10. 06 trillion, an increase of 9. 8% compared to 2010, and GDP per capita reached RMB 64, 240.

Following the integrated economic development of PRD and YRD, the BER region, mainly in Beijing, Tianjin and Hebei, is becoming China's "third growth pole". The regional economic integration of BER was mainly through coordinated industrial distribution and multi-level cooperation between local governments as well as enterprises in industries, infrastructure construction, etc. However, the regional integration of BER has just started and it still has a considerably long way to catch up with PRD and YRD. In 2011, the GDP of BER reached RMB 5. 21 trillion, an increase of 19% from 2010, and GDP per capita reached RMB 49, 057. 9.

Besides the three major economic regions, four smaller economic zones have been formed in the east coastal region, namely, Shandong Peninsula Economic

Zone, Jiangsu Coastal Economic Zone, Guangxi Beibu Gulf Economic Zone and Western Taiwan Straits Economic Zone respectively. Although these economic zones are not as sophisticated as the three major economic regions, they are important for enhancing the eastern region's competitiveness and its pilot function, as well as narrowing the development gap inside the region. By 2011, the GDP of the eastern region had reached RMB 27. 16 trillion, accounting for 52% of national GDP and the GDP per capita reached RMB 53, 350. Urban employed population reached 67. 84 million, accounting for 47. 1% of national urban employment. Total fixed asset investment was RMB 13. 03 trillion, accounting for 42. 6% of the country. The total import and export of goods hit USD 3. 14 trillion, accounting for 86. 2% of the country.

B. The Western Development Strategy

China's western region has a vast area and abundant natural resources. It also includes various minority groups and their diverse cultures. The region includes six provinces(Gansu, Guizhou, Qinghai, Shanxi, Sichuan, and Yunnan), five autonomous regions(Guangxi, Inner Mongolia, Ningxia, Tibet, and Xinjiang) and one municipality(Chongqing). Containing 71. 5% of the national area(6. 87 million square kilometers), the area has only 27% of the population. The non-equilibrium development strategy adopted since the Reform and Opening up had created a big development gap between the East and West while boosting the economy of the east. The Western Development Strategy was adopted to gradually eliminate the gap. A variety of policies in finance, law and tax were taken to support the development of the western region, as well as to enhance the overall strength of the national economy.

The promotion for western development was called for by Former CPC Secretary General Jiang Ze-min in Xi'an on June 19, 1999. The 5th Plenary Session of the 15th CPC Central Committee put forward the western development plan in October 2000. The *Declaration of Policies and Measures for Implementing Western Development* issued by the State Council on December 27, 2000 manifested the official start of western development strategy. The objective of the strategy is to accelerate the reform and opening up and strengthen the capacity of development in the western region through national support and regional cooperation. Major strategic measures include infrastructure development, energy and mineral resources development, environmental protection, local industries development with comparative advantages, resources transforming, promotion of equal access to public services, poverty alleviation, human resource development and technological innovation.

From 2000 to 2010, the western development program initiated 143 key projects with a total investment of RMB 2.9 trillion. Over 40% of the infrastructure investment and the financial transfer payment from the central government during this period were given to the West. By 2011, the main lines of the state highways were completed with a total length of 18.6 thousand kilometers, 7.4 times longer than they had been ten years before. Through a series of investment and construction, the western economy was developed and people's living standard was raised substantially. In 2011, the GDP of the western region reached RMB 10.02 trillion, accounting for 19.2% of national GDP, and the GDP per capita reached RMB 27,731. Urban employed population reached 31.64 million, 21.9% of the total urban employment. Total fixed asset investment was RMB 7.21 trillion, accounting for 23.6% of the country. The total import and export of goods reached USD 183.9 billion, accounting for 5% of the country.

C. The Strategy of Revitalizing Old Industrial Bases in Northeastern China

The share of industrial output of the three northeast provinces kept falling since the start of Reform and Opening up, decreasing from 16% to 9.3%. A lot of natural resources were nearly exhausted due to the long and intensive development. The report to the 16th CPC Central Committee brought out the concept of rejuvenating Northeastern China in November 2002, indicating that the government would definitely "support the adjustment and transformation of old industrial bases in the northeastern and other regions, and development of alternative industries in the cities that used to depend on resource exploration. " In October 2003, the State Council issued *Guidelines for Implementing the Revitalizing Plan of the Old Industrial Bases in Northeastern and Other Regions*, marking the official start of the plan.

The old industrial bases cover the three provinces of Heilongjiang, Jilin, and Liaoning. The region has 8.2% of the national territory (788, 000 square kilometers) as well as the same percentage of national population (109.66 million in 2011). The old industrial bases used to be "the eldest son of the republic" and the "armed forces of the republic", but after more than 20 years since the reform and opening up, they encountered a lot of economic and social problems such as the decline of the state-owned economy and a large number of laid-off workers. The revitalizing plan aimed to solve these problems, focusing on promoting innovation in the institutional system, industrial structure adjustment, state-owned enterprises reform, tax reform, and social employment.

In August 2007, the *Northeastern Revitalization Plan*, aiming to fully rejuvenate the region in ten to fifteen years, was approved. The *Liaoning Coastal Economic Zone Development Plan* and *Tumen River Regional Cooperation Development Guidelines: Changchun-Jilin-Tumenas Leading Development and Opening Areas* were approved by the State Council in 2009. In the same year, the Guidelines for Promoting Northeastern Revitalization Plan was issued. In April 2010, the Shenyang Economic Zone was designated by the National Development Reform Committee as National New Industrialization Reform Pilot Zone. Economic growth was accelerated in the three northeastern provinces, gradually catching up with the national economic growth rate. Especially in 2008, the GDP growth rate reached 13.4%, which was 1.7% higher than the national average growth rate. With the fastest growth of the region since reform and opening up, the growth rate ranked No.1 among the four regions. In 2011, the GDP of the northeastern provinces reached RMB 4.54 trillion, accounting for 8.7% of the national GDP. GDP per capita reached RMB 41,400. The urban employed population was 13.24 million, 9.2% of national employed population. Total fixed asset investment was RMB 3.26 trillion, accounting for 10.7% of the country. The total import and export of goods reached USD 156.62 billion, accounting for 4.3% of the country.

D. Rise of Central China Plan

As the various strategies promoted the development in the east, west, and northeast, the development of the central region was relatively backward and became the main problem of China's regional economy. The central region covers six provinces: Shanxi, Henan, Anhui, Hubei, Hunan and Jiangxi. With 10.7% of the national area (1.03 million square kilometers) and 26.7% of national population, the central region is a densely populated area. It acts as a link between the East and the West in the strategic plan of China's regional development. The central region contributes 40% of China's grain output. It has a rural population of 244 million, nearly one-third of the national rural population. To adopt the Central China Plan, the investment on agricultural infrastructure would be increased so as to enhance the agricultural productivity. It would also help solve the problems of agriculture and rural areas in China, and increase the income of farmers. Food and energy safety would also be enhanced.

The concept of "the rise of central China" was first brought out by Premier Wen Jia-bao in his government report in March 2004. The Central Economic Work Conference in December 2004 mentioned the promotion of the development of the central region again. In April 2006, the *Guidelines for Promoting the Rise of Central China* was issued, indicating that the region would be built into a national important grain production base, energy and raw material base, modern equipment manufacturing and high-tech industrial base, and integrated transport hub ("three bases and one hub"). In May 2006, *Policies and Measures for Implementing Guidelines for Promoting the Rise of Central China* brought generated 56 guiding policies. In September 2009, the State Council executive meeting discussed and passed in principle the *Plan for Promoting the Rise of Central China.*

The Rise of Central China Plan aims at making use of the region's geographic advantages and resources so as to promote industrialization and urbanization. With the emphasis on building a featured economy of the region, the plan proposes to construct a growth pole of the region so as to form a coordinated economic development pattern between the east, central and west. The investment growth rate in the central regions has grown considerably in recent years, over 30% for three years in a row from 2007 to 2009. In 2011, the GDP of the six central provinces reached RMB 10.45 trillion, accounting for 20% of national GDP. GDP per capita reached RMB 29,229. The urban employed population was 31.42 million, 21.8% of the national employed population. Total fixed asset investment was RMB 7.08 trillion, accounting for 23.2% of the country. The total import and export of goods reached USD 162.67 billion, accounting for 4.5% of the country.

3.3.2 The Strategy of Development Priority Zones and Interaction of Regional Economies

In order to foster the growth poles of each region and accelerate the "four-wheel-drive" strategy, the government issued a series of specific development policies for some cities, provinces and big regions since 2005. These specific regional development policies were conducive to the comprehensive and coordinated development of the regions that greatly supported the regional reform and opening up in China. In June 2005, the State Council approved the Shanghai Pudong New Area for the integrated and comprehensive pilot reform. In August 2010, the State Council approved the establishment of eight comprehensive pilot reform zones, including Shanghai Pudong New Area, Chongqing, Chengdu, Tianjin Binhai New Area, Wuhan Urban Agglomeration, Xiangtan Urban Agglomeration, Shenzhen, Shenyang Economic Zone. Shanghai Pudong New Area, Tianjin Binhai New Area, and Chongqing Liangjiang New Area were upgraded as sub-provincial areas. In addition, a number of regional or special plans were carried out to develop the 16 areas, including Guangxi Beibu Gulf, Yangtze River Delta, Pearl River Delta, Shanghai (as an international financial center and international shipping center), West Economic Zone of Taiwan Strait, Jiangsu Coastal Economic Zone, Hengqin New Zone, Guanzhong-Tianshui Economic Zone, Liaoning Coastal Economic Zone, the central region, Tumen River area, Yellow River Delta, Poyang Lake area, Hainan International Tourism Island, Anhui City clusters, and the Greater and Lesser Khingan Mountain areas.

These special plans were conducted under three principles: to accelerate the development of key areas, to push forward the significant development strategies, and to extend the scope of certain areas. Some of the plans were programming for important development priority zones, e. g. Shanghai Pudong New Area, Tianjin Binhai New Area, and Chongqing Liangjiang New Area. Some were focusing on the development of certain provinces and cities, for example, the plans for Xinjiang, Tibet, Ningxia, and Qinghai, in order to boost the west development, and the reform schemes for cities of Chongqing, Chengdu, Shanghai, and Shenzhen. Some plans aimed at promoting the coordinated development in a larger scope, for example, the development framework of Greater Pearl River Delta, Yangtze River Delta, Beijing-Hebei-Tianjin Urban Agglomeration, Wuhan Urban Agglomeration, Changsha-Zhuzhou-Xiangtan Urban Agglomeration, West Economic Zone of Taiwan Strait and so on.

To realize the development priorities of each region, it is necessary to strengthen economic integration and cooperation and create a new pattern of complimentary and coordinated development between the east, central, and west. Regional economic relations should be reshaped under market economy conditions to build multi-level economic cooperation. Regional cooperation should also promote the development of minority areas and poverty-stricken areas, exploring new development plans for the backward areas so as to help alleviate poverty.

Case 3. 1   Shenzhen: A Name Card for China's Special Economic Zones

Established as the first Special Economic Zone(SEZ) in China, Shenzhen is also the most successful and most influential SEZ of its kind. Evolving from an unknown fishing village into a modern big city that has the highest GDP per capita of China and an urbanization level of over 70% , Shenzhen produced a miracle in the world history of industrialization, urbanization, and modernization. How did Shenzhen SEZ, the experimental and pilot ground for Reform and Opening up, create the transition to "Chinese miracle"? What progress has it gone through?

The Birth of Shenzhen SEZ

On August 26, 1980, the NPC Standing Committee approved the Guangdong Provincial Regulations on Special Economic Zones, declaring the establishment of Shenzhen SEZ, the first one in China. This was the "birthday" of Shenzhen. However, the gestation of the modern Shenzhen could date back to 1979, when three great events happened, which were the foundation of Shenzhen's blueprint in the future 30 years. The first was that the central government decided to establish SEZs. In June 1979, in response to the applications of conducting foreign economic activities and taking flexible policies proposed by Guangdong and Fujian provincial governments, the central government decided to found pilot special zones in Shenzhen, Zhuhai, Shantou and Xiamen. The second was the initial idea of Shekou Industrial Zone in July, which was the first action of Reform and Opening up. The third was that in March, Shenzhen, then known as Baoan County, was promoted to municipal level, governed by both Huiyang Prefecture and Guangdong Province. In November 1979, Shenzhen was appointed as a direct-controlled city by Guangdong CPC Committee.

In 1979, the urban area of Shenzhen only contained three square kilometers with a population of over 20,000. The GDP was RMB 196 million, and the national income RMB 160 million. Residents' incomes were very low. The per capita net income of rural households was as low as about RMB 300, the net income was RMB 152.2, and the per capita net income of urban household was RMB 759. There were only 19 kindergartens, 226 primary schools, 24 middle schools, and one continuing study college for teachers, with 65,300 students and 2,388 teachers. Shenzhen SEZ had only one polytechnic school, 7 middle schools, 38 primary schools with 12,000 students and no university by then. In 1979, there were only a little over 4,000 people with either a polytechnic school degree or above. There were 466 health care workers and only 12 were attending physicians.

In August 1979, the first joint venture in China, East Lake Hotel, invested by Hongkong Carnival Company Limited, was established in Shenzhen. On November 7, 1979, the agreement for the first Sino-foreign cooperative enterprise in Shenzhen, Wu Shi Gu Quarry, was signed among Shenzhen Metals & Minerals Import and Export Group, Guangdong Building Materials Import and Export Group, and Hongkong Kaixuan Trade Company with an investment of HKD 46.44 million. In 1979, there was only one registered trademark in Shenzhen, the Nanshan brand, which was used for soy sauce. In November 1979, the leaders of Baoan Cannery rode bikes to meet the Pepsi-Cola representative Li Wenfu for they didn't even have a business car. Pepsi-Cola set up a factory in Shenzhen in 1981, the first investment of a Fortune 500 company in Shenzhen.

The Generation of Pioneers in Shenzhen

"Flies, mosquitoes, and Shajing oysters, these 'three treasures' we owned; moved away nine out of ten households, leaving behind the young and the old. " The ballad is a true portrait of Shenzhen before the Reform and Opening up. At that time, Shenzhen had no universities, no local newspapers, no broadcast or TV stations. The only cultural facilities were a Xinghua Bookstore and a cinema built in the 1950s. The local farmers' daily income was only one RMB, but Hongkong farmers, on the other side of the sea, could get more than HKD 60 in one day. The huge gap and the special policies of the central government given to Shenzhen inspired great passion of reform and innovation and set up a dream for Shenzhen. People from all over the country with dreams for the future were attracted to pioneer the land. What they brought with them was just fervent hope for the future. Walking beside the sea in the Shekou Industrial Park, wood cabins and rods for drying fish could be seen everywhere at that time. It took up to six hours to drive anywhere, even for simple tasks like shopping. However, the pioneers didn't shrink from the arduous conditions. The aspiration for success encouraged them. It was these builders and entrepreneurs that continued to create the legend of wealth. In 1982, Hao Lianyu, the manager of Labor Service Company of Third Beijing Computer Factory went to Shekou Industrial Zone with 18 unemployed young men. They started by selling Youtiao and pies, and then opened Beijing Restaurant. The restaurant adopted the kind of operation that was very flexible at that time. For example, dumplings were sold by number, and the restaurant remained open after ten o'clock in the evening. The restaurant's turnover kept rising and they eventually opened five chain restaurants. In a time when everyone could possibly be successful, Ma Ming-zhe, an ordinary driver with only junior middle school education when he was transferred to Shekou, eventually became the Chairman and CEO of Ping An Insurance (Group) Company of China, Ltd. because of his wisdom and ambitions.

In 1992, the series of speeches Deng Xiao-ping made in his inspection tour to South China triggered a round of government officials, teachers, and scientific researchers going into business. The Vice Chairman of Shekou Industrial Park's Youth League Committee Shou Peiping resigned from his position and took over a state-owned enterprise on the verge of collapse. As the general manager, Shou used his rich management skills and turned the losing enterprise into a profitable one, earning more than two million RMB in the first year. The enterprise has been selected by Famous Brands Times as the top ten female garment brand that has influenced the garment market in China. Shou, also the Deputy Director of Shenzhen Garment Association, was honored as one of the 50 Most Influential People in China's Garment Market. In 1993, Ma Hua-teng, the founder of internet giant Tencent Company, graduated from the Department of Computer Science at Shenzhen University and began to work on the development of an internet paging system at Shenzhen Motion Telecom. In 1997, Ma found that the instant chat software ICQ designed by three Israeli young men was difficult to promote among Chinese users because of its English interface. In the next year, he created Tencent Company with his university classmate Zhang Zhidong, introducing a point-to-point instant chat software, which soon defeated ICQ with practical functions of offline messaging and server-side information storage. Registered users reached 130 million in the same year, and they soon sealed a risk investment of USD 2. 2 million from IDG and Pacific Century Cyber Works.

After Hong Kong's return to China in 1997, Shenzhen benefited from the international bridge with Hong Kong, attracting more talented people from Hong Kong, the U. S. and other places around the world to work and explore business opportunities in Shenzhen. When Velia was sent by a South African trading company to work in Shenzhen in 2001, he quickly found a business opportunity trading Video Compact Disc (VCD) products between China and Africa. He started his own company selling VCD produced by a Shenzhen factory to Africa and the profits exceeded one million USD in the next year. Later he expanded his business to electronic security facilities, MP3, etc. Currently, 60% of the international students in Shenzhen are from Hong Kong while over 60,000 Hong Kong people live in Shenzhen. U. S. president Barack Obama's brother Mark Ndesandjo opened a BBQ restaurant in Shenzhen in 2002.

The Reform Achievements of Shenzhen

After 30 years' development, Shenzhen has been a pioneer of China's Reform and Opening up. In the 1980s, Shekou first proposed the opinion "time is money and efficiency is life" and applied the incentive of "shipping one more cart of mud for the additional four cents bonus", which broke up the rules of the old planned economy. No one expected that this could attract the central government's great attention. Perhaps, it was the "four cents bonus" that triggered the butterfly effect and created the "Shenzhen speed" of constructing one floor of a building in three days in Shekou Industrial Park. Thus, a market-oriented reform breaking through the management system and the pricing system began to sweep Shenzhen SEZ. It was the first place in the country to reform the enterprises' salary distribution system, labor system, social insurance system, employment system of government institutions and the structure of governmental agencies. For opening up, Shenzhen SEZ "crossed the river by feeling the stones" and carried out bold explorations. Shenzhen founded the Shekou Industrial Zone and carried out large-scale urban infrastructural construction. In addition, it opened Man Kam To, Shekou Port, Meisha, Sha Tau Kok, Chiwan, Daya Bay and other ports. In the financial sector, it developed capital markets and introduced a number of foreign banks. In 1983, the first stock of PRC, "Shen Bao An", was issued, and the first joint-stock enterprise in Shenzhen was born. In 1984 when Deng Xiaoping visited Shenzhen in his first South China inspection tour, Shenzhen had changed from the fishing village to a modern town with every household living in a well-built house. In 1986, Shenzhen took the lead in changing state-owned enterprises into stock companies; in 1987, China Merchants Bank and Shenzhen Development Bank, China's earliest regional shareholding banks, were founded; in 1988, China's first Foreign Exchange Regulation Center was set up; in 1990, a Stock Exchange was established; in 1991, the non-ferrous metals futures market was created. Besides, in 1988 the housing system reform was first carried out in Shenzhen; in 1993, Hong Kong Hutchison Whampoa Limited was introduced to build Yantian port; in 1995, the first Foreign Investment Service Center was established; in 1996, Shenzhen was the first to give national treatment to foreign investors and resident foreigners; in 2001, the Foreign Complaint Center was founded, which actively promoted Shenzhen and Hong Kong's investment and trade cooperation, infrastructure and port economic cooperation. In 2002, a two-way settlement business with the Hong Kong dollar, checks, and foreign currency real time gross settlement was opened.

The first remarkable feature of Shenzhen's Reform and Opening up was the "Shenzhen Speed". In 2010, Shenzhen's GDP reached RMB 958.15 billion, nearly three times that of China's total economic output in 1978, while the figure for 1979 was only 196 million. From 1979 to 2010, Shenzhen's economic output grew 4,878 times. During the 30-year development, Shenzhen created a world miracle in industrialization, urbanization and modernization. From 1979 to 2010, its GDP grew from RMB 196 million to RMB 958.15 billion, ranking fourth among the major cities of China, with an average annual growth of 25%. GDP per capita grew from RMB 606 to RMB 94,296, ranking first with an average annual growth of 12%. Total import and export volume rose from USD 16.76 million to USD 346.75 billion, with an average annual growth of 33.2%. Secondly, Shenzhen has been the city with the highest output and largest export of high-tech products in China. The high-tech industry is the most important pillar industry in Shenzhen. In 2010, high-tech products output value reached

RMB 1.02 trillion, of which RMB 611.59 billion was created by products with independent intellectual property rights, accounting for 60.1%. The total import and export value of high-tech products reached USD 197.7 billion, of which exports were USD 108.75 billion, imports were USD 88.97 billion. Last, independent innovation created another miracle. In 2010, the number of patent applications in Shenzhen reached 49,430, ranking second in Chinese cities; among which invention patent applications was 23,956 (9,615 patents granted), with the patents granted accounting for 48.46% of the total patent applications, ranking first.

Shenzhen also gained remarkable achievement in modernization. Shenzhen was upgraded from a county-level city to a prefecture-level city in 1979, and became a sub-provincial city in March 1981. In November 1988, it was listed as one of the specifically designated cities in the state plan and conferred provincial level authority of economic management. The system reform and administrative upgrading promoted the gathering of personnel, capital, technology, and other economic factors in Shenzhen. Among these factors, personnel was the most important for Shenzhen's development. As the only "immigrant city" in China, Shenzhen is the best demonstration of "the law of talents gravitation". It has grown from a small border fishing village to a modern city with millions of residents. Shenzhen is not only a fully functional and international metropolis with habitable and beautiful environment, but also has the biggest number of ports and the only Chinese city with ports of land, sea and air. With its strong economic development dynamic, modern urban infrastructure and transportation network, Shenzhen is one of China's main windows to the world. Shenzhen airport is China's fourth largest airport, the passenger throughput in 2010 reached 26.71 million. It has the world's fourth largest container hub port, with port container throughput of 22.51 million TEUs. Among the mainland cities, Shenzhen ranks No. 1 in its comprehensive competitiveness. The City Competitiveness Blue Book 2009: China City Competitiveness Report released by the Academy of Social Sciences analyzing 294 cities based on the statistics in 2008 showed that Shenzhen ranked No. 2. In 2010, according to the Global Financial Centers Index released by City of London, Shenzhen ranked No. 9, ahead of Shanghai (No. 11) and Beijing (No. 15), becoming the best financial center in mainland China. Shenzhen has won the China Habitat Environment Prize, UN Habitat Award and Sir Patrick Abercrombie Prize.

Case 3. 2   Yangtze River Delta: A Model of the Integration of Regional Economy in China

The Yangtze River Delta (YRD) area, where the longest river in China drains into the East China Sea, is an important gateway connecting mainland China and the world. It is the most urbanized and most developed area in China. It also has the most densely distributed towns and cities in China. According to The *Regional Plan for Yangtze River Delta* issued by the State Council, the YRD area comprises Shanghai, Jiangsu province and Zhejiang province with an area of about 0. 21 million square kilometers. The area has 16 key zones including Shanghai, eight cities in Jiangsu (Nanjing, Suzhou, Wuxi, Changzhou, Zhenjiang, Yangzhou, Taizhou, Nantong), and seven cities in Zhejiang (Hangzhou, Ningbo, Huzhou, Jiaxing, Shaoxing, Zhoushan, Taizhou) . In March 2010, Hefei, Ma'anshan, and four other cities joined the YRD Economic Zone. How have industrial agglomeration and the regional structure developed in the formation process of YRD?

The Development of Industrial Agglomeration in YRD

Yangtze River is the third longest river in the world. The Yangtze River estuary was an important starting point for China's Maritime Silk Road in history. Nowadays, with nearly 1, 000 kilometers' coastline and waterway, YRD has formed a group of Chinese distinctive ports including Shanghai port, Ningbo port, Zhoushan port, Zhangjiagang Port, Nantong Port, and so on. It lies at the heart of the Jiangnan region(literally the south of Yangtze River). However, the economic center of the Jiangnan region used to be the cities along the Beijing-Hangzhou Grand Canal rather than Shanghai. It was not until modern times after the Opium War that Shanghai was forced to open, and foreign investment began to establish plants in Shanghai. The Westernization Movement after the war promoted the development of ordnance industry in Shanghai and Nanjing, and other industries like textile, flour, and machinery in Wuxi, Suzhou, Changzhou and other cities. In the 1930s, Shanghai became the most active industrial and commercial city in the Far East, attracting the talents and capital to Jiangsu and Zhejiang. The spontaneous economic integration and economic factors' flow laid the foundation for YRD to become the base for the rise of China's national industries. As a result, Shanghai quickly grew into the pioneer and center of YRD.

After the founding of PRC, the government made great efforts to promote the development of YRD economic zone, especially after the Reform and Opening up. On December 22, 1982, the State Council decided to set up the Shanghai Economic Zone, which was the prototype for YRD economic circle. There were three objectives for the establishment of the Shanghai Economic Zone. The first was to break the regional blockades between Shanghai and the surrounding areas. In the early stage of Reform and Opening up, the management system of the planned economy caused a lot of conflicts for the local economy, which had to be solved by regional cooperation. The second was to accelerate the development of the surrounding areas of Shanghai. At that time, Shanghai was a leading city in China, a group of small and medium-sized cities in Jiangsu province and Zhejiang province were the satellite cities. Although they were not in the same administrative zone, there were close economic connections between them. The third was to undertake an experimental exploration for building economic zones with a network based on large cities in the country. On March 22, 1983, the Planning Office for Shanghai Economic Zone was officially established. With its heart in Shanghai, the zone included nine other cities, namely, Suzhou, Wuxi, Changzhou, Nantong, Hangzhou, Jiaxing, Huzhou, Ningbo and Shaoxing. In August, the Shanghai Economic Zone Planning Conference, held in Shanghai, decided to establish a mayors and governors joint meeting system in the zone. Later, Anhui, Jiangxi and Fujian applied to join the zone. The establishment of the zone and the lateral economic ties between the cities and provinces played an important role in reducing the cost of economic factors flow within the region.

The YRD region has the largest port cluster and urban agglomeration in China, and has become the main area for "headquarters economy" and multinational companies with a strong advantage of industrial agglomeration. Of the 35 cities with the strongest economic strength in China, ten cities are located in YRD. It has about half of the top 100 Chinese cities or counties with the most powerful comprehensive strength, thousands of large enterprises and nearly one thousand industrial parks, each with an industrial output exceeding RMB 10 billion. More than four hundred Fortune 500 companies have set up headquarters, plants, or operation centers in YRD.

While actively developing modern service and advanced manufacturing industries, Shanghai is moving towards an international center for economy, finance, trade and shipping. As a comprehensive reform pilot zone and an international economic center, Shanghai Pudong New Area will continue to play its role of opening and exploring. A national business center providing service to YRD and the whole country will be established relying on the Hongqiao Transportation Hub. To build the new industrial layout in Shanghai, the urban area will concentrate on developing a modern service industry, while the suburban area will support advanced manufacturing, high-tech industry and modern agriculture. In the future, Shanghai will promote the development of Jiading New City with the auto industry and modern service industry as the support, Songjiang New City as a base for the high-tech industry, modern service industry and higher education, and Linggang New City focusing on modern equipment manufacturing supported by the container seaport and airport.

Jiangsu has nurtured more than 100 industrial clusters, of which there are traditional industries of textile, garment, and other light industries, and emerging industries of IT, metal products, building materials, electrical appliances, environmental protection and garden flowers. Typical clusters include the petrochemical industry in Nanjing, electronic information in Suzhou and Wuxi, garment in Changshu, silk in Wujiang and crystal in Donghai. In the future, Jiangsu will make efforts to strengthen the city function of Nanjing as a regional center, and make full use of its seaports and river ports along with its culture, science and education resources. With advanced manufacturing and modern service as the pillar industries, Nanjing will accelerate the construction of Nanjing Metropolitan Area, Yangtze River Shipping Logistics Center and the Science and Technology Innovation Center. Suzhou and Wuxi will be the first two candidates to undertake the industrial transfer from Shanghai to develop a high-tech industry, advanced manufacturing and service outsourcing. The culture and tourism industries will also be developed. Changzhou, Zhenjiang, Nantong, Yangzhou and Taizhou, making use of their own advantages, are becoming the other major cities in the YRD region with complementary functions.

The "block economy", characterized by professional division of industries, is active in Zhejiang province. The developing mode of "one town, one production, and one county, one industry" has been a substantial economic feature of Zhejiang province. Typical industrial clusters include shoes and clothing in Wenzhou, dyeing and weaving in Shaoxing, low-voltage electrical appliances in Yueqing, fiber in Xiaoshan, leather in Haining, ties in Shengzhou, hardware in Yongkang, buttons in Yongjia, pens in Tonglu, socks in Zhuji, etc. In the future, functions of a high-tech industrial base in Hangzhou will be strengthened. In addition, Jiaxing will focus on the development of high-tech industries and port industry. Shaoxing will boost new textile, biomedical and cultural tourism industries. Wenzhou will highlight equipment manufacturing and trade within the private economy. Taizhou will focus on auto and motorcycles, ships, pharmaceuticals and the petrochemical industry, etc.

Development Status of the YRD

The YRD region has become one of most energetic regions in China due to its geographical location, abundant natural resources, solid economic foundation, well organized urban structure, prosperous education and cultural background. According to the Regional Plan for the Yangtze River Delta, the strategic plan for YRD is to become an important international gateway in the Asian-Pacific region, the world's major modern service industry and advanced manufacturing center, as well as a world-level city agglomeration with strong international competitiveness. The development objective is to attain a moderately prosperous society in all aspects, first in the country by 2015 and then first in the country to realize modernization by 2020. The YRD region has the largest ports group in China, which is composed of Shanghai Port, Ningbo and Zhoushan Port, Zhapu Port, Nanjing Port, Zhenjiang Port, Zhangjiagang Port, Jiangyin and Nantong Port. These ports account for 70% of China's port throughput, of which 35% are contributed by Shanghai Port. Shanghai has established economic and trading business with more than 160 countries or regions and 300 international ports. In addition to its international outreach, the YRD region is also the artery of the Yangtze River's waterway, and a broad and well-developed market in the Yangtze River basin which produces one half of grain, cotton and industrial production in China. The geographical? advantage of "golden coast" and "golden waterway" has helped Yangtze River Delta to reach a higher level of development than other parts of China, and also led China's regional economic integration.

The YRD region boasts China's fastest-growing economy and the most promising economic sectors with the largest economic aggregate. According to the statistics in 2010, the YRD region with 2.2% of the national territory and 11.65% of the population in China, created 21.7% of the national GDP, 19.1% of the total retail sales in social consumer goods, 23.5% of local fiscal revenues, 36.6% of the foreign trade turnover and utilized 47.9% of the foreign capital. It also had 22.81% of deposits in RMB and foreign currencies in all financial institutions and 19.8% of the resident savings deposits(see Table 3.8). On this most abundant area of China, a series of vibrant city clusters are constantly rising. In 2011, the GDP of Shanghai, "the super-giant", was specifically RMB 1.92 trillion. Suzhou, "the heavyweight giant", also created a GDP of more than one trillion, and with a similar economic scale, Hangzhou, Wuxi, Ningbo, and Nanjing reached RMB 600 billion −800 billion respectively. A group of "young giants", including Shaoxing, Nantong, Changzhou, Taizhou and Jiaxing boosted their GDP to RMB 250 billion −400 billion.

With nearly half of China's 100 most powerful counties in this region, the county economy of the YRD region has been in the leading position for a long time. Nearly 100 industrial parks in the region have industrial output over RMB

10 billion. They are home to thousands of giant companies like Wanxiang Group, Jinshan Petrochemical, Yangzi Ethylene, Volkswagen, Shanghai Alcatel Lucent, and Eastern Communications. These companies have not only a dominant share in the domestic market, but also a considerable share in the international market. Nearly 90% of the Fortune 500 companies have established business in this region. Over 200 of these companies set up their regional or Chinese headquarters in Shanghai. Eighty-one of them have invested in 188 projects in Suzhou. Incomplete statistics shows that the utilization of foreign investment is approaching as much as USD 150 billion. The YRD region has become a strong magnetic field for international capital and technologies.

Table 3. 8   Economy of YRD and its Proportion in National Economy

Item	Volume	Proportion(%)
Land Area(10,000 square kilometers)	21. 1	2. 2
Population(10,000 persons)	15,619	11. 65
GDP(billion RMB)	8,631. 38	21. 7
Total Retail Sales of Social Consumer Goods(billion RMB)	2,992. 27	19. 1
Imports and Exports(billion USD)	1,088. 16	36. 6
Fixed Asset Investment(billion RMB)	4,087. 8	14. 7
Actual Utilization of Foreign Capital(billion USD)	50. 62	47. 9
General Budget Revenue(billion RMB)	956. 19	23. 5
Deposits in RMB and Foreign Currencies in All Financial Institutions(billion RMB)	16,725. 12	22. 81
Resident Savings Deports(billion RMB)	6,087. 6	19. 8

Source: *Provincial and Municipal Statistical Yearbook.*

As the infrastructure system in YRD is basically completed, the region has stepped into the stage of urban integration. The rapid transportation network within the region has helped in constructing the "one-hour commute" and "three-hour economic circle". The distances between the cities have been shortened to realize the "one-city effect". The urban integration has been strengthened through four respects. The first is to promote the integration of the transportation system. The *Memorandum for Promoting Integrated Management of Road Transportation in YRD* and *Guidelines for Integrated Development of Road Freight Transportation* were signed between Jiangsu province, Zhejiang province and Shanghai to coordinate the transportation management policies and regulations. Mutual recognition of vehicle operation qualification is realized among the YRD cities. The second is to accelerate the development of intercity high-speed rails. The Shanghai-Hangzhou high speed rail will construct a "one-hour economic circle" in YRD and promote further regional integration when the work is done. The third is to construct cross water bridges to make shorter connection between the cities, for example, Hangzhou Bay Bridge, a trans-oceanic bridge and also the world longest bridge, Jiangyin Bridge, Zhenjiang-Yangzhou Bridge and Suzhou-Nantong Bridge across the Yangtze River. The fourth is to construct highways along the river and coast. A number of highways were constructed or expanded, including Shanghai-Ningbo Highway, Shanghai-Hangzhou-Ningbo Highway, Hangzhou-Pudong Highway, Shanghai-Jiangsu-Zhejiang-Anhui Highway. It is planned that by 2020 there will be ten highways connecting Shanghai and the other two provinces in the region.

The YRD region has favorable conditions and opportunities to become the first world-class city agglomeration in China. Based on Shanghai's leading function, YRD has striven to bring Nanjing, Suzhou, Wuxi, Hangzhou, Ningbo and other major cities into an international level. An urban network with megacities and big cities as the main body, small and medium cities and counties as the coordinated parts has been established by taking a new road of urbanization and fully speeding up the pace of modernization and integration. YRD has been the most energetic region in China as well as a world-class city agglomeration with international competitiveness(see Table 3.9).

Table 3.9　Introduction to Major Cities in YRD

City	2011		Introduction
	Population	Industrial Output (million RMB)	
Shanghai	23,019,148	1,919,598	One of the four direct-controlled municipalities in China, one of the five national central cities, and the largest city in China. Sitting at the middle portion of China's arc-shaped north-south coastline, it is also a global financial center and one of the world largest cities.
Nanjing	8,001,680	614,552	Sub-provincial city, regional central city, and the capital of Jiangsu province. Located in the lower Yangtze River basin and the hub of the East and West, Nanjing plays an important role in influencing the development of the central and western regions. Nanjing literally means "southern capital". It has the title of "Ancient Capitals for Six Dynamics", and is recognized as one of the Four Great Ancient Capitals of China.

Cont.

City	2011		Introduction
	Population	Industrial Output (million RMB)	
Nantong	7,282,835	408,022	A prefecture-level city in Jiangsu province. Located on the northern bank of the Yangtze River, Nantong is an important port in the lower basin of the river. Nantong is the first modern city planned and constructed by China, and is honored "Northern Shanghai".
Jiaxing	4,501,700	266,806	A prefecture-level city in Jiangsu province. Located in northeastern Zhejiang province and the hinterland of Hangjia Plain, and the only city surrounded by the Grand Canal River, it is an important city in YRD and along the Grand Canal River.
Ningbo	7,605,689	601,048	A sub-provincial city, separate state-planning city, and a famous seaport city. Located in the northeastern Zhejiang province, and the southern part of YRD, it borders Hangzhou Bay to the north, Shaoxing to the west, Taizhou to the south and Zhoushan to the northeast across a body of water.
Changzhou	4,591,972	358,042	A prefecture-level city in Jiangsu province, previously known as Dragon City or Pi Ling in ancient times. Located in the northwest of Taihu Lake Plain, and the only Chinese city lying at longitude 120° east. Changzhou borders the Yangtze River to the north, Taihu Lake to the south, Anhui province and Nanjing to the southwest, Wuxi to the east, and Zhenjiang province to the west, and lies right in the middle area between Shanghai and Nanjing.
Wuxi	6,372,624	688,015	A prefecture-level city in Jiangsu province. Lying on the Grand Canal of China, it borders the Yangtze River to the north, Taihu Lake to the south, Suzhou to the east and Changzhou to the west. As one of the birthplaces of China's modern industry, it has been praised as "Mini Shanghai".

Cont.

City	2011		Introduction
	Population	Industrial Output (million RMB)	
Hangzhou	8,700,400	701,180	Sub-provincial city and capital of Zhejiang province. The Chinese character Hang literally means ship, especially the ship that Empire Yu took or had taken in controlling the flood in Chinese legend. As a renowned historical and cultural city in China, it is beautiful and prosperous and especially famous for its natural scenery like the West Lake, Qiantang River, etc. An old Chinese saying praises the scenery of Suzhou and Hangzhou as "paradise on the earth".
Huzhou	2,893,500	151,883	A prefecture-level city in Zhejiang Province. Lying in northern Zhejiang, it is surrounded by Suzhou and Wuxi in Jiangsu province, Hangzhou and Jiaxing in Zhejiang province, and Xuancheng in Anhui Province. On the southern bank of Taihu Lake, it is the only city surrounding the lake area chosen to be named after the lake.
Shaoxing	4,912,200	329,123	A prefecture-level city in Zhejiang province, formerly known as Kuaiji and Shanyin, and called Yue for short. It is now a national and even global center for manufacturing of textiles, electronics, and energy efficient lighting.
Zhoushan	1,121,300	76,530	A prefecture-level city in Zhejiang province, the first administrative division set for a group of islands. It has a state-level new zone—Zhoushan Archipelago New Zone. Sitting in Zhoushan Archipelago on the south of the mouth of the Yangtze River and the East China Sea outside Hangzhou Bay, it administers all the islands of Zhoushan Archipelago, composed of 1391 islands, 103 of which are inhabited.
Suzhou	10,465,994	1,071,699	A prefecture-level city in Jiangsu province. Located in the lower reaches of the Yangtze River and the center of Taihu Plain, it is a renowned historical and cultural city in China, and the birthplace of Culture of Wu. It has been famous for its beautiful natural scenery and elegant gardens, as the saying goes "Jiangnan has the best gardens in the world, while Suzhou has the best gardens in Jiangnan" and "Paradise on the earth."

Cont.

| City | 2011 | | Introduction |
	Population	Industrial Output (million RMB)	
Zhenjiang	3,113,384	231,040	A prefecture-level city in Jiangsu province. Sitting on the southern bank of the Yangtze River in Southwest Jiangsu, it is a famous port city near the intersection of the Yangtze River and the Grand Canal. It used to be the capital of Jiangsu province during the period of the Republic of China(1912 − 1949). It was once known as Jingjing or Jingkou.

Case 3. 3   The Chengdu-Chongqing Economic Zone: A New Highlight of Western Development

In China's southeastern and coastal areas, the Yangtze River Delta, the Pearl River Delta and the Bohai Economic Rim have undoubtedly become the three major growth poles in today's China. But in the vast western region, which area will undertake the essential task in regional development and become the fourth pole to boost the nation's economic growth? The Chengdu-Chongqing Economic Zone(CCEZ) is ready to take off.

When the Leadership Group for Western China Development was established by the State Council and the first working meeting was held in 2000, the clarion call of western development was officially sounded. A series of economic and social development was carried out, including infrastructural construction, cultivation of the special industries with local advantages and environmental protection. The three key economic zones, CCEZ, Guanzhong-Tianshui Economic Zone and Guangxi Beibu Gulf Economic Zone, were initially formed and became the new growth pole for the development in China. With the unique historical background, advantage of location and quite mature industrial base, CCEZ has been the biggest highlight of the western development.

Historical Accumulation and Basic Conditions

Located in the Sichuan Basin in the upper reaches of the Yangtze River in Southwest China, CCEZ borders Shanxi and Gansu to the north, Yunnan and Guizhou to the south, Qinghai and Tibet to the west, and Hunan and Hubei to the east. With its center in Chengdu and Chongqing and 15 cities in Sichuan and 31 districts or counties in Chongqing, CCEZ is a densely populated city agglomeration in the west. CCEZ is of strategic importance for enhancing the inland opening up, developing the western economic regions, coordinating urban and rural development, environmental protection and social stability.

Sichuan and Chongqing have been the most profoundly nurtured areas by the Ba-Shu culture. Chengdu is the core of the Shu Culture while Chongqing is the crystallization of the Ba Culture. The twin megacities, 300 kilometers away from each other, have deeply linked and shared common culture and history. In the ancient Chinese cultural system, a number of local cultures, like Bashu, Qilu(in Shandong province) and Sanjin(in Shanxi province), jointly built the brilliant Chinese civilization in the past 5,000 years. In 316 BC, after the State of Qin conquered the State of Ba and the State of Shu, Ba(Chongqing) and Shu (Chengdu) respectively became the political and economic centers of eastern and western Sichuan, which lasted for the following 2,000 years. The old Bashu Culture has closely integrated the people in Sichuan and Chongqing. They drink water from the same river and are as close as family members. Having the same dialect(Sichuan Dialect), drama(Sichuan opera) and food, the jointly created culture and folklore have already made Sichuan and Chongqing inseparable.

CCEZ has tremendous potential for development that includes fertile land, rich natural resources, large deposits of coal, bauxite, natural gas, phosphorus, brine, water, etc. Its water resources, mineral resources, natural gas and forest covered area are ranked at the top in China. There are six places recognized as World Heritage Sites or world geological parks. Good agricultural conditions make it an important production base for grain, pigs, citrus, tea, vegetables, silk and traditional Chinese medical materials. In CCEZ, a sound industrial system has been established with strong industrial base and supporting capacity, of which the equipment manufacturing industry, automobile and motorcycle industries, electronics and information industries, bio-pharmaceutical industry, energy and chemical industries, metallurgy and building materials industries, textile and food industries and aerospace industry have basically become the region's leading industries. The development of the tertiary industry is very fast in recent years. Logistics, commerce, finance and tourism have also developed rapidly. CCEZ is becoming an important center of materials distribution and finance in the western region and an important tourist destination in the country.

Starting from Concept to National Planning

It had been a dozen years' waiting and expectation before the initial concept was turned into a final plan. In 2000, when the Western Development Strategy was proposed, Sichuan and Chongqing were only set as the main body of the upper Yangtze River economic belt, but the CCEZ was not explicitly conceptualized.

In 2001, the Chongqing-Chengdu Economic Cooperation Talk Minutes first proposed to jointly build a "Chengdu-Chongqing Economic Corridor", which was the first time that a "Chengdu-Chongqing Economy" concept came into view. In 2003, the Preliminary Research on China's Western Development Key Regional Planning released by the Institute of Geographic Sciences and Natural Resources Research made a systematic study on the major economic growth areas in the western region, which first proposed the concept of CCEZ and highlighted the "construction of the largest two-core city agglomeration as the largest anchor of the Western Development Strategy".

In 2004, Sichuan and Chongqing made the first step from concept to action to set up their own cooperation leading group of CCEZ respectively. Since then, the two sides have conducted high-level exchanges every year through cooperation fora and joint conferences between mayors, district heads and county chiefs. In February 2004, the two sides signed the Framework on Strengthening the Cooperation of Chengdu-Chongqing Economic and Social Fields and Developing the Upper Yangtze River Economic Zone and the "1 + 6" Chengdu-Chongqing cooperation agreements. Based on the agreements, they sought cooperation on transportation, energy, tourism, radio and television, culture, agriculture and police service. In April 2007, Sichuan and Chongqing signed the Agreement on Promoting the Cooperation and Construction of the CCEZ, declaring the two sides would work together to create the new growth pole of China—the "fourth pole" and clarified that CCEZ included 14 cities and 23 counties.

In 2005, the National Development and Reform Commission (NDRC) included CCEZ in the preliminary plan for the 11th Five-Year Plan period, manifesting that CCEZ came into the view of the central government. In 2007, NDRC started to compile the plan for CCEZ, marking that the zone was officially upgraded to a national strategy. In the same year, Western China Development Office of State Council issued the *Eleventh Five-Year Plan for West Development Plan*, emphasizing the construction of CCEZ, Guanzhong-Tianshui Economic Zone and Guangxi Beibu Gulf Economic Zone, making them the strategic highland of West Development. In July 2010, the *Regional Plan for CCEZ* compiled by NDRC was finally finished. In May 2011, the plan was approved by the State Council, explicating the function, overall layout, and objectives of CCEZ from a state-level.

The Development of "Two Cores and Five Belts"

In accordance with the strategic positioning of CCEZ, the zone is given priority as the foremost pivotal economic core of Western China, followed by key national modern industrial base, and lastly the inland pilot area to undergo in-depth opening up, the area where coordinative urban-rural development is to be demonstrated, and the zone in upper reaches of the Yangtze River under the protection of ecological security. It will be built as an important economic center of West China by 2015 and one of the strongest areas in the country by 2020.

According to the plan, CCEZ would construct a layout of "two cores and five belts" to promote the coordinated regional development. As Chengdu and Chongqing both constitute the core cities, the five belts are Yangtze River Coast Belt, Chengdu-Mianyang-Leshan Belt, Chengdu-Neijiang-Chongqing Belt, Chengdu-Nanchong-Suining-Chongqing Belt, and Chongqing-Guangyuan-Dazhou Belt.

As the only direct-controlled city in West China and the core city of CCEZ, Chongqing has been selected as a target area where comprehensive urban-rural reform will be demonstrated. It would be particularly onerous to perform the mission to reconcile the growing sharp contradiction in the urban-rural dual structures, transform and revitalize the outmoded industrial bases and strike a sound balance between urban and rural developments.

Chongqing brought out six major reforms, including the development of one-hour commute circle and two sub-regions, expanding opening up, upgrading industrial structure, promoting science and education as the impetus for development, and protecting the environment. In 2011, Chongqing's GDP reached the level of trillion for the first time, the total amount being RMB one trillion, 5. 5 times that of the beginning period of West Development. In 2000, the GDP was only RMB 179 billion. Urban population increased from 10. 14 million in 2000 to 16. 06 million in 2011, increasing by 50% in ten years. Local fiscal revenue increased from RMB 10. 4 billion to RMB 290. 89 billion. Therefore, after twelve years' development, Chongqing's economic aggregate and social development has made tremendous progress.

As the capital of Sichuan province and the other core of CCEZ, Chengdu strives to be the "strategic highland of opening economy in the inland area" by focusing on the modern service industry, high-tech industry, advanced manufacturing and local-featured agriculture, and promoting headquarters economy. In 2012, Chengdu Tianfu New Area and Chongqing Liangjiang District were both listed as the key new urban area construction plan in the 12th *Five-Year Plan for West Development Plan*. Thus, Tianfu New Area, supported by the state-level Chengdu Hi-tech Industrial Development Zone and Economic and Technological Zone, entered into a fast starting period. Chengdu Hi-tech Industrial Development Zone, with an area of 130 square kilometers, has begun to form a world-class and international influential IT industry base. The year 2011 witnessed a GDP of

RMB 70 billion with Chongqing, higher than the gross GDP of Chengdu by more than one tenth; whereas the gross financial revenue reached RMB 22 billion, contributing to one tenth of the indicator of Sichuan province. The foreign trade import and export volume of the Chengdu Bonded Area reached USD 18 billion, ranking first in the comprehensive bonded areas in the central and western region.

The other five economic development belts are all making use of their natural endowments, industrial bases and location advantages to develop their competitive industries. For example, the Yangtze River Coast Belt, with its center in the urban area of Chongqing, takes the advantage of the golden waterway, the expressways and railways along the river to develop equipment manufacturing, metallurgy, clean energy, new materials, textile and food industries, commerce and logistics industries. The Chengdu-Mianyang-Leshan Belt, centered in Chengdu, relies on intercity high speed rails, Baocheng-Chengkun railway, Chengdu-Mianyang expressway, Chengdu-Leshan expressway and Chengdu-Yaan expressway and gathers the electronic information industry, biological medicine, equipment manufacturing, technology services, commerce and logistics and local-featured agriculture. Chengdu-Neijiang-Chongqing Belt, depending on the Chengdu-Chongqing railway and expressways, developed pillar industries, such as fine chemical, electronics and information, textile and food, new building materials, commerce and logistics. The Chengdu-Nanchong-Suining-Chongqing Belt focuses on machinery manufacturing, oil and gas, fine chemical, textile and food industries, and depends upon the network of the Lanzhou-Chongqing railway, Chongqing-Suining railway, Chengdu-Nanchong expressway, Chongqing-Suining expressway, Chongqing-Nanchong expressway and Jialing River as a link. Chongqing-Guangyuan-Dazhou Belt develops machinery manufacturing, natural gas, salt chemical, metallurgy and building materials, textile, and food industries on the network connected by Xiangyang-Chongqing railway, Dazhou-Wanzhou railway, Chongqing-Dazhou expressway and Chongqing-Yichang expressway as a link.

Improvement of Transportation Infrastructure

When Sichuan's transportation was mentioned in the past, people first thought of the famous poem by Li Bai in the Tang Dynasty. "The Sichuan Road. What heights! It is more difficult to take the Sichuan Road than climbing Heaven." However, the situation has been greatly changed after a decade of construction in Western Development. Sixteen ways connecting Sichuan has been completed, including seven railways, eight expressways and one waterway. In addition, Chengdu has been connected with 128 Chinese and foreign cities by air transport.

According to the design of rail transportation planning for the Chengdu-Chongqing Economic Zone, major cities with population of half a million or more will be connected by high-speed railways, and two-thirds of the cities with population of 200,000 or more will be linked by non-stop high-speed railways. A high-speed railway transportation network connecting Chengdu, Ya'an, Leshan, Neijiang, Yibin, Luzhou, Chongqing, Wanzhou, Guang'an, Nanchong, Dazhou, Bazhong, Guangyuan, Mianyang, Deyang will be established in Chengdu-Chongqing Economic Zone. The duration of distance between the two core cities, Chengdu and Chongqing, and their neighboring cities will be reduced to one hour, and there will be four non-stop railways linking these two cores, especially the Chengdu-Chongqing high-speed railway and Suining-Chongqing intercity lane, whose construction will shorten the time and space distance to the largest extent and help the integration and interaction of the two core cities.

In addition, G93 Chengdu-Chongqing Ring Expressway, the longest expressway connecting the largest number of cities in China, has been completed. It is more than 1,200 kilometers in length, linking Chengdu, Mianyang, Ya'an, Leshan, Yibin, Luzhou, Suining, Chongqing and other cities in CCEZ. The expressway is important for CCEZ's development into the "fourth pole" of China's economic growth. For example, the G93 expressway has cut the distance between Luzhou and Chongqing from 250 km to 150 km, which particularly facilitates acceleration of logistics and demographic and capital flows between both cities.

After a decade of West Development, the population of CCEZ (206,000 square kilometers) reached about 100 million in 2010, and its GDP reached RMB 2.2 trillion. The two core cities' economic aggregates ranked the top in western and central regions. But the development is imbalanced. Except Chengdu and Chongqing, the total GDP of all the other cities hasn't reached RMB 100 billion. There is still a considerable gap between CCEZ and the other three poles in the east, Yangtze River Delta, Pearl River Delta and Bohai Economic Rim. However, as national programs continue to enhance infrastructures, urban construction and environmental protection in the area, CCEZ will make better use of its resources and favorable geographical position to become a shining point in China's Western Development.

Questions for discussion:

1. Since the founding of PRC, how many stages has the regional economic development strategy gone through? What are the characteristics of each stage?

2. Is there a big developing gap between China's eastern, central and western regions? What are the causes of the gap? To change this disparity, what relevant policies have been issued?

3. What are the three major economic growth poles currently in China? Where are they? And what are the characteristics of their development?

4. How do you evaluate the history and strategic initiatives of China's regional economic development?

After the founding of PRC, a realistic choice for social development was to give priority to supporting the development of heavy industry by implementing the policy of "industry nurturing agriculture", which then led to the urban and rural differences. When the economy had developed to a certain degree, urban-rural gap influenced the progress of development. Therefore, much urbanized construction had been done in large-scale in China. During that period, problems such as rural urbanization, farmer's migration into cities, urban real estate market and rural migrant workers aroused public concern and city malaise increasingly appeared.

Chapter 4

China's Urbanization Process and Urban Problems

Urbanization is an inevitable stage in China's social and economic development. During the urbanization progress, particular attention must be paid to a series of crucial issues, for example, the urban-rural gap and its causes, the current situation of China's urbanization, the city problems brought by urbanization as well as the policies and measures the government has made to deal with those problems. The answers to the above questions will help us deeply understand the process of China's urbanization.

4. 1　Urban-rural Gap, Urbanization and China's Economic Development

4. 1. 1　Urban-rural Gap in China

A. Reasons for Urban-rural Gap

It was a necessary choice to let urban areas develop first in social development after the founding of PRC. Why? Posed by a large population and a weak economic foundation, China had to adopt the policy of developing heavy industry first to change its backwardness. Much funding budget, raw materials, agricultural and sideline products were badly needed to promote the development of heavy industry. If the market failed to solve the demand-exceeding-supply problem of resources, it was required to adopt the highly-centralized planned economic system to allocate the limited resources in order to ensure that the development of heavy industry was given priority. However, the result was that the agricultural and rural development in China was left behind compared with that of industrial and urban development.

Firstly, a unified purchase and sale system had been carried out since 1953 for agriculture products to accumulate capital for industrial development. The government regulated and controlled the grain market and adopted the policy of planned purchasing and supply to balance the supply and demand. After the founding of PRC, the conflict of demand exceeding supply caused by large-scale industrial construction was becoming increasingly severe. Input on agricultural production reduced, while the grain used for industry and consumption increased. During that period, industrial capital was accumulated at the cost of agricultural development, improvement in rural areas and farmers' interests.

Secondly, the household registration system was carried out in order to guarantee the employment rate of urban residents and impose restrictions on the migration of rural residents. The *Regulation of the People's Republic of China on the Household Registration (1958)* marked the establishment of China's household registration system. According to the regulation, the agricultural population could not be transformed into a non-agricultural population in principle, except the specific cases of college enrollment and unified recruitment by the official labor department, which meant that it was impossible for farmers to find jobs at their own will in cities. Meanwhile, residents of different household registration categories enjoyed different employment and welfare treatments and the household registration category was of hereditary character. Non-agricultural population, living in urban areas, could acquire various social resources and enjoy more rights, while the agricultural population had to work hard in the fields, facing the loess back down. The Household Registration System artificially led to bigger rural-urban differences. Furthermore, the corresponding social management systems, concerning employment, input on educational resources, social welfare and security system, medical and health care as well as food supply marked a boundary line between rural and urban areas. From then on, an urban-rural segmentation framework had been established as the result of the from-top-to-bottom official system and the resource allocation mechanism had been worked out, with cities having the priority to use more resources. It is clear that those systems and mechanism enlarged the gap between rural and urban areas.

Thirdly, large amounts of capital flew from counties to cities as a result of the implementation of financial, fiscal and revenue systems. Statistics showed that the net flow from rural to urban areas amounted to RMB 1. 87 trillion in terms of taxes of township enterprises and agriculture under fiscal and taxation systems and RMB 6. 24 trillion through net balance between deposits and loans in rural banks. It was clear that too much capital outflowing from rural places was an important reason for the increase in rural-urban differences. Besides, other reasons included budget transfer, agricultural input affecting price between industrial and agricultural products. To some extent, tuition fees for higher education, high medical expenses for health care in rural areas and the lack of subsidies for arable lands also exerted negative influence on the gap-widening after the implementation of reform and opening up policy.

B. Harms Brought by the Rural-urban Gap

Firstly, traditional lower-efficient industries set obstacles for the development of modern higher-efficient ones, which restricted the upgrade of industrial structure and brought with it problems such as unfair income distribution, lack of effective demand and irrational allocation of factors.

Secondly, rural and urban residents respectively took different economic status and had different opportunities in social development, which violated both the principle of "fairness and justice" in the field of society and the principle of "freedom and equality" in the field of economy as well.

Thirdly, the organic ties were cut off between counties and cities and fell into a mutually-constrained vicious circle, which had a negative effect on the coordinated development of rural and urban areas.

The planned economic system gave rise to the rural-urban gap and a series of relevant rules and regulations sped up the formation of the boundary line between rural and urban areas. The pursuit for urbanization reinforced the rural-urban gap. Industrialization that greatly relied on heavy industry development failed to promote urbanization; instead, it reinforced the rural-urban differences with distinct Chinese characteristics.

4. 1. 2   Shift towards Urbanized Mode: Changes of Rural Areas and Farmers

A. "Local Urbanization" with Chinese Characteristics

In China, urbanization in rural areas means the transition from a traditional agriculture-dominated society to a modern industry-oriented society, as well as the industrialization of production in rural areas, urbanization in farmers' daily life and modernization in their concepts.

Rural urbanization with Chinese Characteristics concerns the concept of "local urbanization". "Local" means the original residential places, including natural villages, administrative villages and new communities merged by several villages. "Local urbanization" refers to the situation where the rural population still live in rural areas instead of migrating to cities. Meanwhile, they can live in the same way as urban residents do, with improvement of infrastructure, promotion of production, increase in income, improvement of the quality of agricultural population, lifestyle changes and development of social undertakings.

Why did China adopt the "local urbanization" policy? The reasons are listed below: a) "Cun Cun Tong" (project of improving highway network and extending radios and TV broadcast coverage to every village) in rural places raised the density of the transportation network and the majority of rural areas were covered by integrated road systems. b) Mechanization and industrialization enhanced the proficiency of agricultural producing. Farmers have more choices besides agricultural production because they have plenty of time to do non-agricultural work. c) Basic infrastructure in rural areas gradually improved due to the government's huge input into rural construction and the increase of farmers' income. In addition, medical care, educational and cultural undertakings developed quickly so that farmers got more access to education, acquired medical services and enjoyed their colorful life. d) The population density in China is relatively high, especially in eastern and middle regions, which makes it impossible for cities to absorb a large number of rural residents. e) Farmers always hold the concept of provincialism. They are more likely to have jobs in their hometowns and meanwhile, live an urbanized life.

Nowadays, there are more than 200 million migrant rural workers and their family members who migrate across different provinces or regions every year. Through the migration, they have gained experiences and skills and become used to urban lifestyle. When they go back to their hometowns, they bring the advanced culture and urban civilization back and try to live as urban residents do, which accelerates the course of "local urbanization".

Traditional urbanization gave rise to city malaise, such as high population intensity, traffic jams, low employment rate, environmental degradation and expensive housing rents. Therefore, the appearance and continual development of de-urbanization in China provided some references for "local urbanization" in rural areas.

B. Changing from Farmers to Urban Residents

In the early period of urbanization, owing to the migration of rural population to cities, farmers' ideology, democratic rights, status, lifestyle and behaviors had been quietly changed, thus they were gradually turned into urban residents.

Farmers who belonged to the following groups had become urban residents: Firstly, labor force of the new generation(the second generation of migrant rural workers); secondly, college graduates originally from rural areas, most of whom wanted to find jobs in cities; thirdly, farmers who used to live near the cities but lost their arable lands. The above groups of farmers shared a common feature: they were curious about being urban residents and hoped the cities would accept them.

From the urban residents' views on the rural population's migration, on one hand, they were willing to accept rural workers to do low-end labor work that they were not willing and refused to do, work that was of great necessity. On the other hand, urban residents were worried that so much rural population rushing into cities would cause housing, traffic, social safety problems as well as fierce competition in the urban labor market.

On the other side, farmers hesitated about whether to become urban residents or not. Firstly, migrant rural workers and farmers who lost their arable lands were excluded from urban social securities. They lacked the sense of safety and mainly relied on themselves and their families for medical care. Secondly, to a certain degree, lack of specification for rural land rights and potential function of arable lands still attracted farmers who had been actually influenced by urbanization. The *Land Administration Law of the People's Republic of China* failed to clarify the ownership and the right to use rural lands or the rights and responsibilities between contractors and the collective; therefore, farmers' interests could not be guaranteed through the implementation of rural land circulation. Meanwhile, farmers did not want to abandon the farmlands, because the compensation fees were unreasonable. Thirdly, China carried out the system of unified policy-making and classified management through the whole society, that is to say, local and central governments shouldered different responsibilities on social undertakings, taking employment rate and social security as the examples. In order to protect local residents' interests, local governments always held negative attitudes toward granting urban residency to rural people through formulating repulsive and restrictive policies. According to relevant policies, service management and urban residents' employment was emphasized, but those of rural residents were ignored in the process of the rural population's transition to urban residents. Due to the implementation of the rural-urban segmentation system, until now there have been several discriminatory regulations, especially for the migrant workers in cities in terms of work categories and even the proportion of migrant workers in a company. Although some restrictions are not clearly described, in fact it is unfair to ask rural workers for various certificates and charge different kinds of fees from them.

Both the household registration system and farmland property rights system were the crucial reasons that impeded the rural population's transition into urban residents.

4.1.3   Urbanization and China's Economic Development

A. Urbanization Level in China

The Sustainable development strategy research group from the Chinese Academy of Sciences (CAS) released the *China New-type Urbanization Report (2012)*, which revealed that the urbanization rate in mainland China reached 51.27% in 2011, the first time exceeding 50%. That means, the number of urban residents exceeded that of rural people and China has stepped into a key stage of urbanization development(see Table 4.1).

Based on the "motive force of development in urban and rural areas", "fairness in urban and rural development" and "quality of rural and urban development" index, the report worked out a list of 50 representative cities from China's mainland based on the new-type urbanization level, with Shanghai, Beijing, Shenzhen, Tianjin, Chengdu, Guangzhou, Suzhou, Chongqing, Hangzhou and Wuxi ranking the top ten.

The *China New-type Urbanization Report(2012)* also briefly divided the course of China's urbanization development into six stages, including initial development (1949 – 1957), tortuous development(1958 – 1965), sluggish development (1966 – 1978), resumptive development(1979 – 1984), stable development (1985 – 1991) and fast-speed development(1992 – now). Based on statistical analysis, this report concluded that China's urbanization development was stepping onto a much healthier road after the concept of Scientific Outlook on

Development was proposed in 2003(see Table 4. 2).

Table 4. 1 Statistics on Urbanization Rate in China(1949−2012)

Year	Urbanization Rate(%)	Year	Urbanization Rate(%)
2012	52. 57	1980	19. 39
2011	51. 27	1979	19. 99
2010	47. 50	1978	17. 92
2009	46. 59	1977	17. 55
2008	45. 68	1976	17. 44
2007	44. 94	1975	17. 34
2006	43. 90	1974	17. 16
2005	42. 99	1973	17. 20
2004	41. 76	1972	17. 13
2003	40. 53	1971	17. 26
2002	39. 09	1970	17. 38
2001	37. 66	1969	17. 50
2000	36. 22	1968	17. 62
1999	30. 89	1967	17. 74
1998	30. 40	1966	17. 86
1997	29. 92	1965	17. 98
1996	29. 37	1964	18. 37
1995	29. 04	1963	16. 84
1994	28. 62	1962	17. 33
1993	28. 14	1961	19. 29
1992	27. 63	1960	19. 75
1991	26. 37	1959	18. 41
1990	26. 41	1958	16. 25
1989	26. 21	1957	15. 39
1988	25. 81	1956	14. 62
1987	25. 32	1955	13. 48
1986	24. 52	1954	13. 69
1985	23. 71	1953	13. 31
1984	23. 01	1952	12. 46
1983	21. 62	1951	11. 78
1982	21. 13	1950	11. 18
1981	20. 16	1949	10. 64

Source: National Bureau of Statistics of People's Republic of China.

Table 4. 2   Six Stages of China's Urbanization Development

No.	Year	Feature
1	1949 − 1957	initial development
2	1958 − 1965	tortuous development
3	1966 − 1978	sluggish development
4	1979 − 1984	resumptive development
5	1985 − 1991	stable development
6	1992 − now	fast-speed development

Source: *2012 China New-type Urbanization Report.*

Concerning the quality of China's urbanization development, there are distinct features from the aspect of region and scale. The regional feature is mainly represented as follows: the urbanization quality in eastern regions was apparently higher than that in northwestern, middle and western regions and the urbanization quality almost matched the level of economic development. That is, economically fast-developed areas always embraced urbanization of high-quality, and vice versa (see Table 4. 3).

Table 4. 3   Urbanization Quality Index in China(From the Aspect of Region)

Region	East	Northwest	Middle	West
Urbanization Quality Index	0. 5419	0. 4860	0. 4632	0. 4643

Source: *China's Urbanization Quality Report, China Economic Weekly.*

The feature of scale is mainly represented as follows: the urbanization quality improved with the expanding scale of the city. The reason is attributed to the fact that metropolises with more accumulated resources always contributed more to improving urbanization quality in terms of economic and social development, urban construction, industrial structure, etc(see Table 4. 4).

Table 4. 4   Urbanization Quality Index in China(From the Aspect of Scale)

City Size(Population)	Over 2 million	1−2 million	0. 5−1 million	0. 2−0. 5 million	under 0. 2 million
Urbanization Quality Index	0. 5920	0. 5368	0. 4825	0. 4680	0. 4496

Source: *China's Urbanization Quality Report; China Economic Weekly, China Urban Construction Statistical Yearbook(2010).*

B. Urbanization Propelling China's Economic Development

Firstly, urbanization benefited from China's high saving rates. In the past 30 years, the high saving rate was a vital force pushing China's economic development. For decades, the saving rate of Chinese people maintained at 40%

or more. After 2003, this rate increased significantly and exceeded 50% . In addition, the saving rate of Chinese companies grew even more quickly. In recent years, profits of enterprises, especially the profit increase of state-owned enterprises, reflected the cyclical disequilibrium of China's economy. Further urbanization development will mainly rely on the release of cyclical excess savings.

Secondly, urbanization promoted the innovation and application of technology, increased the total factor productivity rate and enhanced the capability of long-term economic growth. Global historical experience also proves that cities are the pioneers that innovate and promote advanced technology, not the rural areas.

Thirdly, urbanization raised China's general consuming demands. Underconsumption was a tough problem in China' economic growth, which caused the "non-balanced expansion" with Chinese characteristics. Additionally, it was hard to eliminate this kind of non-balanced increase in a short period. In the long run, the key point of economic growth in China would be determined by the increase of consumption, domestic demands in particular, therefore, urbanization would play a significant role in stimulating consumers' consumption.

Fourthly, urbanization gave rise to more demands in infrastructure construction and other investments. In China, enormous investment demands will be generated in the future 20 years if the estimated 500 million rural population are involved in the urbanization process. Subsequently, the corresponding infrastructure, municipal construction and improvement in functional facilities in urban areas will push up the amount of investment in some relevant industries. To sum up, urbanization has positive effects on solution-making targeting surplus productivity in economic development. In the long term, however, many industries in China still cannot reach the productivity peak; therefore, the apparent capacity excess will be eased with the course of urbanization.

4. 2   Urbanization and China's Property Market

4. 2. 1   Cities Merger Villages and Land Supply under Multi-track System

A. Expansion of Urban Land in China

Reform of the land system is of great importance in China's economic and social reform progress. It is also a major driving force for China's fast urban expansion, high-speed industrial development and space optimization. For one thing, earlier cheap land resources attracted foreign investment and stimulated private investment, which accelerated the pace of industrialization from the top down in China. For the other, the reoccurrence of differential land rent accelerated the process of "suppressing the second industry and developing the third industry"[1] in urban areas, land function transfer and urban spatial structure optimization, which continuously pushed forward city expansion. In recent years, land supply shrinkage and skyrocketing real estate prices made it possible for local governments to gain huge benefits from lands surrounding the cities through land bid invitation, auction and listing procedure[2], which offered necessary material basis in return for fast urbanization development.

The up surging increase of urban land demand is a significant feature in the process of urbanization. Zhang Li, et al (2011)[3] has researched the land expansion degree index from 1997 to 2007, covering 222 cities at prefecture-level and above in China. According to his analysis, the urban expansion index (UEI) is represented as small cities < medium cities < large cities < mega cities. The number of cities with higher land expansion growth speed than the national average speed is represented as mega cities > large cities > medium cities > small cities. The expansion speed of urban land use also coincides with the size of cities, namely, small cities have the lowest UEI while megacities have the highest. The system of city size tends to be imbalanced(see Table 4.5).

Table 4.5   Land Expansion Situation in Cities of Different Scale in China

City Scale	Built-up Acreage (square kilometers)	Number of Cities	Expansion Degree Index	Higher than the Average Speed Increase	
				Number of Cities	Percentage (%)
Small city	S <50	66	39.2	13	19.7
Medium City	50≤S <100	88	64.4	32	36.4
Large City	100≤S <200	40	79.5	19	47.5
Megacity	S≥200	28	143.1	19	67.9

Source: Zhang Li, et al. The features and influencing factors of urban expansion in China during 1997 −2007, *Progress in Geography*. 2011.5.

---

1   Suppressing the second industry and developing the third industry in the process of industrial restructuring, see details: Circular of the General Office of the State Council Transmitting and Issuing the Opinions of the State Planning Commission on Policy Measures for Accelerating the Development of the Service Industry During the "Twelfth Five-Year" Period. (guobanfa [2001] No. 98)

2   According to the *Land Administration Law of the People's Republic of China* and regulations of Ministry of Land and Resources, the profit-oriented lands shall be open to the public and granted by means of bidding, auction and listing, which is named as the land bid invitation, auction and listing system.

3   Zhang Li, et al. The features and influencing factors of urban expansion in China during 1997 − 2007, *Progress in Geography*. 2011.5.

In terms of regional aspects, eastern cities witnessed the highest expansion degree with the built-up areas in cities at prefecture-level and above increasing from 6,685 square kilometers in 1997 to 14,677 square kilometers in 2007. The overall expansion degree index of western regions reached 74.2% with one-third cities of these regions surpassing the average speed. Cities from the central parts had the lowest expansion speed and the overall expansion degree index during those ten years was only 62.1%, with the smallest percentage of cities growing faster than the national average increasing speed. From the above datum, it can be seen that there were distinct differences of land expansion among various regions(see Table 4.6).

Table 4.6   Expansion of Urban Lands in China's Different Regions

Region	Number of Cities	Expansion Degree Index	Higher than Average Speed Increase		Lower than Average Speed Increase	
			Number of Cities	Percentage (%)	Number of Cities	Percentage (%)
Eastern	96	119.5	50	52.1	46	47.8
Central	78	62.1	17	21.8	61	78.2
Western	48	74.2	16	33.3	32	66.7
National	222	92.8	83	37.4	139	62.6

Source: Zhang Li, et al. The features and influencing factors of urban expansion in China during 1997 −2007, *Progress in Geography*. 2011.5.

Dramatic reduction of arable lands in China was caused by urban land expansion. Based on statistics, 120 million mu arable lands diminished during the eight years from 1997 to 2005, which amounted to 6.6% of the total arable lands in China. China is a large country with 21% population of the whole world but only 7% arable lands; therefore, the reduction of arable land resources is really a tough problem to deal with.

B. Urban Land Supply: Under Multi-track System

A Multi-track system has been adopted for urban land supply in China. Urban land trade includes such modes as land grant in the first-level market and possession transfer, mortgage and renting in the second-level market. Since the Shenzhen Special Economic Zone had been appointed as the pilot city for land grant in 1987, the land grant volume was fluctuated each year, with a tendency of increase. The total volume reached the peak in 1993, 1998 and 2002 respectively, and it coincided with the variation of urban land use expansion and influenced by relative land policies of the government. The second-level market of urban lands was almost dominated by possession transfer in the early 1990s, but was replaced by land usage rights mortgage instead. Land usage rights renting accounted for only a small proportion with a decreasing tendency. Total trading volume of urban lands in the second-level market was on the rise.

4. 2. 2   Urban Property Market: Hottest Topic in Today's China

A. Aerial View on China's Real Estate Price

In recent years, the urban real estate prices in China fluctuate frequently with the tendency of increasing continuously. Table 4. 7 and Figure 4. 1 illustrate China's urban housing price index, land-trading price index and house-renting price index from 1998 to 2008 respectively, with the price increase of land-trading the highest and house-renting the lowest.

Table 4. 7   Statistical Table of China's Property Price Index(1998−2008)

Year	Housing Price Index	Land-trading Price Index	House-renting Price Index
1998	101. 40	102. 00	102. 40
1999	100. 00	100. 00	98. 50
2000	101. 10	100. 20	102. 40
2001	102. 20	101. 70	102. 80
2002	103. 70	106. 90	100. 80
2003	104. 80	108. 30	101. 90
2004	109. 70	110. 10	105. 50
2005	107. 60	109. 05	106. 73
2006	105. 51	105. 78	103. 48
2007	107. 60	112. 30	103. 80
2008	106. 50	111. 10	102. 00

Source: Data Center of the National Development and Research Center.

Note: last year = 100

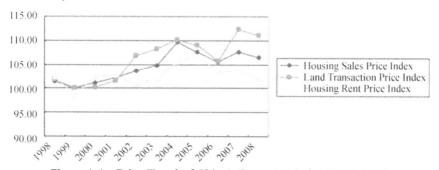

Figure 4. 1   Price Trend of China's Property Market(1998−2008)

Source: Data Center of the National Development and Research Center.

Internationally, the ratio of housing price to family income is a crucial indicator of whether the housing price stays at a reasonable level or not. In the early 1990s, the World Bank did research on over 50 cities around the world and concluded that if the housing price was 3−6 times that of the family income, the former was at an appropriate level; if the housing price was equivalent to or exceeded 6 times the family income, houses were unaffordable for the majority of people. Taking China's statistics for example, the average transaction price of common residential buildings among 17 districts or counties of Beijing was RMB 6,048 per square meter in the second half of 2004, a RMB 540 per square meter increase compared with the price of the latter half of 2003, with the year-on-year growth being 9.8%. However, the average disposable income in Beijing was about RMB 15,637.8 in 2004. It meant that the price of a residential apartment covering 60 square meters in Beijing was equivalent to the total disposable income of 20 years for a common resident. Another example can be taken from a remote county—Yong Feng, Jiangxi province. The average price of commercial residential building rose from RMB 400 per square meter in 2000 to RMB 800 per square meter in 2004. In other words, it might take 20 to 30 years for a common working-class resident to spend all his income to purchase a residence, without any other consumption expenditure.

In China, the price of a commercial residential building was constituted by four parts: land premium, construction cost, property taxes, management cost and profits. Based on an estimation in 2004, the following results can be concluded: 1) As far as small and medium cities are concerned; the standard unit price of a multi-storey residence was approximately RMB 300,000 per mu. Taking FAR(floor-to-area ratio) of the building, residential communities' fittings and equipment and planning designs into consideration, the unit price of building areas was about RMB 180 per square meter. 2) The construction cost of a common residence, villa and multi-storey building ranged from RMB 500 to 800 per square meter, from RMB 500 to 600 per square meter and at most RMB 2,000 per square meter respectively. And there would be the possibility of a price hike of about 2%, if various factors were considered. 3) Property taxes and management cost altogether were no more than RMB 150 per square meter. At present, taxes levied in the property market are sales tax(5.5%) and profit tax (33%). Real estate investors were good at making full use of preferential taxation policies for High-tech and Development Zones, therefore, taxes could be reduced to a minimum amount. In a common county, the business tax and income tax paid by property investors was about 10%. 4) The advisable and reasonable proportion of profits was 8% or 10%, which did exceed the average profit level among relevant industries. According to that data, the housing price in small and medium cities should be around RMB 1,000 per square meter, while the actual average price was about RMB 3,000 per square meter. Facing the soaring housing price, many residents felt powerless and frustrated, besides those who have borne house mortgages.

B. *Factors that Influence the Housing Price in China*

Factors that influenced the housing price in China involve many aspects, such as social, economic, political and legal system elements. From the views of economics, there are two kinds of factors playing dominating roles. One is the basic house value determined by national or local social and economic fundamentals, including local GDP and grawth rate, population variation, employment or unemployment rate, average disposable income of residents and income increase speed, public service, living quality and so on. This basic value has long-term effects on housing price. The other kind of factors that influence the property market price are short-term ones, including credit and taxation policies, markets' expectation, price fluctuation of construction materials, market supervising ability, exploration cost, markets' transparency, maturity of market service system and so on.

C. *Performances of the Government*

Aiming at controlling the housing price, a series of market regulative policies were introduced by the Chinese government in recent years. From the aspect of regulatory purpose, the implementation of those policies helped stabilize housing prices and guaranteed residents' demands through standardizing the development of the real estate market and reducing the potential financial risks in the undue development. From the aspect of regulative means, market-oriented measures such as land supply control, interest rate and taxation were adopted at the earlier stage, while administrative means like controlling the proportion of different types of apartment layout and asking local governments to shoulder responsibilities for stabilizing the housing price were adopted at the later stage. From the aspect of regulatory objectives, investors were targeted through adopting methods of increasing the threshold for project exploration at the earlier stage and raising the interest rate of personal loans, squashing speculative demands as well as controlling land supply and restricting land usage by local governments at the later stage.

The goals of the central government's regulation mainly focused on preventing financial risks, controlling land supply and stabilizing housing price. However, those goals were mutually contradictory. Control on land supply led to the decrease of housing supply and housing price rose on the condition that demand was fixed. Therefore, the goal of stabilizing housing price could not be easily achieved.

Specifically, the goal of stabilizing housing price was not achieved through adopting the market-oriented means of adjusting interest rates and taxation, since market-oriented means failed to work. Housing price was still surging up and residential problem became a crucial challenge that affected social stability. As a result, the central government turned to administrative means to strictly regulate the property market. In the short term, administrative means had effective results; however, over the longer period they would result in reduction of housing supply, higher implementation cost, corruption phenomenon on rent setting and seeking and exerting negative effects on establishing the market with multiple supplies.

Concerning the choice of regulatory objectives, investors were firstly targeted in order to normalize their behavior and prevent financial risks. Then the focus were shifted to house buyers and policies of restraining demands, speculative demands in particular, were adopted to help stabilize the price. These policies had dual effects: although the policy of restraining speculative demands could help stabilize the housing price temporarily, it also laid constraints on rigid demands and solutions for residential problems with the result being purchasing cost increase.

4. 2. 3   Urbanization and Property Market: From an Interactive Developing View

In today's China, urbanization is vigorously pushed forward and the property industry is flourishing. Urbanization and the property market influence each other.

A. Housing Price and Urbanization Degree: Push and Pull Game

Forward stimulating function: on one hand, the fast increase of property prices stimulated the expansion of housing construction, which improved the urban living environment and attracted the rural population. The large number of rural migration accelerated the process of urbanization. On the other hand, the construction industry was a kind of labor-intensive industry, meaning that the scale of property exploration was heavily dependent on the number of rural migrant farmers working as building laborers. The construction of a project always lasted for more than half a year and the rural migrant workers were classified as permanent residents in cities and towns during the construction period, which expanded the size of the population and improved the degree of urbanization.

Backward repelling function: If housing prices increased excessively and exceeded the income growth rate as well as the actual purchasing ability of rural and urban residents, they would feel powerless and frustrated in the face of the excessively high housing price and give up the will of migrating to urban areas. Additionally, high housing prices drove up the rental price, set up obstacles for population floating and constrained the urbanization process.

B. Influence of Urbanization on Real Estate Price: Multi-element Blending

After the implementation of reform and opening up, it was clear that the process of urbanization was overwhelming and urbanization and the property market developed flourishingly, keeping pace with each other. Nowadays, cities in China are developing quickly; therefore, the property industry will definitely develop to a higher degree. The urbanization process mixed up various elements related to society, humanism, the economy, population and government's behavior, which directly or indirectly pushed up housing prices.

Imbalance between supply and demand is an important factor that influenced real estate prices. China's economy is just at the fast developing stage of industrialization and urbanization. From the experience of developed countries, the demand for real estate and automobiles emerged progressively at this stage. As far as residential demand is concerned, there are 155 million households in China at present. Supposing that each household needed an apartment of 90 square meters, it could be estimated that residential demand covering an area of 13.95 billion square meters would need to be met. The residence inventory in urban and rural areas in China is 9 billion so far. Therefore, the gap is 4.95 billion, indicating that it would take 20 years of residential construction with 247.5 million square meters as the annual target. What's more, at that time the amount of households will reach 261 million assuming a growth rate of 64%. If each household needs a residence with 90 square meters, the total demand is 23.49 billion square meters. In that case, compared with the house stock, the shortage will be 14.49 billion square meters and in order to cover that shortage, new apartments covering 724.5 million square meters need to be built up each year in the future 20 years. Even more, if the resettlement projects in cities and towns and the transformation of old towns are taken into consideration, 875 million square meters of newly-built residence need to be built up each year. Nevertheless, in recent years the newly-built residential acreage in urban and rural areas was about 500 million −600 million square meters annually, which could never meet the demand.

Population structure and consuming elements are other important factors that influenced property price. Over the last ten years, the population of China migrated frequently in a large scale; therefore, the traditional household registration system could not effectively impose restrictions on population floating. Besides the rural migrant workers who were rushing to cities for jobs, highly-competent talents with higher education background and bachelor or master's degrees were also attracted to cities. Population size in urban areas rapidly expanded. As a result, the practical and potential demands for residence had effect on real estate prices in cities. Additionally, the upgraded demands of house purchase was growing step by step, due to income increase, living condition improvement, optimization of housing structure and enlargement of living accommodations. A World Bank study reported: the real estate market will step into the fast-growing period, if GDP per capita reaches USD 1, 300; reach the growth speed peak, if GDP per capita exceeds USD 1, 500; enter the stably developing period, if GDP per capita approaches USD 3, 000, with the growth rate slowing down. In 2003, GDP per capita in China was USD 1, 270 and the residential consumption correspondingly entered into the fast-growing period. In 2005, GDP per capita reached USD 1, 750 and the growth rate exceeded 20% . The rapid growth of residents' income drove up the upgraded demand of housing consumption.

4. 3   Issues Arising from Urbanization and Population Development in China

4. 3. 1   Urbanization and the Aging Population

A. Ten Percent Urban Senior Citizens

Since the beginning of the 21st century, the age structure of Chinese population began to change greatly, indicating that China had entered into an aging society. In recent years, China has been witnessing the largest-scale population aging process and the fastest speed in the world ever. Meanwhile, China has also been facing a population growth pattern transformation with low birth rate, low death rate and low growth rate as its characteristics. Typically, this kind of transformation takes more than a hundred years to fulfill in developed countries but only less than 30 years in China, which brought with it population aging problems. Internationally, the criteria indicating whether a country or a region has entered into an aging society is the proportion of the aged population over 60 years old to the total population surpassing 10% , or the proportion of the aged population over 65 years old to the total population surpassing 7% . According to the latter criteria and based on the data from the 5th National Census, the proportion of senior people over 65 years old to the total population was 7% and this percentage increased to 8. 5% in 2009. And China's Population and Development Research Center estimated that the percentage would reach 12. 17% , 15. 19% , 21. 15% and 23. 10% in the years 2020, 2030, 2040 and 2050 respectively. The aging population will be a big challenge for economic and social development. Taking the labor force supply as the example, the urban demand for labor force increased with the rapid development of China's economy and relied heavily on rural migrant workers; however, the aging of the population suggests a decreased working age labor force. According to the data from the national population sample survey in 2005, the total number of the aged above 65 was 150 million, with 90 million rural population accounting for 58% . The decreasing output of cheap labor force from rural areas constrained the development of the economy and the course of urbanization. Fast development of China's economy in the past 30 years is also closely related to demographic dividend brought by the abundant supply of cheap labor force.

B. "4 +2 +1" Family Pattern and Urban Elderly Care

Since the central government promulgated and implemented the one-child policy nationwide in the late 1970s, the number of only-child families has sharply increased with the proportion of the only child to the newly-born children increasing quickly. Based upon the data provided by relevant departments, the number of the single children in 2000 exceeded 100 million. With millions of first generation only-child adults entering into the marriageable and childbearing age in succession, the brand new living and working pattern of their family members becomes a kind of "4 +2 +1"one, that is, the family is constituted of the parents of the young couple, the young couple themselves and their one child. In China, the majority of the post-1980s generation faces the challenge of caring for their aging parents. A renowned newspaper, *Southern Weekly*, conducted a survey on difficulties in caring for elderly parents with 2, 765 participants born after the 1970s. The results reflected that some felt they were under great pressure from day-to-day living and working, so it was really hard for them to look after their parents; some thought it was unaffordable for a couple to take care of four elderly people at the same time; some were living far away from their parents and there was no close residence for their parents to live in; and some found there were obstacles concerning the differences and reimbursement of social pension insurance and medical insurance among different cities.

Nowadays, China has gradually built up an elderly caring pattern with households as the foundation and communities as backup in urban areas. Senior citizens do not have to move out of the community they are used to living in. This pattern combines the advantages of family caring and professional institutions, and various kinds of services for the elderly can be provided by community service staff at home or in institutions. Therefore, this kind of elderly caring method is full of prosperity. The promotion of this pattern requires suitable and advanced community services, but China lacks such community services. As a consequence, most senior people still rely much on themselves and their family members.

At present, the service for the aged in cities is deficient in China. The current situation can be roughly viewed through the research on elderly caring institutions in Harbin, Heilongjiang province. The rooms were bright in private institutions with special nursing service provided at night, with facilities such as Happy Farmland(an activities-driven service of cultivating and harvesting fruits and vegetables), college for the aged, calligraphy and painting as well as recovery rooms. Yet, the caring and nursing charges were very high in private institutions, which was unaffordable for most elderly people to live in. Taking a four-person room for example, each senior people was charged RMB 1,200 per month for the bed, RMB 4,800 per month for nursing service, RMB 700 per month for catering(altogether monthly RMB 6,700), while RMB 7,600 per month for a double room. On the other side, state-owned institutions lacked beds severely. One should pay RMB 1,000 for a bed, RMB 450 for nursing and RMB 400 for catering according to the charge standard in a state-run nursing home, which was provided with considerate nursing care and equipped with gymnasiums, internet bars, reading rooms, central air-conditioning, elevators, televisions, telephones, an emergency call system and 24-hour hot water. However, if one wanted to live in a state-run facility, there would be a long but uncertain waiting period. It is said that altogether 200 beds were occupied, with over 100 people waiting for beds. After 2011, the lack of beds for the aged became worse, so nursing homes had no other choice but to convert activity and meeting rooms into living space as a response.

4.3.2   Urbanization and Rural Migrant Workers in China

A. The Employment of Rural Workers: Learning through Work

Basically, there were three typical categories in regard to employment cost in China's medium and large cities. The first category was the expense on outplacement of laid-off personnel of state-owned enterprises. In order to find work for those unemployed people, many re-employment centers were established in various localities and the government subsidized such kind of social undertakings. In addition, all sectors of society including the business circle provided some capital support for re-employment of laid-off workers. The second category was the expense on outplacement of redundant government officials. Taking the central organs for example, such kind of cost included the expenses on courses in colleges and training in foreign countries as well as the expenses born by state-owned enterprises and companies attached to governmental organs that shoulder responsibilities of taking in the reduced employees. Relevant fiscal expenditures on the outplacement increased accordingly, which were much more than that on laid-off workers. The third category was the cost of employment of rural migrant workers. The governmental finance covered little on this part, so the rural workers had to bear the burden by themselves. What's worse, rural workers' employability was naturally gained through the working process without targeted job-transfer training given to laid-off workers as mentioned above. With respect to employment policies for rural workers, China mainly adhered to the principle of "making use of less average input cost to create more employment opportunities", which might offer more chances for people at the bottom of the society to find jobs.

B. Migrant Workers' Employment in Cities: Temporary Workers

The floating population is mainly constituted of rural migrant workers and classified under informal employment. Informal employment consists of employment of informal sectors and informal employment of formal sectors. That kind of situation means the employees do not have formal job identity or stable career status and are called "temporary workers" in China. Compared with formal employees, it is obvious that the employment quality of rural migrant workers is relatively lower.

Based on China's practical situation, informal employment has the following characteristics. Firstly, migrant workers could not be accepted by the urban formal employment system because they did not have permanent urban residence certificates or special working skills gained by training. Informal employment reflected the segmentation in the labor force market. Secondly, urban residents always had negative impressions about rural workers because they were deeply influenced by the traditional planned economy system and employment models. Even more, local governments held negative and discriminatory attitudes towards the informal employment of rural workers in terms of management policies. According to estimation, China had an approximate 710 million − 720 million labor force population. The capacity for formal employment in formal sectors was about 200 million, while positions concerning agricultural production and informal employment were 500 million. Among those, there were 80 million – 100 million rural population migrating into cities for jobs, most of which belonged to informal employment. Facing the challenges generated from surplus labor, informal sectors and informal employment had tremendous potential of providing job opportunities. In addition, China was also facing the stresses of a growing employable and floating population. To a certain extent, it needed to rely on the potential performance of informal employment.

4. 3. 3   Issues of Urban Medical and Health Care in China

A. China's Input on Medicare and Sanitary Service and Residents' Medical Expenses

For a long time, it was a common phenomenon that large and medium medical and health institutions were attached great importance to, while support for construction and development of primary-level institutions were always ignored. The disparity of inputs led to a medical service capability gap between medical institutions of primary-level in communities and other levels. Therefore, development of the urban sanitary service system was unbalanced with a prevalent feature of "difficult access to quality medical services and expensive medical bills" (see Table 4. 8).

Table 4. 8   Expenditure Pattern of Urban and Rural Total Health Care in China

Year	Total Expenses on Health (RMB 100 million)				Expenditure Pattern of Total Health Care(%)		
	Total	Government	Society	Individual	Government	Society	Individual
1991	893. 49	204. 05	354. 41	335. 03	22. 8	39. 7	37. 5
1992	1, 096. 86	228. 61	431. 55	436. 70	20. 8	39. 3	39. 8
1993	1, 377. 78	272. 06	524. 75	580. 97	19. 7	38. 1	42. 2
1994	1, 761. 24	342. 28	644. 91	774. 05	19. 4	36. 6	43. 9
1995	2, 155. 13	387. 34	767. 81	999. 98	18. 0	35. 6	46. 4
1996	2, 709. 42	461. 61	875. 66	1, 372. 15	17. 0	32. 3	50. 6
1997	3, 196. 71	523. 56	984. 06	1, 689. 09	16. 4	30. 8	52. 8
1998	3, 678. 72	590. 06	1, 071. 03	2, 017. 63	16. 0	29. 1	54. 8
1999	4, 047. 50	640. 96	1, 145. 99	2, 260. 55	15. 8	28. 3	55. 9
2000	4, 586. 63	709. 52	1, 171. 94	2, 705. 17	15. 5	25. 6	59. 0

Cont.

Year	Total Expenses on Health (RMB 100 million)				Expenditure Pattern of Total Health Care(%)		
	Total	Government	Society	Individual	Government	Society	Individual
2001	5,025.93	800.61	1,211.43	3,013.89	15.9	24.1	60.0
2002	5,790.03	908.51	1,539.38	3,342.14	15.7	26.6	57.7
2003	6,584.10	1,116.94	1,788.50	3,678.66	17.0	27.2	55.9
2004	7,590.29	1,293.58	2,225.35	4,071.35	17.0	29.3	53.6
2005	8,659.91	1,552.53	2,586.41	4,520.98	17.9	29.9	52.2
2006	9,843.34	1,778.86	3,210.92	4,853.56	18.1	32.6	49.3
2007	11,573.97	2,581.58	3,893.72	5,098.66	22.3	33.6	44.1
2008	14,535.40	3,593.94	5,065.60	5,875.86	24.7	34.9	40.4
2009	17,541.92	4,816.26	6,154.49	6,571.16	27.5	35.1	37.5

Source: *China Public Health Statistical Yearbook 2011.*

Notes: ① The above statistics are based on the prices for the corresponding year. ②Expenditure on higher medical education has been no longer calculated since 2001 and expenditure on urban and rural medical aids has been calculated since 2006.

Table 4.9   Urban-rural Disparity, Capitation Fee and GDP Proportion of Total Expenditures on Health in China

Year	Urban and Rural Expenditures on Health(RMB 100 million)			Capitation Fee(RMB)			GDP Proportion (%)
	Total	City	Country	Total	City	Country	
1991	893.49	482.60	410.89	77.1	187.6	45.1	4.10
1992	1,096.86	597.30	499.56	93.6	222.0	54.7	4.07
1993	1,377.78	760.30	617.48	116.3	268.6	67.6	3.90
1994	1,761.24	991.50	769.74	146.9	332.6	86.3	3.65
1995	2,155.13	1,239.50	915.63	177.9	401.3	112.9	3.54
1996	2,709.42	1,494.90	1,214.52	221.4	467.4	150.7	3.81
1997	3,196.71	1,771.40	1,425.31	258.6	537.8	177.9	4.05
1998	3,678.72	1,906.92	1,771.80	294.9	625.9	194.6	4.36
1999	4,047.50	2,193.12	1,854.38	321.8	702.0	203.2	4.51
2000	4,586.63	2,624.24	1,962.39	361.9	813.7	214.7	4.62
2001	5,025.93	2,792.95	2,232.98	393.8	841.2	244.8	4.58
2002	5,790.03	3,448.24	2,341.79	450.7	987.1	259.3	4.81
2003	6,584.10	4,150.32	2,433.78	509.5	1108.9	274.7	4.85

Cont.

Year	Urban and Rural Expenditures on Health(RMB 100 million)			Capitation Fee(RMB)			GDP Proportion (%)
	Total	City	Country	Total	City	Country	
2004	7,590.29	4,939.21	2,651.08	583.9	1261.9	301.6	4.75
2005	8,659.91	6,305.57	2,354.34	662.3	1126.4	315.8	4.68
2006	9,843.34	7,174.73	2,668.61	748.8	1248.3	361.9	4.55
2007	11,573.97	8,968.70	2,605.27	876.0	1516.3	358.1	4.35
2008	14,535.40	11,251.90	3,283.50	1,094.5	1,861.8	455.2	4.63
2009	17,541.92	13,535.61	4,006.31	1,314.3	2,176.6	562.0	5.15

Source: *China Public Health Statistical Yearbook 2011*.

Notes: ①The above statistics are based on the prices in the corresponding year; ② Expenditure on higher medical education has been no longer calculated since 2001 and expenditure on urban and rural medical aids has been calculated since 2006.

The statistics of the Third National Health Service Survey showed that the average cost to a resident was RMB 163.5 per visit for medical diagnosis and treatment in urban hospitals and RMB 97.7 per visit in rural medical institutions. Medical expenses were increased by 55%, with 38% and 75% in urban and rural areas respectively, compared with the statistics of the Second National Health Service Survey in 1998. Statistics also revealed that 20.9% of out-patients as well as 33.2% in-patients considered the high expenses as the most unsatisfactory aspect in the process of seeking medical services. Journalists from *People's Daily* conducted interviews in ten selected hospitals in Shandong province, Fujian province, Shanghai, etc. and results manifested that the cost for influenza treatment ranged from RMB 6 to 270. The survey also revealed the concealed diagnosis process-indiscriminate use of antibiotics without advising patients, which had been a prevalent phenomenon in the medical industry.

The statistics of the Fourth National Health Service Survey(see Table 4.10 and Table 4.11) presented that the average medical charges per visit and the average medical charges per case for China's urban and rural residents covered by basic medical insurance were RMB 242 and RMB 415 respectively. The average cost was distinctly different among different regions. The average medical expenditure in large cities was two times higher than that in small cities and it was almost the same as that in large and medium cities. The median medical charges in large and medium cities were twice as high as that in small cities. The condition of skewed distribution on medical cost was more prevalent in large and medium cities than in small cities. The average hospitalization expenses were

RMB 5,020 per case and RMB 409 per day. It also varied from cities to cities, higher in large cities and lower in small cities.

Table 4.10   Medical Expenses of Urban and Rural Residents covered by Basic Medical Insurance in 2008(in Two Weeks)

City Size	Average Medical Expenses (RMB)		Medical Expenses per Case (RMB)		Medical Expenses per Patient(RMB)
	Mean	Median	Mean	Median	
Total	242	110	415	150	419
Large	359	150	619	200	650
Medium	321	140	501	200	501
Small	133	70	254	120	254

Source: *Analysis Report of the Fourth National Family Health Survey in 2008.*

Table 4.11   Average Hospitalization Expenses of Urban and Rural Residents covered by Basic Medical Insurance in 2008

City Size	Average Hospitalization Expenses per Day (RMB)		Average Hospitalization Expenses per Case(RMB)	
	Mean	Median	Mean	Median
Total	409	350	5,020	4,000
Large	500	400	5,712	6,000
Medium	425	350	5,511	4,000
Small	339	280	4,145	3,000

Source: *Analysis Report of the Fourth National Family Health Survey in 2008.*

B. Treating "Difficult Access to Medical Services and Expensive Medical Bills" Rationally

"Difficult Access to Medical Services" might be divided into two kinds: absolute difficulties and relative difficulties. For the first kind, the difficulties resulted from the absolute insufficiency of medical resources, because residents' needs for basic medical health services could not be met due to the shortage of doctors and medicine. Since the founding of the People's Republic of China, especially since the Reform and Opening up, many achievements had been made in the health service and medical service system covering both urban and rural areas. The condition of "Difficult Access to Medical Services" usually appeared in remote and western rural areas with backward economic development, inconvenient transportation, vast lands and sparse population. The second kind was relative difficulties. Compared with residents' needs for medical care, medical resources of high quality were in shortage. Under that condition, many patients rushed to large state-owned hospitals to seek medical consultation and treatment from experienced experts instead of doctors of primary-level medical institutions, even if they just had a minor illness. Therefore, third-level grade-A hospitals were crowded with patients and medical staff and registration opportunity was very hard to get.

On the other side, "Expensive Medical Bills" might be represented from three perspectives. From the perspective of personal subjective feelings, patients judge whether the medical treatments were worthy of the expenses in terms of their prospective target costs and the effectiveness of the treatment. From the perspective of family economic condition, if the total medical charges surpassed the payment capability of a family, the family members' daily lives would be greatly affected. In that situation, some families used their savings on medical care and even sold their residence in search of a cure for their illness, which would lead to the problem of "becoming poor or return to poverty because of illness. " The essence of this kind of difficulty is inherent in the heavy economic burden caused by diseases and the lack of effective social medical insurance. From the perspective of social development, the total medical expenses of the whole society increased continually with a certain higher growth rate, but it was hard to adjust and control. If the overall level of medical care charges exceeded the whole society's bearing capacity, it would exert negative effects on substantial development of the society and economy. [1]

C. China's Medical and Health Service System Reform

The *Working Plans on Medical and Health Services System Reform 2011* pointed out: "Annual government subsidies for the new cooperative medical care system and basic medical insurance for urban residents will be raised from RMB 120 to 200 per person respectively and the per person payment standard for public health services will be increased properly. The reimbursement rate for hospitalization expenses should be raised to around 70% . In all coordinated regions that are covered by the basic medical insurance for working urban residents, the basic medical insurance for non-working urban residents and the new type of rural cooperative medical care, the maximum payment limit of consolidated fund targets to reach at least six times the amount of the local employees' average annual salary, the local residents' annual disposable income and the national farmers'

---

1   Chen Zhu. Dialectical views on the problem of "difficult access to quality medical services and expensive medical bills", *China Daily.* 2011. 2. 24

average annual net income respectively, with the baseline of RMB 50, 000. We should continue to accelerate the capacity expansion of the coverage of medical insurance system as well as extend the coverage of the national basic system of drugs to all grass-roots medical and health-care institutions. Policy-based efforts to encourage private capital into the medical service field and guide non-governmental bodies to operate hospitals should be increased to promote the development of non-public medical institutions. Efforts should also be made to introduce social capital into the operation of high-end medical institutions and control the ratio of special demand for medical treatment in public hospitals. " [1]

The *Working Plans on Medical and Health Services System Reform 2012* pointed out: "The coverage of the basic medical insurance for working urban residents, the basic medical insurance for non-working urban residents and the new type of rural cooperative medical care should be raised to 95% . Annual government subsidies for the new cooperative medical care system and basic medical insurance for urban residents will be raised to RMB 240 per person respectively and the per person payment standard for public health services will be increased to approximately RMB 300. In all coordinated regions that are covered by the basic medical insurance for working urban residents, the basic medical insurance for non-working urban residents and the new type of rural cooperative medical care, the maximum payment limit of consolidated fund targets to reach at least six times the amount of the local employees' average annual salary and the local residents' annual disposable income respectively and eight times the amount of the national farmers' average annual net income, with the baseline of RMB 60, 000. We should work hard to raise the reimbursement rate for hospitalization expenses covered by the basic medical insurance for non-working urban residents and the new type of rural cooperative medical care to above 70% and about 75% respectively and narrow the gap between the target reimbursement rate and actual rate. We will further strengthen the efforts to increase input on medical aid, and build up a bottom line for medical care insurance firmly. The establishment of funds of emergency medical assistance should be carefully studied to help the patients who have no payment ability and unidentified patients to pay for the emergency medical expenses, making full use of governmental funds, social donation and other funding sources. In order to provide a guarantee for urban and rural families, we should actively explore and establish a kind of critical illness insurance system, in which certain amounts of money are earmarked in the basic

---

[1]   Circular of the General Office of the State Council on Printing and Issuing Medical and Health System Five Key Reform 2011 Annual Main Organization of Work. (guobanfa [2011] No. 8)

medical insurance fund to buy critical illness insurance policies from commercial insurance companies so as to effectively raise the standard of guarantee, relieve urban and rural residents of the heavy burden of catastrophic medical spending and prevent the tragedy of ' becoming poor or return to poverty because of illness' from happening". [1]

4. 4　"Large City Malaise" in China and Sustainable Development of Cities

4. 4. 1　Urbanization and City Pollution in China

A. Overall Condition of City Pollution

Over the past 20 years, the growth rate of urbanization had risen from 20% in 1980 to 38% in 2002, which was twice as fast as the world's average speed. With the development of urbanization, the air quality in some large cities in China rapidly deteriorated; therefore, air pollution became one of the most serious and emergency urban problems in present China. In northern China where the climate is dry and vegetation coverage is limited, soil particles have become the main resources of urban air pollution. Recently, because of urban infrastructure being in peak period, construction and transportation dusts have become the main reasons for urban air pollution. Especially in winter when coal-burning is needed for heating, the total air pollution volume might increase by 30% to 40%. In addition, acid rain is another potential threat for environmental protection with 40% of the territory in China having been polluted. SO_2 (sulfur dioxide) and NO_2 (nitrogen dioxide) are the two other kinds of gases that will affect air quality. SO_2 is a regional pollutant which is usually caused by local industrial production, energy consumption and residents' daily lives and is detected mainly in North, Central, East, Southwest as well as South China. The average density of NO_2 is relatively lower. Monitoring results showed that NO_2 density in all the target cities was not very high and could meet the secondary level of The National Ambient Air Quality Standard, while the density in large cities such as Beijing, Shanghai, Guangzhou, Shenzhen and Chongqing was relatively higher.

With the rapid development of industrialization, urbanization and vehicle PARC(the total number of vehicles in a country) in China, pollution emission

---

volume increased at a high speed, which led to the formation of a disastrous weather-smog. The smog frequently occurs in large cities like Beijing, Guangzhou and Nanjing. It was(and still is) harmful for people's health and also excreted bad influence on people's work and daily lives. The Yangtze River Delta was one of the most thickly populated, urbanized and polluted areas in East China and unfortunately was becoming the most serious smog-polluted area in the country. Heavily emitted SO_2 and NO_X (nitrogen oxides) were the primary pollutants and air pollution in those areas was of regional and complex characteristics. The southern parts of Jiangsu province were considered the urbanization core region among cities located in the Yangtze River Delta. The city areas along the river in Jiangsu province in 2008 had been expanded 2.5 times as against 1978. However, rapid economic development brought about serious regional air pollution at the same time.

B. Sources of City Pollution in China

Particles were the primary pollutants that affected air quality of cities in China and also the biggest obstacles for 113 key cities to meet the 2010 overall pollution control standard. Compared with SO_2 and NO_X, particles had so many sources and complex ingredients that they were hard to prevent and control. The particles in the air were mainly caused by primary pollutants such as soil wind dust, coal smoke dust, construction dust, vehicle exhaust, garbage incineration industry, concrete manufacturing and metal smelting industry as well as secondary pollutants such as urban transportation and construction dust. The research on China's ecological and environmental problems presented that exhausts from industrial furnaces, vehicles and coal-burning by local residents sharply increased the concentration of suspended particles, SO_2 and CO_2 (carbon dioxide). The suspended particles threatened the health of urban residents. The increasing production rate, the usage of vehicles and motor bikes were the other causes of air pollution in cities. Since the mid 1980s, the yield of cars, motorcycles and trucks increased at the speed of over 10% annualy, while the usage of vehicles gave rise to the content increase of lead in the air. [1] The analytic results from studies of Wang Dongyu(2006) and others on emergency water source pollution events in China demonstrated that the number of emergency pollution events and the potential risk of water resources pollution were both increasing with chemicals and polluted water as the main pollutants and traffic incidents, leakage of factories and

---

[1]   Hu An-gang. Ecological environment and environmental protection planning in China, *Journal of Safety and Environment*, Vol. 1, No. 6, 2001. 6.

sudden pollution discharge as the main risk sources. [1]

C. Policies and Measures on City Pollution in China

In May 2011, *Guiding Opinions on Promoting the Coordinated Air Pollution Prevention and Control and Improving the Regional Atmospheric Quality* (hereinafter referred to as the "Opinions") was issued. It required local governments to promote all-round and coordinated air pollution prevention and control and to improve the regional and urban air quality. Concrete measures included: unified coordination and management of regional air environment as a whole; making efforts to build a regionally coordinated prevention and control working mechanism; adhering to the principle of "unified planning, unified monitoring, unified supervision, unified evaluation and unified coordination". Unified planning meant to organize and make plans for regional air pollution prevention and control in a coordinated way, according to the regional air quality and characters of the pollutants. Great efforts should be made to balance regional environmental bearing capacity, pollution discharge volume, the current situation of economic and social development and mutual influence between cities, set up goals scientifically for environmental quality improvement among related regions, work out measures to prevent and control pollution and designate the key projects that are badly in need of pollution treatment. Unified monitoring meant to push forward the establishment of a regional air quality monitoring network, to share the monitored information among different regions and raise the monitoring capability of regional air quality with the monitoring focus on acid rain, particles and the ozone. Unified supervision meant to strengthen the work on the online monitoring system construction of regional key pollution sources, boost its enforcement efforts and organize special improvement programs to treat regional air pollution. Unified evaluation meant to establish the evaluation system for coordinated air pollution prevention to supervise and evaluate the working effects of regional air pollution prevention and control as well as to reveal the results open to the public. More strict reward and punishment measures concerning air quality controlling would be promulgated in the cities where the planned tasks were not fulfilled on time and the air quality condition was getting worse. Unified coordination meant to establish a cross administrative region mechanism of joint pollution prevention and control in a holistic way, intensify the organization and

---

1   Wang Dong-yu. Statistical analysis on drinking water source and supply system contamination threats and incidents for urban areas in China during 2006. *Journal of Safety and Environment*, Vol. 7 No. 6, 2007. 12.

cooperation and joint forces to treat pollutions.

Considering the disparity of air quality condition and the urgency of air pollution prevention and control among various localities, *the Opinions* also made Beijing-Tianjin-Hebei region, Yangtze River Delta and Pearl River Delta the key regions of coordinated air pollution prevention and control. As the main subjects responsible for preventing and controlling air pollution, local governments should strengthen the organization and leadership as well as supervision and evaluation. The Ministry of Environmental Protection, jointly with other relevant departments, should evaluate and examine the working effects of prevention and control on air pollution. New approval for construction projects which would cause air pollution should be strictly restricted in cities where the planned tasks were not fulfilled on time and the air quality condition was becoming worse. [1]

In December 2012, the central government approved the 12th *Five-Year Plan for Atmospheric Pollution Prevention and Control in Major Areas*. It was required in the plan that 47 cities including Beijing, Shanghai, Tianjin, Chongqing and other 15 provincial capitals should put strict restrictions on highly-polluted projects in steel, cement, petrochemical, chemical and non-ferrous industries. On one hand, as far as industries that highly rely on geographic locations were concerned, effects should be achieved in promoting industrial transformation and updating through increasing investments on energy conservation and emission reduction. On the other hand, initial steps had be taken on the movement of enterprises from first-tier and second-tier cities to third-tier cities and from eastern regions to central and western regions sooner after the plan was issued. The plan came up with several measures that could be adopted in the process of industrial structure and distribution upgrading, energetic structure optimizing, clean utilization of coal, implement of joint control on different kinds of pollutants and the establishment of regional atmospheric joint prevention and control mechanism. [2]

4. 4. 2   Urbanization and Urban Traffic Congestion

A. Overall Condition of Urban Traffic Congestion in China

After entering the 21st century, the speed of urbanization and mechanization has accelerated. During the 10 years from 2000 to 2009, the motor vehicle

---

[1]   *Guiding Opinions on Pushing Forward the Joint Prevention and Control of Atmospheric Pollution to Improve Regional Air Quality.* (guobanfa [2010] No. 33)

[2]   Twelfth Five-Year Plan for Atmospheric Pollution Prevention and Control in Major Areas. (guobanfa[2012] No. 146)

PARC of first-tier cities such as Beijing, Shanghai, Guangzhou, Hangzhou, Chengdu and Shenzhen has surpassed one million and the national total number of vehicle PARC increased by 16. 3% per year from 16. 09 million to 62. 81 million with a net growth of 46. 72 million. Under that background, urban transportation problems, with traffic congestion as the representative, gradually became a common problem in China's large cities. At first, traffic congestion appeared in mega cities like Beijing, Shanghai, Guangzhou, Chengdu, etc. and then spread quickly to big and medium cities where the population exceeded one million. What's more, the traffic condition in some small and medium cities was worsening.

B. Features of Urban Traffic Congestion in China

Traffic congestion is a commonly seen phenomenon in China and differentiates in cities at different urbanization stage and in different functional regions of the same city. The features of traffic congestion in China can be specified as the following types: a) Traffic congestion regularly taking place and spreading out. Taking Beijing for example, the traffic congestion index rose from 5. 1 after the Beijing Olympic Games to the current 6. 7. It reached the medium level of congestion and even serious level at some peak periods. The speed was lower than 15 km/h on some parts of the main roads during the morning and evening rush hours and the everyday congestion hours on work days on all roads exceeded 4 hours. b) Serious traffic congestion during commuting hours. This outstanding phenomenon, with the characteristics of unidirectional congestion, always appeared in large cities with a population of more than one million at morning and evening peak hours, where traffic demands were accumulated. c) Traffic congestion appearing at parts of the road network points. Traffic congestion usually appeared at certain key points of the road network or at a road crossing alone. If this kind of point congestion could not be settled effectively, it would expand to point-line-area congestion. The point congestion affected the connected roads and nearby road crossings and it would cause regional traffic congestion, which might exert negative influence on the functional performances of the whole road network. d) Decrease of traffic capacity caused by mixed motor vehicle and non-motor vehicle lanes as well as traffic disorder. This phenomenon was frequently observed in small and medium cities with the characteristics of mixed lanes for cars, motor bikes, bicycles and pedestrians which interrupted each other and reduced the driving speed on the roads.

Urban traffic congestion in China is resulted from many factors, two of which are significant ones. Firstly, the growth rate of urban population exceeded the overall control target. The *Beijing City Master Plan(2004 – 2020)* required that the actual residential population should be controlled to less than18 million; however, it reached 17. 55 million in 2009, ten years earlier breaking the control target. The permanent resident population in Shanghai reached 19. 21 million in 2009, surpassing the planned control target of 16 million. The total number of population in Hangzhou was 4. 24 million, also ten years earlier breaking the control target of 4. 05 million according to the plan. That kind of breaking through the target would surely result in the condition that traffic needs were in excess of overall planning and put the traffic system constructed according to the overall plan under great pressure. Secondly, the expansion of cities enlarged the commuting distance. From 1990 to 2002, the urban built-up areas of 16 cities located at the Yangtze River Delta increased on average by more than 10% annually, with the highest expansion speed of 28% in Hangzhou and the lowest 11% in Ningbo, Zhejiang province. From 1997 to 2007, new construction lands covering 49 square kilometers were expanded annually, which was nearly equivalent to the acreage of old Guangzhou city before 1949. Correspondingly, the average commuting distance in Guangzhou increased from 2. 54 kilometers in 1984 to 6. 42 kilometers in 2005, while the distance in Shanghai increased from 4. 5 kilometers in 1995 to 6. 9 kilometers in 2004. The expansion of urban areas reflected in the rising volume of the turnover of residents and commodities and the expansion speed far surpassed the capacity of the urban road system.

C. Policies on Traffic Congestion Formulated by Chinese Government

In order to alleviate the severe traffic congestion in cities, several local governments worked out measures to deal with the traffic problems. Firstly, implementing the transportation system of odd-and-even License Plate Rule to relieve urban traffic pressure. During the period of Good Luck Beijing Olympic Test Events, Beijing carried out the odd-and-even License Plate Rule. Cars with the tail number on the license plate being odd could be driven on odd dates, and vice versa. Effective achievements were gained after implementing this rule. From October 8 to November 7, 2012, the traffic management department of Lanzhou launched a one-month trial on tail number limitation for taxis. From January 16, 2013, Jinan carried out the tail number limitation on heavily polluted days. Secondly, granting car registrations via a lottery system. Private car buyers were required to apply first and then take part in the lottery procedure. The computer provides ten numbers randomly, from which the buyer selects one number. Considering the worsening traffic jam in Beijing, car registration began to be allocated by a license-plate lottery system on January 26, 2011. Of the total

180, 000 private car applicants, only 17, 600 of them were awarded the rights for car registration. Thirdly, raising the proportion of public transit. Efforts should be made to improve the public traffic capacity, raise the proportion of cycling trips and reduce the usage of private cars. Beijing has worked out a policy with the purpose that the proportion of public transit in the city center should be raised to 50% , the proportion of cycling should be kept at 18% and the proportion of passenger cars should be controlled below 25% .

4. 4. 3   Urbanization and Green Growth

A. Lifting the Veil of Green Growth

The key point of "Green" Growth is to develop a circular economy, which is also a kind of sustainable economy. The United Nations Conference on Environment and Development(1992) approved the *21ˢᵗ Century Agenda*, which was the symbol of making "sustainable development" the common target and the strategy of joint actions of human beings from the whole world. Circular economy, characterized by high efficiency, low emission and low consumption, takes the effective and cyclic utilization of the recourses as its core and follows the principle of "reclamation, reduction and recycle". It is coherent with the economic growth mode guided by the concept of sustainable development. The ultimate goal is to protect the scarce environmental resources and improve the efficiency of environmental resources allocation.

The pursuit of a circular economy cannot only improve the gradually deteriorating ecological environment, but also play an important role in propelling the process of urbanization. China is a developing country with a large population and vast territory. For many years it has adopted the growth mode of extensive economy; therefore, many enterprises produced with low efficiency and high resources consumption and heavily polluted the environment. The fast growth rate and development of the economy relied more and more on resources that were becoming increasingly scarce and depended on imports to meet domestic needs. At present, China has become the second largest importing and consuming country for crude oil. Resource shortage became a major obstacle for economic development, thus the process of urbanization. Besides, the economic development level of the central and western parts of China is relatively low. As the large-scale development in western China is on its way, it is necessary to step on the road of sustainable development and pursue a circular economy which can help enhance employment quality and promote the development of relevant environment-friendly industries. In addition, the processes of production, maintaining, service and recycling of products with durability and stability belong to labor intensive industries, which can provide a large amount of employment opportunities.

B. Achievements in Pursuit of Green Growth in China

During the 11th Five-Year Plan period(2001 – 2005), energy consumption grew at an average annual growth rate of 6.6%, supporting the 11.2% annual growth rate of the national economy. The energy consumption elasticity coefficient dropped from 1.04 to 0.59 and the amount of saved energy consumption reached 630 million tons of standard coal. a) The growing trend of energy consumption intensity and major pollutant discharge were reversed at the stage of fast industrialization and urbanization development. Energy consumption per unit of GDP was reduced by 19.1% during the 11th Five-Year Plan period. Total sulfur dioxide(SO_2) emissions and total COD(chemical oxygen demand) emissions were reduced by 14.29% and 12.45% respectively. b) Traditional industries were reformed and upgraded. The proportion of thermal power generating units with a generation capacity above 300,000 kw each in China's thermal power installed capacity increased from 50% in 2005 to 73% in 2010; the proportion of large iron production blast furnaces with a capacity above 1,000 cu m each increased from 48% to 61%; the proportion of new dry process cement production each increased from 39% to 81%. c) Advancement of technology was propelled. From 2005 to 2010, the popularity rate of coke dry quenching technology in the iron and steel industry rose from less than 30% to above 80%, the popularity rate of low temperature waste heat power generation in cement production from trials reached 55% and the popularity rate of ionic membrane caustic soda technology increased from 29% to 84%. d) The capacity of energy conservation and emission reduction was strengthened. During the 11th Five-Year Plan period, the total energy conservation capacity was equivalent to 340 million tons of standard coal; newly increased sewage treatment capacity in urban and rural areas was 65 million tons and the sewage treatment rate reached 77%; desulfurization in coal-burning power plants was carried out with a production capacity of 578 million kilowatts and the proportion of that unit capacity each in total thermal power generating units reached 82.6%. e) Level of energy efficiency was enhanced. From 2005 to 2010, coal consumption in thermal power supply dropped 10.0% from 370 to 333 g/kwh; comprehensive energy consumption per ton of steel decreased 12.1% from 688 to 605 kg of standard coal; that in cement production, down by 28.6%; that of ethylene production, down by 11. 3% ; and that of synthetic ammonia production, 14. 3%. [1]

C. Policies and Measures on Green Growth

China has launched a series of policies and measures to promote Green Growth, including: a) Reducing the energy consumption. The 11th Five-Year Plan required that the demand of energy consumption should be reduced by 20%. b) Improving modes of energy transport. Efforts should be made to construct the fastest railway network in the world, build subway and bus rapid transit systems in dozens of cities and turn trains into the kind of transportation similar to the intensive carbon emission efficiency as planes. c) Raising the energy efficiency in fields of manufacture, construction industry and so on. d) Investing in clean energy. Work should be done continually to invest more in storage experiments for wind power, solar power, nuclear power and carbon. e) Exploring and formulating new policies. Actually, China has issued some policies to control CO_2 emission. f) Setting up goals, quotas and standards as well as providing enough financial support for new technologies. Although there were some opposite opinions on the measurement system of carbon emission internationally, a general consensus has been reached in China regarding the effective measurements and reports, which has laid a basic foundation to achieve the goals of Green Growth. Such measurement systems has been mentioned and referred to in some governmental documents.

Additionally, relevant departments of the State Council are establishing an accountability system which will be implemented according to division of work, assignments and working achievements. Efforts should be made to address the root causes of pollution and low efficiency, put strict restrictions on the approval for new projects in high-polluted and energy-intensive industries, fulfill the task of speeding up to remove the backward energy capacity and promote the energy reduction of key projects in implementing the policies of energy conservation and emission reduction.

Case 4. 1   Real Estate Speculative Groups in Wenzhou

The huge power of private capital from Wenzhou first aroused public attention through Wenzhou investors' performances on real estate speculation. Based on the past 20 to 30 years' wealth accumulation, Wenzhounese, who are

---

[1]   Twelfth Five-Year Plan for Energy Saving and Emission Reduction. (guobanfa [2012] No. 40)

known as "Chinese Jews", have grasped enormous private capital with the amount reaching RMB 600 billion. The aggressive and hardworking Wenzhounese searched for investment opportunities everywhere, and with a large amount of money started their trials in the Wenzhou property market in the beginning. From 1998 to 2001, the enormous private capital of Wenzhounese were invested into the local property market, with the annual growth rate of real estate price being 20%. The downtown housing prices rapidly increased from about RMB 2,000 per square meter to above RMB 7,000 per square meter. In August, 2001, the first Wenzhou house-purchasing group left for Shanghai and purchased more than 100 commercial residences with RMB 50 million cash flowing into the Shanghai property market in just three days. At the same time, another group set out for Hangzhou. Afterwards, altogether RMB 200 billion was invested into real estate markets of various localities, half of which was accumulated in Beiijng and Shanghai.

Every coin has two sides, however. There were not only triumphs, but also failures among the real estate speculative groups. Once a group could earn millions per day during the peak period, there was also a possibility of failure under domestically strict restrictions on the real estate market. The following is a vivid example of one such failure that resulted from severe regulatory policies.

Introduced by an anonymous investor, the journalist had the chance to interview Xu Tong and listen to his legendary experience. "You took the train here, right? There are countless tunnels from Lishui to Wenzhou. I had drilled many tunnels and I knew sunlight was not far ahead. But now, it enters into a long and dark tunnel, without seeing the end." Xu Tong started the conversation.

Xu Tong was formerly a traditional peasant in Ruian, a county-level city of Wenzhou. His house is a three-storey building located in the town of Ruian. The building is shabby and lacking maintenance. Compared with other buildings, it is miserable except that the water area in front of it can passably save face. "All the houses I have purchased were much better than this one; unfortunately, I have never lived in any one yet." After Xu met the journalist and spoke a few words, he hurried to move away: "The journalists can be seen by the neighbors, but I can't be seen and intercepted by them." "Them" refers to his relatives and old friends, who are creditors now. In the end, Xu and the journalist moved to a sand dredger 2.5 kilometers away. Xu told the journalist except the farmland covering several mu, this boat was his only one asset that has remained.

Xu was a bit later than others to set foot in the property market speculation in 2005. He expanded his speculative group quickly in three years. Meanwhile, he explored and invested from one city to another in most of the first-tier cities in

China with more than RMB 100 million and purchased houses ceaselessly in bulk. Where he invested the real estate price soared. When he left, he had gained huge profits. However, at that time the housing price was still increasing in spite of the much stricter regulations. He invested in Hangzhou with two million on a trial and earned 0. 5 million in only half a year. It seemed that this was a much easier way to get money compared with laborious sand excavation. When he got back to his hometown, he was envied by many villagers, thus more private investors with capital were attracted and join in his speculation. Followed by seven villagers, he entered into the Shanghai property market with a principal of RMB 20 million. They made up their minds to spend all the money on purchasing apartments in a luxury building, and then they sold them two months later making profits as high as 25% . From then on, they rushed to southern cities like Guangzhou and Shenzhen and northern cities like Beijing and Dalian. Xu's total asset including the principal and profits was in excess of RMB 100 million and he had more than 20 followers at that time. Like any other speculative group, if the group members were satisfied with a building, they would purchase the houses in bulk. On one hand, they roughly investigated other projects. On the other hand, they observed the market trend. Once there would be profits, they listed the properties and sold them with the help of intermediary agents. One thing he remembered most clearly was that he sold about a dozen houses at one time in May, 2007. At that time, he never worried about the market. Real estate prices were continually increasing and the intermediary agents even required him to raise the price. He sold six residential units at the average price of RMB 14, 000, while it only cost him RMB 9,900 per unit six months prior. The price was raised twice in the three-day listing period. Xu could sell several houses per day in those days with millions in profits. Several waves of relatives and friends visited him in a single day and wanted to join in his speculation with a lot of money. While he was pleasantly enjoying the huge profits, the same as other real estate speculative groups did, he also gained trust and respect from others. On the contrary, he was also jealous of those who were much richer than him. Their total capital reached 100 million and had a financial group with hundreds of millions of capital. The greedy desire made him neglect the potential risks.

Now, it seems that Xu has come back to earth. The money he had earned is totally tied up, what's worse, he owes others RMB 30 million. Putting aside the frequent annoyance of over 20 households' complaints to him for better or worse, they are his followers and responsible for their own profits and losses, he has borrowed 30 million in cash. He was figuring out while lighting a cigarette: 18 million from five relatives in the form of private loans, with monthly interest rate differentiating from 2% to 5% according to the length of repayment period; 12 million from a friend who raised the funds from several of his colleagues; 12 million from his own bank account. Altogether more than 40 million is tied up in the property market. Complex feelings of gratitude and resentment are mixed up among the members of speculative groups. Xu's cousin, who loaned him six million for speculation, now considers Xu his enemy because he has earned no bonuses. A week ago, his cousin even sent his wife to meet Xu. With a critical attitude and full of anger, she scratched Xu's face.

Dating back to last May, Xu had already observed the risks behind the soaring real estate prices and sold most of his houses. But after a three-month observation, the price was still as high as before. He purchased again at a high price. Unfortunately, he has become the last runner in the relay-race with no buyers taking over the baton and had no choice but to run constantly, till now. The most important thing is that he has put the entire principal and profits he had gained before on these residential buildings.

What is the reason for the sacrifice? Xu lit another cigarette and continued telling his story. The currency policies were tightening, interest rate on private loans was increasing and the trend of more and more severe adjustment and control was getting clear. He was infatuated by the extravagant profits. Last September, after he spent all the capital on another round of purchasing houses, he suddenly felt regretful and unconfident. Actually, just as soon as he purchased the houses of a project called "Fuli Newtown" in Guangzhou, even when he had not received the housing ownership certificates, he tried to find new buyers, with regret. The listed price was certainly set high, but he failed. Then he suddenly found out that his fellow villagers, peers, people surrounding him and even the building developers were determined to sell their houses, while the formerly potential buyers hesitated to make the decision. At that point, he felt things beginning to skid and began to smoke cigarettes heavily. In addition, several members of the speculative group started to sell houses in bulk individually. The price was raised in the first month, but none were sold. The price was adjusted to the former level in the second month, only one flat was sold. In the next two months, the price remained, but still none was sold. From the beginning of this March, he was totally living in panic. The listed housing price was lowered several times, but without any effective results. Until this May, his houses devalued by more than 20%. He decided to sell the houses at the cost of 30% of the total price, but there was still not a single buyer. He was totally in despair and under the pressure of high interest rates on his loans. Every cent of the total RMB 30,000 interest must be paid per day and all his assets were changed into houses. If Xu needed some comfort, he could just think about people around him whose money was also tied up and retreat may lead to disastrous results. They felt hopeless about the property market. Even if it would recover a little after this round of adjustment and control, there was not much room for speculation. Observation and retreat as quickly as possible were of great significance. He heard that some speculative groups would investigate the real estate markets in second-tier or third-tier cities, but he only smiled bitterly as a response. He said he had already died. The only reason for him to live on was trying to pay the interests back through tilling lands and excavating sands laboriously.

This is a common example from hundreds of Wenzhou speculative groups; however, it also represents the experiences of Wenzhou speculators hiding in the background of this conspired wealth-game along with numerous others.

Excerpted from: Gong Peijia. Real estate speculative groups in Wenzhou, *China Times*, June 27, 2008.

Questions:

1. What is the influence of real estate speculative groups on China's property market?

2. What are the implications of the phenomenon of real estate speculative groups?

Case 4. 2 Migrant Workers Shortage in Cities—Strategies Adopted by Enterprises

The phenomenon of migrant workers shortage, which involves both general and skilled workers, appears in some major southern cities at first, especially during the period of Spring Festival. No matter which shortage pattern it is, the shortage is relative, partial and of structural reasons.

The phenomenon of migrant workers shortage mainly has the following five features: a) The phenomenon appears in some areas. Original equipment manufacturers(OEM) located in the Yangtze River Delta and the Pearl River Delta stay at the bottom of the "Smiling Curve" and have low profits as well as a reputation for ill-treatment. Therefore, it is hard to recruit employees. b) The phenomenon appears in some industries. For workers hired by labor-intensive industries such as feather or eiderdown processing, textile, garment processing and catering services, the labor intensity is high and working hours is long. Therefore, the recruitment for employees is relatively difficult. c) The phenomenon appears in some enterprises. Small and medium enterprises without satisfactory management practices find it more difficult to recruit employees. Most importantly, due to the remote position of these enterprises, transportation is difficult, while cultural life is not rich and lacks attraction. On the other hand, job hunters pay great attention to the reputation and brand of enterprises, so they are not willing to work in small and medium enterprises. d) The type of work is also a factor. Serious shortage of workers, involving operating certain types of machines like lathing, pliers, mill, and electro welding, has resulted in the shortage of skills and is directly related to the enormous effects of large-scale investment for railway, road and airport construction on the development of the machine building industry. e) The shortage of workers is also a result of the imbalance of workers' age and sex. In recent years, the overall number of new generation of migrant workers is gradually decreasing with the post 1980s and 1990s generation as the representatives. All kinds of production lines are badly in need of young workers, who are irreplaceable by elder workers. Meanwhile, some industries such as garment processing and catering services only hire young women, but the labor force of this group are in short supply. Therefore, the recruitment difficulties stand out prominently.

A mainstream viewpoint on the shortage of migrant workers is that the employment situation for rural migrant workers is not very optimistic because the supply of rural labor exceeds the demand as a whole. This viewpoint is also verified from the micro-level by an investigation conducted by a research group in some selected cities and counties of Anhui province, an advanced agricultural province. Taking Chaohu city as the example, 70,000 people hunt for jobs every year, but the number of new positions is only about 40,000, indicating that there is a 30,000 labor surplus .

There are many kinds of strategies that Chinese enterprises usually adopt to tackle the shortage. Three typical ones are listed below:

Firstly, carry out business outsourcing to cope with the shortage of general workers. A private textile enterprise can be taken for example. This enterprise is engaged in garment processing and exports its entire products to Europe, the U. S. and Japan. Benefited from the improving economy recently, more products are booked, which leads to the shortage of seamers on the production line. This enterprise carries out the following measures: On one hand, adopting the mode of business outsourcing. It selected nine companies to cooperate with and outsourced the surplus orders to them. Through this strategy, it successfully transferred the recruitment difficulties to its partners. On the other hand, strive for mutual and beneficial development through cooperation. Here, another factory can be given as the example. It is a typical garment manufacturer and has easier access to recruit nearby employees. The above mentioned private textile enterprise provides its surplus lockstitch sewing machine and some other specialized equipment for the clothing factory to use and places a stable number of product orders so as to ensure the continuity of its production. In order to guarantee the quality of the products, the company also appoints technical staff to provide assistance for the factory, check the whole production process and provide advice on operating management, manufacturing and processing.

Secondly, organize on-the-job training to tackle the shortage of skilled workers. Nowadays, many enterprises are badly in need of skilled, experienced, high-qualified and practical technicians with middle or high level certificates, especially specialized high-ranking technicians. The research group studied a company that produces measuring and cutting tool, which explored a new way to deal with the shortage of skilled workers. This company recruits a batch of apprentices from unemployed junior and senior high school graduates and cultivates them to be skilled workers through on-the-job training. Each apprentice can earn about RMB 600 per month as the basic salary. Assigned qualified technicians are responsible for instructing the apprentices in the technical key points and the corresponding workload of the technicians are credited to the apprentices. The enthusiasm of the qualified technicians is stimulated and the newly recruited employees are trained this way. Additionally, the demand for skilled workers is met and the recruitment difficulty of skilled technicians is effectively resolved.

Thirdly, take long-term measures to improve the benefits and treatment of employees. Essentially, the root cause of migrant workers' shortage lies in the relatively low benefits. The workers are in lack of the necessary sense of security. An electronics corporation explored some effective and long-term solutions by seizing the essence of the problem and focusing on the improvement of employees' benefits. Facing the serious situation of an increasing number of orders and difficulties in recruitment, the corporation raises the salary standard of workers by 5% to 10% compared with other companies, strictly implements the normal "5-day plus 8-hour" working time and proactively raises the subsidies for overtime work. What's more, the corporation also tries to provide better livelihood welfare regarding workers' lives including their career, treatment and emotions, which helps the corporation not only persuade veteran staff not to leave, but also attract more potential job hunters. At a recent job fair, this company successfully fulfilled the task of recruiting 500 people and stably coped with the problem of "migrant workers' shortage".

Excerpted from: Yin Yunsong and Li Jinong. On the situation and strategies of "migrant workers shortage"—based on a survey conducted in strong agriculture provinces, *China Development Observation*, 2010(10).

Questions:

1. It is well known that China is a country with a large population. Why does the phenomenon of "migrant workers shortage" still happen? What are the underlying reasons?

2. What should the government do to tackle with the "migrant workers shortage", besides the strategies adopted by enterprises.

Case 4. 3   The "Legacy" of the First Photochemical Haze Pollution in China: Prequel of Smog from Lanzhou to Beijing

Thirty-nine years ago, photochemical smog pollution took place the first time in Lanzhou, China, which opened the ceremony for studies on atmospheric pollution. The purpose for us to date back to that contaminative event is to forecast the trend of the recently large-scale atmospheric haze in most China's cities.

Just after the celebration of the Spring Festival, atmospheric haze revived in many metropolises. The results of research conducted by the Chinese Academy of Science aroused public attention about the disastrous smog. Recently, the special research group named "The Causes and Controls of Atmospheric Dust-haze" from Chinese Academy of Science published brand-new results. Wang Yuesi, a researcher at the Institute of Atmospheric Chemistry and Physics, was the director of that research group. He explained that the heavily smoggy pollutants that took place in central and eastern China were the mixture of the pollutants of photochemical smog pollution events that took place in London and Los Angeles in the 1940s and 1950s respectively and the dust aerosol with Chinese characteristics. After this explanation was reported, topics related to the atmospheric pollution were getting hotter and hotter. Some of the public simply regarded the recent haze in China as photochemical smog and fears were aroused. Several experts in the fields of atmospheric environment all hold the opinion that although the nitrogenous organic compound was monitored, it can not be concluded that it was photochemical smog pollution. There were tens of thousands of particle types of nitrogenous organic compounds, which should be further analyzed, to determine if they are harmful or not.

To put the disputes aside, Chinese people are very familiar with this kind of pollution. An expert introduced that photochemical smog pollution took place in several cities in China, such as Beijing, Shanghai, Nanjing, Guanghzou, Jinan and Lanzhou. Among them, the one took place in Xigu District of Lanzhou thirty-nine years ago started the research on atmospheric pollution in China.

The smog was so heavy that people could see nothing around them. The air pollution made people feel very uncomfortable. When the atmospheric pollution took place in 1974, it caused spontaneous teary eyes due to the effects of the pollutants. That event became the watershed of studies on atmospheric pollution in China. In the same summer, residents in Xigu District felt that their eyes were stimulated and full of tears. In addition, some plants were affected by the pollutants. "It was not like the sulfur dioxide pollution; instead, it looked the same as the photochemical smog pollution in Los Angeles to some degree. " Until now, professor Tang Xiaoyan, who is about 80 years old, can even remember the above words by his student Wu Renming at that time. Tang Xiaoyan, an academician from the Chinese Academy of Engineering and a professor of Environmental Science Faculty, Peking University, is the pioneer in the field of atmospheric environment and technology. The implication behind Wu's words was that the residents in Xigu District were suffering from the pollution. The XXL hand-made gauze masks people wore covered from the eyehole to the chin, with two black circles at the position of the nose. The city was enveloped by haze for days, or even the whole winter. An unknown strange smell was permeating through the air. Chen Guangting, a researcher at Cold and Arid Regions Environment and Engineering Research Institute, Chinese Academy of Science was a local resident in Lanzhou. In his opinion, the pollution in Lanzhou at that time was much more serious than that in current Beijing, as if the top of the tea-pot was covered by a hand, which made people feel breathless. It was Wu's doubt that drove the Chinese people who were not willing to accept the fact of air pollution to the subsequent 40-year prevention and control on pollution. Afterwards, Tang and researchers from the same group went to Lanzhou and conducted research together with the Environment Protection Institute of Gansu province.

This was obviously a tough battle. There were no studies or foreign literature on photochemical smog pollution in China during that time, so it was hard to identify the nature of the pollution. In fact, the theoretical basis of photochemical smog was first described in 1951 by Dr. Haagen Smit, California Institute of

Technology. He believed that photochemical smog was the chemical reaction of strong sunlight, nitrogen oxides and hydrocarbon of vehicle exhaust in the atmosphere, which belonged to the category of secondary pollution. Ozone and Peroxyacyl nitrates (PANs) were usually considered the distinct index of photochemical smog pollution.

A researcher at China Environmental Monitoring Station Wei Fusheng, an academician from the Chinese Academy of Engineering, told a journalist from *Southern Weekly* that he was impressed by the experience of the research on photochemical smog pollution. As a significant national research project, the research on photochemical smog pollution of Xigu District in Lanzhou lasted for several years and the scholars who participated in the scientific research were all the backbones from various institutes, with Peking University and the Environment Protection Institute of Gansu province as the first two practitioners. Under the guidance of Tang Xiaoyan, his team started to identify the nature of the pollutants. According to the recorded documents, the concentration of ozone per hour in the air exceeded the standard greatly, which was much higher than that of photochemical smog monitored in the severely polluted areas in Japan. The research lasted four years and in 1978 it first revealed that photochemical smog did exist in China and found out the causes of the smog were different from those in other countries.

At that time, Wang Shigong, the director of Atmospheric Science Faculty of Lanzhou University, was deeply impressed by the national driving forces on the research. More and more experts participated in the related studies on pollutions in Xigu District in the 1980s. From 1981 to 1983, a study of *Rules of Photochemical Smog Pollution and the Comprehensive Prevention and Control in Xigu Area* was jointly conducted by the following institutions: Chinese Academy of Environmental Sciences, Peking University, Environmental Protection Station and Monitoring Station of Gansu province, Lanzhou University, Lanzhou Petrochemical Company and Lanzhou Refinery, with more than 120 experts involved in this study. A large number of concrete suggestions on pollution prevention and control were given and the decision was made to move away the pollution sources: Lanzhou Iron and Steel Plant and Lanzhou Coking Factory. Coal was gradually replaced by natural gas as the major energy source for heat supply. Prudent planning was made on the site selection of a newly-built industrial zone in order to ease the air pollutant dispersion.

Now, many graduates who majored in environmental protection were very familiar with the long-lasting research. Actually, the studies on atmospheric pollution continually pushed forward the research objectives of differentiating from identification and investigation of simplex pollutant, acid rain in the 1980s as well as the confirmation of composite pollutants in China compared with Europe and America in the 1990s. From Tang Xiaoyan's point of view, the most significant thing was that the research during those years laid great foundation for the latter exploration. It was based on those research findings that we can study the acid rain in the 1980s as well as the mechanism and transformation of PM 2. 5.

Moreover, experts had already pointed out that the air pollution forecast should be adopted as an effective measure to prevent and control air pollution, especially while the pollution was taking place. They also suggested that air pollution forecast should be published through news media like the weather report, which has been realized today.

As the urbanization fast develops, photochemical smog pollution appears in Guangzhou, Beijing and Shanghai, following the step of Lanzhou. An anonymous expert of atmospheric pollution in the Pearl River Delta said that some scientific references recorded that there were some monitored data of photochemical smog in the summer of 1986 in Beijing. And other references showed that Shanghai had experienced photochemical smog pollution for the first time on June 2, 1995. People traveling at the Bund felt that their eyes and noses were stimulated by something in the air, which made them shed tears unconsciously. The statistics revealed that the concentration of carbon monoxide was extremely high.

The above mentioned experts concluded that the atmospheric pollution in China was a kind of complex and large-scale one with a group of cities involved. The polluted cities were mainly located in areas of the Pearl River Delta, Yangtze River Delta and Beijing-Tianjin-Hebei region. The cause of urban atmospheric pollution was changed from coal firing pollutants to vehicle exhaust emission or the mixture of the both, so that it became more difficult to prevent and control such kinds of pollution nowadays, compared with the pollution in the 1970s. What's worse, the studies on the influence of photochemical smog pollution on human beings health were scarce and sporadic. "Not a single city can deal with the pollution by itself, unless joint forces carried out", said the expert. Tang Xiaoyan also shared the same opinion. It seemed that the pollution in Zhuhai was not serious, but extremely high ozone concentration was detected there. The reason was that the pollutants could transfer from one place to another. In her opinion, emission reduction itself was not enough. What's more important, the energy structure and industrial structure should be adjusted. "Can the developed areas lower the GDP growth and develop at a moderate speed?" she questioned.

Statistics of the regional atmospheric monitoring of Guangdong province, Hong Kong and the Pearl River Delta illustrated that the overall air quality of the

Pearl River Delta regions was improved step by step, however, the concentration of ozone increased by 21% and became the only rising index of air pollutants, which was the root of the occurrence of photochemical smog pollution in the Pearl River Delta. The reality is cruel. "Based on our observation and the limited research findings, photochemical smog pollution in China has became a realistic problem, but not a potential threat," said Chai Fahe, deputy dean of Chinese Research Academy of Environmental Sciences, as the response to a journalist's question.

Excerpted from: Yuan Ruirui. The "legacy" of the first photochemical haze pollution in China: prequel of smog from Lanzhou to Beijing, *Southern Weekly*, February 21, 2013.

Questions:

1. Can the atmospheric haze affect the course of urbanization in China?

2. What kinds of measures should the Chinese government adopt to deal with the problem of air pollution?

Finance, which is the core of modern economy, is essential. If finance works well, all the other things go well. ——By Deng Xiao-ping, chief architect of China's opening and reform, when inspecting Shanghai in the spring of 1991 and highly praised Pudong new area for implementing "finance first" in its development.

Chapter 5

Evolution of Interest Rate and Exchange Rate and the Chinese Currency Policy

5. 1　China in the Beginning of Interest Rate Liberalization

If financial practice can be simply interpreted as a course of capital inflow and out, then interest rate stands for the price of capital borrowed or lent in investment and financing, namely the using price of the capital. From the macro financial point of view, since the policy of interest rate is directed by the state, the interest rate as an important variable in the economic system is a major means for the state government to generally regulate and control the system. To find out the basic information about China's interest rate policy, the website of The People's Bank of China with pages introducing Chinese interest rate policy can be consulted. According to this website, The People's Bank of China is the interest rate policy setting body in China. In response to the requirements in implementing Chinese currency policy, it makes timely use of interest rate as a tool, adjusts the level and construction of interest rate so as to influence supply and demand of social capital and eventually realize the stated objectives of the currency policy. Meanwhile, this website introduces the interest rate tools currently widely-used in China. They are mainly: First, regulating the base rates of the central bank, including: refinance rate, namely the interest rate applied when The People's

Bank of China provides re-lending to financial institutions; rediscount rate, namely the interest rate applied when the financial institutions conduct rediscount of the discounted notes to the People' Bank of China; deposit reserve rate, namely the interest rate the People's Bank of China pays to the financial institutions for the legally required reserves they deposit; the excess deposit reserve rate, namely the interest rate the People's Bank of China pays to the financial institutions for the part that exceeds the legally required reserve they deposit. Second, regulating the legal deposit and lending rates of the financial institutions. Third, setting range to the deposit and lending rate for the financial institutions. Forth, formulating corresponding policies to regulate the construction and grade of various interest rates. [1]

5. 1. 1   The Interest Rate Policy in China before the Reform and Opening

A. 1949 − 1952: Transitional Interest Rate Policy in Early Years of New China

On the first day of December 1948, the People's Bank of China was founded. When it was newly founded, the People's Bank of China played the function of interest rate policy setting. [2] Just coming out from the darkness, the primary task of the Chinese society at that time was to recover from the war injuries. But with different policies still in deficiency, many unscrupulous traders were in existence. They cornered the market which resulted in soaring prices, leaving the common people unbearably miserable. To curb the soaring prices, The People's Bank of China firstly conducted the policy of soliciting deposit with high interests, setting a very high level of interest rate. According to the interest table issued by The People's Bank of China in May 1949, the fixed-term deposit rate for 6 months was as high as 150% monthly; if the deposit time was longer than 6 months the deposit rate could be further negotiated, and the demand deposit rate was also as high as 30% . [3] This was obviously a special policy for a special time. But with the interest rate much higher than the price increases, the hoarding practice of illegal traders was cracked down, and at the same time the

---

1　http:// www. pbc. gov. cn/publish/zhengcehuobisi/623/index. html

2　The Central Bank of China at that time was only the nominal policy maker, to be more exact, it is more like an actuator. In case of important issues, The Central Bank of China reports to the State Council which make the decisions and the central bank conveys and carries out the decisions.

3　From July 6, 2012 to now, the yearly demand deposit rate was 0. 35% , the yearly deposit rate was 3% .

idle money in large amounts was deposited in the bank, strengthening it by providing it with more currency sources.

Because of soaring prices and goods and materials in scarcity, people had to buy necessities in this way.

Of course, such high interest rates could only exist in special historical periods. It is true that the high deposit rate in 1949 had a good governance effect on the national economic order, but inversely, according to the law of economy, in time of high deposit rates, loan interest rates naturally goes high. Based on the records, the loan interest rate at that time was very high, which mainly refers to the loan interest rate to private businesses. Of course, other loan interest rates were also very high. This obviously restrained the operation and development of industry and commerce. Therefore, at the beginning of 1950, with prices steady and going down and the national economy gradually back on track, The People's Bank of China made timely regulation on interest rates based on the price level and industry profit level of that time. In May 1950, it stipulated that the fixed-term deposit rate for 1 month was 15%, and the loan interest rate was accordingly lowered to no higher than 30%. Thereafter, according to the actual situation, interest level was twice further regulated, respectively in February 1951 and July 1952. Till July 1952, the fixed-term deposit rate for 1 month was lowered to 7.5%, and that for 1 year was only 12%. The interest rate was on the way to normal.

B. 1953−1957: Upside Down Interest Rate
Upside down interest rate is also termed negative interest rate. It refers to the

phenomenon of the actual yield of deposit being "negative". For inflation rate higher than deposit rate, the value of money deposited in the bank not only decreased but also depreciation by inflation of prices. "Negative interest rate" can also be called upside down interest rate, which means the personal actual profit rate being a negative number.

Since the 1950s, influenced by the Soviet Union and the socialist countries of Europe, the Chinese government tried to change the inefficient status of the centralized economy system and made some adjustment on the economic system. Accordingly, the interest rate policy was adjusted in two aspects.

In the first place, the interest rate was greatly lowered. Leadership of that time believed that to carry out large scale economic construction, it was necessary to lower the interest rate continuously. Under such guiding ideology, the government instructed The people's bank of China to lower the interest rate substantially. For state-owned businesses, the industrial loan monthly interest rate was lowered from 69.9% to 4.5% within ration and 4.8% over ration, and commercial loan monthly interest rate from 10% to 6.9%. For businesses of other ownerships, the loan interest rate was also lowered correspondingly. Contrary to this, the deposit interest rate was generally not regulated, except that the deposit interest rate for state-owned businesses was a little bit lowered. The government hoped to draw up the idle money in society by means of high deposit rates and meanwhile support the economic construction and development by means of low loan rates. However, although it is true that negative interest rates may promote investment, the imbalance between deposit and lending rates can destroy the normal order of the financial market. People may borrow money from the bank and then deposit it into the bank to gain the price difference; secondly, the condition of negative interest rate results in the wasteful use of capital. When deposit and lending interest rates are greatly different, the borrowed money may not be made full use of and even the idle money won't be returned to the bank, causing credit capital to fall short; thirdly, it does no good for the economic calculation of the bank and other financial institutions. When in negative interest rate, the more money the bank draws in and lends out, the greater loss it suffers. This may prevent it from developing and its business from operating.

In 1955, the yearly interest rate for government bonds was 4% and that for loans was 10.8% and 12%, while the yearly deposit interest rate was as high as 14.4%, which was obviously unreasonable. Therefore, realizing such a situation, to deal with the inversion phenomenon, since September 17, 1955, the government began to sharply lower the deposit interest rate. After the adjustment, the yearly interest rate for deposit longer than a year was 7.92%, and the interest rate for other terms was also lowered accordingly, by a large margin.

C. 1958−1978: Leftist Interest Rate Policy

1958 to 1978 in China was the period for national economic adjustment. Meanwhile, it was a special period—called the culture revolution. This period was seriously influenced by leftism. [1] The law of value was ignored in economic operation, and interest rate policy was gravely interfered with. As all issues in China politicized, so was the interest rate policy. This is shown in the following two aspects:

First, interest rates were partially lowered by large margins. In the Great Leap Forward Movement [2] period, with the industrial and agricultural increase objectives unreasonable, regulators blindly believed that the high interest rate affected people's passion for fund-raising. Therefore, beginning November 1958, the government decided to lower the deposit rate, with the monthly savings account interest rate lowered from 2.4% to 1.8%; and the interest rate for 1 year from 6% to 4%. Up until 1965, politics had even greater influence on the economy; everything was under political purpose and the law of economy was ignored. Under such conditions, deposits needed to be mobilized. Thus, on April 21, the deposit rate was lowered again. Deposit interest rates were imposed uniformity in all cases, with the interest rate for 1 year lowered to 3.3%, and deposit rate classification for 3 months, 2 years and 3years was canceled. Meanwhile, the so-called "cash custody" was provided, which was in effect interest-free deposit. This trend went further and further during the "cultural revolution", which resulted in the total neglect of interest rate policy leading to denial of interest for a time. Interest was seen as exploitation, and some deposits were even frozen while others were inspected. "Lower and lower interest rate, smaller and smaller interest difference and fewer and fewer levels of interest rate" was absurdly taken as the advantages of socialism and the interest rate policy entirely strayed away from economic law. In August 1971, interest rates was

---

1   From a philosophical point of view, if the routes and policies are in accord with practice, they are correct; if they overpass the objective facts and conduct immature doings, they are called left adventurism.

2   The "Great Leap Forward Movement" was from 1958 to 1960. The target of economic development at that time was impractical, aiming to raise the industrial and agricultural productivity by many times. For example, steel production double from 1958 to 1959, namely from 33.5 million tons to 107 million tons; and double again from 1958 to 1959, namely from 107 million tons to 300 million tons. Grain production increase by 80% from 1957 to 1958, namely from 3900 billion Jin to 7000 billion Jin, and increase again by 50% from 1958 to 1959, from 7000 billion Jin to 10,500 billion Jin.

again greatly lowered. The monthly interest rate for 1 year was lowered from 3. 3% to 2. 7%, pushing the originally low interest rate sharply downward by 20%. In some places, free-interest deposit still continued. In addition, there was no interest for deposits from the Party, the Youth League and trade unions, as well as deposits from the management departments. Loan interest was also free.

Second, classification of interest rate was oversimplified. Under the guidance of interest rate denial, canceling of interest rate levels continued throughout the time of interest regulation, leaving finally only three levels of 6 months, 1 year and due on demand. Rates were blindly generalized at 6% for settlement of the loans, agricultural loans, industry and commence, and credit loans to individuals.

To conclude, the interest rate policy in China of this period totally strayed away from the law of economic development and was completely directed by politics and the ideology of leaders. The upside down interest rates due to human error, the lowering interests rates by large margins, the simplification of interest rate levels, as well as free-interest deposits are all big stains in the history of Chinese interest rate policy.

5. 1. 2 Interest Rate Policy under Planned Commodity Economy

The ten-year cultural revolution brought serious damage to the national economy, close to the brink of collapse. With billions of people being persecuted, after this disastrous period, most Chinese people felt disappointed with the system of "all-round dictatorship". As the well-known Chinese leader Deng Xiao-ping said, "There is no way out if we do not reform and open the door. The closed state in the past 20 years has to be changed. All of us unanimously agree to carry out the reform and opening policy, for which we should give credit to the ten-year "great cultural revolution. "

A. 1978–1985: Interest Rate Policy in the Years of Bringing Order out of Chaos

After many times of futile reformation and turmoil under the planned system, recalling the painful experience, the Chinese government felt it necessary to make new changes. On December 18 to 22, 1978, an important meeting was held in Beijing which was seen as a milestone in Chinese economic development. It was the Third Plenary Session of the 11th Central Committee of the Chinese Communist Party; thereafter the leftism in all walks of life was rectified. The same thing happened to the interest rate policy, in which the Chinese government rediscovered the important function of interest rate as an economic lever, and managed to put the interest rate policy back on the right track. From 1979 to 1985, the People' Bank of China raised the deposit interest rate five times respectively in April 1979, April 1980, April 1982, and April and August of 1985. With the national economy in serious imbalance after the Great Leap Forward, a large amount of money was in need to readjust it. Therefore, raising the interest rate to a reasonable level at that time gave full play to its function as an economic lever, and massive funds was drawn to the bank in this way. By 1985, the national economy was in positive trend, a wage level system reform began to be carried out. Rising income led to rising prices, then rising price index. Since the inflation rate was much higher relative to deposit rate, raising deposit rates protected the depositors' interest. Till August 1985, the interest rate was nearly restored to the reasonable level of 1955. [1] Meanwhile, interest rate levels were completed, with 3-year, 5-year and 8-year term levels being added to meet depositors' various needs.

In addition, the right of interest rate management at that time finally fell into the hand of The People's Bank of China. Before that, the management right had belonged to the central bank on the surface, but in case of important modulations, it had to report to the State Council for approval. Under such planning system, the central bank was but the executor of interest rate policy. In January 1982, the State Council awarded The People's Bank of China 20% interest rate floating right, which provided the central bank with management right in the true sense and made it possible to set reasonable rate levels in accord to time and place in a flexible way.

B. 1986−1989: Unsteady Interest Rate Policies

In this time span, for the real economy, some coastal regions with ideal conditions to open the door to the outside were taken as Test Areas(such as Guangzhou, Foshan, Jiangmen, and Zhanjiang in Guangdong province). The government basically gave up the pricing methods created for the planned economy, played price liberation on prices of small commodities, and enlarged the range of market regulation prices of general consumer goods. However, in this period, the over-heated economy resulted in double inflation in investment and consumption, and excessive issue of currency led to credit expansion, and the age-long accumulated contradiction between larger general social demand and less supply became even more intensified. Therefore, the hidden inflation broke out

---

1   The monthly deposit rate of demand deposit rose from 1.8% in 1971 to 2.4%; the interest rate for a one-year term deposit rose from 2.7% in 1971 to 6.0%.

because of the pulling of demand. This was the first inflation period in the true
sense since the foundation of new China. Take Zhejiang province as an example,
the increase in consumer price exceeded 6% every year, with average yearly
increase as high as 13.8%. The interest rate regulation in this period showed an
obvious feature, namely to regularly fluctuate with the periodic fluctuation of the
national economy, in which the interest levels were once up and once down, at
small amplitudes.

The first rising wave, as stated before, occurred beginning in 1985. Due to
wage system reform, prices rose excessively fast, the central bank increased the
interest rate twice that year. In the years following, to cope with the inflation
caused by the over-heated economy, approved by the State Council, on
September 1, 1988, The People's Bank of China increased the deposit and loan
interest rate all roundly. [1] However, with the phenomenon of the over-heated
economy still existing, inflation became even more serious from the end of 1988 to
the beginning of 1989, causing a buying spree and a run on banks in big and
medium-sized cities all over China, The increment of savings deposits dropped
significantly. To restrain such situation, the government had to conduct improvement
and rectification. On February 1, 1989, the deposit and loan interest rate was
increased again, [2] pushing the interest level to the top of that wave of regulation.

The effect of the first wave of regulation did not show until the second half
of 1989 when the over-heated economy was curbed. But due to the rapid
shrinkage, the national economy market became weaker and the increasing speed
of industry dropped sharply, negative sides of sharp shrinkage occurred.

To conclude, the planned commodity economy of this period put the
"commodity" property of currency into play, and interest rate was seen as the
economic lever of effective resource allocation. However, it should be noted that
in the double regulation system of interest rates in China, too much government
guidance still existed. For instance, professional banks had to give "preferential
interest" rates to those enterprises supported by government, no matter whether
beneficial or not. Another example, the professional banks did not have the right
to decide on deposit and loan interest rates. The interest rate policy of this period
presented the fact that the "professional bank" of China was not "of independent
management, responsible for its own benefit or loss" yet. In actual practice of
interest rate, there was still right "erosion" on the part of the central bank to the
professional bank. With the development and prosperity of the social economy,

---

[1]   For example, the interest rate of 1-year term rose from 6% to 7.2%.

[2]   For example, the deposit interest rate for 1 year rose to 9.45%.

interest rate liberalization was almost certain.

5. 1. 3   The "Thrilling Leap" and Ice-breaking Trip of Interest Rate Liberalization

Worrying about the malignant rate war or bank bankruptcy risk caused by interest rate liberalization, the Chinese government never carried out the last push for interest rate liberalization. But on June 8 and July 6 of the year 2012, the deposit and lending base rate for RMB and its floating interval of Chinese financial institutions were adjusted twice, and it was also said that The People's Bank of China would announce implementation of short-term liquidity operations(SLO). [1] Analysts believe this showed that the Chinese central government meant to develop a new short-term market benchmark interest rate, which was a significant step toward all-round interest rate liberalization. This also signified that after the planned economy interest rate guidance policy , to meet the needs of Chinese economic and financial development and the opening of financial markets after entering WTO, the Chinese central bank forwarded the "procedure of foreign currency first, and domestic currency after; loan first, deposit after; large amount of long-term first and petty short-term after for deposits, gradually setting up the interest forming system of deposit and lending interest rate decided by supply and demand of the market. The central bank adjusts and guides the market rate, leaving market mechanism playing the chief function in allocation of financial resources. "

Table 5. 1   The process of interest rate liberalization in China

Time of reform	Events of reform
June 1, 1996	Start the inter-bank rate among banks
June 1997	Start bond repurchase rate among banks
August 1998	First time for China Development Bank to issue liberalization bonds in bond market among banks
The year 1998	The People's Bank of China reforms the generative mechanism of discount rate
October 1998	National debt issuance by means of market bidding, therefore the realization of liberalization in market interest rate among banks and the issuance interest rate of national debt and policy-guided financial bond

---

1   Public market short-term liquidity operations focuses on less than 7-day short-term repurchase (Reverse REPO), after sort-term product of 7-day and the like, super short-term product of overnight and the like will be constructed.

Cont.

Time of reform	Events of reform
October 1999	The People's Bank of China approved of the representative of Chinese-funded commercial bank to provide pilot project of large deposit on fixed term to representative of Chinese-funded insurance company with interest rate negotiated by the two sides(minimum deposit amount being 30 million yuan, and term span longer than 5 years, excluding 5 years)
November 2003	Rural credit cooperative under commercial banks can open agreement deposit of postal savings(minimum deposit amount being 30 million yuan, and term span over 3 years, excluding 3 years)
July 2003	Loosen the management of interest rate on retail deposit of foreign currencies such as English pound, Swiss Franc and Canadian dollar, leaving it to the autonomy of the commercial bank
November 2003	Carry out upper limit management on retail deposit rate of US dollar, Japanese yen, Hong Kong dollar and Euro, the commercial bank can define it based on the levels of interest rate in the international financial market so long as not exceeding the upper limit
January 1, 2004	The People's Bank of China enlarge the floating range of deposit interest rate again
August 2006	Enlarge the floating expansion of interest rate on commercial individual housing loan
June 2012	Further enlarge the floating range of interest rate, with the upper limit to deposit interest rate reaching 1. 1 times of the base rate, and the lower limit of loan interest rate reaching 0. 8 times of the base rate

Source of document: the website of the People's Bank and policy news.

Website: http://www. pbc. dov. cn/publish/ zhengcehuobisi/624/index. html

A. Voice—the Interest Rate Liberalization Have to be Carried Out

a. Connotation of Interest Rate Liberalization

The system of interest rate liberalization consists of three parts: the first being the policy interest rate of the central bank, which is also the operation target of currency policy. The central bank policy rate is virtually the price of supplying and taking back base money by the central bank and adjusting base money among banks. Since the central bank's power of supply of the base money is literally limitless, and it is the monopoly supplier, therefore, it can adjust and control the price of base money by means of open market operation, like the federal fund rate of the USA.

The second being the market interest rate, the middle target of currency policy, including currency market, bond market and deposit and loan rate, with various terms, risks and counterparties. The market rate is formed through supply and demand of funds, in which the central bank cannot impose direct adjustment or control but indirect influence.

The third being the rate transmission channel. The policy interest rate of the central bank should play an extremely important part in the whole interest rate system. Rate transmission should be unimpeded, financial institutions carry out market operation, risk-based pricing and arbitrage mechanism be in function. Rate transmission involves complicated theoretic problems, such as Alan Greenspan's (former US Federal Reserve Chairman) "long-term interest rate puzzle" (the relevancy degree between the federal rate and the long-term rate drops), for which Ben Bernanke (former US Federal Reserve Chairman) put forward the "Operation Twist".

b. Voice of Support from all Directions

The liberalization of interest rates is supported by experts and learners from different fields. Some learners believe that the People's Bank adjusts the interest rate so as to cope with the financial crisis of the world and the Euro debt crisis and to minimize the impact of the crises on the Chinese economy. To define an upper limit to the floating span of the deposit rate and a lower limit to that of the loan rate, the major purpose is to grant the financial institutions greater power to set prices by themselves. The purpose of such doing is to lead the interest rate system of our country to develop in the direction of liberalization, and meanwhile, enable our financial institutions to adapt to interest rate liberalization of the future. It is a kind of slight exploration. [1]

At the same time, many experts hold that China is more qualified to carry out interest rate liberalization than in the 90s. The bank system has met the requirements, and the banks have established better risk-control mechanisms and improved the ability to set prices. The whole thing is speeding up now, but some basic things need yet to be done. The somewhat microscopic deposit insurance system is one of the obstacles. After loosening the steps toward interest rate liberalization, the deposit rate especially formed two levels, for the big banks as a team, they almost maintained the original level after the downward regulation; and for the medium and small banks and the like, they increased to the top once and forever, no matter for deposits shorter or longer than 1 year. As for individual risks, it is not necessary to worry. From the 90s of last century till now, only one bank was liquidated in the economic market, Hainan Development Bank. Some of the liquidation was carried out until recent years, in which the depositors' interests were basically protected. If a deposit insurance system was not established,

---

[1] From a speech by Zhang Jian-hua, the director of the Research Bureau of the People's Bank of China, at the Lujiazui Forum in Shanghai on June 28-30, 2012.

it would be unlikely for the financial institutions to distinguish its own risk profile and the market state. The interest rate liberalization in countries like the U. S. aims to protecting the deposit.

"With the rapid development of the financial products and the expansion of direct capital-raising, the realistic demand of interest rate liberalization stands out. The actual launching of interest rate liberalization is approaching. Within these two years, the breakthrough or progress of interest rate liberalization will beyond our imagination. " [1]

"The deputy director of the financial committee of National People's Congress Wu Xiao-ling believes that the year 2013 is more eligible for promoting the interest rate liberalization. For one thing, the extent of floating downward can be further widened, and for another, the prevailing way in market can be introduced, namely to replace the way in which the bank issues the base deposit rate with that of forming deposit rate by adding a number of base points. In the world interest rate liberalization, the prime rate of each commercial bank is formed by adding points on the basis of London interbank offered rate. We may go for interest rate liberalization and eligible to form our deposit prime rate by adding points on this standard. The central bank focuses on cultivating interbank offered rate. When money is in need now, why does the central bank carry out repurchase in open market—both sell repurchase and reverse repurchase, instead of lowering the reserve interest rate? In my eyes, the central bank definitely intends to cultivate the policy target rate and the inter-bank offered rate of our country. As for the deposit, I think we need to have some control over it for a period of time. The floating range can be enlarged, but not too much. The reason for this I won't say. As a matter of fact, if we control the upper limit of deposit rate, firstly the financial institutions can be restrained from over-competition, since the small institutions are likely to do so; and secondly, the fixation of the rising range of deposit rate can actually lead more direct financing tools to facilitate the development of direct financing. " [2]

The financial restructuring and joint-stock system reform of the commercial banks are reaping staged achievements. This is greatly removing problems of soft control and introducing price setting on products and services in market competition, which laid essential foundation for further interest rate liberalization. "It is pointed out in the national financial work conference that presently the

---

[1]   By the Deputy director of Financial Research Institute in Development Research Centre of the State Council Ba Shu-Song at the Spring Forum of Overseas Bank (China), May 2012.

[2]   Wu Xiao-ling at Sanya Finance International Forum, December 15, 2012, Sanya, China.

conditions for establishing deposit insurance system are provided, the scheme for its completion needs to be studied in time. " The completed reform of commercial banks concentrated on solving problems of capital adequacy level and quality. Capital quality is a general index of healthy condition, so in the future we need to pay much attention to the qualities of financial products and financial services, which eventually depend on the comments of the clients. On the other hand, in the premise of controllable risks, we will open our financial market to a greater extent and at a higher level, and improve the exchange rate formation mechanism of RMB, and enforce the two-way floating elasticity of RMB exchange rate [1].

B. The Status quo—Preparations and Voice of Worry

At present, the currency market, the bond market and the deposit and loan interest rate for foreign currency are all basically open. Control over interest rate is mainly reflected in what was established in 2006 which stipulated that for deposit interest rate of RMB, "the lower limit is open and the upper limit controlled", and for loan interest rate, "the upper limit open and the lower limit controlled".

In view of the Asian financial crisis, the following points can be reviewed on the interest rate liberalization of China.

Firstly, the deposit and loan rate of foreign currencies. The deposit and loan rate of foreign currencies in China were opened by several steps, which mainly took place before 2004.

Secondly, to expand the loan pricing power and deposit pricing power of the banks. Before 2003, the floating range of the banks' pricing power was limited within 30%, and in 2004 the rising range of loan interest rate was expanded to 1.7 times of the base rate. In October 2004, the upper limit of deposit rising range was removed, and the lowering range was to 0.9 times of the base rate, not totally open yet. Meanwhile, the deposit interest rates of the banks could all float downward, with no limits set.

Thirdly, market pricing was carried out in all activities of enterprise bonds, financial bonds, commercial bills, and market transactions of currencies, no limits were set on prices. With the development of various bills and corporate bonds and the expansion of transactions in OTC (over-the-counter) and secondary markets in specialty, prices were increasingly market-driven. Many enterprises,

---

1 From an essay published in the journal China Finance written by the President of People's Bank of China and "Mr. RMB"—Zhou Xiao-chuan.

especially those of high quality, could choose to issue bills and bonds for capital-raising, with the prices free from the limit of the benchmark interest rate for loan.

Fourthly, to enlarge the floating range of commercial personal housing loan rate. In August 2006, the floating range reached 0.8 times of the base rate; and after the May 2008 great earthquake of Wenchuan, to support the post-disaster reconstruction, The People's Bank of China furthered the autonomous pricing power of the financial institutions of home mortgage, lowering the rate of commercial personal housing loan to 0.7 times of the base rate. However, it could be seen that the financial enterprises were not so willing to set prices for home mortgage on their own.

5.1.4   Icebreaking—Interest Rate liberalization Entering Abyssal Area

After years of standstill, interest rate liberalization resumed with force. On June 7, 2012, the central bank declared to adjust the floating range of deposit and loan rate, namely to increase the upper limit of deposit rate to 1.1 times of the base rate, and to decrease the lower limit of loan rate to 0.8 times of the base rate.

As Mr. Li Dao-kui—the former member of Monetary Policy Committee see it, enlarging the rate floating span, especially allowing 10% up floating of the deposit rate, is a big step toward interest rate liberalization and it bears great significance by restarting the reform.

More surprisingly, a month later, the central bank made further progress in interest rate liberalization. On July 8, it declared to further lower the floating range of loan rate to 0.7 times of the base rate.

Adjustment statement of RMB benchmark interest rate for loans

"The central bank means business this time", in the eyes of a senior executive of a joint-stock bank, the commercial banks seldom lower the loan rate to 0.7 times, therefore, the interest rate liberalization in China is near to being accomplished.

As for the deposit rate, it has always been seen as the last protection of the banking industry, and it's also the essential symbol of interest rate liberalization. This time the central bank uncommonly increased the upper limit of the deposit rate to 1.1 times, leaving commercial banks feeling chilly, but brought hope of interest rate liberalization to the financial industry as a while.

After the two rate adjustments of June and July of 2012, some people say "The wolf is coming" or "The good days of the bank is over".

**The banks live leisurely in
time of fixed interest rate.**

A. Half Honey

Interest rate liberalization raises efficiency of the capital market, and the banks can benefit a lot from it.

Firstly, from the perspective of assets and liabilities, interest rate liberalization provides the banks with a freer management environment than when the interest rate were controlled, leaving the commercial banks operating more autonomously. For instance, as for the liabilities, with the pricing power in hand, the banks may choose to be in debt initiatively and optimize the liability structure so as to minimize the operating cost. As for the assets, according to the requirements of their own business, the banks can set different interest rates for different assets and match the price with the risks, following the differentiation pricing strategy.

Secondly, interest rate liberalization helps the commercial banks to carry out financial innovation. Facing the new challenge of interest rate liberalization, considering from the perspective of clients—both enterprises and individuals, the banks need to know how to effectively control the interest risks caused by interest rate liberalization. This need to hedge risks makes it necessary for the banks to research and develop a lot of innovation derivatives. According to other countries' experiences, the course of interest rate liberalization is also the course of financial innovation for the banks. With the direction of interest rate liberalization clearer and clearer, the banks gradually launch new products including structural deposits, interest rate swap, and fixed interest rate loans, etc. to meet new requirements of the clients. Financial innovation naturally leads to changes in income structure. Therefore we can see the increase of non-interest-rate spread in the course of interest rate liberalization. For example, before the deregulation of 1997, from the start of interest rate liberalization in the 80s to the 90s, the proportion of this part reached 32. 2% . In recent years the intermediate businesses of Chinese banks develop quickly, which is also closely relevant to the acceleration of the course of interest rate liberalization.

B. Half Distressed

Then, why do they say that the good days of the banks are over?

In the meanwhile of bringing opportunities to banks, interest rate liberalization changes the accustomed traditional business model of the banks, hence exerts deep influence and impact on the management and risk control of the commercial banks. For the Chinese commercial banks that had long operated under controlled interest rate, the influence and impact can be even fierce. For quite a long time, the interest margin of Chinese banks has been bigger than that of the mature markets. The present deposit and loan rate money in China is as high as over 300 basis points, while it is usually over 25 basis points in the mature markets. As a matter of fact, in the six interest rate rises since 2012, the central bank mostly enlarged the interest margin. The naturally formed interest margin under interest rate control enables the banks to live on the traditional deposit and loan business. So long as the credit scale expands, the interests of banks are liable to increase. Such profit is equal to monopoly profit. However, under interest rate liberalization, the interest rate space of deposit and loan will be minimized, so it will become difficult to depend too much on interest margin. Therefore, the commercial banks have to do essential regulations on their policies.

Interest rate liberalization grants the banks the pricing power, so whether able to exert the power properly forms a challenge to the Chinese banking industry. Against the background of long-time interest rate control, Chinese banks are short on experience with no accumulated data at hand. As is reflected in the markets, after the upper limit of loan rate was removed, most of the commercial banks would rather lower the rate to grab big clients and large projects, leaving the medium and small enterprises inadequately served. A major reason for this phenomenon is that the banks' pricing power has not caught up with the changes of the situation, for which they could not timely and accurately set prices for clients and programs. The ability of pricing is an essential component of core competence, in which the foreign trades are much more advantaged.

Interest rate liberalization may also extend the credit risks, including problems like the adverse selection of high-risk clients expelling low-risk clients, default risks because of enterprises failing to bear the changes in interest rate, and the moral risks on the part of the banks for their blindly pursuing a risky portfolio.

Bank crisis may also reflect the systemic risks caused by interest rate liberalization. Therefore, the commercial banks need to enhance their functions of autonomous pricing and control of interest rate risks, and meanwhile make due efforts on financial innovation which is the only way of coping with interest rate liberalization.

5. 2   Exchange Rate Liberalization of RMB

According to the definition given by Wikipedia, in economics, exchange rate refers to the conversion ratio between currencies of two countries. To put it in a common way, exchange rate is the ratio when one changes the monetary unit of one country into that of another country.

The characteristic of exchange rate lies in that it is the rate of floating. So long as the currencies can be traded by the exchange rate, the exchange rate of the alternate day will be influenced. Therefore, some people make profits by gaining the exchange rate differential—buy in a certain foreign currency at a lower rate today, and sell it on the alternate day when a higher rate occurs.

Under economic globalization, being an important link of international economy, politics and social relations, exchange rate plays an essential function and is reflected in every aspect of the national economy. With the deepening of the opening policy, and the strength of the Chinese economy getting increasingly enhanced, the exchange rate of RMB attracts more and more attention of domestic and foreign learners and industrial and commercial enterprises. Is RMB underestimated? Is Chinese trade surplus related to exchange rate? How should we look at the huge foreign exchange reserve? These are all the problems we discuss in this section. Of course, to answer these questions, we may start with the historical review which may help us systemically understand the history of foreign exchange in China and the formation of foreign exchange policy.

5. 2. 1   A Historical Review of the Exchange Rate Policy of RMB

A. 1979−1993: The Period of Multiple Rate System

At the initial stage of the opening policy, the value of RMB was greatly over-estimated. This gravely impacted Chinese foreign trade of that time, since the over-estimated exchange rate of RMB could not reflect the supply-demand relationship in the market. Therefore, the trading companies suffered heavy loss, causing China's foreign exchange to be in severe shortage. To respond to such shortage, the government urgently needed to increase the foreign exchange income which required the RMB to be devalued. But on the other hand, to increase non-trade foreign exchange income and protect the interest of imports, the value of RMB needed to be increased. Facing this dilemma, as a member of the IMF, the Chinese government followed the IMF regulation of multiple foreign exchange rates which allows the member countries to carry out more than one exchange rate for a short period and transit to single exchange rate after adjustment. The dual exchange rate system in China began on January 1, 1981, in which the export exchange rate of enterprises was divided into two parts: the first part was required to be handed over to the state at a lower official exchange rate while the rest could be sold at regulated market exchange rates or be used to import profitable goods depending on the supply-demand signal in the market.

B. 1994−1997: The Period of Unification of Exchange Rate and Soft Pegging on US Dollar

At the beginning of 1994, the official exchange rate of RMB and the foreign exchange swap prices were unified, and a system of single, supervised floating exchange rate based on supply and demand in the market was implemented. This change was seen as a strategic reform of Chinese exchange rate policy. Then, what was the motivation for the timing of this reform? It should be said that the big background is that enterprises deposited much foreign exchange while the state was short of foreign exchange reserve. This is exactly the shortcoming of a dual exchange rate system. Under the dual rate system, there was a big difference between the price in the foreign exchange swap market and the official price, with the official exchange rate of USD and RMB being 1: 5. 7 while that in the foreign exchange swap market being 1: 10 or even higher. In such conditions, the foreign trade companies naturally chose to sell the foreign exchange in the market instead of selling it to the commercial banks. In order to break through the foreign exchange control and grab the opportunity in the market, some enterprises would rather buy foreign exchange at the foreign exchange swap market. Thus, what occurred was that private entities possessed much foreign exchange while the state controlled small foreign exchange reserve, in which the foreign exchange swap market got bigger and bigger while the official market shrank smaller and smaller. At that time, the foreign exchange transactions in the swap market took up 80% −85% of the whole, while that in the official market only 15% − 20%, and the foreign exchange black market was rather active, leaving the official market playing a seemingly supporting role.

Against such situation, to increase its foreign exchange reserve and narrow the difference between the swap market and the official market, the government implemented exchange rate unification and the system of forced settlement and sales, resulting in the concentration of foreign exchange from the enterprises to the commercial banks to the central bank, leading the foreign exchange reserve of the central bank increasing constantly. Consequently, the official exchange rate was uniformed with that of the swap market to 1:8.7. Thereafter, the over-the-counter market, which was less controlled by government, dealings set freely by sellers and buyers with big amplitude disappeared gradually, leaving the floor trading market—China Foreign Exchange Center to trade, extend credit, and liquidate. Under this mechanism, the central bank takes charge to clear the market when supply and demand are out of balance. In case of devaluation of RMB, even if the central bank offers an over-low price to buy foreign exchange, enterprises and commercial banks are forced to sell the foreign exchange to it. In this way the central bank buys the vast majority of the foreign exchange in market by the forced settlement and sales rate. In case of appreciation of the RMB, in order to keep the exchange rate steady, the central bank may offer a comparatively higher price to buy foreign exchange. As well, it cannot prevent enterprises, residents and the commercial banks from selling all the foreign exchange to it, not even private entities. Thus, the central bank buys the vast majority of the foreign exchange in the market at a rather high price.

This exchange rate system shows advantages as well as disadvantages: the first is that it can conceal the pressure of devaluation, but not appreciation; the second is that it concentrates the foreign exchange in the hands of the state, but removes the possibility of keeping foreign exchange among common people when the value of RMB increases; the third is that the total control of exchange rate by the central bank can avoid sharp price fluctuation in the foreign exchange swap market, but leaves the market impact on exchange rate rather insignificant.

C. 1998−2005: The Period of Rigid Pegging to US Dollar

In face of the above situation, from 1998 to 2005, China began to restore open market operations and enhanced market intervention, resulting in the gradual growth of the base monetary system, the progressive optimization of export construction, and the steady increase of foreign exchange reserve. China officially joined WTO on November 17, 2001. From then on, China entered the all-round opening period with its economy developing rather quickly. Foreign investment poured in at the rate of USD 600 billion every year, which on the one hand enlarged the foreign exchange reserve, and on the other hand posed challenge to the central bank concerning liquidity. Therefore, depending on the weighted average price of exchange rate in the previous-business-day inter-bank foreign exchange market, the People's Bank of China made timely announcements of the basic exchange rate of USD, Japanese Yen, Hong-Kong Dollar and Euro with RMB of that day. The interbank foreign exchange rate and the nominal rate were allowed to fluctuate within certain ranges. Pegging to basket currencies around the USD and focusing on an exchange rate target zone, taking the present exchange rate as the central exchange rate, stipulating a comparatively narrow fluctuating area, the central bank kept the exchange rate of RMB in a steady state. It could be said that from 1998 to July 21, 2005, before the exchange rate reform of RMB, it was basically sensible to keep the exchange rate between the USD and RMB unchanged. In that period, the fluctuation margin of exchange rate between the two currencies was less than 1%.

D. 2005-Present: The Period of Referring to a Basket of Currencies

Reviewing what has happened since the exchange rate reform from 1994, the objective of the reform was basically realized, namely to keep the exchange rate of RMB steady through adjustment by stipulating certain fluctuating ranges of the exchange rate. However, with the development of the Chinese economy, the absence of an actual foreign exchange market resulted in the fact that the volume of foreign exchange transactions did not match the scale of foreign trade and capital. [1] Therefore, on July 21, 2005, a new round of reform was launched, aiming at a system of foreign exchange rate based on supply and demand in the market, adjusted in reference to basket of currencies and under

---

[1]   In 2005, the average daily transactions of the China Foreign Exchange Centre was estimated to be USD 3 to 4 billion, and that of 2008 being no more than 10 billion.

administration. The exchange rate of RMB is no longer pegged to the USD only, but forming a more flexible system of RMB exchange rate. Before this reform, the learners and enterprisers had different opinions on whether to make gradual progress or to adjust once and for all. In the end, since the authorities worried that the impact on the economy might be too much if completed at one time, following the learners' advice, the model of "small steps forward" was adopted, namely adjusting many times and at small ranges. After the beginning of opening and reform, the exchange rate of RMB against the USD increased 2% one time, and the rate between USD and RMB was adjusted to 1:8. 11. At the end of 2005 it reached 1:7. 007, with the exchange rate of RMB against the USD increasing 2. 5% that year. From July 2005 to June 2008, the accumulative appreciation rate of RMB against the USD was about 21%, the yearly increase being as high as 7% on average. The dispute over whether to make gradual progress or to make the change once and for all never stopped, but history could not be reversed and no comparison could be conducted. However, one thing was for sure, the model of gradual appreciation did arouse strong expectation for increase in the value of RMB.

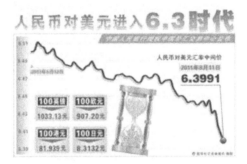

RMB against USD hits a new height

In 2008, the US subprime crisis led to the world financial crisis which interrupted the progress of RMB exchange rate reform. To deal with the impact of the crisis, as the president of the People's Bank of China, Zhou Xiao-chuan said, "The world financial crisis caused a lot of negative impacts and uncertainties. In this special time, the policies may consider differently from common times. " Taking the later actions by the central bank into consideration, the difference resided in neither raising the value at large margin again nor lowering it at large margin. Thus, starting from September 2008, the RMB returned to the pegging to the USD, the exchange rate of RMB against USD was fixed around 6. 8235, with a very narrow fluctuation margin.

With the impact of the world financial crisis fading away, on June 19, 2010, the exchange rate reform restarted. The People's Bank of China aimed to enhance the elasticity of RMB exchange rate, enlarge the fluctuation span of RMB exchange rate, and exert dynamic administration and regulation on the fluctuation of RMB exchange rate. Up to March 26, 2012, from the starting of exchange rate reform in 2005, the accumulative appreciation of RMB against the USD was 30%.

5. 2. 2   Distortion and Reality—Dispute on RMB Devaluation and Hot Foreign Exchange Reserve

A. *The Foreign Exchange Reserve " Being Increased"*

Foreign exchange reserve refers to the capital possessed by a country which can be used to exchange currencies of other countries at any time. In the narrow sense, foreign exchange reserve refers to the foreign exchange accumulation; in the broad sense, foreign exchange refers to assets by price of foreign currencies, including cash, gold, securities of foreign countries, etc. The Chinese shortage in foreign exchange reserve we mentioned previously refers to shortage in these assets. An essential requirement of being an international reserve assets is being a currency which can be freely used to exchange into other reserve assets, that is a currency which takes an important part in the system of international currency. At present, the frequently used major currencies in international clearance are USD, Euro, Japanese Yen, and Pound, etc.

Starting from 2002, the foreign exchange reserve in China exploded. The fast increase of foreign exchange in China began in the 90s of the 20th century, with 1996 being over 1,000 billion dollars, and 2005 adding up to over 8,000 billion dollars. It increased 7 times in nine years. Although there is no uniform international measurement for a reasonable reserve of foreign exchange in theory as well as in practice, China's foreign exchange obviously exceeded the practical need with too large an amount and extremely fast increase.

To explain and solve problems in the management of overly high foreign reserve, we must first find out the formation mechanism of foreign exchange reserve. First, the long-time foreign trade surplus is the major reason for foreign exchange reserve. Secondly, in order to invite investment, the Chinese government constantly issues favorable policies for foreign trade and investment. Under the system of tax distribution, to promote the local economy, the local government adds more of such kinds of policies. The preferential policies of "two exemptions and three diminutions" (exemption of enterprise income tax on the first and second year, half diminution of enterprise income tax from the third to fifth year) is not only implemented in the tax-protected zones and economic development zones, but becomes a basic condition for the local government to attract foreign investment. Thus, a lot of foreign businesses directly entered through investment, resulting in continuing surplus in capital accounts in international payment. Thirdly, the "gradual progress policy" in exchange rate reform discussed previously renders the system of exchange rate short of elasticity, adding to the pressure of RMB appreciation on the one hand and inflating the foreign exchange reserve on the other. Fourthly, under the current system of foreign exchange settlement and sale, the central bank is responsible to buy back all the foreign exchange. With the fast increment in foreign exchange, foreign exchange supply increases continually which not only restrains the effectiveness of macroeconomic regulation and control in general, but also weakens its effect by structure.

B. "The Hot Potato" that is Hard to Handle

It seems most suitable to describe the large amount of foreign exchange in China's hand by the old saying that "Too much money burns the hand". According to data issued by the People's Bank of China on January 10, up to December 2012, China's foreign exchange reserve balance was 33, 100 billion dollars, an increase of 1, 300 billion dollars compared with that at the end of 2011. Since 2006, China surpassed Japan in foreign exchange reserve, becoming the first in the world, and consistently being so for seven successive years.

The hand-burning foreign exchange reserve

It is true that large amounts of foreign exchange reserve strengthened China's ability to pay in foreign trade and raised China's international standing, but it cannot be neglected that it posed challenges to the management of foreign exchange and the macroeconomic regulation and control. As put by Zhou Xiao-chuan, the current foreign exchange reserve had exceeded the required level of China.

Besides, the over-large foreign exchange reserve provided reason for politically attacking the RMB as "being artificially underestimated", causing a lot of trade frictions, and increasing appreciation expectation of the RMB.

To see it objectively, adequate foreign exchange reserve brings advantages to the Chinese economy. For instance, being rich in foreign exchange reserve helps to avoid the infectious capital outflows and to keep the exchange rate steady, especially at times of crises; in international balance of payment, the big foreign exchange reserve can ensure payment of import and debt; in keeping the financial steadiness of the country, adequate foreign exchange reserve enables the country to effectively respond to the financial risks caused by external impacts.

However, as is pointed out by Zhou Xiao-chuan, unreasonably high level of foreign exchange reserves naturally causes problems.

First of all, the biggest risk caused by a large foreign exchange reserve is its effect on the nation's economy and finance. Now let's look at the components of high levels of foreign exchange reserve, which consists of three parts: favorable balance of trade, direct foreign investment, and "hot money". According to a learner's estimation, favorable balance of trade takes up only half of the foreign exchange reserve of China, [1] the rest being foreign capital including direct foreign investment and "hot money" which has always been difficult to estimate. And the harm of hot money to the economy is obvious since "hot money" itself is venture capital which is unsteady and fluctuates with the change of exchange rates. When RMB is expected to appreciate, the short-term speculative capital pours in quickly, while when RMB is expected to depreciate, it withdraws quickly. Besides, China's deficiency in supervision of short-term capital causes more and more floating money to enter China through legal or illegal means, shaking the steadiness in quantity of foreign exchange reserve. The most impressive display of the power of "hot money" is the Asian financial crisis. On July 2, 1997, with the Thai government's announcement of abandoning the fixed exchange rate system, the exchange rate of Thai baht depreciated 20% on that very day. Then the Philippine Peso, Indonesian Rupiah, and Malaysian ringgit were successively attacked by international speculators. In August of the same year, Malaysia gave up protection of the Ringgit, and the Singapore dollar, which had always been strong, was impacted too. It is reported that from July 1997 when the Asian

---

[1] Tang Yong-zhong, vice dean of the Law school of Huazhong University of Science and Technology.

financial crisis started to August 1998, the MSCI (Morgan Stanley Capital International) emerging market index slumped 57%, and the Standard and Poor's 500 index accumulatively increased 8%, the USD index increased 4.5%, thereby the hot money escaped from the stock market of emerging markets and poured into the American stock or exchange market. [1]

In addition, the trade friction risks caused by large amounts of foreign exchange reserve also stand out, and the economic bubble risks gradually appear as time goes by. Many people believe that "bubbles" in the real estate and stock markets are relevant to "hot money", which are after all problems of exchange rate.

5.2.3 Disputes on Appreciation of RMB

A. Voices of " RMB Being Underestimated" Heard Constantly in the World

On September 2, 2003, the 73rd US Treasury Secretary John Snow visited China. Immediately after he took office, Snow expressed more than once that he hoped China would implement a more flexible exchange rate system. He pointed out meanwhile that America must take into consideration the complexity of RMB exchange rate management, and the American government should not impose on the Chinese government how to handle problems of the value of RMB. Although he stressed again and again that by this visit he intended to promote the "continuous growth and prosperity" of US-China trade, international media mostly held that Snow's visit aimed at appreciation of RMB exchange rate, some even termed his Asian visit as "trip of exchange rate".

RMB and USD

---

1   From the Bloomberg database.

The Chinese government took this opportunity to identify its stand—then Premier Wen Jia-bao of the Chinese State Council made it clear that to keep the RMB exchange rate at a reasonable and equilibrium level is in the common interests of both countries. China implemented a floating exchange rate system based on supply and demand in the market, a unitary and controlled system. This system suited China's reality and international society. According to the development level of the economy, the economic development status, and the international balance of payment, China will continue to explore and improve the formation mechanism of RMB exchange rate by deepening the financial reform.

As a matter of fact, long before Snow, China's neighbor, Japan, continually demanded China's exchange rate appreciation. In 2002, the Japanese government began to blame China for "deflation export" and required China to increase the value of RMB. On August 26, 2003, the Japanese finance minister again said that he would negotiate the problem of Chinese exchange rate with Snow at the Japan-America finance ministers meeting on September 1, and he would "exchange opinions" with other countries on the meeting of International Monetary Fund in September, and he suggested he would discuss the same problem at the APEC finance ministers meeting.

B. *True Surplus or False Trade*

As for China's trade surplus, the former Minister of Commerce Chen De-ming once pointed out that the level of trade deficit between America and China had been over-estimated. The reasons for statistical differencec include: Firstly, some Chinese products are transported to America through other economic means, and the added value in this course is counted as surplus on China's part; secondly, in processing trade export to America, Chinese enterprises usually make to order only, taking no hand in designation, transportation, and sales, etc. Therefore, the import customs clearance price of America is higher than the Chinese export price, pushing up China's surplus. [1]

Previously, when interviewed by the Washington Post, Chen said that "China and America are in balance on general trades, and the surplus is mainly caused by processing trade. Viewing from enterprise entities, in 2009, in the 140 billion surplus of China toward America, nearly 76% is created by foreign enterprises which are mostly America-invested businesses. Viewing from the products, 67% of China's surplus comes from electronic information technology

---

[1]   Guo Li-qin, WTO: Chinese Surplus Rather Small in Fact, from China Business News, June 14, 2012.

and electronic instruments which are processed and assembled in China. "

Besides, China's trade surplus is the surplus of trade in goods issued by the General Administration of Customs. With statistic technology lagging behind, China could not carry out fully-covered statistics as in the developed countries like America and the European continent. As a matter of fact, according to the balance of international payments which reflects payment flow of a country in all the economic transactions with other countries in a certain period, current items include: trade in goods, services, earnings and unilateral transfer. In other words, it includes not only trade in goods which is traditionally stressed by China, but also services in trade.

Foreign capital flows into China in
false trade in the way of ants move

The trade surplus issued in China is the surplus of trade in goods, excluding the large deficit in trade service, therefore does not reflect the actual situation of China's trade. In 2012, China's surplus of trade in goods was USD 115.1 billion, and by incomplete statistics, the deficit in trade service was USD 60 billion. Above these, if the huge consumption on high-grade consumer goods overseas is taken into consideration, China's overall trade surplus can be significantly reduced.

C. Dissolve Expectation of Appreciation, Guard against "Hiroshima agreement"
Trap

Every country in the world is scrupulous and takes everything into consideration in the reform of their exchange rate system since it is not only related to finance, but integrated with politics, economy and the society. Appreciation of the RMB concerns not only the policies of exchange rate and finance, but more deeply, it causes economic and social adjustment and leads to far-reaching social results. When considering the "where to go" of the exchange rate system, the Chinese government has to first answer the question "are the governments, enterprises and common people ready for the appreciation of RMB". Presently, in face of various pressures, the intellectual circles and the government agree on the basic point that the expectation of appreciation should be dissolved before the liberalization of exchange rate.

Why should the expectation of RMB appreciation be dissolved? There are two reasons that cannot be neglected: the expectation theory and the Price-sticky Monetary Approach. The exchange rate expectation theory holds that when the exchange rate turn from fixed to flexible, the nominal rate naturally begin to rise, and such rise may intensify people's expectation that the nominal rate would continue to rise. International capital, private capital as well as household savings rush into the Chinese market continuously, causing waves of investment booms. Foreign capital all have confidence in RMB, so they buy assets of RMB so as to get the benefits caused by RMB appreciation. The investment booms lead to gradual increase in asset value, and meanwhile attract more foreign capital that has not entered China. When another round of foreign capital entrance comes, the value of RMB is forced to go up and its international purchase power is strengthened. But internal of China, inflation is created and the domestic purchase power of RMB decreases continuously.

According to the Price-sticky Monetary Approach, the market may over-adjust the exchange rate. That is to say, in market adjustment, when the exchange rate is underestimated, the appreciation may rise up too high; while if it is overestimated, the market may lead the exchange rate to decrease too much. Although it is hard to anticipate an accepted equilibrium exchange rate value, over-adjustment does happen frequently. When a certain exchange rate is over-adjusted, although everyone in the market can see it, it is not immediately corrected. It usually goes on for some time until a certain economic period appears in which the turning point occurs and a new over-adjustment in the opposite direction happens. The over-adjustment of exchange rate has grave impact on the economy.

Therefore, considering either of the above two theories, for the healthy and stable development of China's economy, the expectation of RMB appreciation should be dissolved. The "Hiroshima agreement" of Japan is a lesson we should learn. In September of 1985, the five finance ministers from America, Britain, Japan, Germany and France held a meeting at the Plaza hotel in New York and signed the "Hiroshima agreement". The main point of the agreement was to greatly appreciate the Japanese Yen and Mark and to lower the over-estimated US dollar. After the agreement, the appreciation of Japanese Yen was highly expected so that the five developed industrial countries began to sell USD in big quantities, leading the USD to depreciate and the Japanese Yen to appreciate quickly. After that, the American finance minister still believed that there was appreciation space for the Japanese Yen, so that consequently the Japanese Yen doubled its value against the USD in three years.

What resulted was not only depreciation of the Japanese Yen, but also impact on the Japanese economy. To prevent economic depression following the appreciation of the Japanese Yen, the central bank of Japan had to lower the interest rate five times, from 5% in 1985 to 2.5% in 1987. Low interest rates created huge bubbles in the entity economy and real estate. To prevent the bubbles from bursting and ensure the healthy development of the economy, the Japanese government increased the discount rate five times from March 1989 to May 1990. This on the one hand pricked the bubbles and mauled heavily on the economy, and on the other hand led the stock price to decline precipitously, leaving the Japanese economy in a "roller coaster" for more than a decade.

History has shown us how terrible it is to depend too highly on a country's currency value. Therefore, taking history as a mirror and taking its own characteristics into consideration, China must effectively dissolve the appreciation expectation of RMB.

5.3   Money Policy of China and Internationalization of RMB

5.3.1   Historical Review of Chinese Money Policy

A. The Nominal Money Policy before the Opening and Reform

Compared with finance policy, there is no history for money policy. Before the opening up, finance was the main body in national income distribution and played a dominant role in economic operation and adjustment. Being the dependency and cashier of finance, the People's Bank of China played all the functions of the central bank, professional bank, and other bank and non-bank financial institutions. Money policy was actually the policy of comprehensive credit. All the economic indicators were under program control. Price setting, money supply and investment scale were all controlled by the Development Planning Commission and the Ministry of Finance, emphasizing "money goes with goods". With resource distribution mainly decided by the nation's administrative order, the function of the People's Bank of China was to supply money according to the national economic plan, namely to "keep the plan and forbid the outflow". Therefore, there was in fact no actual money policy.

B. 1984−1992: Expansionary Alternatively-elastic Money Policy

Only after the foundation of a secondary bank system in 1984, did the money policy in symbolic meaning occur. Of course, by American standard, there is actually no independent money policy in China up to now. For one thing, the People's Bank of China has only the right to make suggestions in making money policies.

Since 1984, with the nation's economic system turning from planned management to macro-management under state adjustment, The People's Bank of China began to symbolically perform the central bank's function. The indirect money policy as a tool was put into use, with the management of credit scale plan as the major means of regulation. However, the credit scale is not totally stipulated by the People's Bank of China. It can only make suggestions. Especially after the failure in price breakthrough in 1988, severe inflation occurred. As a result, starting from the latter half of 1989, the right of The People's Bank of China was further taken and the central government greatly tightened the credit scale. The money policy then existed in name only.

C. 1992−1997: The Money Policy Aiming at Curbing Inflation

Since the third quarter of 1994, the People's Bank of China began to declare the quarterly money supply indicators. At the beginning of 1995, it declared to enlist money supply as one of the control objectives of money policy. And starting from 1996, it began to declare the annual regulation goal of money supply. At that time, controlling credit scale remained the major means.

D. 1998−2007: Stable and Healthy Money policy

Money policy in the common sense turned up in January 1998. After years of bold and resolute reform in finance and state-owned enterprises, unstable situation caused by macroeconomic depression occurred in which the national consumer price index showed constant negative growth, enterprises were working under capacities, and the jobless population kept increasing. The central bank gave up control of the credit scale and greatly lowered the interest rate. The central bank lowered the interest rate three times in 1998. It lowered the rate twice on July 10, 1999 and February 21, 2002, residents' deposit rate being 1.98%. Meanwhile, the floating span of loan interest rate was enlarged, the open market operation was enhanced to regulate the monetary base, and the credit limit was cancelled. Credit policy was made flexible and the loan structure was regulated(it actually means that the local government imposed on the banks to issue loans for stability and unity). In April of 1996, the open market operation was first launched and when it was restored in 1998, it gradually became the major means to carry out money policy. In 1999, the volume of bond operation in open market was RMB707.6 billion, with net availability of monetary base being RMB191.97 billion. This kind of money policy resulted in the rapid growth of credit. In some places and enterprises, blind investment and expansion intensified significantly, therefore the input and output efficiency dropped greatly.

In 2003, China started to raise the deposit reserve ratio and implemented the system of deposit reserve ratio of difference. On February 21, 2002 the deposit and loan interest rate of the financial institutions was lowered for the last time, and after that the interest began to be raised; the management of real estate credit business was strengthened; window guidance to the financial institutions was timely carried out; experimental units of interest rate liberalization was established; the ability to regulate monetary base through open market operation was enhanced, etc. Up to the end of 2007, interest rate was increased eight times and the reserve ratio was raised fourteen times.

In the latter half of 2007, the national economy was over-heated, with prices and inflation rising. Therefore, the Central Economic Working Conference held at the end of 2007 clearly put forward that starting from 2008 the money policy would change from "steady" to "tightened". Until then, the "steady" money policy implemented for ten years by the central government was replaced by the "tightened" policy.

E. "Roller coaster" Period of Money Policy in Financial Crisis

To cope with the international financial crisis, the Chinese government carried out the expansionary monetary policy which is still in dispute now. It should not be denied that the expansionary money policy of China could effectively bring about the increases in Chinese industries and consumption.

The expansionary policy is dominated by expansion of credit and realized by enlarging money supply, aiming at increasing industry and improving the level of consumption. The expansionary policy dominated by credit expansion in China causes smaller inflation than that dominated by enlarging money supply. This is because in the cause of loose monetary policy, money is not retained in financial sectors but put in the entity economy(the financial loan spreads are the major driving force for financial institutions to offer loans). Just as Mr. Zhou Xiao-chuan expressed at the Annual World Meeting of CEOs in 2009, since The People's Bank of China always keeps the bottom line of benchmark deposit rate at

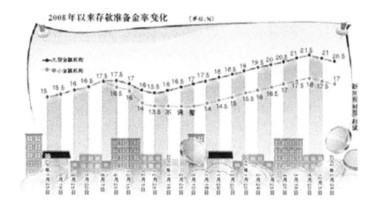

2008年以来存款准备金率变化   (单位:%)

Table of Change in Deposit Reserve Ratio Since 2008

2. 25% , the financial institutions in China have the impetus and pressure to put the deposit into use. Therefore, in a financial crisis, the financial institutions in China do not hoard money as the financial institutions in other countries, but invest in the entity economy to bring back benefit instead, so as to compensate payments in interest. It is just the exogenous quality of the Chinese interest rate policy that effectively overcome the liquidity trap, forcing the financial institution in China to lend out money even at severe credit risks in order to gain profit to compensate the payment in deposit interest. In other words, comparatively, the tight-money policy of China is strongly administrative, while in the expansionary money policy, the government need only to let go of the credit gate, then the financial institutions will autonomously provide a large quantity of money supply.

The expansionary money policy of China may bring about inflation to some extent, but there is a time-lag, because in an economic depression monetary deflation occurs before inflation. It should be noticed that in the course of loose money policy in China, only those investments dominated by the government was stimulated, the private investments may not be moved completely. In the first three quarters of 2009, most of the long-term loans were offered to the government dominated infrastructure construction, taking up RMB2. 1 trillion and 50. 5% of the whole new medium and long term industry loans. And it is difficult for this part of an investment to bring along private investment and to promote steady and rapid development of the entity economy. In November 2009, the People's Bank of China, China Banking Regulatory Commission, China Securities Regulatory Commission, and China Insurance Regulatory Commission together issued the "Instruction on Improving Financial Service to Support Adjustment and Revitalization of Key Industries and Restrain Overcapacity of Some Industries", and pointed out that the moderately loose monetary policy would be insisted. But under the premise of moderately loose monetary policy to assure economic growth, in order to prevent potential inflation, the government required the promotion of industrial regulation by means of money policy.

Concerning the inflation caused by expansionary money policy, Mr. Zhou Xiao-chuan pointed out at the 2009 China Finance Conference that "for Chinese economy is at the transition period, China's money policy should be different from the unified money policies of the western countries which aim at controlling inflation. China's money policy is designed for the four purposes of low inflation, economic growth, higher employment and general equilibrium in international balance of payment. Since the Chinese economy is turning from planned economy to market economy, the money policy has to take optimizing of resource allocation into consideration, and accept some inflation as a cost. " In other words, China's particularity at the period of transition caused its different specialty in transmission mechanism and policy efficiency compared with other countries. China's money policy is not only effective in the entity economy, but can also promote economic and financial reform and keep them developing continuously. Therefore, while keeping moderately loose monetary policy, the central bank should pay more attention to its function in regulating industrial construction and promoting economic steady growth.

Since the beginning of 2011, the money policy of China turned into "steady" from the previous "moderately loose". This was an important change in the keynote of money policy. The "moderately loose" money policy in the previous two years was a "special measure" taken in the world financial crisis. At that time, the economy of China had been stabilized and begun to grow, the "moderately loose" money policy should timely drop out.

Data from the Statistical Bureau showed that in the first three quarters of 2010, the year-on-year growth in gross domestic product(GDP) of the Chinese economy was 10. 6% . The increase rate improved 2. 5% than the same period of the previous year. And the newly issued purchase management index(PMI) of China's manufacturing industry showed that the PMI of November was 55. 2% , increased 0. 5% than the previous month and had increased constantly for four months. The positive momentum of the Chinese economy intensified. Meanwhile, with the second round of quantitative easing monetary policy of America, worldwide liquidity occurred and pressure of imported inflation further improved. Pushed by various factors, the domestic price increases was also under great pressure. The latest data showed that China's consumer price index for October was 4. 4% , creating the new highest of 25 months.

At such a moment, the monetary policy turning from "moderately loose" to "steady" sent out a clear signal to the market. By putting in a reasonable amount of money and credit, the aim of stabilizing prices could be reached and risks of excessive price rises prevented. Therefore, the central bank raised the deposit reserve ratio several times and tightened the money supply. This can be said to be slamming brakes on the previous money policy.

Upon until the completion of this book, China's money policy is still considered "steady". However, in the background of various new quantitative easing international relay money policies, the present money policy of China is still under great pressure. "being vigorous" may not stabilize the high material price and high housing price, while "being steady" has to face pressures of economic growth and international competition. The makers of China's money policy need to be wise and courageous enough to confront and dissolve the pressures and challenges.

5. 3. 2   Readjustment of International Money Policy: Strategy of RMB Internationalization

Internationalization of RMB refers to the process in which RMB crosses national boundaries and circulates abroad and becomes generally accepted in the world as currency for pricing, settling accounts and reserve. Although the present circulation of RMB abroad does not equate to RMB internationalization, the expanding of its world circulation will consequently result in the internationalization of RMB, turning it into a world currency.

A. Progress of RMB Internationalization

Since 2011, "RMB internationalization" and "Hong Kong offshore RMB center" have become hot topics in the economic and financial circles of Hong Kong. Many economists and famous financial institutions have done analysis, research and predictions on the subjects.

The basic development path of RMB internationalization:

Firstly, in a medium period(5 to 10 years) it will gradually become a widely accepted currency of settlement in world trade; secondly, in a medium or long period(10 years later), after gradual opening of controls under capital items, it will become an increasingly important international investment currency; thirdly, in a long period(20 years later), it will gradually become reserve currency. To realize the above purposes, the offshore Yuan market must go through three major stages: Forming, Developing, Maturity.

To conclude, in the internationalization of RMB, "two large steps after three small steps" should be carried out. Three small steps include gradually releasing RMB to go outside its boundaries, permitting RMB to circulate abroad, and opening channels for RMB's backflow on the mainland. It is said that two of the three small steps have been taken, if introduction of "small QFII" can be realized in the third, then the two large steps can be carried out.

"Setting sail"is used to express people's hope for the "two large steps" which refer to "expanding of capacity and quantity", namely to develop RMB products, to provide plenty of space for RMB, and then to further scale up RMB circulation. "Capacity" and "quantity" are believed to be of relevant relation: so long as the scale of RMB in the market is big enough, the issuers and enterprises are willing to put out large quantities of RMB products.

Table 5. 2   The Process List of RMB Internationalization

June 2007	The first RMB bond landed on Hong Kong, and after that, several mainland banks successively issued two or three years RMB bonds in Hong Kong several times, amounting to 20 billion Yuan.
July 10, 2008	The State Council approved of the armed scheme of the People's Bank of China, a new department in charge of exchange rate was set up, one of its functions being "developing RMB offshore market depending on the progress of RMB internationalization".
December 4, 2008	China and Russia negotiated to speed up using domestic currency for settlement; on 12th of that month, the People's Bank of China and National Bank of Korea signed bilateral trade swap agreement; by currency swap, the two countries can provide each other with short-term liquidity support as much as 180 billion Yuan.
December 25, 2008	The State Council decided to carry out RMB settlement pilot projects for trades in goods between Guangdong and Yangtze river delta area and regions of Hong Kong and Macao, and between Guangxi, Yunnan and the ASEAN; besides, China signed agreement on bilateral currency settlement of autonomous select with eight neighboring countries including Mongolia Vietnam, and Burma, RMB regionalization sped up.
February 8, 2009	The size of trade swap agreement between China and Malaysia reached 80 billion Yuan/40 billion Ringgit.
March 9, 2009	Assistant governor of the central bank, Guo Qing-ping, declared that the State Council had confirmed that the Cross-border RMB settlement center would open pilot area in Hong Kong. The specific pilot plan and administrative measure are under study, not published yet.
March 11, 2009	The People's Bank of China and National Bank of Belarus signed bilateral trade swap agreement, aiming to push forward bilateral trade and investment to promote economic growth of the two countries.

Cun.

March 23, 2009	The People's bank of China and Central Bank of Indonesia signed bilateral trade swap agreement to support bilateral trade and direct investment so as to promote economic growth, and to provide short-term liquidity for stabilizing financial market.
April 2, 2009	The People's Bank of China and Central Bank of Argentina signed bilateral trade swap agreement.
July 2009	Six departments issue administrative measure of pilot areas of cross-border trade RMB settlement, China's pilot RMB settlement in cross-border trade formally launched.
June 2010	Settlement pilot areas expands to 20 provinces and areas and cities from the coast to the hinterland, and the settlement areas abroad extend to all countries and regions.
July 21, 2011	The central bank issues "Notice on Problems Related to Cross-border RMB Businesses", which clarified for the first time the tentative way of direct foreign investment to RMB settlement businesses. This is another major initiative to promote RMB cross-border flows.

Data source: web of The People's Bank of China and the finance and economics website of Sina.

B. Speeding up of RMB Internationalization

In fact, we have obviously seen the speeding up of the convertibility process of RMB. On August 17, 2011, the then vice Premier Li Ke-Qiang visited Hong Kong and announced a series of new policies and measures to support Hong Kong's further development, and to deepen the cooperation between the mainland and Hong Kong in trade and finance, etc. including enlargement of service and opening, permitting the mainland to implement Hong Kong stock ETF, permitting the RMB of Hong Kong enterprises to invest in the mainland in way of FDI and "small QFII" and other important measures to promote capital account liberalization and to develop RMB offshore market. [1]

Following Hong Kong, Singapore and London also promised to set up RMB offshore center. As for Singapore, China will allow it to implement RMB liquidity through Chinese-funded banks as early as possible(*To Accelerate the Process of RMB Convertibility in Due Course*, April 26, 2011). And London showed great interest in setting up RMB an offshore market. This reflects the need for RMB offshore is spreading and it will provide favorable opportunity for expanding overseas RMB trades and settlements.

---

[1]   Stimulating the New Breakthrough of RMB Convertibility, August 17, 2011.

RMB Internationalization

September 6, Nigeria declared its plan to convert about 10% of the 33 billion Dollars of foreign exchange into RMB assets. However, because the RMB project is not open yet, it is still in progress. It is likely that China will commit to maintain the security of RMB assets to Nigeria as it did to Malaysia many years ago.

There are several advantages for RMB to become international reserve currency: a) It suits the economic status of RMB; b) It can cope with the dilemma of world reserve currency and mitigate the damage of foreign exchange reserve; c) Speed up the change in the way of Chinese economic growth, especially the construction of the future international finance center; d) Avoid large amount of capital inflow and minimize the operation difficulty of the central bank; e) Enjoy the profit of seigniorage; f) Ease international criticism of China's "exchange rate manipulation" and "trade protectionism".

It can be seen from the latest measures issued by the government, the internationalization of RMB is accelerating. It can be predicted that during the 12th Five-Year Plan, with the gradual opening of capital accounts and the construction of RMB offshore market in Hong Kong, together with the reform of exchange rate and interest rate liberalization, the process of RMB convertibility may be faster than expected. This also lays good foundation for RMB to become international reserve currency in the later 10 years. [1]

Can RMB be internationalized? Maybe the choice should finally be made by the market, since it is an issue of the whole world and a product of the market economy. Therefore, we may well go forward following Mr. RMB —Zhou

---

1 An Exploration on RMB Convertibility Path, April 19, 2011.

Xiao-chuan's words: do our best for homework and respect the choice of the market.

Case5. 1   The housing price of China which gets higher with each adjustment

We can see from the diagram that housing prices in Tianjin have been basically been going up since 2008 except for a low point in 2009. However, compared with the housing policies of the same time, it is found that prices did not rise in time of bailout and soared in time of rein. The deviation of the price trend from that of regulation presents an interesting scene. Through this case, we try to let the readers learn something about China's housing policy and how it is implemented. We cannot give definite explanation for the reason of "the severer the regulations, the higher the prices ", we only try to provide some explanations for people to think about and discuss.

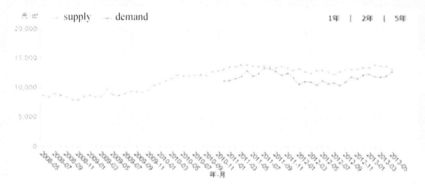

Figure 5. 1   Chart of housing price trend of Tianjin from 2008 to 2013

October 10, 2008, the finance ministry declared it would reduce or remit taxes on personal housing consumption, and loosened the control over the lower limit of loan interest rate, and meanwhile lower the ratio of down-payments. [1]

---

[1]   Since November 1, 2008, when buying ordinary houses smaller than 90m for personal use, the deed tax rate temporarily lowered to 1% , the stamp duty suspended, and the value-added tax of land exempted. The local government may make taxation reducing policy. The financial sectors can provide loans for the first personal house and ordinary housing for improvement. The lower limit of loan interest rate can reach 70% of the benchmark rate, the minimum down-payment ratio adjusted to 20% . Meanwhile, the personal accumulation fund loan interest rate lowered too, with each level dropping 27% . Construction of low-rent housing was sped up, entity with rent was enhanced, range of low-rent housing rent subsidies extended, and shanty area transformation accelerated.

Almost at the same time, the People's Bank of China made the same decision and lowered the personal housing loan interest rate to 70% of the benchmark loan rate, with the minimum down-payment ratio being 20%.

After the 2008 financial crisis, in face of the Chinese economy which was impacted at the real economy level, the rescue policies were frequently released from the government. The local governments all rushed to rescue; some officer of the building department and the national development and reform commission went everywhere to ask for help; and the finance department and the central bank formulated a lot of policies. It can be seen that the subjects of market rescue were not merely the finance department and the central bank. Then why did we mainly introduce the rescue policies of these two departments at the beginning of this section? To understand this, We need to learn something first about about the strength and important status of the two departments in regulation. In a critical moment, the vested interest groups in the housing market demonstrated strong strength. Then, what is the result of the regulations? As is shown in the diagram, around February 2009, there was a nadir of the housing market in five years. Thereafter, the housing market climbed all the way, and the regulation policies did the same thing.

In 2010 "ten items of national housing policy" were issued. And the executive meeting of the State Council held on April 13, 2010 requested that for those families that purchase a second house on loan, the down-payment should be no less than 50%, and the loan interest rate no lower than 1.1 times the benchmark rate. For those families that purchase the first house on loan and the house is bigger than $90m^2$, the down-payment should be no less than 30%. April 17, the State Council issued "the notice on resolutely curbing the fast-rising housing prices of some cities", and pointed out that in those places where the housing price was too expensive, loans for the third or more houses can be suspended.

The executive meeting of the State Council again issued eight items of housing market regulation (the eight national new items hereafter), requiring to enhance different housing credit policies: for those families that purchase the second house on loan, the down-payment should be no less than 60%, and the loan rate no lower than 1.1 times of the benchmark rate. After that, the deposit reserve ratio rose again and again. Till 2003, the five national items was issued, and the personal income tax of a second hand house dealing rose from 1% of the total trading volume to 20% of the price difference. This is said to be the biggest bright spot of the policy. However, regulated as the housing policies were, the housing prices went up, not down. Then, how did the problem that puzzled both the policy-making governments and the common people come into being? This author tries to explain it in the following way.

First, security housing and low-rent housing was not enough

Almost every new policy pointed to "speeding up the construction of security houses and intensify real object with rent", however, whether it was actually carried out remains unknown. By 2010, China's gap of security housing was 1. 25 million, and that of low-rent housing 0. 7 million. Furthermore, the signal sent out by this policy may easily be mistaken by the interest bodies: some property developers may begin to deny discount and fare reduction again; some local governments may refuse to reduce the income level of land grant fee. They may gamble with the populace with the mentality of violence and looting. These all may lead to the hideout of the house price adjustment that has once appeared.

Second, The battle between the local government and the central government

Although the central government emphasized again and again to keep the policy of housing market regulation "unmoved", the local governments on the other hand constantly "move" in different ways. Why do the local governments behave this way? It is really forced by the difficult situation they faced. The national income from land sales in 2010 was about 2, 700billion Yuan, amounting to 66. 5% of the local financial revenue. Especially in Wuhu, the number reached 90%. If the housing price goes down, the decline of trading volume will bring down the land price, then the fiscal income will have too many problems to deal with. So it is well reasoned for the local governments to bailout.

Third, the functions of the local government authority

Tracing the source, it can be found that a large majority of the fiscal income of the local government was used to invest instead of spent on people's livelihood. Since there is no limit for the size of investment projects and for capital required, the local government will continuously push up land price to gain more capital for investment. When such impulse is closely related to personal interest, it is difficult to restrain. Obviously, the basic power for the local governments to frequently shake the policy of regulation comes from the distortion and dislocation of the government functions. The function of the government is not to dominate the economy, but to provide public products, public services and public welfare. If the function of the government goes back to people's livelihood, it will be powerless in shaking regulation policy.

Case 5. 2   The annoyance of RMB appreciation—the benefit black hole of Chinese toy industry caused by RMB appreciation[1]

Two toy factories in Guangdong closed down. The reasons include rise in labor cost, increase in European standard for toys, and rising raw material cost. Another more important reason was the fast appreciation of RMB. The National Federation of Industry and Commerce reported that the difficulties faced by medium and small industries were graver than 2008. Meanwhile, yesterday the Administration of Exchange Control reclaimed that the foreign exchange reserve won't disappear. There are some reasons for saying so. But one thing the Administration forgot to make clear—if appreciation of RMB rises to a certain degree, the foreign capital may make forced harvest. If China cannot resist it, big loss will be inevitable.

Prosperity of the toy industry in the past

Only one year ago, exchange rate was but an obscure concept in Lu Zhong-ping's mind, however, it has become a tiger that bites.

"I no longer care so much for the change of exchange rate, it's useless to see. " As the Chairman of Kai Le Toys Company Lit. of Jiangsu province, Lu Zhong-ping said in distress, "in the last year I lost more than 300 thousand Yuan just because of RMB appreciation, that is over 10% of the total yearly benefit".

Yesterday, the central bank announced that the middle price of RMB against USD to be 7. 7293. Since the exchange rate reform on July 21, 2005, the exchange rate has accumulatively risen 6%. Insiders believe that appreciation can promote regulation of industrial structure, but forms great challenge to labor-intensive export enterprises.

---

1   From *First Financial Daily*.
(Website: http://www. cnstock. com/rdzt/rmb/2007 −04/25/content_2102192. htm)

As a matter of fact, there are already a lot of people as depressed as Lu
Zhong-ping. They worry that their export earnings may someday be eaten out by
the ruthless tiger—the exchange rate.

Worry on exchange rate appreciation

"The cost of raw material and labor are all increasing, while the price of
export goods is declining, therefore profits drop severely. "

Lu Zhong-ping who is attending the 101st Canton Fair in Guangzhou said,
"Now the only way to negotiate with the clients is to raise the price a little. And
it is best to drive up the amount, that's the only way out. "

Thinking of the loss caused by the appreciation, Lu feels painful. "At the
end of last year, we received an order from the Nest coffee of Italy. The original
profit was 5% . But when we settled account after the spring festival, RMB
appreciated, so the profit dropped to about 3. 5% . The original profit being only
40 thousand dollars, in such cases, more than 5,000 dollars are lost. "

The general manager of Shenzhen Company of the New Century Underwear
Factory in Nanchang —Yu Guowen is equally frustrated. "Appreciation made us
profitless. I feel like weeping but have no tears. " At the Canton fair, he could
not feel happy even when obtaining orders, "The clothes company nearby also
feel sad about appreciation. We are almost at zero profit like a welfare factory.
After paying taxes and employee salaries, almost nothing left to us. "

The depression of toy industry today

He once thought of dissolving the pressure by means of raising prices, but it
is not the fundamental way to solve the problem. "In that case, the clients won't
come here to buy goods. Nowadays India is developing especially fast and the
clients may go there to buy what they want, " Yu said, "Our original profit was
6% to 7% , with the RMB appreciation being 6% , no profit left to us. "

Facing the appreciation and price rise of raw materials, Professor Lan Yi-
sheng of the College of Business Administration of Shanghai University of Finance

and Economics pointed out that these factors have more influence on those enterprises with high proportion of export and low added value of the products. For example, enterprises of textile, clothes, shoes, toys, etc. They may feel greater pressure.

"By the ' flooding effect' of exchange rate adjustment, the nation hopes the medium and small enterprises with low added value to retreat from the market, so as to reverse the vicious circle of price competition among small enterprises. " The Vice Dean of Economics School of Fudan University Sun Li-jian believes, "But, since the price of labor in our country is still rather cheap, there is no reaction taken by the most of the industries yet. When the advantage of labor price no longer make up for the loss caused by appreciation, the small enterprises will be forced to close down or move abroad. "

Difficulty in internal digestion

Presently, enterprises in foreign countries can still transfer or avoid exchange rate risks by means of pricing power, currency option, and hedging. In fact, avoiding exchange rate risks by means of mental tools is a major means taken by the foreign enterprises, but not inside China.

"I don't know much about finance and nor did I ever use any tools, " said Lu Zhong-ping. And Yu Guo-wen thought that using metal tools to avoid risks means to sign contract with the client to deliver goods at the exchange rate of the settlement time.

The foreign trade salesman of a clothes export enterprise—Ms Yin said that for big orders they usually try to avoid risks by signing forward contract on settlement of exchange, but the effect is limited. "When trading with European clients, I usually try to persuade the clients to settle by Euro. So long as RMB continue to rise in value, the risks of loss cannot be avoided unless to settle by domestic currency. "

On this point, Sun Li-jian thinks that because the Chinese enterprises and banks have long been under fixed rate system, they basically know nothing about avoiding risks by means of mental tools. "For medium and small enterprises, there are costs to make the choice of using tools. Since they know little about this, they'd rather stay the same as before, " said Sun, "RMB appreciation in a narrow range to some extent protected these enterprises which have not been driven out of business. "

"On the other hand, it is true that enterprises can go to buy forward contract in the market, but the premise is that some people expect to rise and some expect to fall. However, the present condition is that all expect RMB will rise so there is no seller. Therefore, this tool is invalid, " said Sun, "at present, this is the only financial derivative that can be used, and for medium and small enterprises there is none. "

"Although we can avoid risks by purchasing forward exchange settlement products from the bank, it is not enough to resist the pressure of RMB appreciation, " a business personnel on condition of anonymity from Boyu Daily Necessities co. Ltd said, "so for small orders the cost may be increased, not cost-effective. "

Sun Li-jian pointed out that because China is still in the period of price competition, and RMB is not yet an international settlement currency, and the enterprises' overseas business capacity is poor, many popular methods in other countries cannot be employed in China.

The danger of transferring abroad

"What we can do now is to lower the profit, and then manage to obtain big amount, the pressure caused by appreciation need to be dissolved all by ourselves, " Lu said, "to shorten the time of getting back money, we cancelled long and medium terms of contracts and only accept orders under three months. We hope to negotiate with the clients on this Canton Fair, there may be no problem to raise 2% of the prices"

Jin Xiao-li, the international trade department clerk of Kunshan Rongguang Carpet co. Ltd. Also said that in the short run, the only way out is to talk with the upstream firms like the raw material suppliers, and meanwhile, raise a little bit of the rate toward clients. "After all, the foreign tradesmen that RMB will raise before they come, so they may well understand the rice in price. "

"In the long term, I ask the development department to create new things to attract the clients, " Lu said, "for fashionable products like the plush toys we made, we can only make more effort on design to attract customers. "

Facing the current dilemma in export, some enterprises tried to adjust the proportion between export and domestic sale, increasing that of domestic sale. However, in Zhang Xue-song's(Zhang is the salesman of Kunming Jiuren Import Expor co. Ltd) opinion, exploring the international market is the trend. He holds that the enterprises should enhance design and innovation to increase technology content.

On this point, Lan Yi-sheng holds that innovative products do not only refer to high technology products. The enterprises can develop some innovative and labor-intensive products, such as popular consumer goods like "rice dumpling balls". Although there is no new high technology inside, but there are new ideas to gain high profit.

Both Yu Guo-wen and Lu Zhong-ping never thought of building factories abroad. "It is said that Vietnam is not bad, but I don't know very well, " said Yu, "before finding suitable partner we won't go there, for what we know is limited, it may be risky to go Vietnam blindly. "

Sun Li-jian claimed that since it is difficult to readjust the industrial structure for the medium and small enterprises, it is an effective measure that can be considered for long term development to build factories in countries such as Vietnam and India. "But Chinese enterprises are short of overseas business experiences, lack of social security system, and the domestic staff may resist transferring abroad, therefore, few enterprises did so. "

Lan Yi-sheng pointed out that if enterprises cannot directly go to build factories abroad, they may first consider to buy raw materials abroad. "Now the markets are linked and there are only import tariffs. " Lan said, "and recently the tariff level is gradually going down, and the prices of some raw materials should continue to drop to encourage import. This is also helpful in reducing surplus. "

Case 5. 3   Foreign exchange certificate of RMB

Starting from January 1, 1994, China carried out unification of foreign exchange rates, stopped issuing foreign exchange certificate. Since then, the foreign exchange certificate that had circulated for 13 years inside china quit the historical stage. As a special certificate of special historical period, the occurrence, development and extinction of it are all epitomes of that period of history. On April 1, 1980, approved by the State Council, The People's Bank of China began to issue foreign exchange certificate. Foreign exchange certificates are mainly held by foreigners, overseas Chinese and Hong Kong and Macao compatriots, circulated within the specified range at the same value with RMB. It is not a currency, but a note with the function of planned circulation in a certain area, a special bank payment voucher. In the beginning period of the opening and reform, visitors and merchants from abroad poured in. To meet the need of the development in foreign communication, and to make it convenient for foreigners, overseas Chinese and Hong Kong and Macao compatriots to consume in China, and to stimulate China's foreign economic exchange, the foreign exchange certificate was issued by The People's Bank of China on April 1, 1980, approved by the State Council.

Background:

At the beginning of the opening and reform, foreign visitors, overseas Chinese and Chinese compatriots from Hong Kong, Macao and Taiwan came to

China in increasing numbers. But the market supply inside China was very limited. Domestic residents' daily supplies (such as oil, meat and cloth) were supplied according to rations. To satisfy the need of these visitors, China constructed some hotels and department stores. However, foreign currencies were forbidden to circulate inside China then. To make them able to buy things and consume in those places, and at the same time to distinguish them from the domestic residents, the State council granted right to The People's Bank of China to issue foreign exchange certificates. Those visitors needed to exchange their foreign currencies into foreign exchange certificates at Bank of China or other specified places for exchange. It was used as the equivalent of RMB. When departing mainland of China, they may choose to change it back into hard currencies or keep it for use on their next visit to China. Many foreigners called the foreign exchange certificate "money for travel".

Privileged currency

Foreign exchange certificate includes notes of 100 Yuan, 50 Yuan, 10 Yuan, 5 Yuan, 1 Yuan, 5 Jiao, and 1 Jiao, altogether seven face values like notes of RMB. Just as is written in the book ' Bring out the Critical Point' by Kenneth Starck—a journalism Professor from the University of Iowa, "If money speaks, the foreign exchange certificate speaks 50% louder than RMB. " Kenneth Starck came to China in 1986 and taught writing to postgraduates majoring in English News at Chinese Academy of Social Sciences. He had profound understanding of the use of foreign exchange certificates. With it, people could buy imported goods, consume in specified places, and exchange it into dollars, etc. which could not be done with RMB. But gradually, it was no longer enjoyed alone by foreigners. Some mainlanders obtained some foreign exchange certificates from overseas relatives and friends. On obtaining it they became objects of envy among their colleagues, neighbors and friends, because foreign exchange certificates was the pass card in and out of friendship stores.

Foreign exchange certificate of 100 Yuan

Scalpers

For the whole of the 80s and beginning of the 90s, the most frequently heard greeting in Beijing and other tourism cities was "Got money to change?" At the risk of jail, the scalpers found business opportunity between the mainland residents' crave for foreign exchange certificates and foreigners' need for RMB. Once they got RMB, foreigners could consume in every hotel and restaurant. And the price difference between RMB and foreign exchange certificate made speculating foreign currencies a lucrative profession—although illegal.

Before 1994, Chinese exchange rate system was s double-track system. Take the end of 1993 as an example, for the exchange rate stipulated by the State Administration of Foreign Exchange, one dollar was converted to 5.7 Yuan; while that in the enterprise foreign exchange market, one dollar was to 8.7 Yuan. Only about 20% of the foreign exchange transactions were done at the official exchange rate. On January 1, 1994, the double-track system was abrogated.

Before the double-track system was invalidated, one could exchange hard currencies such as USD at the official exchange rate by using foreign exchange certificates. If people possessed only RMB, they could only exchange USD on the black market. The exchange rate on the black market was usually higher even than that in the foreign exchange market serving for the enterprises, which was usually 1 dollar to 9 Yuan of RMB. Corresponding to the exchange rate of USD on the black market, the price of foreign exchange certificates on the black market was 130 Yuan of RMB for 100 Yuan of foreign exchange certificates.

Black market transactions were usually conducted in dark alleys or behind the booths of free markets. When dealing with each other, the two parties both would look alertly behind the other party to make sure no policemen were following. Once the deal was done, the scalpers would quickly exchange the certificates into hard currencies and then sell them to mainland residents in urgent need of USD. And the foreigners holding the illegally obtained RMB began to enjoy the freedom of accessing to any restaurants and stores.

The thriving black market business quickly spread to the whole country. You could see figures of scalpers all over the tourism cities like Beijing, Shanghai, Guangzhou, Hangzhou, and Kunming, etc. old or young, men or women. They waited day and night near the prosperous business districts and tourist hotels for business opportunities. At the same time, outside branches of Bank of China, scalpers could always be seen stopping anyone they thought might become their customers and to automatically ask "Want some foreign exchange certificates?"

Even after the central bank announced the unification of the exchange rate and stopped issuing foreign exchange certificates in 1994, the scalpers did not vanish. The mainland residents did not have an official channel to buy USD, although their need for USD was getting greater and greater. Therefore, the scalpers still could find space to live, only that their question was changed from "want any exchange certificate?" to "want any USD?"

Black market of foreign exchange

Till 1998, things changed since personal foreign exchange purchase was gradually opened. In that same year, the State Administration of Foreign Exchange stipulated that an individual going abroad on private business could purchase USD 2 thousand once. In September 2003, it was adjusted to USD 3 thousand within 6 months and USD 5 thousand over 6 months. In August 2005, the above two numbers were respectively raised to USD 5 thousand and USD 8 thousand.

Starting from May 1, 2006, China implemented the annual foreign exchange purchase management system. Residents can purchase USD 20 thousand and on February 1, 2007, it was raised to USD 50 thousand.

With the increase in the amount of residents' legal foreign exchange purchase, the scalpers' business which was once prosperous depressed, so they had to find other ways to make a living.

Collection value

However, the foreign exchange certificate became a new favorite—this time in the collection market. In the stamp and money market in Beijing, the price of a whole set of 7 face-valued foreign exchange certificates could be RMB10 thousand. In Xiamen, a note of 5 Jiao face-valued certificate with the Design of the temple of heaven at its back could be sold at 9 Yuan, while the one with the design of the Great Wall at its back and 100 Yuan face-valued was priced at RMB1 thousand. Experts believe that since most of the certificates were taken back by the People's Bank of China, those remaining in residents' hands are very limited in number, therefore, foreign exchange certificates as a collection item still has great space for appreciation.

Compared with the first and second sets of RMB, foreign exchange certificates are less in variety and low in price, suitable for small and medium collectors. In addition, the designs of its notes are all pictures of places of historic interest in China, having high taste of art and collective value. Presently the value of all kinds of foreign exchange certificates has greatly increased, with the less being five or six times the original price and the more dozens of times the original price. Especially the low face-valued notes of 1 Jiao, 2 Jiao, 5 Jiao and 1 Yuan, the market prices for them are comparatively low so there is great space for appreciation potential. They are strong items in foreign exchange certificates.

Questions for discussion:

1. Tell how many cases of interest rate upside-down occurred since the founding of new China. How has these cases influenced the economy?

2. What are the standards for all-covered statistic trade surplus and trade surplus according to China's general administration of customs? What is your interpretation of China's trade surplus? Do you agree that the trade surplus of China is overestimated?

3. What do you think needs to be done before RMB becomes world currency?

Before reform and opening up, China's economy was a typical revenue-dominant economy without the financial system or financial service in the modern sense under the traditional planning economy system. The initial establishment of China's financial system commenced from 1984, which was symbolized by the formation of a "double-leveled banking system" represented by the central bank and four specialized banks. After the 1990s, with the prosperous development of financial markets involving stock, bond, currency markets and so on, the diversified financing system in China gradually came into being. The complementary development between indirect and direct financing pushed the entire elevation of financial institutions and financial markets in China.

Chapter 6

The Structure and Reform of Financial System in China

In the history of human development, China used to be a big and influential country in terms of finance and made eminent contribution to the development of thee global financial industry. For example, the first paper currency came into the world in the Northern Song Dynasty in China and was called "Jiao Zi" by the Chinese. Paper currency exerted an important effect on solving the shortage of revenue and promoting economic development. Even Marco Polo, who came from Europe to do business here, has documented the necessity of moving from gold coin to paper currency by the Venice merchants in order to purchase on the market. But the excessive financial expansion brought about tragedies to many regimes in China. The latest example can be traced back to the defeat of the Kuomintang government in mainland China in the 1940s. Due to the chaos caused by the financial reform, the government not only lost the support of the people, but many were hurting at that time from the depressed economy in

China, shortage of materials, shortage of financial resources, soaring prices, and masses of people living on the edge of starvation.

After the founding of PRC, under the planning economy, the financial system was just a part a meager part of the whole. With the highly centralized planning, financial development was out of the question. The reform and development of financial system over the next three decades played a giant role in the cause of reform and opening up and also laid a solid foundation for the prosperity of China's economy. The future continuing development and reform of the financial system will also determine the China's fate.

6. 1   China's Financial Industry in the Times of Planning Economy

The People's Bank of China was founded in 1948 which unified the RMB issuance nationwide. From the end of 1952, China's financial system commenced to stride into unitarization and was eventually incorporated into the system of the People's Bank of China. Bank of China became the international financial business department under the People's Bank of China. Agricultural Bank of China was canceled soon after the establishment. Bank of Communications tended to shrink and became "non-banking". The People's Construction Bank of China became "non-banking", too. Most of the foreign banks withdrew from China. The insurance industry was more concentrated and foreign insurance companies were cleared from China. Rural Credit Cooperatives underwent rapid development but with a very strong official-operated color. Theoretically, in the first 30 years of the founding of PRC, the operation of China's finance was characterized by restrainted the overall restraint of finance. The main reason for this phenomenon was the absence of market mechanism. China's economy in the first 30 years after the founding of PRC was virtually the highly-materialized planning economy and the "highly centralized unification" financial mechanism was implemented by the People's Bank of China to monitor all the financial businesses. China's financial industry not only bore the typical restraining presentations externally but also demonstrated the characteristics of a materialistic planning economy internally.

6. 1. 1   The Highly Centralized Unification of Financial System

Before reform and opening up, China's economy was a typical revenue-dominant economy without the financial system or financial service in the modern sense. After the founding of PRC, the People's Bank of China adopted a four-level differentiating banking structure and reorganized the central banks set up by the Kuomintang government across the country. Thus, the business departments of the People's Bank of China came into being. At the same time, the banking system of PRC was gradually set up. After reorganization, Bank of China and Bank of Communications both adopted the three-level system including a general managing department, branch and sub-branch. People's Insurance Company of China established afterwards and branches were built in various regions of China in succession. But this kind of co-existence of various financial institutions did not last long. In 1952, the remaining commercial banks and insurance companies were incorporated into the system of The People's Bank of China, one after another. Bank of China co-worked with the foreign business bureau of the People's Bank of China. Bank of Communications and People's Insurance Company of China were put under the administration of the Ministry of Finance. Agricultural Bank of China was cut and incorporated into the General Managing Department of the Bank of Joint State-Private Ownership Cooperative. Hence, a centralized and unified financial system monopolized by the People's Bank of China was initially established. In this period, The bank was not divided in terms of its professional systems, and every bank was a constituent part inside The People's Bank of China. The People's Bank of China not only functioned as a commercial bank dealing with deposits, loans and remittances, but also took on the responsibility of central bank to conduct macro-regulation. Under this system, The People's Bank of China acted as the financial administrative office and the economic entity dealing in financial businesses as well.

During the "Cultural Revolution", economic construction was put in the second place, so the financial system in China was weakened to a large degree and the independence of banks faded away. The People's Bank of China was even incorporated into the Ministry of Finance and became the next tier of institution attached to the Ministry of Finance in September 1969. It basically descended to the "Big Treasury" and "Cashier" of the government. The leaders at that time failed to realize the importance of banking so that they just regarded the bank as "a Big Treasury" to conduct receiving and paying. Banks were not called to mind unless money was in need. Some even mixed up the financial and credit capital and resorted to administration means, resulting in many violations of economic law. The turmoil of the "Cultural Revolution", which lasted for 10 years, came to an end in October 1976 and the banking system of China commenced its restoration and reconstruction. The State Council decided to separate the People's Bank of China from the Ministry of Finance, again. The financial institutions under provinces, cities and autonomous regions followed suit.

During the development of China's economy and finance in the first 30 years after the founding of PRC, the essential function of finance—financing—only worked on the verge of the planning economy to an extremely limited degree and this kind of function was always denied as well.

6. 1. 2   Financial Product in Short Supply

China's financial structure can be called bank-oriented. Under this financial framework, deposit monetary banks and similar institutions occupied the dominant position in the financial system so that deposits and cash almost became the only financial tool. This characteristic was highlighted during the first 30 years of financial development in China.

In November 1949, the authority made a decision that anyone holding RMB could deposit the number of units of certain commodities converted from their amount of money in accordance with the prevailing unit price index of certain commodities issued by the People's Bank of China day by day in order to control the rising prices. When money was withdrawn, payment would be made based on the unit price index of certain commodities in order for the depositors not to suffer loss from the rising prices.

In March 1950, the People's Bank of China launched a variable term deposit (time-demand optional deposit) which bore the convenience of the current deposit and the benefits of fixed deposit, so depositors were very enthusiastic about it. In Late May, the People's Bank of China launched the capital-protected and inflation-protected deposit. When deposited, the amount of money was received and kept. When paid, if the prevailing price index of certain commodities increased, the payment would be adjusted to ensure the protection of inflation according to the prevailing price index of certain commodities. If the prevailing price index of certain commodities maintained the same rate or decreased, the money could be capital-protected according to the original amount of money deposited and the interest would be counted.

In 1952, the People's Bank of China confirmed various basic currency deposit patterns: fixed deposit and withdrawal in lump sum, fixed deposit in installments and withdrawal in lump sum, fixed deposit in lump sum and withdrawal in installments, fixed deposit in lump sum and withdrawal of the interest periodically, current deposit, prized fixed-amount deposit and so on. At the same time, the People's Bank of China lowered the deposit interest rate nine times successively and declined the bracket of interest rate in order to adjust the deposit flexibly.

But, because of the shock of the "Great Leap Forward" in 1961 and 1962, the deposit in both urban and rural areas of China kept decreasing. The deposits of residents rose again after some measures taken in 1969. "The Cultural Revolution" severely devastated the original policies to protect and encourage deposits. The savings and deposits of the people under examination were frozen, grabbed, withdrawn or transferred. During that period of time, savings agencies located in towns were condensed to 4,300 and the number of employees cut to 10,300. The frozen deposits did not thaw until 1972 and the interests were paid accordingly.

The financial industry in the first 30 years after the founding of PRC was under continuous adjustment, but what maintained the same was the successive absorption of deposits from residents. The main means at that time to adjust the deposit variable involved increasing the varieties of savings deposit, successively adjusting the deposit interest rate, providing preferential treatments to clients with high credit, actively absorbing foreign remittances and savings and so on. Those measures offered valuable capital for the economic construction at the initial stage after the founding of PRC.

6.1.3   Financial Operation Framework Centered by Credit Planning

The conception of "macro-regulation" was not introduced in the first 30 years after the founding of PRC. So, the overall credit planning embodied the content of financial macro-regulation at that time.

The overall credit planning system established in the People's Republic of China in 1952 included two constituent parts, the sources and utilization of capital. Deposit plan, cash-issuing plan and credit distribution plan constituted the basic measures of financial macro-regulation in the first 30 years after the founding of PRC. Under such a system, although the commercial banks still dealt with deposit and loan, all the deposits were handed in to the People's Bank of China and all the loans were planned and determined by the People's Bank of China so that there was only one balance sheet for all of China at that time. Under this highly centralized and unified system, the primary means of financial management were "credit plan" and "cash plan". If the loans were higher than the deposits, it was called "credit imbalance", which required the issuance of a net amount of cash to make up for the imbalance. Thus, the corresponding operation of the macro-economy might be subjected to the pressure of inflation. On the contrary, if the deposits were higher than the loans, it was called "deposit imbalance", which would result in the flow back of net amount of cash from circulation so that the corresponding operation of the macro-economy might fall into recession. Evidently, under this kind of system, the difference between deposits and loans was a key index to measure whether the financial operation of the whole society was loose or tight and whether the financial operation of the whole society was good or bad. Therefore, ascertaining the scale of deposit and loan in every part of China, mobilizing capital and distributing a cash issuing plan between different regions based on the scale of deposit and loan had become a main task of financial regulation of the People's Bank of China.

In the first 30 years after the founding of PRC, the national economy was highly materialized. Just under the operation framework determined by credit planning, abiding by the instruction from the higher level became the basic principle of the operation of banks in China at that time. This was different from the operation mechanism of seeking profit optimization of commercial banks in most of the countries in the world. On the basis of credit planning determining the loan issuing and cash issuing, the head office of the People's Bank of China decomposed all the loans and transmitted the loans to each of the branches and sub-branches for them to issue. All the deposits were estimated by the People's Bank of China, which requested each of the branches and sub-branches to organize and absorb the deposits. For the branches and sub-branches, whether they granted the loan or not, how much to grant and whom to grant depended on the loan quota distributed by the higher bank rather than the amount of deposit they attracted.

The capital distribution at that time was actually one means to accomplish the instructive economic planning. In addition, there was the shortage of capital and the financial activities were quite simple so that it was suitable for the People's Bank of China to use the difference between deposits and loans to depict the macro-operation of finance. But the conditions which were applicable to ensuring the conception of difference between deposits and loans were altered by every change concerning the traditional system after 1984. There is little difference between China's financial system and that of countries with developed market economies, so the rationality of using the difference between deposits and loans for measuring the activities of financial institutions basically disappeared.

6. 2   Establishment of the Framework of Modern Financial System

The reforms of the financial and economic systems were put on agenda almost at the same time in 1978. It was determined on the 3rd Plenary Session of the 11th Central Committee of the Communist Party of China that the emphasis should be shifted to the economic construction in the new historical period and banks would go through a succession of reforms with the financial system covering institutional, business range, capital management and loan systems.

6. 2. 1 Establishment of the System of Deposit Monetary Banks

A. Establishment of Specialized Banks and Preliminary Confirmation of the Function of Central Bank

Agricultural Bank of China reestablished in June 1979 (which was originally the Rural Financial Bureau of the People's Bank of China). Bank of China, which used to be the International Business Department of the People's Bank of China, separated from it. The People's Construction Bank of China (which was later changed to China Construction Bank) upgraded into a first class bank (it used to be a unit of the departmental level subordinate to the Ministry of Finance). After the People's Bank of China executed the function of Central Bank, the Industrial & Commercial Bank of China set up in January 1984, which dealt in the business of industrial and commercial credit and deposit separated from the Central Bank. People's Insurance Company of China became an independent operation group and disconnected from the People's Bank of China. Up to this point, the People's Bank of China had been divided into six parts, so the original one was divided into six financial institutions. The "highly centralized unification" by the People's Bank of China in the first 30 years after the founding of PRC was gone forever.

Head Office of the People's Bank of China Located on Chang'an Avenue

B. The Establishment of Shareholding Banks

Pushed by the reform and opening up, the Bank of Communications was reorganized to become a nationwide comprehensive shareholding bank which was dominated by public ownership in July 1986. From then on, twelve shareholding banks were set up successively including CITIC Industrial Bank, China Merchants Bank, Shenzhen Development Bank, Yantai Housing Savings Bank, Bengbu Housing Savings Bank, Fujian Industrial Bank, Guangdong Development Bank, China Everbright Bank, Huaxia Bank, Shanghai Pudong Development Bank, Hainan Development Bank and Minsheng Bank. By the end of 1996, these thirteen shareholding banks possessed 3, 748 institutions and 85, 500 employees.

The birth of shareholding banks created feasibility of the introduction of a competitive mechanism under the "wholly state-owned" ownership system. At the same time, the establishment and development of shareholding commercial banks contributed to the exploration of experiences of commercialization for the state-owned banks. But in terms of the stock equity structure, operation mechanism and administrative structure, there was no essential difference between the shareholding banks and specialized banks at that time.

C. The Restoration of Rural Credit Cooperatives

The development of rural financial institutions underwent two stages in China. The first stage was from 1977 to 1984, which was the restoration period of rural finance in China. In 1977, the State Council issued *Several Regulations Concerning Rectifying and Strengthening the Work of Banks*, which specified clearly that the rural credit cooperatives (abbreviated as "RCC" hereafter) were under the administration of the People's Bank of China. In 1979, the State Council specified in Notice Concerning the Restoration of Agricultural Bank of China that Agricultural Bank of China would concentrate on handling rural credit, manage the rural credit cooperatives, which would become the basic institutions of Agricultural bank of China. Due to the fact that all the deposit and loan businesses of Agricultural bank of China were arranged according to the instructive planning of the country at that time, this kind of planning economic instruction conspicuously did not conform to the need of the rural financial development. So, in the following 20 years, the problems of the reform of rural financial development had not been solved completely.

From 1985, the rural financial system of China entered into a rapid development stage and the reform of rural credit cooperatives kept moving forward. By the end of 1995, the rural credit cooperatives with independent accounting across the whole country amounted to 50, 219 and the number of county union cooperatives reached 2, 409. Owners' equity reached RMB 63. 2 billion, among which the paid-in capital was RMB 37. 8 billion and the total assets reached RMB 985. 7 billion. The balance of all kinds of deposits was RMB 717. 3 billion and the savings deposit was RMB 616. 9 billion, taking up more than 60% of the rural savings. All kinds of loans reached RMB 517. 6 billion, which accounted for more than 60% of the whole agricultural production loans, more than 80% of the framer's loans and more than 70% of the loans of township enterprises.

6. 2. 2   Establishment and Development of Trust Companies

The China International Trust and Investment Corporation (abbreviated as "CITIC" hereafter) was announced to setup in Beijing in October 1979, symbolizing the official restoration of the trust industry in China. In the same month, the head office of Bank of China took the lead in building the Trust Consulting Department and the Trust Consulting Company of Bank of China was later structured on the basis of the former. The primary objective of the establishment of CITIC at the very beginning was to explore the new channels of introduction of foreign capital and financing outside the bank. On the other hand, it aimed at introducing new forms of elements with certain market regulating function to push the reform of economic and financial systems outside the highly-centralized planning economy and the traditional financial system.

The State Council did not clearly specify the definition of trust business in the *Notice of Pushing the Economic Union* nor did it elaborate how to carry out such a business. So, the first trust company after the restoration of the trust industry and the founding of PRC started on the path of mixed operation dominated by banking business and the simultaneous development of the financial industry. Although the branches of the People's Bank of China launched the trial trust business in the economically developed cities one after another, most of the varieties were employed by the banks as the tool to break through the credit planning management. By the end of 1981, 241 cities in 21 provinces throughout the country launched trust businesses successively. The rapid development of trust institutions, especially the financial trust institutions in the short term, brought about the phenomenon of decentralized fund, disordered business, scrambling for capital with the original bank business and grabbing turf. This resulted in the large scale improvement and rectification carried out four times by the central government on the trust companies from 1982 to 1993. The incentive of every improvement and rectification initiative was to stop the violation of capital absorption by the trust companies.

6. 2. 3   Initial Establishment of Financial Market

A. Currency Market

The currency market in China sprang up at the beginning of the 1980s. Seen from the varieties of transaction, the currency market mainly involved inter-bank borrowing, buy-back and bill market.

In 1982, the People's Bank of China initiated the implementation of "three bills plus one certificate" (bill of exchange, promissory note, check and letter of credit), which marked the beginning of the bill market in China. In the same year, Shanghai took The lead in carrying out the business of acceptance and discounting of bills and the People's Bank of China began to make a trial on the business of rediscounting the bills. The acceptance and discounting of commercial bills basically ceased from 1988 to 1995 in China due to the fact that the credit system was seriously destroyed so that the parties to a bill worried about the emergence of "triangular debts". Plus, the absence of experience in manipulation and management of the commercial banks, the violation of regulation, and fake bills were rampant. All the commercial banks basically stopped the bill business in 1988.

Inter-bank borrowing market was the earliest organized currency market formed in China. The original target of the construction of inter-bank borrowing market was conceived in the short-term horizontal capital regulation between financial institutions. But in the initial stage of financial system reform, the function of the currency market for the short-term capital transaction alienated gradually. Before 1984, the surplus or deficiency of capital between banks could only be regulated vertically by administrative means. The layout of a new financial network with the two-level banking system came into shape in October 1984. After the start-up, the amount of the inter-bank borrowing was small and did not achieve scale. Until the 1990s, with the improvement of the macro-surroundings, the inter-bank borrowing market turned out to be active accordingly.

With the development of inter-bank borrowing achieving scale, the buy-back market began to sprout. The earliest buy-back of treasury bonds initiated from 1988, but the response from the market was indifferent because of improper preparation. In order to promote the circulation of treasury bonds, after repeated argumentation and thorough preparation, the STAQ [1] system commenced the trial operation of the business of buy-back of treasury bonds in July 1991 and gradually reversed the sluggish situation of transaction of treasury bonds in the organized market.

B. Bond Market

The first issuance of treasury bonds was at the end of 1949 after the founding of PRC and this type of government bonds issued only 6 times before it ceased in 1958. The Ministry of Finance renewed the issuance of treasury bonds 22 years later in 1981 in order to make up for the financial deficit. Ever since then, the issuing mode of treasury bonds transformed from the original administrative distribution to selling to residents relying on the counter of the banks. The secondary market of the transaction of treasury bonds came into shape accordingly.

The issuing of the corporate bond was later than that of treasury bonds. Some local enterprises conducted financing by spontaneously raising funds from society or employees inside the enterprises, which was similar to the issuing of corporate bonds. This was 1984. Afterwards, the scale of local corporate bonds enlarged rapidly. In order to standardize the corporate bond market which developed so quickly, the Chinese government continuously strengthened the administrative control. Unfortunately, that did not restrain the enthusiasm of issuing corporate bonds . Under the circumstance of an unsound legal system and social credit system, the violations of regulation pertaining to issuing corporate bonds became a problem as it grew in scale, which led to more severe supervision. With tougher administrative control, the varieties of corporate bonds which used to flourish declined swiftly and the issuing scale decreased sharply.

C. Stock Market

1982 to 1992 witnessed the budding and spontaneous development stage of the stock market in China. In this stage, there were no unitary administrative measures or regulations for the issuance and transaction nor a uniform entity of supervision for stocks, a new emergence. Under the extremely loose circumstance, the entity for issuing stocks covered all types of enterprises including state-owned, collective, big-sized and small-sized businesses. The places for transaction in

---

1   STAQ System: the National Securities Transaction Automatic Quotation System. It is a comprehensive over-the-counter transaction market based on computer networks to conduct the transaction of negotiable securities. The system's core operation is located in Beijing.

people's memory involved the informal civil "fair" and the more formal counter market and the formal exchange. The stocks for transaction included individual shares as well as "corporate shares" [1] with very evident Chinese characteristics.

"Feilo Acoustics Co. , Ltd. " was the first company to issue stocks publicly, on November 18, 1984 after the reform and opening up in China. After that, the stock market in China zigzagged as it moved forward with twists and turns. With the birth of A-share denominated by RMB, B-share, the transaction of which was denominated by foreign currency, came to the world as well. The first B-share emerged on November 30, 1991, which was issued to overseas investors by Shanghai Vacuum Electron Devices Co. , Ltd.

For the stock market in China, two dates will be mentioned again and again. One is November 26, 1990 when the Shanghai Stock Exchange was established. The other is December 1, 1990 on which the Shenzhen Stock Exchange was founded.

The establishment of Shanghai Stock Exchange and Shenzhen Stock Exchange can be called the milestone event in the history of financial development in China. Direct financing became an indispensable part of the financial system, which greatly enriched the financial structure of China.

The Hall of Shanghai Stock Exchange

---

1   Corporate share: It refers to shares formed by the investment of the legal person of enterprises or institutions and social groups with the qualification as legal persons with their disposable property in conformity of law under the non-listed circulation equity of shareholding limited companies.

Shenzhen Stock Exchange

6. 3   The Deepening Development of Financial Institutions and Financial Market in China

Entering the 1990s, the situation of "unitary domination" in banking was broken by the establishment of Shanghai Stock Exchange and Shenzhen Stock Exchange. Especially since the 21st century, with the thriving development of the financial market including stock, bond, currency market and so on, the diversified financing system in China gradually came into being. The complementary development of channels of direct and indirect financing pushed the whole promotion of the financial institutions and financial market in China.

6. 3. 1   Reform and Development of Chinese Banking

Thanks to the favorable opportunity of deepening of reform and opening up and the sustained high growth of the economy, China timely accomplished the stripping of the bad assets of the main commercial banks and the supplementation of capital before the ending of the WTO transitional period. China reconstructed the capital basis of banks to create favorable conditions for the subsequent shareholding system reform and going public. According to statistics from the China Banking Regulatory Commission, the total domestic capital of RMB and foreign currencies of financial institutions in Chinese banks increased from RMB 27,660 billion to RMB 95,300 billion between 2003 and 2010, growing 2.45 times in seven years. The total liabilities ascended from RMB 26,590 billion to RMB 89,470 billion and owners' equity went up from RMB 1,060 billion to RMB 5,830 billion. The market value of Industrial & Commercial Bank of

China and China Construction Bank amounted to USD 233. 5 billion and USD 220 billion respectively in 2010, which occupied the first and second place in the ranking of market value of global banking.

A. Shareholding System Reform of State-owned Commercial Banks

China officially joined the WTO on December 11, 2001 which meant that Chinese-owned banks would compete with foreign-owned banks under the same environment after the five-year transitional period starting from that date. The entry into the WTO increased the urgency of further deepening the reform of the wholly state-owned commercial banks.

By the end of 2003, the Chinese government decided to choose the Bank of China and China Construction Bank to be the first trial entities for shareholding system reform and injected USD 45 billion to the two banks through the Central Huijin Company on December 30 that year. The two banks initially used the capital, reserve and the current year profit to write off all the lost-loans and loss from the non-credit capital (RMB 407 billion) and then stripped all the doubtful loans (RMB 278. 7 billion) to the capital management company. On the basis of financial reorganization, the two banks transformed from wholly state-owned to shareholding limited companies on August 26 and September 21, 2004 respectively.

China Construction Bank signed a subscription agreement with Bank of America and Singapore Temasek Holdings (PTE) Co. , Ltd. on June 17 and July 1, 2005. As per the agreement, the two strategic investors held 9% stake and 5. 1% stake of China Construction Bank respectively. With all the capital from the two strategic investors in place, the introduction of investment of private equity in China Construction Bank was completed and announced before the listing. China Construction Bank Corporation went public officially on the Hongkong Stock Exchange on October 27 and the total funds raised amounted to about HKD 62. 2 billion.

Bank of China signed strategic investment and cooperation agreement with Royal Bank of Scotland Group on August 18, 2005. Royal Bank of Scotland, together with another two cooperative partners, invested USD 3. 1 billion to purchase a 10% stake in Bank of China, among which Royal Bank of Scotland paid USD 1. 6 billion to purchase a 5. 16% stake while the investment bank of American-Merrill Lynch and Li Jiacheng made a joint investment of USD 1. 5 billion to purchase a 4. 84% stake. On August 31, Temasek invested USD 3. 1 billion to purchase a 10% stake of Bank of China through its wholly owned subsidiary – "Asia Financial Holdings Ltd. " United Bank of Switzerland invested

USD 500 million in Bank of China on September 27 and became the third strategic investor. Bank of China's stock was listed on the Hongkong Stock Exchange and Shanghai Stock Exchange on June 1 and July 5, 2006 successively. The total funds raised amounted to HKD 86 billion and HKD 20 billion respectively.

The shareholding system reform of the Industrial & Commercial Bank of China was initiated in April 2005 and the bank was officially renamed Industrial & Commercial Bank of China Ltd. on October 28, 2005. Overseas strategic investors were selected. Goldman Sachs Group, Allianz Group and American Express Company invested USD 3.78 billion to purchase about 10% stake, which was about 24.185 billion shares in January 2006. The Industrial & Commercial Bank of China signed the Strategic Investment and Cooperation Agreement with the National Social Security Fund Council and the latter invested RMB 18.028 billion to the former in June 2006. A-share and H-share of the Industrial & Commercial Bank of China were listed on the Shanghai Stock Exchange and Hongkong Stock Exchange on October 27, 2006 simultaneously, a pioneer event for the synchronous listing of A + H shares, and the funds raised amounting to RMB 26.622 billion and RMB 124.948 billion respectively.

Dust settled about the shareholding reform scheme of Agricultural Bank of China on October 2008 and the bank's shareholding system reform launched officially. The writing off of Agricultural Bank of China's bad debts of was in full swing from November 2008. On November 6, 2008, the Central Huijin Company officially injected RMB 130 billion into the bank and held its 50% stake, tying with the Ministry of Finance as the biggest shareholders of Agricultural Bank of China. Agricultural Bank of China Ltd. was formally founded on January 15, 2009 and the registered capital was RMB 260 billion. Agricultural Bank of China initiated its IPO (Initial Public Offerings) procedure on April 7, 2010 and 21 underwriters submitted elementary underwriting plans to the banking institution. On July 15 and 16 of the same year, Agricultural Bank of China officially listed on the Shanghai and Hongkong Stock Exchange. The total funds raised from A-share and H-share amounted to USD 22.1 billion, which broke the record set by Industrial & Commercial Bank of China.

B. The Development of Shareholding Commercial Banks

The organization of shareholding commercial banks was the inevitable result of China's financial system reform. In order to promote the overall servicing level of the financial industry, introduce a competition mechanism and explore the experiences of the reform and commercialization of state-owned banks, China set up some shareholding banks and regional commercial banks one after another beginning in 1986.

According to the requirement for reform of the economic system, The State Council approved the restoration of the establishment of the Bank of Communications on July 24, 1986 and Bank of Communications became the first national commercial bank with a shareholding system in China, but in reality it was the state-owned shareholding commercial bank. The first genuine national shareholding commercial bank whose shares were completely held by the enterprise legal person was China Merchants Bank, which was set up in Shenzhen Special Economic Zone on April 8, 1987. In the same year, CITIC Industrial Bank, with its stake held by China International Trust and Investment Corporation, was established. Since then, shareholding commercial banks including Shenzhen Development Bank, Yantai Housing Savings Bank, Fujian Industrial Bank and Guangdong Development Bank setup and did business in succession. From 1992 to 1996, China Everbright Bank, Huaxia Bank, Shanghai Pudong Development Bank, Hainan Development Bank and Minsheng Bank were setup one after another in China. Entering 2000, Yantai Housing Savings Bank, which was converted to Evergrowing Bank, together with the newly-established Zheshang Bank, The Bank of Bohai, Huishang Bank and CITIC Bank (formerly CITIC Industrial Bank), stepped into the parade of national shareholding commercial banks in succession.

Within the Chinese banking industry, shareholding banks have always been famous for their light burden and good quality of capital. But because of various reasons, like scale, the market position of shareholding banks was far from being the rival of the four big banks. In the 1980s, the shareholding banks at that time were quite fragile and could only played a supplementary role in filling the business gaps left by the four major national banks. Entering the 1990s, with the successive establishment of shareholding commercial banks like China Everbright Bank and Minsheng Bank, the institutions and business of shareholding banks expanded rapidly and their strength consolidated continuously. Especially during the past decade, in terms of the growth rate of capital and profit, the shareholding banks far outstripped the four major national banks. From January 1, 1998, the People's Bank of China canceled the quota control on the volume of loan increases by state-owned commercial banks. With the development of the economy in China, the degree of financial marketization was greatly enhanced and various financial institutions and financing channels emerged so that loans could not reflect the changes in the society's ability to pay. The credit capital management system characterized by "planning management, self pursuit of equilibrium, proportional management and indirect regulation" conducted radical reform on the credit capital management system characterized by "quota management". By the end of 2013, the national shareholding commercial banks in China amounted to 12 including CITIC Bank, China Everbright Bank, Huaxia Bank, Guangdong Development Bank, China Merchants Bank, Shanghai Pudong Development Bank, Industrial Bank, China Minsheng Bank, Evergrowing Bank, Zheshang Bank , the Bank of Bohai and Ping An Bank.

Since the reform and opening up, especially after the 21th century, the commercial banks in China had made remarkable progress in their development. However, there was no denying that a big gap still existed when compared with their international peers.

a. Profitability Still Needed to Be Promoted

From the profit point of view of the banks, the higher the loan-to-deposit ratio, the better. Interest should be paid for deposits, if there are more deposits than loans, it means that the cost for the banks is high and the income is low, therefore, the profitability is relatively poor. As commercial banks' aim is to make profits, they will try their utmost to increase the loan-to-deposit ratio. The Chinese banking industry used to pay arbitrarily to attract deposits, but is now distressed by the ever-decreasing loan-to-deposit ratio. After 2001, there was excess liquidity in Chinese commercial banks, which was highlighted by the trend of declining loan-to-deposit ratio. On one hand, social capital flooded into the domestic banks, increasing deposits sharply. On the other hand, housing, car and enterprise loans were declining, so banks could not loan out the money at hand. Since 1998, the annual deposit growth rate was higher than the loan growth rate (except for 2009 which was affected by the financial crisis). Entering 2010, the economy recovered and deposits rose again and excess liquidity swept back a second time. The huge difference between deposit and loan demonstrated that plenty of exercisable capital of the banks was in idle status, resulting in the decline of the profit level of the commercial banks. Moreover, compared with the large-scale banks worldwide, the profit margin of Chinese commercial banks still had a long way to go.

b. The Credit Capital Orientation Was Too Unitary

With the growth of economy, if the loans of commercial banks are too concentrated, the loans will mainly go to the privileged state-owned enterprises or official financial institutions and the utilizing efficiency of the credit capital that should serve various aspects of economy will be lowered. The too unitary orientation of credit capital will bring about two issues. One is low profit margins caused by excess capital of the state-owned enterprises. And credit is liable to be at risk, which could result in bad assets of the commercial banks coming into being. The primary assets of the Chinese commercial banks are loans and the bad assets of the banks are mainly non-performing loans. Non-performing loans vary with the change of macro-economic cycle, macro-regulation policy and the operation mode of the banks. The concentration of credit capital on large-scale national projects lays the seeds for bad assets. The second issue is the earnest aspiration from numerous medium and small-sized enterprises for capital. For most of the medium and small-sized enterprises in China, bank loans are the main financing means for them to acquire capital. Request for capital from these enterprises is characterized as "swift, small-scale and frequent". However, for the time being, the loan examining and approving mechanism of the Chinese commercial banks is unfavorable for the financing of medium and small-sized enterprises. In addition, the banks have relatively strict requirements for mortgages and relatively high credit level requirement from guarantors. Thus, medium and small-sized enterprises find it difficult to meet the standard specified by the banks. The above-mentioned three points bring about the problematic financing for medium and small-sized enterprises.

   c. Poor Internal Credit Management

Chinese commercial banks are facing up to the ever-increasing market risk, but in practice, the objective of risk management always simply comes down to security management. There is deviation in terms of direct supervision objectives and supervision efficiency is neglected so that the efficiency of bank supervision is low and the cost for supervision is too high. The commercial banks fail to take timely effective measures to defuse credit risk so that the possibility of banks having bad loans is increased. There exist lags in between every step of the following: exploring the risk, reacting to the risk, taking measures and producing the ultimate effects. In addition, the absence of effective risk analysis tools restricts the prediction and precaution of the potential risk to a great extent so that the prior control and coping ability of the credit risk by the bank is weakened.

Besides, inside of the commercial banks, the credit authority distribution is unreasonable, the punishment measures are unclear, the organizing structure of the personnel is unreasonable, the overall quality of the credit personnel is not very high, the mobility of credit personnel is too big and the credit risk information system is unsound. The above-mentioned, and other similar aspects, are to be perfected and promoted.

C. Three Policy Banks

China Development Bank, China Import & Export Bank and Agricultural

Development Bank of China are the three policy banks of China. Seen from the business operation, they mainly deal with low rate and long term policy loans and they have their specific clients and business objectives. Based on the initial establishment, the policy banks primarily play roles in the non-profit field to promote the implementation and execution of national policies. With the deepening of the market reform in China, the range of policy business shrank little by little so that the policy banks commenced trial on commercial business and the development of business demonstrated the tendency of diversification. Among them, the commercial operation of China Development Bank is the most outstanding.

The transformation from policy banks to commercialization was confirmed at the National Financial Conference in 2007. The first step was to push the reform and realize the overall commercial operation of China Development Bank to deal in medium and long term business. The further deepening of the internal reform of China Import & Export Bank and Agricultural Development Bank of China was conducted at the same time. It meant the gradual separation of the Chinese policy banks from the national finance. The policy banks would carry out commercial reform to achieve the ultimate target of independent operation, self-financing and self-assumption of risk as per their own conditions.

The reform scheme of China Development Bank was eventually approved by the State Council in February, 2008. According to the scheme, China Development Bank was oriented as a "commercial bank" and the main path of reform was initially designed as "reorganization-shareholding transformation-listing". China Development Bank Co., Ltd. was officially founded on December 15 in the same year. Hence, China Development Bank formally became a commercial bank and would gradually face the same regulatory treatment as other commercial banks. By the end of 2011, the total amount of capital in China Development Bank was RMB 3,821.2 billion and the bank became the fourth biggest banking institution in China.

D. The Internationalization of Chinese Banking

Since entering the WTO, China has been sticking to the reform and opening up policy of achieving equity, mutual benefits and win-win cooperation and continuously deepening the reform and opening up of the banking industry. Completely fulfilling the commitment of entering the WTO, the service level and the competitiveness of the whole banking industry have been significantly enhanced and the internationalization of Chinese banks has been furthered. One measure is to actively push forward the layout construction of overseas institutions and set up a global service network that matches the internationalization of China's economy. By the end of 2011, the policy banks and China Development Bank set up 6 overseas institutions and owned a stake in 2 overseas institutions. Five big commercial banks established 105 overseas institutions and purchased (or owned a stake in) 10 overseas institutions. Eight medium and small-sized commercial banks setup 14 overseas institutions and 2 medium and small-sized commercial banks purchased (or owned a stake in) 5 overseas institutions. The second measure is to increase the capital supplementation channels to speed up the pace of conforming to the international practice by means of listing overseas. By the end of 2011, 5 big-sized commercial banks, 3 shareholding commercial banks and 1 rural commercial bank publicly listed on the Hongkong Stock Exchange. The third measure is to strengthen the business tandem to set up the interchanging servicing network of mutual tandem and mutual support among the head office, domestic and overseas branch institutions and overseas agents so that the servicing coverage range can be expanded. The increasing numbers of institutions of local head offices of overseas banks, branch institutions and sub-branching institutions were 21, 183 and 389 respectively. The number of cities with the establishment of these banks expanded from 20 to 50. One hundred and twenty-five business sites were founded in the Midwest and Northeast regions. The fourth measure is the sustainable and stable increase of the business input. After the outbreak of the International Financial Crisis, there were more than 40 overseas banks in total by then actively providing consultation and service for Chinese enterprises to "go globally" by introducing products and services suitable for the local demand. On the other hand, they set up the role model in terms of management conception and management method to promote the overall servicing level of local banks. In addition, by the end of 2011, the regulatory grace period of the loan-to-deposit ratio terminated for foreign corporate banks and all the 39 overseas corporate banks reached the standard. By then, all the regulatory grace periods for overseas banks in China ended completely and the uniform regulatory standard of both the Chinese and overseas banks was realized.

6. 3. 2　Chinese Insurance Industry of Rapidly Sprang up

A. The Exploration and Initial Formation of the Development Path of Insurance with Chinese Characteristics

Entering the 21ˢᵗ century, with China's entry into the WTO and the introduction of a series of measures to deepen reforms and enlarge opening up, "reform, opening up and development" became the primary features of the development path of the insurance industry with Chinese characteristics and the development path of insurance with Chinese characteristics initially formed. See Figure 6. 1.

Since 2000, the industrial chain of Chinese insurance has been gradually perfected and a complete industrial chain including insurance group, professional insurance company and insurance agency has initially come into being. Firstly, the integrated operation of insurance group of China was promoted. Ping An Insurance Company of China and China Pacific Insurance Company setup the collectivized operation architecture in 2000. Since 2003, People's Insurance Company of China (PICC), China Life Insurance Company and China Reinsurance (Group) Corporation setup insurance groups one after another and covered all the fields of the insurance industry successively. Secondly, professional insurance companies were developed. A procession of professional insurance companies were built in succession including professional health insurance, professional car insurance, professional liability insurance, professional agricultural insurance, professional endowment insurance and so forth. Thirdly, the insurance agency market was encouraged. The first insurance brokering company—Jiang Tai Insurance Brokering Company established in 2000. The rapid development of part-time agency, especially the banking insurance channel, has become the main channel of the development of insurance business in China.

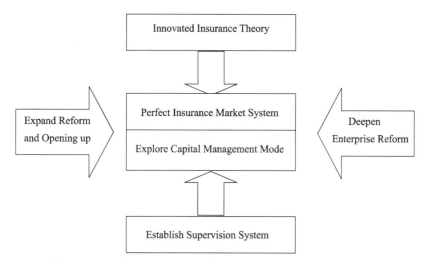

Figure 6. 1   Systematic Exploration of Development Path of Chinese Insurance

B. Prospects for Development of Insurance Industry in China

The stable and rapid growth of the national economy has laid a solid foundation for the insurance industry in China to keep the fast – growing development. Over the past three decades, the national economy in China has maintained an average 9.7% high growth rate and by 2020, the GDP per capita in China will stride into the ranks with other upper-middle income countries. At that time, the urbanization will be greatly enhanced, the dualistic economy between urban and rural areas will be obviously improved and the various objectives of establishing the overall well-off society will be basically achieved. Accordingly, the Chinese insurance industry will walk on the connotative development path with self-innovation as the main body to realize the fundamental change of the development pattern.

Seen from the capital scale of the insurance industry, the Chinese insurance industry plays a vital role in the collection of social capital and financial management along with the development and expansion of the main body of insurance and the insurance industry as a whole. The total capital of the insurance industry in China is expected to demonstrate an explosive growth tendency. It is predicted that by 2020, the total capital of insurance industry is expected to exceed RMB 20,000 billion and China will become one of the three largest insurance markets worldwide.

Among the world's top 500 of 2012, Chinese insurance enterprises occupied four seats including China Life Insurance Company, Ping An Insurance Company of China, PICC and China Pacific Insurance Company. In the future five to ten years' time, there will be more Chinese insurance enterprises to step out of China to open up the international insurance market by means of purchasing stake, merging and establishing new institutions. And we believe more insurance tycoons of world-class rank will emerge in China in the future.

6.3.3 The Rough Road for the Capital Market in China

A. Comprehensive Management and Nurturing the Superior and Eliminating the Inferior of the Securities Industry

Share split reform, a significant breakthrough in the Chinese capital market system initiated in 2005. Before the reform, state-owned shares could not be circulated and the equity of the listed companies were deliberately divided into circulating shares and non-tradable shares so that the management structure of the listed companies was flawed and the issues of same shares with different rights and dominating position of state-owned shares were highlighted. The successful launch of the reform of share split removed the institutional obstacles which had perplexed the development of A-share market for many years and enabled the Chinese securities market to enter into a brand new development stage. New regulations concerning key businesses like self-operation of securities companies, treasury bonds buy-back, securities issuance of listed companies and so on successively emerged from the second half of 2005 to the first half of 2006. The formulation of rules and regulations concerning risk supervision, risk disposal and net capital calculation of securities companies was accelerated as well.

With the overall pushing of the assessment of standardized and innovative securities companies, innovation and reorganization became two major themes of the securities industry, which intensified the fragmentation and competitive environment of securities companies. The modernized securities companies vigorously promoted all kinds of innovative businesses while the securities companies with plenty of problems left over from history and having difficulties in operation carried out reorganization. The Central Bank and China Securities Regulatory Commission set up China Jianyin Investment Ltd. and China Securities Regulatory Commission Investors Protection Fund Corporation to implement the reorganization of securities companies with relatively bigger scale. Galaxy Securities, China CITIC Construction and other big securities companies reappeared after reorganization and innovative securities companies like CITIC Securities and China Merchants Securities enlarged their scale of business by acting as the custodian of the weak securities companies. Reorganization directly led to the further enhancement of the concentration of the whole industry. Market share of the brokering business of the top 10 securities companies was quite close to 60% and market share of the underwriting business of the top 10 securities companies was very close to 90% by the end of 2012. And the top 10 securities companies almost swept all the capital management business.

The capital quality and the profit of the whole securities industry had been evidently improved. Seen from the income structure, the income from brokering, underwriting and self-operated business was the primary source of the income of securities companies. In 2012, the brokering income accounted for 60%. After the accomplishment of share split reform and with the restart of initial public offering, additional offerings and rationed shares and the gradual opening up of the underwriting of short-term financing bonds, the percentage of income of underwriting gradually increased to 13%. The innovating business of securities companies set sail rapidly and new business-like collection of financial products, securitization of capital and short-term financing bonds made pioneering progress and the innovating securities companies took early lead in these businesses.

B. Significant Policies and Reform Measures of Capital Market

Chinese capital market is an "emerging plus transitional" market which develops with the reform of the economic system. Due to the overall environment of the initial establishment and limitation of the system design of the market itself, the Chinese capital market has accumulated some deep-rooted problems and structural contradictions. The problems and contradictions restricted the effective play of market function and hindered the market from further development. Over the past several years, China Securities Regulatory Commission launched a series of reform measures aimed at perfecting the basic market system and resuming the function of the market to push forward the profound changes of the Chinese capital market.

a. Share Split Reform

Share split primarily originated from the inconsistent recognition of the shareholding system and function and orientation of the capital market in the early stage. The reform of the management system of state-owned assets was in the initial phase so that the conception of operation of the state-owned capital was not established yet. The settlement of share split is to realize the transformation of mechanism, which is conducted through a consultative mechanism of balancing the benefits between circulating shareholders and non-tradable shareholders to eliminate the systematic difference of the transfer of shares in the A-share market. In the reform, consideration is employed to balance the mutual benefits between circulating shareholders and non-tradable shareholders. The smooth advancement of the reform of share split solved the problems concerning interests split and price split of state-owned shares, corporate shares and circulating shares so that all sorts of shareholders could enjoy the same rights of listing circulation and stock return. The price of all kinds of stocks is worked out by the uniform market mechanism and the secondary market begins to reflect the actual value of the listed companies and becomes the common benefits basis for all sorts of shareholders. Share split reform lays a marketization basis for the optimization of resource distribution of the Chinese capital market so that there is no essential difference between the Chinese capital market and the international market in terms of the market basis level.

b. Overall Promotion of the Quality of Listed Companies

Over the past several years, the China Securities Regulatory Commission has launched special activities to further promote the standardized operation, strengthen the management and increase the quality of listed companies. The activities primarily include perfecting the supervision system of listed companies, standardizing management of companies, clearing up the capital of the listed companies which has been illegally occupied and setting up an incentive mechanism of equity. With regard to the long-term accumulated problems of securities companies, the Commission carries out comprehensive administration on the securities companies by means of a three-pronged approach, namely risk disposal, daily supervision and pushing the development of the whole industry.

c. Reform of Issuance System

Part of the reform was to make the issuance examination and verification system transparent. In 2004, the recommendation system of main underwriters for issuing and listing was converted to a sponsorship system and the sponsoring institutions and accountability mechanism of sponsoring representatives were set up. The regulation of keeping the identity of the commissioners of the Securities Issuance Examination Commission confidential was cancelled in the same year. The principle of assuming respective responsibility and risk of the market participators under the examination and approval system was implemented and the first step of achieving the objective reforming the issuing system marketization was realized.

The restriction of the securities issuance market was consolidated. The successive launches of a procession of managerial approaches to securities issuance and a system of corresponding complementary regulations formed the IPO system under the full circulation pattern. Thus, issuance efficiency was enhanced.

The pricing mechanism of issuance was marketized. The examination and approval of price-fixing of issuance of shares were cancelled and an inquiry system was implemented. In 2006, the links of inquiry, price fixing and allocation of shares were put under key emphasis for further standardization. As a result, the inquiry system was perfected and the supervision on activities of issuers, securities companies, securities servicing institutions and investors engaging in securities issuance was strengthened.

C. The Development and Evolution of Bond Market

The circulation market of Chinese bonds started from the restoration of government's issuing treasury bonds in 1981. It has undergone three main stages during the development including the physical bond counter market, floor trading bond market represented by Shanghai Stock Exchange and over-the-counter bond market represented by inter-bank bond market.

a. Physical Bond Counter Market (1988−1993)

The start of the Chinese bond market can be dated back to the time when 61 cities were chosen by the Ministry of Finance in 1988 as the trial places for the circulation and transfer of treasury bonds. It was the over-the-counter trade of cash bonds at bank counters and also the official origin of the Chinese treasury bonds circulation market.

The Shanghai Stock Exchange was founded in December 1990. It commenced to accept the custody of physical bonds and conducted book-entry bond trading after opening an account in the exchange to form the market layout with the coexistence of floor trading and over-the-counter trading. But at that time, the bond market was mainly characterized by the fact that there was no uniform custody institution of the bearer's physical bond. Custody was dispersed to custody institutions after issuance so that the transaction could only be conducted in the place where the custody institution was located and could not be done trans-regionally.

After 1994, the excessive issuance and short selling of treasury bonds in the form of custody policies became popular and the market risk was very high. The physical bond counter transfer market was closed down due to the over-issuance of fake treasury bonds custody policies. Regional treasury bonds buy-back markets represented by Wuhan Securities Trading Center and so forth were ordered to close down by the department in charge because of fake treasury bonds mortgage and violation of capital operation in 1995.

b. Floor Trading Bond Market Represented by Shanghai Stock Exchange (1994 – 1997)

In 1994, treasury bonds futures trading was launched in the exchange and the spot transaction of bonds in the bond market enlarged, obviously because of the effect of the futures trading. The situation maintained to May 1995 and because of the "327" treasury bonds event afterwards, the treasury bonds futures market was shut down and the transaction volume precipitously shrank. The State Council officially ceased all the over-the-counter bond market in August 1995 and the securities exchange became the only legal bond market in China.

The Ministry of Finance issued book-entry treasury bonds in trial places for the securities exchange market in 1995. By 1996, book-entry treasury bonds were issued in large quantities in the Shanghai Stock Exchange and Shenzhen Stock Exchange. At the same time, with the spread of the buy-back transaction of bonds, the exchange bond market system was initially formed.

In the first half of 1997, with the surge of the stock market, a great deal of bank capital flew into the stock market to make it overheated by means of bond buy-back in the exchange. Hence, according to the unified deployment of the State Council, the People's Bank of China made a decision for all the commercial banks to quit the bond market in the Shanghai Stock Exchange and Shenzhen Stock Exchange completely. This symbolized the development of the floor trading bond market represented by the Shanghai Stock Exchange was affected to a relatively large extent. The exploration of new patterns of organization and transaction in the Chinese bond market was required.

c. Over-the-counter Bond Market Represented by Inter-bank Bond Market (1999- Now)

After June 1997, commercial banks withdrew from the exchange bond market and the treasury bonds, financing bonds and policy financial bonds held by these banks were under the custody of the Central Government Treasury bonds Registration and Clearing Corporation. The buy-back of bonds and buying and selling of cash bonds could be conducted, so the inter-bank bond market commenced.

In 1999, the Ministry of Finance, China Development Bank and other policy banks issued treasury bonds and policy financial bonds in the inter-bank bond market. The total amount was RMB 442. 6 billion, accounting for 74% of the total issuance of bonds in China that year. In 2000, the same institutions issued RMB 390. 4 billion bonds again in the inter-bank bond market, accounting for 62% of the total issuance of bonds in China that year. With the enlargement of the scale of the inter-bank bond market, the over-the-counter bond market gradually evolved into the leading force in the Chinese bond market.

After 2001, the departments in charge such as The People's Bank of China, China Securities Regulatory Commission and Ministry of Finance accelerated the unification and interconnection between the exchange bond market and inter-bank bond market. In the first place, the unification of the two participating institutions of the two markets was a priority. In the second place, the Ministry of Finance began trying to issue trans-market treasury bonds (trans-exchange and trans-inter-bank bond market).

It can be said that the national inter-bank bond market constructed by the People's Bank of China in June 1997 is the primary constituent of the Chinese bond market at present, which makes up the basic characteristic of the Chinese bond market. The construction and development of the Chinese bond market highlights the characteristics of China's market-oriented reform. The construction and development of the inter-bank bond market is the rare successful case of government's building market in the history of China's economic system reform.

Compared with the inter-bank bond market in China, the development of the corporate bond market was full of frustrations. It experienced brilliance at the beginning of the 1990s and the low tide of 1994 and 1995. Generally, the Chinese corporate bond market moved forward from non-standardized to standardized and the issuance mode and interest setting strode forward to the marketization direction. The influence and scale of the corporate bond market gradually enlarged. Although, in contrast with the total amount of treasury bonds, it is in the absolute weak position and the fluctuation of price is basically subordinate to the trend of treasury bonds, it has unique features. The development of the Chinese corporate bond can be summarized into the following four stages.

(a) Budding Stage (1984 – 1986)

As mentioned above, from 1984, financing of enterprises emerged by enterprises' raising funds spontaneously from society or inside the enterprises, similar to issuing corporate bond. According to rough estimation, by the end of 1986, the total issuing amount of this kind of bond had reached some RMB 10 billion. During this period of time, the country had not conducted standardized management on it and there was no corresponding law or legislation, either.

(b) Rapid Development Stage (1987 – 1992)

On March 27, 1987, the State Council promulgated Provisional Regulations on the Management of Corporate Bonds which specified that the issuance of enterprise bonds should be under the examination and approval of the People's Bank of China and the State Planning Commission. At the end of 1989, the State Planning Commission and the People's Bank of China jointly issued *Notice on Examination and Approval Procedures of the Limit Declaration of the Issuance of Corporate Bonds* which specified that the limit of the issuance of bonds by the enterprise should be declared and incorporated into the national annual bond issuance plan. From 1989 to 1992 the annual issuance plan for corporate bonds was RMB 7. 5 billion, RMB 2 billion, RMB 25 billion and RMB 35 billion respectively. The issuance scale rapidly enlarged and corporate bonds could be put into seven categories including national investment bond, national investment corporate bond, central enterprise bond, local enterprise bond, local investment corporate bond, residential construction bond and internal bond.

(c) Basically Halting Stage (1993 – 1995)

On August 2, 1993, the State Council revised and promulgated the Regulations on the Management of Corporate Bonds and began to standardize the issuance of bonds. On December 29, 1993, the National People's Congress issued the *Company Law of the People's Republic of China* to standardize the issuance of corporate bonds. In 1993, the corporate bond issuance plan was altered to be settled by new bank loans. Varieties of corporate bonds can be generalized into central enterprise and local enterprise bonds. At the beginning of 1993, the country's corporate bond issuance plan was RMB 49 billion but the actual issuance was more than RMB 2 billion. The total issuance volume from 1993 to 1995 was RMB 18. 5 billion.

(d) Standardized Development Stage (1996 — Now)

The total issuance amount of corporate bonds from 1996 to 1998 was RMB 93 billion which was mainly arranged to be used on a batch of key national construction projects such as railway, power, petrifaction, petroleum, Three Gorges Project and so on. In November 1999, the State Council sanctioned the State Planning Commission to conduct unified management on the examination and approval of issuance of corporate bonds and the *Regulations on the Management of Corporate Bonds* began to be revised. On September 18, 2000, the amended *Regulations on the Management of Corporate Bonds* was submitted to the State Council. The total issuance amount of the corporate bonds after official approval in 2001 was RMB 24. 4 billion.

Up to now, the Chinese bond market has included varieties of treasury bonds, corporate bonds, government agency bonds and so on(see Figure 6. 2) .

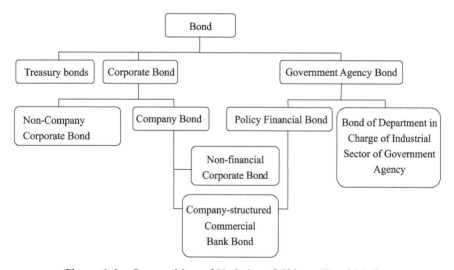

Figure 6. 2   Composition of Varieties of Chinese Bond Market

D. The In-depth Development of Currency Market

a. Inter- bank Borrowing Market

The development of the Chinese currency market started from the construction of the inter-bank borrowing market at the beginning of the 1980s. In 1992, "arbitrary inter-bank borrowing" was cleared up and in 1995 the securities buy-back market was rectified. In January 1996, the People's Bank of China set up the national inter-bank borrowing center in Shanghai. By then, the two-layer network of the inter-bank borrowing market came into being. One was the A-level network composed of institutions such as all the national commercial banks, shareholding commercial banks, urban commercial banks and provincial financing centers. The other was the B-level network with the participation of the branch institutions of commercial banks and other financial institutions tied to local financing centers. In 1996, the total transaction of the national inter-bank borrowing market amounted to RMB 587. 1 billion among which the A-level network achieved RMB 219. 9 billion accounting for 37. 5% and the B-level network achieved RMB 367. 1 billion accounting for 62. 5% . In the two levels, the transaction volume concerning financing centers accounted for 70% . Although the unitary currency market was set up in form, the orientation and function of the inter-bank borrowing market and bond market did not undergo substantial change. As well, the too large inter-bank borrowing volume contained big risk and the bond market trading shrank.

Financing centers played important roles under that circumstance. On one hand, they provided information agency service for the local medium and small sized financial institutions on funds borrowing. On the other hand, as the binding mechanism between big banks and medium and small sized financial institutions, they gathered parts into a whole or broke the whole into parts in terms of amount of capital by means of lending or borrowing of their self-operating capital. But there were some visible problems, especially when the real estate bubble burst. There was a lot of overdue loan capital to highlight the risk of lending and borrowing. In the light of the problems exposed by the financing centers, the Central Bank determined to cease its self-operation business in the fourth quarter of 1997 and commenced to collect the overdue loans. In June 1998, on the basis of clearing up the overdue lending capital, the financing centers across the country were cancelled. Afterwards, the problems of poor information, unclear credit and mismatch between supply and demand arose in the inter-bank borrowing market which led to a dramatic decline of the transaction volume in the inter-bank borrowing market. In 1998, the credit borrowing amount of the national inter-bank borrowing market was just RMB 98. 9 billion which showed an 86% decrease compared with the previous year. Because of new problems occurring in the inter-bank borrowing market, a nationwide uniform market open to all the financial institutions was gradually established from the second half of 1998. Commercial banks with good reputation became the main participators of the inter-bank borrowing market and the transactions between medium and small sized financial institutions and between medium and small sized financial institutions and commercial banks were more connected by the transaction forms such as agency business, bond buy-back and so on.

Since then, development of the inter-bank borrowing market embodied the following aspects. One was to enlarge the electronic transaction information system of the national inter-bank borrowing market. The second was to encourage the commercial banks to carry out financing agent business to provide convenience for the financing of medium and small sized financial institutions. The third was to absorb the eligible securities companies and securities investment funds to participate in the inter-bank borrowing market.

In 1998, under the spread and deepening of the Asian Financial Crisis and the continuing turbulence of the international financial market, the healthy operation of the Chinese currency market had guarded against financial risk and played a proactive role in safeguarding the smooth implementation of currency and fiscal policy. Having experienced the Asian Financial Crisis, the Chinese inter-bank borrowing market stepped into the steady development phase since 2000. Especially with the official launch of Shibor [1] as the basic interest rate system in 1997, the position of the inter-bank borrowing market in the domestic currency market changed radically. The transaction volume underwent a magnitudinal leap that year and reached the level of more than RMB 10,000 billion and kept a relatively fast development speed afterwards. In 2011 and 2012, the annual transaction scale of the inter-bank borrowing market reached RMB 33,000 billion and RMB 46,700 billion respectively.

b. Inter-bank Bond Market

As mentioned before, the Chinese inter-bank bond market was converted from the treasury bonds buy-back market. The Chinese treasury bonds buy-back transaction trial started from 1991. The original intention of the traders taking part in treasury bonds buy-back was to find a financing channel to replace the original illegal borrowing channel plus the lagging and out-of-control supervision in the very initial period after the establishment of the treasury bonds buy-back market. (The management of treasury bonds buy-back transactions was dominated by the local government where the market was located.) The treasury bonds buy-back market was basically in a "laissez-faire" situation for a very long period of time.

In 1997, the People's Bank of China standardized the treasury bonds buy-back market and required all wholly state-owned commercial banks, shareholding

---

1   Shibor, Shanghai Interbank Offered Rate, officially operated from January 4, 2007 which marked the comprehensive start of the fostering of the benchmarking interest rate in the Chinese currency market.

commercial banks and urban commercial banks to cease the buy-back of securities and cash bond in the securities exchange. It was stipulated that buy-back should be conducted in the inter-bank borrowing market nationwide, so the Chinese inter-bank bond market came into shape and became a closed market established for inter-bank financing by means of bond buy-back and cash bond trading. One important objective for the establishment of the market relied on blocking the channel for the violated entry of bank capital into stock market, controlling speculation in the stock market, rectifying financial order, controlling financial risk and ensuring the steady and healthy operation of finance. After 1998, the inter-bank bond market had exceeded the inter-bank borrowing market in the national inter-bank market and gradually became the main part of the currency market. In 2000, the buy-back of the inter-bank bond market concluded transactions of RMB 1,578.2 billion and the average daily growth was 299%.

After that, the Chinese inter-bank bond market took on a relatively faster development that could be demonstrated by the following aspects. In the first place, the main participants were on the increase. According to the statistics of the Central Bank, by the end of 2012, the number of main participants in the inter-bank bond market amounted to 11,287, an increase of 415 compared with number at the end of 2011. Various financial institutions and non-financial institutions constituted the multi-level investor structure with market makers as the center, financial institutions as the main bodies and the joint participation of investors from other institutions. The inter-bank market had become the vital platform for financing and risk management conducted by various market main bodies. In 2012, with the further enrichment of inter-bank market investors, main bodies of non-financial enterprise investment showed a relatively bigger increase. The trials of overseas institutions investing in the Chinese inter-bank bond market saw steady progress. By the end of 2012, there were 100 overseas institutions approved to enter into the inter-bank bond market including overseas central banks, international financial institutions, sovereign wealth funds, clearing banks from Hongkong and Macao, overseas participating banks, overseas insurance institutions, RQFII (Qualified Foreign Institutional Investors who can use RMB to purchase securities) and so forth. In the second place, with the continuous standardization of the market, the basic construction became better and approached perfection day by day. At the same time, the construction of basic infrastructure such as a bond custody system and transaction system was continuously accelerated and the bond settling system and capital clearing system also improved as it reached for perfection. In the third place, the transaction scale was on the increase. Since 2000, the tradable varieties and quantities of securities in the inter-bank market increased rapidly. According to statistics from the Central Treasury Bonds Registration and Clearing Corporation, the number of securities under custody of the corporation in 2001 was only 138, among which 47 were not negotiable and the total market value of the securities under custody was less than RMB 2, 000 billion. While by the end of July 2012, the number of securities under custody had reached 3, 072 and total market value of all the securities under custody was RMB 22, 300 billion. In addition to traditional government bonds, financial and corporate bonds, varieties such as Central Bank Bills, medium-term notes, short-term financing notes and asset-back securities were added and the issuers covered the central government, financial institutions, enterprises and international organizations. In the fourth place, the term limit focused more and more on the short-term and the mobility of the market gradually enhanced so that the function of providing a mobility management platform for financial institutions was more and more brought into full play. In 2011, the short-term transactions of 1 day, 7 days and 14 days occupied the main part of buy-back transactions and the coalition of the three accounted for nearly 97%. Among them, the buy-back transactions of 1 day occupied the largest proportion which accounted for 52. 19%. It demonstrated that the function of both the buy-back and inter-bank borrowing markets was to satisfy the temporary capital shortage of institutions.

c. Commercial Bill Market

In 1980, the very beginning of reform and opening up, The People's Bank of China began to try out commercial bills to conduct payment clearing aimed at the large amount of payment default between enterprises and gradually extended the practice from local to remote areas. In the following 20 − plus years, the development of the Chinese commercial paper market was at a relatively low pace.

Since 1999, the development of the commercial bill market made some progress which could be demonstrated by the following four aspects. First, a batch of medium and small sized financial institutions were qualified for launching bill discount and could apply to the People's Bank of China for rediscounting, which broke the domination of commercial banks in the bill market. Second, commercial banks had generally put emphasis on expanding the bill business and established the institutions or windows specializing in the bill business in a variety of forms. Third, circulation and transfer of bills increased and the percentage of bills with more than three endorsers showed an apparent rise. Fourth, commercial bills had become a dominant settlement means for a batch of big enterprises and its share in sales revenue steadily increased.

In addition, a number of regional commercial bill markets came into being step by step. Since 1999, the Central Bank has actively adopted policies and measures to choose and push some central cities with good business basis, strong ability to branch out and concentrated financial institutions to accelerate the construction and development of the commercial bill market. The commercial bill business of the central cities occupied the higher percentage across the country and the increase was steady. At the same time, the operation was standardized and the endorsement percentage of the bill, credit payment and financing function were much higher than other regions in China. Entering the new century, the financial informatization construction in China made evident progress while the bill business still maintained at the traditional counter paper bill stage. In order to enhance the transparency and time-effectiveness, greatly overcome the drawbacks and significant risk of paper bill operation, economize the transaction cost of all parties involved and promote the formation of a uniform bill market, The People's Bank of China determined to realize the development of an electronic bill business. On June 30, 2003, the Chinese inter-bank market set up "China Bill Network" and was officially opened to provide quotation and consultation services for the transfer discount and buy-back of bills between financial institutions. It marked the very start of the electronization of the Chinese bill market.

At present, the bill market has become a very important part of our Chinese inter-bank market and the varieties of transactions cover transfer discounts and buy-backs with the main transaction being bank acceptance bills. By 2012, the commercial bills signed and issued by enterprises added up to RMB 17, 900 billion, increased by 18.8% compared with the previous year among which the accumulative acceptance amount of electronic bill was RMB 962.75 billion, accounting for 5.37% of the total acceptance amount of commercial bills nationwide. Financial institutions discounts accumulated to RMB 31,600 billion, increasing by 26.4% compared with the previous year among which the accumulative acceptance amount of electronic bill was RMB 800 million, accounting for 3.29% of the total accumulative acceptance amount of commercial bills nationwide.

E. Derivative Market Was Still at the Primary Stage

The Chinese derivative market originated from the opening of the Zhengzhou Grain Wholesale Market on October 12, 1990 and has undergone development for over 20 years. According to the nature of market development and operation characteristics, it can be divided into the commodity futures market and financial derivative market. Seen from the stage of development, both the commodity futures and the financial derivatives can be divided into three stages, from preliminary attempt to improvement and rectification to recovery and standardized development.

a. Commodity Futures Market

The commodity futures market marked by the opening of the Zhengzhou Grain Wholesale Market demonstrated the trend of blind development from the very beginning due to the unclear administrative department in charge, the unavailability of law to conform to and the inadequate reserve of talented personnel and technology. As the whole country was awash with the exchanges and brokerage firms that was extremely disorderly internally, illegal overseas merchants were just like fish in troubled waters, and the fraud was rampant. On November 4, 1993, the State Council issued *Notice of Ceasing the Blind Development of Futures Market* to request to resolutely stop the blind development of the futures market. This symbolized the end of the first stage of the development of the Chinese commodity futures market.

On April 6, 1994, the curtain of the improvement and rectification of commodity futures transactions opened up. The State Council closed futures transactions of big varieties such as steel, sugar, coal and so on one after another. Until April 23, 1996, after merging and rectification, there were only 15 experimental exchanges left nationwide (there were once more than 50 commodity exchanges in the craziest period) and the listed transaction varieties were 35. In August 1998, the State Council appointed the China Securities Regulatory Commission to be unitarily responsible for the supervision of the national securities futures industry, further clarified the principle of "continuing trial, strengthening supervision, abiding by law and guarding against risk" and merged 14 exchanges (Guangdong Joint Commodity Exchange was closed down during clean-up and rectification in 1996) into three exchanges of Shanghai, Zhengzhou and Dalian and only 12 varieties of commodity futures transaction remained. On December 28, 2000, the inaugural meeting of China Futures Industry Association was held in Beijing, supervision and self-discipline systems of the futures industry were completely established and the stage of improvement and rectification came to a comprehensive end.

In March 2001, "to steadily develop the futures market" was written into the planning outline of "the 10th Five-Year Plan" which marked the start of the recovery stage of our Chinese commodity futures market. In January 2004, "the Nine National Articles" clearly put forward "the gradual launch of varieties of commodity futures providing for the bulk commodity manufacturers and consumers to find price and realize the function of hedging". After that, the commodity futures market obtained steady development, more and more varieties of futures were listed successively and the Chinese commodity futures market began to stride into maturity. For the time being, the listed varieties in the Shanghai Futures Exchange, Zhengzhou Futures Exchange and Dalian Futures Exchange are as follows, see Table 6.1.

Table 6.1 Listed Varieties of Chinese Commodity Futures

Exchange	Listed Varieties
Shanghai Futures Exchange	copper, aluminum, zinc, lead, gold, silver, deformed steel bar, wire rod, hot rolled coil, fuel oil, petroleum asphalt, nataral-rubber
Zhengzhou Futures Exchange	strong gluten wheat, common wheat, cotton, sugar, PTA, rapeseed oil, early indica rice, methanol, glass, rapeseed, rapeseed meal, thermal coal, japonica rice
Dalian Futures Exchange	Maize, soybean No.1, soybean No.2, soybean meal, soybean oil, palm oil, egg, plywood, fiberboard, polyethylene, polyvinyl chloride, polypropylene, coke, coking coal, iron ore

b. Financial Derivative Market

Shortly after the establishment of the commodity futures market, the early financial futures emerged in China. In the short two years time from 1992 to 1993, financial derivatives such as foreign exchange futures, treasury bonds futures, stock index futures, warrants and so on were on the stage one after another. But due to lack of supervision, illegal operation, serious speculation and violating manipulation, the first trial of the Chinese financial derivative market ended up a complete failure.

On June 15, 2005, the Industrial & Commercial Bank of China and Industrial Bank successfully made the first inter-bank market bond futures transaction which was the first genuine derivative product in the Chinese inter-bank market and marked the recovery of the Chinese financial derivative market. In August of the same year, the inter-bank RMB forward market was created and RMB forward inquiry transaction was formally introduced. The inter-bank forward foreign exchange transaction variety was officially launched soon afterwards and the representative domestic RMB forward exchange rate initially came into being. The launch of bond forward transaction and forward foreign exchange marked the beginning of the over-the-counter financial derivative market. After that, transactions such as RMB structural financial products, RMB interest rate exchange and RMB foreign exchange swap were launched successively.

In 2005, with the issuance of CSI 300 Index, CSI 300 Index was designated as the first share price index futures target in April 2006. In May 2006, stock options with the option nature and the convertible company bond with transaction separated from the bond were granted to be launched. In September 2006, China Financial Futures Exchange, aiming at the transaction of financial futures, was founded in Shanghai. What bore the significance of the milestone was the respective launch of margin trading and share price index futures on March 31 and April 16, 2010. The launch of the most proactive variety of the global international financial market-option was under intense preparation. On March 28, 2014, China Financial Futures Exchange started the simulated trading of SSE 50 option contract.

F. The Internationalization of Chinese Securities Market

In investment securities, at the end of 1991, the first B-share, Shanghai Vacuum Electron officially made its public offering. The financing function of the Chinese securities market for the first time strode over the national boundary with the issuance of B-share as the starting point. China allowed foreign residents to invest in B-share by using foreign exchange within China's territory in 1992. On February 19, 2001, the China Securities Regulatory Commission made a decision that the residents within Chinese territory could invest in the B-share market with their own foreign exchange.

Over the past several years, the process of internationalization of the Chinese bond market has been advancing. Financial institutions like CITIC, Bank of China, Bank of Communications, China Construction Bank and Shanghai International Trust & Investment Corporation issued international bonds in different currencies like JPY, USD and Deutsche Mark in the international financial market one after another.

On February 18, 2005, The People's Bank of China, Ministry of Finance, the National Development & Reform Commission and China Securities Regulatory Commission jointly composed the *Interim Measures for the Administration of the Issuance of RMB Bonds by International Development Institutions*. The IFC (International Finance Corporation) and ADB (Asian Development Bank) became the first batch of international multi-lateral financial institutions in China to develop the RMB bond, in September. The issuance of long-term RMB bonds by international financial institutions became an important milestone of the Chinese bond market heading for internationalization.

In terms of securities traders and the internationalization of their business, the

China Securities Regulatory Commission allowed joint venture securities companies with minority holdings (the upper limit for foreign investment was 33%) and joint venture fund companies (the initial upper limit for foreign investment was 33% which was increased to 40% three years later) to carry out business in China according to the relative regulations of WTO's entry principles of securities market, national treatment principles and transparency principles. China Securities Regulatory Commission statistics indicated that by the end of 2011, China had approved the establishment of nine joint venture securities companies and 33 joint venture fund management companies among which the fund management joint venture companies accounted for more than half of the fund companies in China. Meanwhile, the domestic financial institutions began to stride into the international market. There were 15 Chinese financial institutions covering banking and insurance who had established branch institutions of comprehensive securities businesses in Hongkong. This promoted the international competitiveness of the Chinese securities industry and accelerated the alignment between the domestic and international capital markets as well.

QFII (Qualified Foreign Institutional Investors) and QDII (Qualified Domestic Institutional Investor) became the innovative transitional measures. Entering the 21st century, the overall function and efficiency of the Chinese securities market had been greatly enhanced and gradually became one of the biggest and most vital markets in the Asia-Pacific region. At the same time, it raised new requirements for the internationalization strategy of the securities market. The establishment of the QFII and QDII systems acted as an important bridge in the process of internationalization of the Chinese securities market up to the present stage.

The People's Bank of China and the China Securities Regulatory Commission jointly issued the *Interim Measures for the Management of Investment of Qualified Overseas Institutions* on November 5, 2002 and QFII emerged with the issuance. In the following several years, the China Securities Regulatory Commission further relaxed the restriction of QFII qualifications and lock-up period of capital in and out. The investment limit was increased. More conveniences were provided for the account opening and investment of QFII and the QFII investment supervision system, in particular, the information disclosure system had been perfected. By the end of 2011, the overseas investors with the QFII qualification amounted to 116 among which 103 QFII institutions had acquired the investing quota issued by China Foreign Exchange Bureau and the total granted quota amounted to USD 20. 69 billion.

As per the approval of the State Council, the People's Bank of China issued a proclamation to adjust six foreign exchange management policies to allow the eligible banks, fund companies and insurance institutions to assemble domestic funds or purchase foreign exchange by their own means to conduct relevant overseas financial transactions and investments according to the regulations on April 13, 2006. The China Foreign Exchange Bureau announced the first batch of banks acquiring qualifications to conduct overseas financial transactions for their clients and the quota to purchase foreign exchange on July 21, 2006. The QDII product, Hua An International Configuration Fund which had been brewed for quite a long time, was issued to domestic investors in China on September 13, 2006 and 10 QDII funds launched successively after that.

Case 6.1   Ping An Bank: Successful Demonstration of the Merging Story of 1 +1 >2 in the Capital Market

On the 32nd floor of the Shenzhen Development Building on August 2, 2012, a simple unveiling ceremony announced the legal merging between Shenzhen Development Bank and Ping An Bank. Shenzhen Development Bank, with 25 years history, was renamed "Ping An Bank" and became the holding bank of Ping An group, which proclaimed the successful accomplishment of the unprecedented merging in the Chinese banking history.

Reviewing the big event of banking lasting for more than two years, people might wonder why the once brilliant Shenzhen Development Bank lagged behind, why it was Ping An who entered into Shenzhen Development Bank and what kind of beautiful flower their connection would blossom. As a matter fact, when Shenzhen Development Bank began to look for the strategic investor 10 years ago, Ping An was their best choice. After 10 years of ups and downs, the two institutions finally came together which was almost arranged by destiny.

1. Development Process

Founded in December 1992, Fujian Asia Bank was a joint venture bank co-founded by Bank of China Fujian Trust Consultative Company and Hongkong Mid-Asia Financial Co., Ltd. as a response to the government as a trial place for foreign investment in the financial field. It was officially approved by the People's Bank of China to start operation on June 26, 1993.

Approved by China Securities Regulatory Commission, Ping An Insurance Group and HSBC officially purchased 100% stake of Fujian Asia Bank together.

According to the purchase agreement, HSBC would spend no more than USD 20 million to purchase 50% stake of Fujian Asia Bank and Ping An Insurance Group would purchase the remaining 50% stake through its subsidiary

Ping An Trust Investment Company. After that, Ping An Insurance Group poured another USD 23 million into Fujian Asia Bank so that the total fund injected amounted to USD 50 million and Ping An Insurance Group held 73% stake of Fujian Asia Bank while the stake held by HSBC was diluted to 27%. The acquisition cost Ping An Trust USD 43 million which was converted to RMB 356 million according to the exchange rate of that time.

Fujian Asia Bank was renamed Ping An Bank on February 19, 2004 and the head office was moved to Shanghai from Fuzhou. Ping An Bank became the first domestic commercial bank in the name of an insurance brand. The acquisition enabled Ping An Insurance to steer clear of the policy barriers to stretch its operation antenna to the rapidly developing Chinese banking industry.

Shenzhen Commercial Bank, founded on June 22, 1995 as the first urban commercial bank in China, was renamed Shenzhen Commercial Bank in June 1998.

In the middle of 2006, Ping An Insurance Group spent RMB 1.008 billion to purchase 1.008 billion shares of Shenzhen Commercial Bank with the price of RMB 1 per share from 11 state-owned shareholders like Shenzhen Investment Holding Co., Ltd., Shenzhen Financial Bureau and so on which accounted for 63% of the total capital stock of Shenzhen Commercial Bank.

At the end of 2006, Shenzhen Commercial Bank issued 3.902 billion additional oriental shares to Ping An Group with the price of RMB 1 per share. In this way the total stock capital owned by Shenzhen Commercial Bank increased to 5.502 billion shares. Plus the acquisition of shares of some small shareholders, the shares held by Ping An Group amounted to 4.917 billion which accounted for 89.36% of the total stock capital of Shenzhen Commercial Bank and the total cost for this transaction for Ping An Group was RMB 3.909 billion. Thus, Ping An Insurance purchased 89.24% stake of Shenzhen Commercial Bank with the total price of RMB 4.9 billion.

China Securities Regulatory Commission approved Shenzhen Commercial Bank to absorb and merge the original subsidiary company of Ping An Insurance Group-Ping An Bank which was renamed Shenzhen Ping An Bank on June 16, 2007. The original head office of Ping An Bank was reconstructed and converted into the Shanghai Branch of Shenzhen Ping An Bank and the original Fuzhou Branch and Shanghai Zhangjiang Sub-branch of Ping An Bank were reconstructed and converted into Fuzhou Branch and Shanghai Zhangjiang Sub-branch of Shenzhen Ping An Bank respectively.

Shenzhen Ping An Bank was renamed Ping An Bank with the authorization of China Securities Regulatory Commission in January 2009.

The renamed Shenzhen Ping An Bank spent RMB 4. 595 billion to allocate 3. 162 billion shares to all the shareholders according to per 10 shares with the allocation of 5. 79 shares and the unit price of per share was RMB 1. 58. Due to the integration of Fujian Asia Bank, Ping An Insurance Group held as high as 90. 75% stake of Ping An Bank.

The whole name of Shenzhen Development Bank was Shenzhen Development Bank Co. , Ltd. which was founded with the integration of several urban credit cooperatives. Shenzhen Development Bank issued RMB common shares publicly in the form of free subscription for the first time on May 10, 1987 and officially announced the founding on December 22, 1987. It is the first commercial bank in China which issued shares to the public and became listed.

Ping An Insurance Group issued 299 million oriental H-share to the big shareholder Shenzhen Development Bank-Newbridge Group as the consideration to the transfer of 520 million shares held by Newbridge Group in May 2010. The transaction cost was approximately RMB 16. 795 billion and Ping An Insurance Group held 16. 76% stake of Shenzhen Development after the transaction.

Ping An Life Insurance spent RMB 6. 939 billion to subscribe for the non-publicly issued 379, 580 million shares of Shenzhen Development Bank with the price of RMB 18. 26 per share in June 2010. After the subscription, Ping An Insurance held 29. 99% stake of Shenzhen Development Bank.

Ping An Insurance announced to subscribe the non-publicly issued 1. 639 billion shares of Shenzhen Development Bank with the price of RMB 17. 75 per share with its 90. 75% stake holdings of Shenzhen Ping An Bank and RMB 2. 692 billion cash in September 2010. After the transaction, Ping An Insurance held 52. 38% stake of Shenzhen Development Bank in total (2. 684 billion shares) and Shenzhen Development Bank held 90. 75% stake of Ping An Bank according to the closing price of RMB 15. 16 per share on August 1, 2012 and the corresponding market value was RMB 40. 689 billion.

Shenzhen Development Bank planned to increase oriental equity to China Ping An with the amount of not more than RMB 20 billion in August 2011 and after the transaction, Ping An Group would hold as high as 61. 36% stake of Shenzhen Development Bank.

On January 19, 2012, Shenzhen Development Bank issued a public announcement that the Boards of Shenzhen Development Bank and Ping An Bank had deliberated and passed the merging scheme and Shenzhen Development Bank absorbed and merged Ping An Bank and renamed the new bank "Ping An Bank". According to the announcement, after the absorption and merging, Ping An Bank would be incorporated into Shenzhen Development Bank and Ping An Bank would be cancelled and no longer independently exist as the legal main body. Shenzhen Development Bank should be the existent company after the merging and the Chinese name of the company should be transformed from Shenzhen Development Bank Co. , Ltd. to Ping An Bank Co. , Ltd.

According to the announcement on the night of July 25, 2012, Shenzhen Development Bank acknowledged the receipt of *Approval Issued by China Banking Regulatory Commission of Renaming Shenzhen Development Bank.* The China Banking Regulatory Commission approved Shenzhen Development Bank Co. , Ltd. to be renamed "Ping an Bank Ltd. "Ping An Bank" would be upgraded to become the national shareholding bank owning RMB 1, 260 billion capital from the urban commercial bank of Shenzhen.

On July 27, 2012, the bank went through the relative alteration procedures with Shenzhen Market Supervision & Management Bureau and acquired the new Enterprise Legal Person Business License. The Chinese name was changed to "Ping an Bank Ltd. " from that day and the English name was altered from "Shenzhen Development Bank Co. , Ltd. " to "Ping An Bank Co. , Ltd. " (Ping An Bank) . As per application, the abbreviation of securities of the bank was officially changed from August 2, 2012.

By then, it can be dated back to August 2, 2012 mentioned in the article before. In the conference room on the 32nd floor of Shenzhen Development Bank Building located on Shennan Middle Road in Shenzhen, the former chairman of Shenzhen Development Bank-Xiao Suining and president of Shenzhen Ping An Bank-Richard Jackson attended the unveiling ceremony of renaming Shenzhen Development Bank as Ping An Bank. Shenzhen Development Bank officially completed the mission of 25 years and the 23-year-old "000001" would continue its legend of K-line of A-share under the name of "Ping An Bank".

On the night of August 15, 2012, Ping An Bank issued the first semi-annual report after merging. According to the report, in the first half of the year, the bank had achieved revenue of RMB 19.626 billion which demonstrated a 61.70% increase compared with the same period of last year. The net profit belonging to the shareholders of the parent company was RMB 6.761 billion which was increased by 42.91% compared with the same period last year.

2. Why It Is Ping An Who Entered into Shenzhen Development Bank?

In 2002, like other Chinese banks, Shenzhen Development Bank was in the tank of non-performing loans. Under such circumstance, Shenzhen Development Bank was chosen as the specimen experiment for the Chinese financial reform and the supervision management decided to give up the control of the bank to introduce the overseas strategic investor-Newbridge Group.

The negotiation with Newbridge went through a series of frustrations and the contract was officially signed at the end of 2004 while the negotiation commenced from 2002. At that time, Ping An once intended to get involved but eventually gave up for various reasons. The negotiation with Newbridge lasted for two years and during that period, the capital complementation plan was suspended and the institutional expansion of Shenzhen Development Bank was halted due to the regulations of the supervision institution. After the formal entry of Newbridge into Shenzhen Development Bank in 2005, the shareholding reform started. As an American institution, Newbridge could not completely understand everything in China, so that the shareholding reform plan failed due to the collective opposition from the small shareholders in the general meeting of shareholders. During that period, the bank lost a lot of time and opportunities. The shareholding reform failed, let alone the capital supplementation of the bank.

It was not until 2007 that the second shareholding reform finally succeeded. Newbridge is a privately offered fund so its identity made it difficult to offer sustainable replenishing capital to the bank. In the second shareholding reform, it was very difficult for them to buy part of the warrants and they made a loan with very high interest rate to complete the shareholding reform. Hence, by 2007, compared with other shareholding banks developed almost from the same time, Shenzhen Development Bank was conspicuously lagging behind.

Reviewing the past decade which was the decade of economic boom in China and also the decade of the rapid expansion of Chinese finance, we can make a conclusion that Shenzhen Development Bank lost the best opportunity for rapid expansion.

After the first failure of Shenzhen Development Bank's shareholding reform in 2006, Newbridge had the intention to quit from Shenzhen Development Bank and Ping An and other institutions were the potential buyers at that time. There were a lot of rumors in the market then, the response from the market was intense, the stock share of the two companies surged a lot. It was kept confidential and came to nothing in the end. If it succeeded that time, the share price of Shenzhen Development Bank was less than RMB 10 which was a very good opportunity.

As the biggest financial merging, the combination of Shenzhen Development Bank and Ping An Bank provided valuable and referential experiences for future mergers and demonstrated the successful merging story of "1 +1 >2" in the capital market and conducted beneficial exploration and trial for carrying out comprehensive financial service in China.

The most difficult part of the whole event did not lie in the integration of system, network, product or other hardware as going through the above-mentioned was tedious but they could be done little by little. It consisted of the integration of people which was the integration of people's "heart" in a more in-depth sense. It was the most difficult part when people were faced with uncertainty. Thus, at the very beginning of integration, the uncertainty had to be eliminated and transparent and fair communication was required. Shenzhen Development Bank initially put forward the "Three No" principles including no staff cut, no pay cut and no demotion. Secondly, employees were clearly informed about the prospects and direction of the future development of the bank. At the same time, the employees clearly knew their positions and job specifications. The uncertainty was eliminated by letting all the employees know the unitary and explicit target.

Entering Ping An, Shenzhen Development Bank became a subsidiary holding company under Ping An Bank from an independently-operated shareholding commercial bank. It not only acquired the sufficient source of capital but also realized the stability of stock right that had been aspired for a long time and the formulation of the long-term objective. What was more important was that Ping An brought resources of more than 70 million individual clients and more than 2 million company clients to the bank. In the future five to eight years time, it will increase at a rate higher than that of the average growth rate in the same industry and become one of the best banks in China. The client resources will become the significant engine of future profit increase for Ping An Group.

In 2012, with the successful integration between the two banks, Ping An Bank would promote its market competitiveness in terms of several fields including scale, innovated product, service and achievement. Keeping advantage on the traditional corporate banking services and capital business, it will focus on enlarging the business with medium-sized and small sized enterprises with trade financing as the main product and further establish the technological barrier to maintain the core competitive advantage. They will try to be in the leading position in the market in terms of the retail business with small and micro finance and credit card business as the main products and comprehensive financial service.

(the case was selected from the interview with the former President of Ping An Bank—Xiao Sui-ning from *Southern Metropolis Daily*)

Case 6. 2   "327" Treasury Bonds Event: the Rare "Financial Earthquake" since the Founding of P. R. C

The futures trade of treasury bonds in China began on December 28, 1992. "327" was the code of the treasury bonds futures contract which corresponded to the three-year treasury bonds due in June 1995 issued in 1992. The whole issuance amount of the bonds was RMB 24 billion. The camps of bull and bear gathered the influential people of the Chinese securities market at that time. The bears in this event were headed by the president of Wanguo Securities Company-Guan Jingsheng who was known as "Securities Godfather in Shanghai" and brothers of "Liao Guo Fa" -Gao Yuan and Gao Ling. The bulls were led by the big private investors of Shanghai, Jiangsu Province and Zhejiang Province headed by "China Economic Development TrustInvestment Company" which was directly subordinate to the Ministry of Finance including Chen Shunlong who later established the Guo Yuan Securities in Anhui, Xu Weiguo-the President of Shenzhen Da Peng Securities and other big private investors from Jiangsu Province and Zhejiang Province.

After October 1994, Bank of China increased the interest rate of more than three-year deposit and restored the deposit inflation-protected subsidy and the same inflation-protected subsidy policy was applied to the interest rate of treasury bonds as well. The uncertainty of inflation-protected subsidy rate provided room for speculation of the treasury bonds futures. The more and more fiery market of treasury bonds futures made a striking contrast with the sluggish stock market at that time.

In February 1995, the price of the "327" contract hovered between RMB 147. 80 to RMB 148. 30. On February 23, according to the announcement issued by the Ministry of Finance, "327" treasury bonds would be redeemed at the price of RMB 148. 50. The same day, China Economic Development Trust Investment Company led bulls to take advantage of the positive news to make a surprise attack to increase the price to RMB 151. 98. Then the ally of Wan Guo-Liao Guo Fa suddenly changed to bull the market and the price of "327" treasury bonds increased by RMB 2 in a minute and increased by RMB 3. 77 in 10 minutes.

Every RMB 1 increase of 327 treasury bonds meant that Wan Guo Securities would lose more than RMB 1 billion. At 4: 22 p. m. , Wan Guo Securities as the bear rose in revolt to resort to 500, 000 lots to make the price come down from RMB 151. 30 to RMB 150 and then to RMB 148. The last giant selling order of 7. 3 million lots hit the price down to RMB 147. 40. The par value of the selling order of 7. 3 million lots amounted to RMB 146 billion which was six times the total issuing amount of this kind of treasury bonds.

At 11:00 p. m. , Shanghai Stock Exchange officially gave orders to announce the abnormity and invalidity of transaction of all the varieties of "327" after 16: 22: 13 on the 23rd. This part was excluded from the range of that day's settlement price, transaction volume and open interest. After the adjustment, the transaction amount of the treasury bonds of that day was RMB 540 billion and the closing price of the varieties of "327" was RMB 151. 30 of that day which was the price of the last transaction signed before the violation. It meant that the loss of Wan Guo Securities reached as high as RMB 6 billion.

In view of the adverse effect of the violation of "327" treasury bonds, the China Securities Regulatory Commission issued *Urgent Circular on Suspending the State Treasury bonds Futures Transactions Pilot in the Range of China* which marked the termination of the state treasury bonds futures market that only lasted for two years and a half. By then, the first financial futures variety in China came to a premature end and the *Financial Times* of UK called it "the darkest day in the history of securities in Mainland China".

People could not help wondering why Guan Jinsheng sold more than 7 million lots to suppress the contract price before the market closed on the last trading day. After the closing of the market, all the contracts of open interest should be conducted in physical delivery but he could not make the physical delivery of so many treasury bonds. Why did he still do so? Probing into the in-depth reasons, it can be analyzed from the following aspects.

The first, it lay in the financial background. The management of the futures market at that time was in chaos and there was an enthusiasm for treasury bonds futures. 1994 witnessed the game of subsidy rate and the whole country was confronted with the high inflation pressure of double-digit and the interest rate of bank deposit was higher than 10% so that people were not very interested in treasury bonds with fixed rate. The inflation-protected subsidy rate announced then was 8% and was continuously increased month by month and broke through the double digit in December. Stimulated by this, the price of "327" treasury bonds futures kept soaring. It was increased from more than RMB 110 in October 1994 to more than RMB 140 at the beginning of 1995 which demonstrated a more than 20% increase.

At that time, the standard of the treasury bonds futures margin was set as 2. 5% which meant the payment of RMB 2. 5 million margin could entitle doing the business of the market value of RMB 100 million. The more than 20% growth rate meant an extravagant profit more than 10 times the principal for the buyer within the very short three months. The investing institutions could earn more than RMB 10 million a day and they were quite overjoyed. There was an episode then that a client representative of an institution called the headquarters of the company to think of a way to raise more funds to invest another RMB 10 billion by taking advantage of the raging market. One hour later, the client representative called the head office again and informed them that there was no need for them to raise the funds as he had already earned 10 million. "327" treasury bonds should be due in June 1995 and every one hundred treasury bonds should be redeemed RMB 132 at maturity with the 9.5% coupon rate and the inflation-protected subsidy rate. Compared with the current bank deposit interest rate and inflation rate, the return of "327" was too low.

The second, the internal rumors affected the decision-making. In view of the low return of "327" in comparison with the current deposit interest rate and inflation rate, there were rumors on the market that the Ministry of Finance would increase the inflation-protected subsidy rate from the beginning of February 1995 and the "327" treasury bonds would be redeemed as RMB 148. Facing up to the rumors, there was rapid differentiation on the market. According to president of Wan Guo Securities-Guan Jinsheng, who at that time was the very influential character known as "Godfather" in the Chinese securities filed, the first of the three targets in the three-year macro-regulation was to administer the persistently high inflation so that there was no need to increase the inflation-protected subsidy rate and there was no need for the Ministry of Finance to pay an additional more than RMB 1 billion interest to make it harder for the government's finance. The view of Guan Jinsheng represented some of the securities merchants so they betted on the bear market.

At that time, China Economic Development Corporation entered into the market and persisted in doing the bulls. The majority of medium and small individual investors and part of the institutions did the bulls as well. Their opinion was that inflation could not be controlled in the short term and the inflation-protected subsidy was bound to increase so that the redemption price of "327" treasury bonds would be increased accordingly. By the middle of February that year, the boundary of the market had been clearly divided in terms of "who were enemies and who were friends". Tens of thousands of individual investors and medium and small sized institutions began to do the bulls following the "commander-in-chief of doing bulls" – China Economic Development Corporation. Wan Guo Securities, Liao Guo Fa and other institutions did the bears. On February 23, every RMB 1 increase or decrease of "327" contract would cause the fluctuation of RMB 400 million profit or loss in the book value of Wang Guo Securities. According to the comments of people familiar with the situation at that time, there was no route to retreat for either the bulls or bears so that the expectation difference of the policy became the capital game in the market.

The third, it lay in the legal level. The law was unsound and the restriction was absent. On November 22, 1994, When the news of interest rate increase of "327" treasury bonds came out, the quotation of treasury bonds futures in Shanghai Stock Exchange experienced the amplitude of RMB 5 and that had not aroused attention, and many violations were not handled fairly and timely. In the earlier stage of transaction of "327" treasury bonds, the expectation of Wan Guo Securities had been wrong. When there was the huge irreparable amount of book value loss, they simply disturbed the market to save the situation. The next day after the event, Shanghai Stock Exchange issued the *Urgent Circular on Strengthening the Supervision of Treasury Bonds Futures Trading* and China Securities Regulatory Commission and Ministry of Finance issued the Interim Measures for the Administration of Treasury Bonds Futures Trading. We finally had the first trading legislation of treasury bonds bearing the legal validity in China but it was too late.

The margin regulation was unreasonable and the cost for speculation was quite low. Before the "327" event, the margin rate for the clients was 2.5% specified by Shanghai Stock Exchange, 1.5% specified by Shenzhen Stock Exchange and 1% specified by Wuhan Trading Center. The setting of margin level was the core of futures risk control. Five hundred margins could conduct the transaction of RMB 20,000 treasury bonds which had enlarged the potential profit and risk of the manipulators by 40 times. The low margin level was far away from the international practice and even less than the margin level of the current commodity futures which would without any doubt increase the possibility of speculation in the market so that the excessive speculation was unavoidable.

In addition, standardized management and proper forewarning supervision systems were absent. Price limit system is a prevailing system in the international futures filed. But before the event, Shanghai Stock Exchange did not adopt this basic means to control the price fluctuation so that an amplitude of 4 RMB difference between the upper and lower price occurred and there was no forewarning supervision system in the exchange. At that time, the circulation volume of the cash bonds of Chinese treasury bonds was very small and the open interest volume should maintain a reasonable proportion to the spot market circulation volume which should be set in the matching system in the computer. From the large number of selling orders at the closing market on February 23 of "327" contract, the exchange evidently did not conduct real-time monitoring of every order placed so thousands of lots of bear orders were concluded in several minutes through the matching system in the computer, thus the market order was disturbed and the drawback of the market management was exploited.

The fourth, there were flaws in the management and the transactions were overdrawn. The Chinese securities exchange used the matching computer system as the main transaction pattern and applied the "daily marking to market" method to control the risk rather than the "marking to per transaction" settling system so that the overdrawn transactions could not be avoided. The securities exchange failed to use the static margin and the settlement price of the previous day to control the dynamic price fluctuation of the present day so that the main force of bear could realize the crazy behavior of casting thousands of lots of contracts illegally.

The fifth, the supervision responsibility was unclear. The business of Chinese treasury bonds was initially launched under the authorization of the local government. Before the issuance of Measures, China did not specify the main administration institution of the treasury bonds in law. The Ministry of Finance was in charge of the issuance of treasury bonds and participated in the constitution of the inflation-protected subsidy rate. The People's Bank of China was responsible for the examination and approval and routine administration of financial institutions including securities companies and meanwhile formulated and announced the inflation-protected subsidy rate. The Securities Regulatory Commission took the responsibility for the supervision of transactions while each of the transaction organizers was mainly under the direct supervision of the local government. The multi-supervision brought about the low efficiency of supervision and even the vacuum in the measures of supervision.

Eighteen years later, Chinese treasury bonds futures known for the "327" event was launched officially on September 6, 2013, over one year after the start of simulated trading. Seen from the insiders, the action not only produced a giant pushing effect on the Chinese interest rate marketization, but also brought about a reform of the capital management market with the hedging and lever mechanisms.

Case 6. 3   Zhanjiang Pattern: Commercial Insurance's Participation in the Health Care System

As one of the top 10 hot issues of the Chinese insurance industry in 2011, the "Zhanjiang Pattern" was typical of the government-entrusted business operation mode. Zhanjiang had the trial implementation of health care reform for more than two years and realized the multi-win situation of "government giving no additional penny, mass people paying no additional penny, the significant enhancement of the guarantee of residents and wider coverage".

In January 2009, Zhanjiang introduced the integrated urban and rural basic health care insurance with the participation of PICC commercial insurance which realized the multi-win situation of the enhancement of guarantee of insured mass people, decrease of the load of government, full utilization of medical resources and development of the business of insurance. The pattern has become a representative sample of construction of new health care reform with the participation of commercial insurance, which is called the "Zhanjiang Pattern" inside the industry.

As the State Council issued Guidance on the Reform of Urban Health Care System in 2000, China Life Insurance commenced to operate the coordinated supplementary health care insurance for the basic health care of the civil servants in Zhanjiang in 2001. Due to the poor management of the company and the absence of on-the-spot supervision of the hospitals, the loss of business amounted to RMB 30 million so that in 2005, Zhanjiang Municipal Government transferred the business to Pacific Life Insurance to administer, and the latter realized a profit of about RMB 5 million in the first year after the transfer. Meanwhile, Zhanjiang Social Insurance Funds made a profit of about 15 million as well. In 2007, Pacific Life Insurance shrank the business for various reasons and terminated the cooperation before the cooperation agreement was due. Although the cooperation unfortunately ended, the government clearly felt that it was a tendency of the pattern dominated by the government with the concrete operation being conducted by a commercial insurance company.

When Pacific Life Insurance terminated the cooperation, PICC Health prepared to setup a branch company in Zhanjiang. Ye Lijian, who was in charge of the cooperation with the government in Pacific Life Insurance, job-hopped to PICC Health and undertook the business again. In January 2009, Zhanjiang further realized a merging operation of a new rural cooperative medical system and the urban residents medical insurance to integrate the farmers and urban residents into a universal health care system with the participation of both the urban and rural residents. During the process, PICC Health won the bidding to underwrite the large amount of supplementary medical insurance for urban and rural residents.

In this way, the cooperation range of PICC Health and government expanded from over 300, 000 civil servants supplementary medical insurance to more than 6 million urban and rural residents in Zhanjiang. Thus, the "Zhanjiang Pattern" realized a giant leap.

"Town + Countryside", Benefiting Urban and Rural Residents

In September 2007, PICC Health coordinated with the local government in Zhanjiang to push the integration reform of urban and rural residents health care insurance by putting their professional advantages of actuarial management, risk management, claim settling management and so on into full play. In January 2009, the merging operation of the new rural cooperative medical system and the urban residents medical insurance was realized and the universal health care system with the participation of both the urban and rural residents was setup. At the same time, PICC Health took part in the construction of the urban and rural social medical insurance system of Zhanjiang which included "large amounts of supplementary insurance for basic medical insurance of urban and rural residents", "serious illness rescue insurance of urban workers", "coordinated supplementary medical insurance for basic medial insurance of civil servants" and so forth. It was known that by November 2009, the medical insurance projects undertaken by PICC Health had covered 11 counties and districts in the whole Zhanjiang, the accumulative responsibility of medical care insurance undertaken amounted to more than RMB 250 billion and the people insured reached 6.44 million, accounting for more than 85% of the population in the whole city of Zhanjiang.

"Management + Operation", Enlarging Guarantee Effect

In the first place, 85% of the individual payment of the original basic medical insurance of the urban and rural residents continued to be used as the insurance expenditure for basic medical care and the remaining 15% was withdrawn to purchase the large amount of supplementary medical insurance from PICC Health. Under the circumstance of the unchanged standard of government revenue expenditure and individual payment, the coverage limit of the urban and rural residents was increased from the original RMB 15,000 by RMB 35,000 and RMB 65,000 according to different payment levels (when each account of the urban and rural residents paid for the annual basic medical insurance premium, each account could choose either of the two kinds of payments-RMB 20 or RMB 50 per person per year).

In the second place, PICC Health provided managerial service free of charge to "Town Workers Basic Medical Insurance" and "Basic Medical Insurance for Urban and Rural Residents", set up professional medical files for the insured, held medical care lectures and provided multi-health management service like the national cooperation medical service network.

"Basic + Supplementary", Decreasing Operational Cost

PICC Health participated in the managerial service of basic health care and supplementary health care and set up the overall medical insurance system dominated by basic health care and supplemented by large amounts of subsidy. In the hall of the social insurance departments at all levels in Zhanjiang, the service window setup by PICC Health could be seen and they provided services to the insured covering paying fund, voucher auditing, expenses reimbursement and so on. Six people from PICC Health were responsible for the medical insurance policy consultation service through the 12333 medial insurance consultation hotline set up by Zhanjiang Social Insurance Fund Management Bureau.

In addition, PICC Health and the social insurance department jointly developed the medical insurance management information system, shared the expenses settlement information, jointly perfected the medical service quality appraisal system, jointly strengthened the management of the designated hospitals and setup the operation mode of "unitary policy, unitary accounting and unitary management" so that the basic medical care and supplementary medical care business could be done in the same place.

"Information + Capital", Increasing the Managerial Level

PICC signed cooperation agreements with designated hospitals to clarify the respective authority, obligations and punishment regulations. Before the end of every social insurance year, PICC Health coordinated with the local social insurance department to carry out the verifying appraisal of the medical service quality of the designated hospitals. PICC also consolidated the restriction and supervision of the medical service and ensured reasonable and effective treatment of the insured through the appraisal choosing mechanism of the designated hospitals.

In addition, the 112 designated hospitals with medical care insurance in Zhanjiang and PICC Health medical care insurance commissioners organized a medical care inspection team to carry out the whole-process of monitoring service and ensuring the timely transmission of medical information to the insurance company through the information management system. If there emerged empty beds in hospital, PICC Health was entitled to refuse to pay for the relevant expenses to the hospital.

PICC Health and the Social Insurance Department adopted the settling method of payment in advance and verification afterwards which included "controlling the whole amount, monthly payment in advance and settling at the year end". Eighty percent of the actual account payable was prepaid to the designated hospitals on a monthly basis, about 10% was used as the settling capital for the end of year and 10% was the verifying capital. After the examination and verification of the compensation case finished, any overcharging would be returned and shortages part would be paid according to the result of the examination and verification. By this way, the insured only needed to pay the expenses that they incurred when they went through the settlement with the hospital and then left. It simplified the settlement of claims and avoided the problem of going through layers of examination and approval with medical certificates and multi-trips for getting reimbursement. So, seeing a doctor had become more convenient for the insured.

The health insurance business, which is connected with and complementary to basic medical care, is a special field with highly specialized levels, large investment of operation cost and strong social sensitivity. The operation of such a business requires the construction of a professional risk management platform and servicing team. Specialization in this kind of business of professional health insurance company can on one hand, overcome short term behavior, put professional advantage into full play and enhance the service quality. On the other hand, the transferred cost allocation of such kind of business with other businesses can be prevented, the actual accounting of this kind of business can be realized, the basis for determining the cost and premium rate and so on can be provided to the government and the company to ensure the stable operation of the business and protection of the immediate interests of the insured.

The medical reform of integration of urban area and rural area has realized a multi-win situation of "government giving no additional penny, mass people paying no additional penny, the significant enhancement of the guarantee of residents and wider coverage" in Zhanjiang, Guangdong Province which fully embodies the amplification effect of commercial insurance on the insurance funds of basic medical care.

The experiences of Zhanjiang fully demonstrates that supplementary medical care insurance and health management service provided by professional health insurance companies together with the basic medical care insurance of government have greatly made it convenient for the insured to accept medical treatment. As well, it has effectively controlled the unreasonable medical behavior and promoted the operation efficiency of the medical care guarantee system. This may provide the best example for the participation of commercial insurance companies in the construction of a medical care insurance system.

(**the case was selected from the** "*Reading Zhanjiang Pattern*")

Questions for discussion

1. Why was there the "highly centralized unification" financial system before the reform and opening up in China and how do you evaluate the situation?

2. Can you talk about the problems confronted by the Chinese banking as

per your understanding?

3. Compared with the Chinese capital market, what are the differences in the capital market in your country?

4. Do you have any recommendations concerning the bigger role played by the insurance industry in the construction of the Chinese social security system?

China is a large trading nation with a long history in foreign trade. This chapter deals mainly with the development course, international position, institutional structures of China's foreign trade and its relationship with national economic growth.

Chapter 7

China's Foreign Trade: History and Development

7. 1   China's Foreign Trade Development Course

Dramatic changes have taken place in foreign trade since the founding of the People's Republic of China on October 1, 1949. The foreign trade system has changed from planning to market oriented, the foreign trade policy from trade protection to international standard, and the foreign trade function from the regulation of supply and demand to one of the three engines (investment, consumption and foreign trade) that drive the national economy. Foreign trade management policies and system, with their transparency continuously improved, have strictly fulfilled China's international commitments. In 2012, the total volume of China's international trade exceeded that of the United States of America for the first time in history and China came to the top of the list among the major trading nations of the world.

The fast development of foreign trade has significantly contributed to the growth of the national economy and the development of society. It has optimized resource allocation and economic structure, enhanced industrial technology, promoted domestic competition, expanded the market space, increased the fiscal revenue, promoted employment and improved the international balance of payments. What is more important is that the rapid development of foreign trade has led China to increased intercultural exchange and helped bring the Chinese economy in line with world economy. In a word, it has exerted great influence on the domestic reforms.

As far as the world markets are concerned, China used to be a backward, excluded and developing country, but now it has become a world processing and manufacturing base, one of the important forces in world trade, an active participator in the multilateral trading system and in regional economic cooperation, and together with other emerging markets, a significant driving force for world economy and international trade. In this section we will take a retrospective view of the development of foreign trade in PRC so that readers can have an overall understanding of it.

Since its founding in 1949, PRC has witnessed the following five stages in terms of foreign trade development: planning economy, exploration and practice, transformation and development, all-dimensional and multilevel opening to the outside world, and new opening era.

7.1.1 Planning Economy Period: 1949–1978

When it was founded in 1949, PRC took the socialist and self-independent approach to the development of foreign trade. For the following three decades, China's foreign trade, although going though a tortuous process, played an important role in the restoration and development of the national economy and gained some positive and negative experiences about socialist foreign trade. In 1950, the total foreign trade volume reached USD 1,135 million, of which export was USD 552 million and import was USD 583 million. In 1978, the total foreign trade volume increased to USD 20,638 million, of which export was USD 9,745 million and import was USD 10,893 million. Compared with that in 1950, the total foreign trade volume in China went up 16.7 times and 17.7 times respectively, ranking 32nd in the world.

In this period of time, as foreign trade was confined to exchange of needed goods and regulation of supply and demand, it was considered a supplementary means to extended reproduction. In the first few years, exports consisted mainly of primary goods such as farm and sideline products, reflecting the economic structure and production levels in China at that time. With the rapid development of industry, export commodity structure changed considerably. More light industrial and textile products were exported than farm and sideline products and became the leading export goods. Export of heavy industrial products were also on the increase. But up to 1978, export of primary products still accounted for 53. 5 percent of the total export volume. As for imports, instead of the consumer goods and luxuries which had been the major imported goods before the founding of PRC, producer goods came to the top of the list, accounting for about 80 percent of total import volume on the year basis. Following the policy of enlisting foreign aid as a supplement to its own efforts, PRC also made some attempt to make use of foreign capital for domestic economic construction in this period of time.

China's foreign trade in this period of time was affected by changes in international situations, international relationships and domestic ideology. It witnessed the progress of unilateral trade exclusively with socialist countries in the beginning, self-enclosedness during the Cultural Revolution and re-opening the door in the late 1970s.

In the early years of the republic, China's foreign trade was predominantly open account trade, conducted mainly with the USSR and other socialist countries in Eastern Europe, as many capitalist countries in the West took a hostile attitude to the newly established republic. In the 1950s, the volume of foreign trade with socialist countries accounted for more than 50 percent of the total foreign trade volume. From 1952 to the end of the 1950s it reached over 70 percent, of which about 50 percent was with the USSR.

From the end of the 1950s to the early years of the 1960s more and more Asian, African and Latin American countries won their national independence. Based on the principle of equality, mutual benefits, and exchange of needed goods, China took the chance to establish trade relationships with these countries by means of negotiating intergovernmental trade agreements, and developing a variety of trade forms such as barter trade, border trade, open account trade and cash payment trade. Meanwhile, China provided loans or free assistance for these newly independent countries and the socialist countries in Eastern Europe. In addition, mainland China persisted in the policy of a steady supply of goods for Hong Kong and Macao and guaranteed such a supply even in times of national economic difficulties. The re-export by way of Hong Kong and Macao became the breakthrough in exporting goods to western countries.

To meet the domestic needs for means of production and livelihoods, China made use of every opportunity to promote non-governmental trade and official trade with Japan and western European countries. Especially in 1960 when the Sino-Soviet relations broke down, China turned to its trade partners Japan and the capitalist countries in western Europe instead of the socialist countries like the USSR. In 1965, the volume of foreign trade with western countries accounted for more than 50 percent of the total foreign trade volume in China.

"The Cultural Revolution", which interrupted the normal development of the national economy, did great damage to foreign trade. In the early years of the 1970s, China resumed its lawful seat in the United Nations and rapidly improved its foreign relations. On the one hand, China gradually eased tensions with the USSR. And on the other, China established foreign relations with leading capitalist countries such as Japan, Germany and the United States of America. As a result, China's foreign trade regained its recovery and development. The status of western countries as China's foreign trade partners was increasingly enhanced, export structure of commodities was improved, and great achievements were made in the introduction of technology to China. In the late 1970s when the international and domestic situations were favorable for development, China entered the preparatory stage of reform and opening up to the outside world, see Figure 7.1.

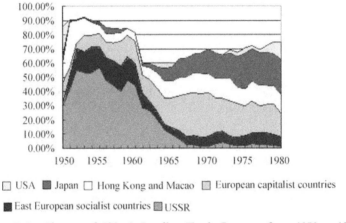

□ USA ■ Japan □ Hong Kong and Macao ▨ European capitalist countries

■ East European socialist countries ▨ USSR

Figure 7.1   Change of China's Leading Trade Partners from 1950 to 1980

7.1.2   Exploration and Practice Period: 1978 – 1991

At the end of 1978, the 3rd Plenary Session of the 11th Central Committee of the Chinese Communist Party was held, which established the strategy and policy of reform and opening up. As a result, foreign trade entered a new stage of practice and exploration. Greater importance was attached to foreign trade. Reform of the trade system and foreign direct investment led to the fast development. From 1978 to 1991, total imports and exports grew from USD 20.64 billion to USD 135.63 billion, of which exports increased from USD 9.75 billion to USD 71.84 billion and imports from USD 10.89 billion to

USD 63. 79 billion. The average annual growth rate was 16. 6 percent and 14. 6 percent respectively.

Processing trade, approved by the State Council, started in coastal areas in 1979 to attract foreign capital, technology and equipment, expand international markets, and generate jobs and foreign exchange income. In the mid − 1980s, with a new round of adjustment emerging in international industrial structure, the government established the coastal development strategy, which focused on a processing trade with both ends of the production process on the world market and on increasing exports of labor-intensive products. The processing trade developed rapidly thereafter.

In that historical context, processing trade enabled China to take over the labor-intensive industries from the world market, which led to the development of the domestic industry, promoted the optimization and upgrading of export commodity structure, and brought about the significant change in foreign exports from primary products and resource products to manufactured goods. In 1986, a radical change took place in foreign trade when manufactured goods became the dominant export commodity instead of the old primary products. In 1991 manufactured goods rose to 77 percent of the total foreign trade volume. The foreign trade market became more and more diversified. Japan, Hong Kong, the U. S. , and members of the European Community were the leading export markets and trade partners while the trade share with Russia and Eastern European countries declined significantly.

Ever since 1979, China established in succession special economic zones, coastal open cities and development areas in which more flexible and more preferential policies were carried out in terms of import and export management and foreign exchange control. These special zones were the liveliest areas in foreign trade and paved the way for the development of national foreign trade and even an open economy. Four special economic zones—Shenzhen, Zhuhai, Xiamen and Shantou—were founded in 1980, and their imports and exports that year accounted for 1. 1 percent of the total volume of national imports and exports and in 1991 their imports and exports increased to 8. 3 percent.

In the years before the reform and opening up, China's foreign trade was conducted under the leadership and control of the Central Government, which formed the main part of the management and operation system established soon after the republic was founded. The government set up successively a series of state-owned companies engaged exclusively in foreign trade. These companies took charge of all national imports and exports and carried out the mandatory plans from the government. Their profits and expenditures, gains and losses were centralized by the government. In 1979, the government began to implement reforms in the foreign trade system including adjustment of leading institutions, establishment of industrial and trading companies attached to industrial sectors, simplification of the content of foreign trade plans, implementation of dual exchange rate system for the competitiveness of exports, and initiation of import-export license system.

In the first few years after the reform and opening up, domestic production capacity and the capacity to earn foreign exchange through exports were so insufficient that foreign exchange was badly needed. Under such circumstances, the government began to attract foreign investment to enhance the capacities. Foreign-invested enterprises were entitled to imports and exports rights. From 1979 to 1991, China's utilization of foreign capital added up to USD 25 billion. Foreign-invested enterprises increasingly expanded their imports and exports and played a more and more important role in foreign trade. From 1979 to 1991, the imports and exports volume of foreign-funded enterprises rose from 0. 1 percent to 21. 3 percent of the total foreign trade volume. Foreign capital contributed considerably to the development of foreign trade in China.

7. 1. 3   Transformation and Development Period: 1992–2001

Deng Xiaoping made an inspection speech in south China in 1992 and the Communist Party of China held the 14th Congress in November, 1993, which established a socialist market economy as the reform target. Since then, China began to absorb western trade and economic thoughts and turn foreign trade from "exchange of needed goods, regulation of supply and demand" to market economy, making the best use of world and domestic markets and resources, taking an active part in international division of labor, competition and economic cooperation, and giving full play to the comparative advantages. The Central Government then put forward a series of strategies such as market diversification, "Big Trade", "attracting foreign investment" combined with "going global", winning the market on the basis of the fine quality of goods, rejuvenating trade through science and techonology, and participating actively in regional economic cooperation and multilateral trade activities.

From this time on, foreign trade in China entered the period of fast development and steady growth. When the financial crisis in Asia hit Japan, South Korea, ASEAN, Hong Kong and Macao in 1997, China's foreign trade also went though serious setbacks and sufferings for the first time after the reform and opening up and had negative imports and exports growth in 1998. But it soon got rid of the impact of the crisis and was rejuvenated. The total volume of imports and exports rose by 11. 3 percent in 1999 and by 27. 8 percent in 2000, of which exports increased by 31. 5 percent.

The establishment and development of a socialist market economy created a favorable domestic environment for the optimization of the export commodity structure. Exports of manufactured goods accounted for over 90 percent of the total volume and capital-intensive and technology-intensive products, gradually replacing resources products and labor-intensive products, became the dominant products for export. In 1995, exports of mechanical and electric products exceeded those of textile products and became the major export goods, changing the export commodity structure another time. Mechanical and electrical products proved to be an important driving force for exports of Chinese goods and led to the rapid development of foreign trade. Meanwhile, industrialization in China began to pick up speed. The rapid growth of fixed assets investment necessitated a great demand on capital goods, imports of machinery and transporting equipment increased rapid considerably.

In the process of attracting foreign investment, undertaking industry transfer and promoting the development of processing, assembling and manufacturing trades, foreign-funded enterprises grew fast and became the main force in China's foreign trade with processing trade as the main trade pattern. In 2001, the imports and exports volume of foreign-funded enterprises accounted for 50. 8 percent of the total volume, exceeding 50 percent for the first time in history. In 1993, exports of processing trade added up to USD 44. 23 billion, exceeding those of general trade for the first time. From 1995 to 2007, exports of processing trade stayed above 50 percent and processing trade thus became the most important trade in China's export.

The development of foreign-funded enterprises and processing trade brought about the internationalization of China's manufacturing. Quite a large number of enterprises were internationally competitive. Meanwhile, with imports and exports based on foreign-funded enterprises and processing trade emerged a trend for foreign trade surplus to increase rapidly year by year. From 1992 to 2001, the total volume of China's imports and exports grew 2. 1 times, from USD 165. 53 billion to USD 509. 56 billion, raising China to the 6th largest trading nation in the world. Foreign trade surplus rose 4. 2 times, from USD 5. 35 billion to USD 22. 46 billion in the same period of time.

International reserves accumulated rapidly. Foreign exchange reserves exceeded USD 100 billion in 1996 and reached USD 212. 16 billion in 2001, which laid a rather solid foundation for China's "going global". Meanwhile, adjusting the national economic structure, making the best use of foreign resources and creating new export growth, all made it necessary for China to "go glabal". In 1999, the State Council endorsed the suggestions made by the State Economic and Trade Commission, Ministry of Foreign Trade and Economic Cooperation, and Ministry of Finance that *"the government should encourage domestic enterprises to engage themselves in processing and assembling business overseas with materials brought from China."* This was the prelude to China's "going global" strategy. Non-financial Foreign Direct Investment (FDI) was USD 1 billion in 2000 and since then, it nearly doubled each year. Overseas investment led to the export of China's technology and equipment and, at the same time, guaranteed a useful addition to the supply of domestic resources.

With the rapid development of trade in goods, China started its negotiations for resuming contracting-party status in GATT (General Agreement on Tariffs and Trade). As the negotiations went on, China made its initial commitments to the opening up of service markets, which promoted the trade in service. From 1992 to 2001, the total volume of import and export trade in service tripled, from USD 18.24 billion to USD 72.61 billion. Due to the comparatively low competitiveness and the big gap between China's trade in service and that of advanced countries, the trade deficit during this period of time, except for the year 1994 when there was a small amount of trade surplus, was surging year by year.

7.1.4 All Dimensional and Multi-level Opening to the Outside World: 2002–2011

China's accession to the WTO in November 2001 marked a new phase in the development of foreign trade. Since that time, China fulfilled its commitments, participated actively in economic and trade cooperation in the multilateral trade system, implemented the strategy of free trade area and advanced trade liberalization and facilitation. Besides, it established, on the whole, a foreign trade policy and system adapted to the market economy and conforming to international practices and rules, established and improved a trade remedy system to safeguard fair trade, established and improved a promotion and service system to standardize the order in foreign trade. The perfection of relevant policies and systems guaranteed the smooth development of foreign trade.

China Import and Export Fair is held in Canton (Guangzhou), and therefore, it is also called Canton Fair. It was first held in the spring of 1957 and since then it has been held in spring and autumn each year. With a history of

The 110ᵗʰ China Import and Export Fair

over 50 years, it is up to now the longest, highest, and largest international trade event in China, characterized by the biggest variety of goods, the largest number of buyers and the most efficious deal-makings.

Since 2002, China has significantly expanded its foreign trade scale, increased its growth rate, and thus become one of the biggest trading nations in the world. The total volume of trade in goods exceeded USD 2 trillion in 2007, putting China third in the world. In 2008, although affected by the financial crisis in the latter half of the year, the total volume of imports and exports for the year added up to USD 2, 561. 6 billion and the growth rate reached 17. 8 percent. From 2002 to 2008, the average growth rate per annum for imports and exports was 26. 7 percent, of which exports accounted for 27. 9 percent and imports 25. 1 percent. From 2001 on, China's foreign trade surplus increased year by year and reached USD 295. 46 billion in 2008.

It was a new task of China's foreign trade to move towards balance between imports and exports. In 2009, China's export and import trade in goods turned out to be the first and the second respectively in the world and its export and import trade in service ranked the 4ᵗʰ and the 3ʳᵈ. In 2011, total exports and imports reached a historical high at USD 3, 642. 06 billion, a 22. 5 percent increase over 2010. Meanwhile, trade imbalance was further alleviated and the trade surplus that year was USD 155. 14 billion, a net reduction of USD 26. 37 billion over the year before, narrowing the gap by 14. 5 percent.

With the expansion of foreign trade, the trade mix was further improved (see Figure 7. 2) . The international competitiveness of Chinese goods was considerably enhanced with mechanical and electrical products and new high-tech products as the major growth points in foreign export. Exports of manufactured goods accounted for 95 percent, and exports of many kinds of commodities ranked the 1ˢᵗ in the world. China, therefore, became the processing and manufacturing base of the world. Major imported goods included raw materials, parts, and high-tech equipment and, influenced by the rise of international market prices of raw materials, imports of energy resources such as oil, iron ore and nonferrous metals increased rapidly, which, brought about another round of increase of import shares of primary products.

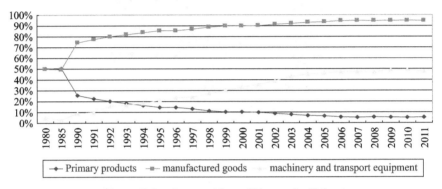

Figure 7.2　Composition of Export in China

Some new changes also took place in enterprise entities and market distribution. Foreign-funded enterprises played a dominant role in imports and exports, state-owned enterprises decreased their shares and other types of enterprises sprang up. In 2010, foreign-funded enterprises and private enterprises accounted respectively for 54 percent and 25.1 percent of the total volume of imports and exports and the shares of state-owned enterprises dropped to 20.9 percent. The European Union became China's largest trading partner. While traditional markets in Europe, the U.S., Japan and Hong Kong remained the major trading markets of mainland China, their shares of trade dropped to some extent, and at the same time, the shares of emerging markets continuously increased. In 2010, due to the adjustment of foreign trade policies and the impact of financial crises, imports and exports of the processing sector fell considerably and exports, for example, in processing trade dropped to 43.7 percent. General trade, however, rose in that year.

With the establishment of a big "goods trade" nation, China's trade in service also developed fast. After joining the WTO, China's trade in service increased rapidly, and just like the trade in goods, it advanced faster than the world's average growth rate and its position in world trade rose steadily. In 2010 service trade exports reached USD 170.2 billion, accounting for 4.62 percent of the world's total and service trade imports added up to USD 192.2 billion, accounting for

5. 47 percent of the world's total. The exports and imports in service occupied the 4th and the 3rd places respectively in the world. However, China's service trade does not match with the goods trade, China's service trade was dominated by traditionally labor-intensive industries such as transportation, tourism and business. New service industries like technology and knowledge-intensive industries were still in their primary stage and needed further development.

Up to now, China's foreign trade and economic cooperation had established a rich and diverse pattern that enhanced mutual integration, mutual promotion and mutual upgrade. In this period of time, the total volume of foreign trade grew rapidly, the foreign trade market expanded steadily and foreign trade practices became more flexible. In addition, utilization of foreign capital, foreign contract projects, labor service cooperation and investment in foreign countries started from scratch and grew steadily, which promoted the development of foreign trade.

7. 1. 5   China's New Opening Era: from 2012 to the Present

China's merchandise exports and imports surpassed those of Germany in 2009. As a result, China became the largest exporter and the 2nd largest importer in the world. In 2010 and 2011, China and the U. S. remained the largest exporter, the 2nd largest importer and the 2nd largest exporter, the largest importer respectively. The U. S. held the 1st place in terms of the total volume of imports and exports. It has been established that China surpassed America in 2012 in the total volume of goods import and export and became the largest country in this aspect. This is another milestone of China's foreign trade development after it became the largest exporter and the 2nd largest importer in 2009.

In 2012, the Chinese economy was faced with great pressure with the European debt crisis, the slower recovery of the world economy and extended downturn of world market demand. Under the correct leadership of the Party Central Committee and the State Council, foreign trade enterprises in all regions and departments adhered to the principle of "making progress while ensuring stability" and earnestly implemented the Party's policy measures concerning the promotion of steady growth of foreign trade by continuous release of "positive energy". As a result, China's foreign trade maintained steady growth and, at the same time, made further progress in promoting the quality, improving the economic performance and optimizing the structure. In 2012, the total volume of imports and exports reached USD 3, 866. 76 billion, a 6. 2 percent increase over that of the year before. To be more specific, exports were USD 2, 049. 83

billion, a 7.9 percent increase, and imports USD 1,817.83 billion, a 4.3 percent increase. The trade surplus was USD 231.1 billion, which expanded by 48.1 percent,

The year 2012 is defined in this book as the beginning of a new stage for China's foreign trade development. In this period of time, foreign trade strategies were adjusted mainly in three aspects. Firstly, China turned its strategy from integration into the world economy by means of WTO's multilateral market openings to a focus on regional economic cooperation and establishment of a Sinocentric East Asian Economic System. Secondly, China established open and competitive Chinese markets featured by Chinese enterprises, Chinese products, Chinese standards, and Chinese technology. Thirdly, China established open, competitive, and county-economy-centered regional markets. In a word, China adjusted its overall opening strategy by participating in the reconstruction of a new world economic system, establishing Sinocentric markets, breaking domestic regional barriers and reducing transaction costs of regional markets to explore new routes of economic growth.

7.2 International Status of China's Foreign Trade

7.2.1 International Status of China's Goods Trade

Goods trade, also called visible trade or tangible trade or international trade in its narrow sense, refers to the exchange of goods between countries. China's foreign trade has developed steadily in recent years. There is no denying, however, that goods trade still plays a dominant role in its international trade. With the development of reform and opening up to the outside world, China's goods trade has kept on growing rapidly on a yearly basis. The total trade volume of China surpassed that of the United States in 2012 for the first time and became the largest country in terms of international trade scale. As a veritable big trading nation, China plays a significant role in world trade. But, compared with other big trading nations, China still has a long way to go. The strategic goal in the near future, therefore, is to transform itself from a big trading nation to a big trading power.

Before the adoption of the policies of "invigorating domestic economy and opening up to the outside world" in 1978, the total volume of foreign trade in China was merely USD 20.64 billion, but the total volume of world trade that year reached USD 2,657.3 billion. In other words, China's foreign trade accounted for only 0.78 percent of the world trade, less than one percent, ranking the 34th. It was not only left far behind the United States, Japan and advanced countries in Europe, but also left behind the "four Asian tigers (Hong Kong, Singapore, South Korea and Taiwan)", of which Taiwan, one province of People's Republic of China, ranked the 19th and Hong Kong (now a Special Administrative Region) the 25th.

China's foreign trade volume turned out to be in the top three in 2008, third only to the United States and Germany. The total volume of imports and exports of the U. S. that year was USD 3, 467 billion, that of Germany USD 2, 671 billion and that of China USD 2, 561 billion with only USD 110 billion less than that of Germany. In terms of exports, China was only second after Germany and accounted for 8. 9 percent of the total volume of world exports. In terms of imports, China ranked the 3rd, and accounted for 6. 9 percent of the total volume of world imports.

International trade all over the world went into a decline due to the world economic crisis incurred by the U. S. sub-prime crisis in 2008. The imports and exports of all countries in the world fell to some extent, but the impact on China's imports and exports was comparatively little. In 2009, China's imports and exports surpassed those of Germany for the first time. China's exports reached USD 1, 202 billion, while Germany's exports were USD 1, 121 billion. China, therefore, became the largest exporter in the world for the first time. In terms of imports, China's reached USD 1, 006 billion, more than Germany's USD 931 billion but less than America's USD 1, 604 billion and ranked the 2nd largest importer in the world. In terms of the total volume of imports and exports, the U. S. reached USD 2, 661 billion and ranked the 1st, and China reached USD 2, 208 billion, only USD 453 billion less than that of the U. S. , and ranked the 2nd(see Table 7. 1).

Table 7. 1   Merchandise Trade: Top 10 Exporters and Importers, 2009

Rank	Exporters	Value (USD billion)	Share (%)	Annual Change (%)	Rank	Importers	Value (USD billion)	Share (%)	Annual Change (%)
1	China	1202	9. 6	−16	1	United States	1604	12. 7	−26
2	Germany	1121	9. 0	−22	2	China	1006	8. 0	−11
3	United States	1057	8. 5	−18	3	Germany	931	7. 4	−21
4	Japan	581	4. 7	−26	4	France	551	4. 4	−22
5	Netherlands	499	4. 0	−22	5	Japan	551	4. 4	−28

Cont.

Rank	Exporters	Value (USD billion)	Share (%)	Annual Change (%)	Rank	Importers	Value (USD billion)	Share (%)	Annual Change (%)
6	France	475	3.8	−21	6	United Kingdom	480	3.8	−24
7	Italy	405	3.2	−25	7	Netherlands	446	3.5	−23
8	Belgium	370	3.0	−22	8	Italy	410	3.2	−26
9	Republic of Korea	364	2.9	−14	9	Hong Kong, China	353	2.8	−10
10	United Kingdom	351	2.8	−24	10	Belgium	351	2.8	−25
	Top Ten Exporters	6425	51.5	−		Top Ten Importers	6683	53	−
	World	12461	100.0	−23		World	12647	100.0	−23

Source: WTO: "World Trade Reports 2010".

The imports and exports of all countries began to recover from the world economic crises in 2011. China's rank remained unchanged that year from the perspective of the total volume, which was USD 3,642 billion, ranking the 2nd in the world (see Table 7.2).

Table 7.2   Merchandise Trade: Top 10 Exporters and Importers, 2011

Rank	Exporters	Value (USD billion)	Share (%)	Annual Change (%)	Rank	Importers	Value (USD billion)	Share (%)	Annual Change (%)
1	China	1899	10.4	20	1	United States	2265	12.3	15
2	United States	1481	8.1	16	2	China	1743	9.5	25
3	Germany	1474	8.1	17	3	Germany	1254	6.8	19
4	Japan	823	4.5	7	4	Japan	854	4.6	23
5	Netherlands	660	3.6	15	5	France	715	3.9	17
6	France	597	3.3	14	6	United Kingdom	636	3.5	13
7	Republic of Korea	555	3.0	19	7	Netherlands	597	3.2	16
8	Italy	523	2.9	17	8	Italy	557	3.0	14
9	Russian Federation	522	2.9	30	9	Republic of Korea	524	2.9	23
10	Belgium	476	2.6	17	10	Hong Kong, China	511	2.8	16
	Top Ten Exporters	9010	49.4	−		Top Ten Importers	9656	52.5	−
	World	18215	100.0	19		World	18380	100.0	19

Source: WTO: "World Trade Reports 2012".

At the end of 2012, China had as many as 220 trade partners, spreading all over the world. The total volume of imports and exports reached USD 3,866.76 billion, a 6.2 percent increase over the year before, of which exports reached USD 2,049.83 billion and grew by 7.9 percent, and imports amounted to USD 1,817.83 billion and grew by 4.3 percent. The trade surplus added up to USD 231.1 billion, an increase of 48.1 percent. The total volume of China's foreign trade surpassed that of the United States for the first time in 2012 and became the largest trading nation in the world.

7.2.2   International Status of China's Service Trade

Since the 1980s, with the development of international division of labor, international service trade has sprung up and grown faster than international goods trade. As an important measure of a country's international competitiveness, international service trade has played a significant role in every country's economic development and has attracted more and more attention. According to the World Trade Organization, the total volume of world service trade in 2011 was USD 8,015 billion, of which exports accounted for USD 4,150 billion and imports USD 3,865 billion. International service trade has become an essential part of present international trade and, predictably, will be an important area of international economic cooperation in which China will participate.

Since China joined the WTO, its service sector has opened up to the outside world. Having established itself as a big trading nation in the world, China has rapidly developed its service trade. Just like goods trade, China's service trade has grown faster than the world's average growth rate and its international status in world trade has risen steadily.

In 2008, the United States was the 1st biggest service trade exporter, with a total volume of service trade exports at USD 522 billion, which was a 10 percent increase over the year 2007, and accounted for 14 percent of the total world service trade. Britain was the 2nd largest service trade exporter, with a total volume of USD 283 billion, accounting for 7.6 percent of the world total. Germany, France and Japan ranked the 2rd, the 4th and the 5th respectively. The total volume of Germany's service trade exports was USD 235 billion, accounting for 6.3 percent of the world total. France's service trade exports came to USD 153 billion, accounting for 4.1 percent of the world total. Japan's service trade exports were USD 144 billion, accounting for 3.9 percent of the world total. Japan took the place of Spain as the 5th largest exporter in the world. China ranked the seventh with a total volume of USD 137 billion, accounting for 3.7

percent of the world total. The ninth largest service trade exporter was India, with a total volume of USD 106 billion, accounting for 2.8 percent of the world total. The Netherlands replaced Ireland as the 10th largest service trade exporter.

As for the imports of service trade, the United States remained the 1st largest importer, accounting for 10.5 percent of the world total, with a total volume of USD 364 billion, and an increase of 7 percent over the year before. Germany ranked the 2nd, with a total volume of USD 285 billion, accounting for 8.2 percent of the world total. Britain, Japan and China ranked the 3rd, the 4th and the 5th. Britain's imports of service trade were USD 199 billion, accounting for 5.7 percent of the world total. The service trade imports of Japan were USD 166 billion, accounting for 4.8 percent of the world total. China's imports of service trade came to USD 152 billion, accounting for 4.4 percent of the world total. The only change to the world top ten importers in 2008 was that the Republic of Korea replaced the Netherlands as the 10th largest importer and the Netherlands became the 11th.

The United States remained the largest exporter of service trade in 2011, with a total volume of USD 578 billion, an 11 percent increase over 2010, accounting for 13.9 percent of the world total. Britain ranked the 2nd with a total volume of USD 274 billion, accounting for 6.6 percent of the world total. Germany, China and France ranked the 3rd, the 4th and the 5th respectively. Germany's exports were USD 253 billion, accounting for 6.1 percent. France's exports were USD 161 billion, accounting for 3.9 percent. China replaced France as the 4th largest exporter of service trade with a total volume of USD 182 billion, accounting for 4.4 percent of the world total. In terms of imports of service trade, the United States remained the largest importer with a total volume of USD 391 billion, a six percent increase over 2010, accounting for 10.1 percent of the world total. Germany ranked the 2nd, with a total volume of USD 284 billion, accounting for 7.3 percent of the world total. China, Britain and Japan ranked the 3rd to the 5th respectively. China surpassed Britain and Japan and ranked the 3rd with a total volume of USD 236 billion, accounting for 6.1 percent. Britain's imports of service trade were USD 171 billion, accounting for 4.47 percent. Japan's imports were USD 165 billion, accounting for 4.3 percent (see Table 7.3).

In spite of the sluggish global economy and the weakness of the world market in 2012, China's foreign trade in commercial services made outstanding achievements by following the principle of "seeking progress in stability" and with administration, service and promotion at the core.

Table 7. 3   Top Ten Exporters and Importers in World Trade in Commercial Services, 2011

Rank	Exporters	Value (USD billion)	Share (%)	Annual Change (%)	Rank	Importers	Value (USD billion)	Share (%)	Annual Change (%)
1	United States	578	13. 9	11	1	United States	391	10. 1	6
2	United Kingdom	274	6. 6	11	2	Germany	284	7. 3	8
3	Germany	253	6. 1	9	3	China	236	6. 1	23
4	China	182	4. 4	7	4	United Kingdom	171	4. 4	7
5	France	161	3. 9	11	5	Japan	165	4. 3	6
6	India	148	3. 6	20	6	France	141	3. 6	7
7	Japan	143	3. 4	3	7	India	130	3. 4	12
8	Spain	141	3. 4	14	8	Netherlands	118	3. 1	12
9	Netherlands	128	3. 1	11	9	Italy	115	3. 0	5
10	Singapore	125	3. 0	12	10	Ireland	113	2. 9	6
Top Ten Exporters		2133	51. 4	–	Top Ten Exporters		1864	48. 2	–
World		4150	100. 0	11	World		3865	100. 0	10

Source: "WTO: World Trade Report 2012".

Firstly, China's foreign trade in commercial services expanded steadily and its percentage in foreign trade further increased. According to the updated statistics issued by the State Administration of Foreign Exchange, China's exports and imports of service trade grew by 12 percent over the year before to a total volume of USD 471. 5 billion in 2012. Its percentage in China's foreign trade grew by 1. 1% to 10. 86%.

Secondly, imports of service trade grew faster than exports and trade deficit further increased. China's exports in 2012 grew by 4. 5% over the year before to USD 191 billion and imports increased by 17. 8% to USD 280. 5 billion. The trade deficit was as high as USD 89. 6 billion and, with a 62. 3% increase over the year before, it hit all-time highs.

Thirdly, exports of high value-added service trade increased relatively fast and the service trade structure witnessed a gradual optimization. In 2012, exports of finance, computer and information services, consultancy and advertising grew by 75%, 18. 8%, 18% and 17. 5% respectively over the year before. The trade surplus of the above-mentioned four items, which displayed a trend to increase year by year, was USD 0. 2 billion, USD 10. 7 billion, USD 13. 4 billion and

USD 2 billion respectively over the year before and the growth rate was, respectively, 100%, 28.9%, 36.7% and 66.7%. Insurance services, proprietary rights and license fee constituted a small proportion, but there was a marked increase in their exports.

Fourthly, there was a steadily fast increase in undertaking service outsourcing, which played a significant role in creating jobs. According to statistics from the Ministry of Commerce, Chinese enterprises signed 125,000 international service outsourcing contracts from January to November in 2012, with the overall contract value coming to USD 51.79 billion and an increase of 38.2% over the same period of the previous year. By the end of November, 2012, there were more than 20,000 service outsourcing enterprises in China which offered 4,180, 000 employment opportunities, 2,847,000 of which were taken by college graduates (or above), accounting for 68.1%.

Fifthly, with the pace of enterprises "going global" accelerated, the export growth rate increased. In 2012, the accomplished turnover of China's contracted projects reached USD 116.6 billion, a 12.7% increase over the year before. The value of newly signed contracts came to USD 156.53 billion, an increase of 10% over the year before. From January to October, 2012, exports of China's leading cultural products reached USD 21.26 billion, an increase of 42.9% over the same period of the previous year.

During the 11 years from 2002 to 2012, the average annual growth rate of China's service trade was 20%. Particularly since 2005, China's service trade developed much faster. The growth rates of 2005 and 2008 were higher than 30% and those of 2007, 2009 and 2011 were all higher than 20%. But on the other hand, the international status of China's service trade did not match up with that of its goods trade because China's service trade had started at a low level and with a weak economic foundation. China's service trade was still predominantly based on traditionally labor-intensive sectors such as transportation, tourism and commerce. New industries like knowledge and the technology-intensive industry were still in their primary development stage. Compared with advanced countries, the international competitiveness of China's service trade was weak. There was still a long way to go in the years to come.

7.3   China's Foreign Trade System

The system of foreign trade, or the management and operation system of foreign trade, is an integral part of the national economic system. It is closely linked with the systems of other economic sectors. To be specific, foreign trade system refers to its system of organizations, institutional setups, administrative rights, specialization of operation and profit distribution. Like other economic systems, it belongs to a superstructure, is determined by the economic base and, in turn, serves the economic base. It consists of two subsystems: national administrative system of foreign trade and the operating system of foreign trade enterprises. As these two subsystems were both founded upon the economic base, they needed corresponding adjustment and reform when changes took place based on economic conditions.

7. 3. 1   System of Foreign Trade before the Reform and Opening Up

A. Establishment of China's Foreign Trade System

China's foreign trade system was gradually established in the transition from the economic system of New Democracy to the socialist economic system. It has grown out of a product economy and a sole planned economy. In other words, upon the founding of PRC, people's political power immediately abolished all the imperialist privileges in China, confiscated the foreign trade enterprises of the Kuomintang government and bureaucrat capital, set up state-run foreign trade enterprises, gradually transformed those of national capital and finally established a single mode of foreign trade enterprises owned by the people. Meanwhile, the Central People's Government set up the Ministry of Foreign Trade to lead and manage all national foreign trade activities.

Having transformed private industry and trade including private import and export enterprises in 1956, the national economy was switched onto the track of product economy and sole planned economy. The national economic system required that sole mandatory planning be practiced and profits and expenditures be centralized by the government. Therefore, a highly-centralized foreign trade system with unified leadership, management and operation was established.

B. Adjustments of China's Foreign Trade System

Such a highly-centralized foreign trade system before the reform and opening up virtually evolved into a big enterprise that not only had the exclusive rights of ownership and management, but also had the executive power in the national foreign trade. To address this issue, some adjustments were made including decentralization of some power.

During the period of "Great Leap Forward" in 1958, the government made some adjustments in the economic system, decentralizing the administrative power of enterprises including some administrative authority for foreign trade management. But later the so-called "disorder" occurred in foreign trade, and, as a result, the government reinforced its control again. In the early 1960s, the government made adjustments in the national economic system, opposing decentralization and enhancing centralization. In the 1970s, the government decentralized the administrative power of enterprises again.

Meanwhile, China recovered and developed its trade relations with western countries due to the breakdown of Sino-Soviet relations in the 1960s. Disadvantages of a centralized foreign trade began to come to light. The adjustments made by the Ministry of Foreign Trade in 1975 included the establishment of foreign trade ports in provinces like Jiangsu in addition to the original five: Shanghai, Guangzhou, Dalian, Qingdao and Tianjin, and authorization of provinces like Yunnan to be engaged directly in border trade or to export to Hong Kong and Macao. These measures played some active role in the recovery and development of foreign trade, but they did not really affect the traditional and highly centralized foreign trade system.

C. Main Content and Features of Foreign Trade System

The main content and features of the sole and highly centralized foreign trade system before the 3rd Plenary Session of the 11th Central Committee of CPC are as follows:

a. State Control over Foreign Trade

The primary means of state control was the practice of foreign trade control system, import and export license system, foreign exchange control system, commodity inspection system, protective tariff system, freight transport supervision system and smuggling prevention system.

b. Mandatory Plans for Foreign Trade

The foreign trade plans (or targets) assigned by the national government were the core content of the foreign trade system, representing the direct state control over foreign trade. The management of foreign trade plans centered on the goods turnover plans including purchasing, allocation, export and import, domestic sales, "exporting on basis of import", foreign exchange receipts and payments and other relevant plans, which were all sole mandatory plans and must be executed to the letter.

c. Unified Management of Foreign Trade

State-owned foreign trade corporations were authorized to deal in imports and exports. The corporations and their branches or subsidiaries were responsible for the imports and exports in accordance with the state plan and their approved scope of business. None of the other institutions, departments or offices had the right to handle imports and exports. Export commodities must all be purchased by foreign trade corporations, that is, the manufacturers or suppliers produced the goods according to the state plan and then sold them to foreign trade corporations for export. Import commodities must all be allocated by foreign trade corporations, that is, foreign trade corporations imported commodities in accordance with the state import plans and then allocated them to the users according to the national allocation plans.

d. Centralization of Both Profits and Losses by the State

All profits and losses of foreign trade enterprises were centralized by the government, namely, all profits must all be turned over to the state treasury and all losses would be subsidized by the state. Most fixed funds and a little amount of circulating funds were appropriated from the national budget and used for free, and a small amount of fixed funds and most circulating funds came from bank loans and were used with interest payments.

e. National Uniform Price

On the basis of the principle of differentiation between inside and outside, domestic market price was severed from international market price. The purchasing price for export commodities was fixed by the state. The price of imported products to be sold domestically was also fixed, in principle, by the state. The export commodities to be sold in the international market and import commodities to be purchased in the international market were priced in accordance with the international market price. Domestic price, fixed by the state, was uniform, usually unchanged, and planned price, which was not affected by international market price and was characterized by stability.

The above-mentioned can indicate the characteristics of China's foreign trade system before the reform and opening up: highly-centralized, state-controlled, and state-monopolized, with profits and losses centralized and government function and enterprise management combined.

D. Advantages and Disadvantages of China's Centralized Foreign Trade System

A Traditional foreign trade system was established in the early years of the republic, under the influence of the domestic and international situation at that time and on the basis of the experience of socialist countries like the former Soviet Union. Four theoretical viewpoints contributed to the establishment of such a system. Firstly, the principle of foreign trade for socialist countries is that the enterprises must be state-owned and foreign trade must be state-monopolized. Secondly, foreign trade must serve the rapidly developing heavy industry.

Thirdly, foreign trade is complementary in the development of socialist countries. Fourthly, foreign trade performs a necessarily auxiliary function in coordinating the various proportional relations in socialist reproduction and in enhancing the harmonious development of the national economy in a planned manner.

Since the system was established under the influence of these theories, it had the following features: a) Foreign trade was state-controlled; b) Foreign trade companies were state-owned; c) Foreign trade institutions and organizations were appointed by the state; d) The mandatory plan of foreign trade was made by the state; all foreign trade activities had to be conducted in accordance with the mandatory plan.

The highly centralized and monopolized foreign trade system fit in with the strategy of national economic development, planned economy, and the import-oriented foreign trade development strategy. Although it played an important role in the economic development of PRC, its disadvantages unfolded themselves with the changes in domestic and international situations. The disadvantages mainly included a) inability to make the best use of China's competitive natural resources; b) lower economic effectiveness compared with foreign trade enterprises of developed countries; c) long-term import-oriented export resulting in irrational import and export structure that affected the improvement of domestic industries, national economy and people's living standard. With the disintegration of the planned economic system and the adjustment of an economic development strategy, reform of the traditional foreign trade system had to be carried out to adjust to the new international and domestic situations.

7.3.2 Foreign Trade System after the Reform and Opening Up

A. Reform of the Foreign Trade System

With the increase of international communication and interaction, routes of reform became widened for China's foreign trade system. Drawing experience from the market economic system and export-oriented foreign trade of the newly industrialized countries and regions, especially the experience of Japan and the "Four Asian Tigers", and reflecting on the sluggish development of domestic economy, China's foreign trade system began to change. It came to be realized that foreign trade enterprises should develop in the direction of specialization and socialization, for the system of sole state-owned foreign trade enterprises was not conducive to arousing the enthusiasm of the employees to seek economic returns, that China's foreign trade should adopt export-oriented development strategy to make up for the disadvantages of the import-oriented development strategy, that foreign trade was the necessity of international division of labor and international exchange rather than a tool to mutually exchange the needed goods and to regulate supply and demand, and that the development of foreign trade and utilization of foreign capital could facilitate self-reliance and enhance the national economy rather than obstructing its development. On the whole, following the overall reform of the economic system, the reform of foreign trade was carried out in alignment with the dynamic evolution of China's reform and opening up and was characterized by obvious stages with distinct features.

a. Preliminary Reform Stage: 1979−1987

The main features of this stage were decentralization of foreign trade rights and implementation of export encouragement policies. The foreign trade system reform started in spring 1979, when the State Council organized a tour to Guangzhou for officials from 7 ministries and commissions. In Guangzhou, these officials met with leaders of Guangdong and Fujian Provinces to discuss issues concerning the practice of special policies and flexible measures in the two provinces. Subsequently, Beijing, Tianjin and Shanghai were endowed with expanded rights of self-management in foreign trade. The State Council held a national working conference on import and export in October 1979 and the foreign trade system reform began nationwide. This process of preliminary reform continued until 1987, which included the following aspects:

（a）Establishing more seaports, decentralizing the right to handle foreign trade transactions, opening more channels and transforming the highly-centralized operating system. Before the reform, seaports for foreign trade were mainly those in port cities like Guangzhou, Dalian, Shanghai, Qingdao and Tianjin. Only a few corporations under the Ministry of Foreign Trade and their branch companies along the coastline had the rights to deal in foreign trade, while other branches located elsewhere did not have such rights, for their major responsibility was acquiring and allocating goods.

After the reform, there were foreign trade ports in every province, autonomous region, municipality with independent planning status and special economic zone. All branch companies of foreign trade corporations had the right to deal in foreign trade. Meanwhile, with the State's approval, some industrial and trading companies were established, CITIC and Everbright companies concurrently engaged in foreign trade were setup, some companies specializing in import and export of local areas were also formed and quite a number of manufacturing enterprises were permitted to conduct foreign trade themselves. By the end of 1987, there were about 3,000 enterprises with the right to engage in foreign trade. Besides, all foreign-invested enterprises could do import and export business themselves. In addition to general trade, other forms of trade also flourished.

(b) The sole mandatory plans were replaced by a combination of mandatory plans, guidance plans and market regulations. Manufacturing and foreign trade enterprises were given more power to engage in foreign trade business in the framework of the state unified plan so that they could work more flexibly to adapt to the changing international market. They were still responsible for collecting the state's export proceeds and other scheduled import and export. The listed items in the state plan were cut down from over 3,000 to 112 and the national acquiring and allocating plans were canceled.

(c) Establishing and improving a foreign trade macro-management system, reimplementing import and export license policies, improving export quota management and establishing a qualification approval system for foreign trade.

(d) Exploring ways for integrating industry and trade, technology and trade, and agriculture and trade. In the very beginning, it was advocated that foreign trade companies and production units should jointly explore the international market, negotiate with foreign companies, arrange production for export, and handle official business. Foreign trade companies should make known to the production units the cost in terms of foreign exchange and production units should make known to the foreign trade companies the cost of production. Although under the condition of state ownership, foreign trade companies and production units shared the same fundamental interests, there were no common interests to link them together. As a result, conflicts arose for the foreign trade companies feared that the production units might ask a higher purchasing price for their products and the production units feared that the foreign trade companies might lower the purchasing price. Such integration turned out to be like a couple "sharing the same bed, but pursuing different dreams".

Later, foreign trade companies were tentatively established in some industrial sectors to settle the problem of "different dreams", but without avail, for the change only involved the relationship of administrative subordination, and foreign trade companies and production units were not unconnected on the basis of common interest. The subsequent explorations included the investment of foreign trade companies in production units in the form of shares or joint venture so that they could share the benefits and take the risks together and the permission given to some qualified manufacturing enterprises to engage in import and export business by themselves. In this way, the problem of "different dreams" was settled. Integration of industry and foreign trade had to be done on the basis of common interest shared between production units and foreign trade companies to settle the problems.

(e) Establishing special economic zones as an experiment, authorizing them more rights to engage in foreign trade business, carrying out special preferential policies and encouraging export. The experiment proved that the enthusiasm for foreign trade was aroused and the channels for foreign trade were expanded. Traditionally, foreign trade enterprises, local governments and relevant departments took responsibility for earning foreign exchange through export. Their export proceeds were all handed into the state and it was the state's responsibility for losses and profits. Such a method separated the rights, responsibility and profits from each other and was not conducive to arousing the enthusiasm and enhancing economic performance. For this reason, in the initial stage of the reform, a benefits distribution system was executed in the field of foreign trade to reduce losses and increase profits. Later on different percentage of benefits distribution was given in accordance to the different regional situations. For example, in Guangdong and Fujian provinces, 30% of export profits could be retained for local development; in ethnic minority autonomous regions and provinces with many ethnic minorities, 50% of export profits; in special economic zones, 100% ; and in other areas, 25% .

In addition, certain percentage of export profits was also distributed in accordance with the difference of industries and the source of export commodities. With the growth of export and the price changes in domestic and international markets, especially after the state gradually lifted the price controls on manufactured goods, the measures previously taken (that is, export commodities like goods sold in domestic markets were taxed by central and local governments) obviously weakened the competitiveness of products in the world market and restricted the structural improvement of export commodities. Since 1985, China adopted the international drawback system for export commodities, namely, when the commodities were exported, the taxes levied at home such as tax on products, value-added tax and business tax would be refunded. In line with the above-mentioned reform, the central government and provincial government both took charge of foreign trade, under the central government's unified leadership, unified policies and unified planning.

In short, the preliminary reform of the foreign trade system and policies broke through the norms of the traditionally mandatory planned economy and the monopoly of Central Government by means of decentralizing foreign trade management and introducing market mechanism. In terms of a foreign trade management mechanism, the monopoly of plans by Central Government and the system of centralized operation of state-owned foreign trade companies were broken through and the right to handle foreign trade transactions was granted to local governments, industrial sectors and enterprises. Multiple management and operation systems brought foreign trade potential into full play. Meanwhile, the association between industries and trade facilitated a closer link between production and marketing and enabled enterprises to establish a direct connection between domestic production and world market. Guidance plans for foreign trade became the dominant plans instead of the previous mandatory plans.

The import agency system went on smoothly. Although export commodities were still dominantly purchased directly, the agency system was already in use. In terms of foreign trade policies, export was encouraged with price mechanism and measures like reduction or exemption of domestic tax and foreign exchange retained. These policies and measures proved to be quite effective. The reform to empower foreign trade enterprises including separation of government functions from those of enterprises and the sole responsibility of enterprises for their own profits and losses was carried out with restricted effects mainly because of the inadequacy of supporting policies such as those for price reform, reasonable tax system and acceptable exchange rate.

Since the reform was in its preliminary stage, some reform measures were unable to be carried out for the inadequacy of supporting policies, and new problems arose. As the underlying problems were not settled, the substantial breakthrough was not realized. These problems mainly were that the financial system concerning enterprise profits and losses centralized by the government or "eating from the same pot" remained untouched, that import and export enterprises did not separate their functions from those of the government, that there weren't effective measures and self-regulating mechanism so that without unified policies, foreign trade enterprises competed with each other under unequal conditions, that macro-management was still executed mainly through direct control for effective regulating system of foreign trade economy suitable for China's national conditions had not been established, and that the integration between industry and trade, technology and trade, and agriculture and trade remained unsettled.

b. Deepening Reform Stage: 1988−1990

The main feature of this stage was the implementation of a contracted managerial responsibility system in foreign trade. More specifically, to overcome the outstanding drawbacks in the foreign trade system, a contracted managerial responsibility system was adopted from 1988 to 1990 for the promotion of foreign trade development. The contracted managerial responsibility, which would be valid for three years, included such items as the enterprises' responsibility for their profits or losses, free operation, integration between industry and trade, implementation of agency system, unified foreign trade, and, based on the enterprises' previous export proceeds, foreign trade profits handed over to the state, and gains and losses, specified the percentage to be turned over to the state. When the contractor completed the amount of contracted foreign exchange, the export proceeds would be distributed in accordance with the original percentage. If there was a surplus, 80% of it would be retained by the contractor and 20% would be turned over to the state. If there was more deficit than before, the contractor would be responsible for the extra; if the original deficit was made up, that part would be retained by the contractor.

Most of the originally state-owned import and export corporations and their local branches were detached from the central government and their management authority was transferred to local government. Economic instruments such as price, exchange rate, tax revenue, tariff, interest rate, and export credit were used to regulate and control foreign trade, improve and perfect a export tax rebate system, and establish and improve foreign exchange swap markets. Meanwhile, pilot reform was also carried out in the areas of light industry, technology and clothing. What is worth mentioning is that, to encourage export and enable foreign trade enterprises to take responsibility for their own profits and losses, the state would refund all the production tax, added-value tax and business tax involved in exporting commodities. The state also adopted certain measures to encourage processing with imported materials, processing materials supplied by clients and assembling on provided parts. In addition, it expanded export credits.

The implementation of a contracted managerial responsibility system in foreign trade is an essential stage in the reform of the foreign trade system. It was carried out after the successful implementation of the contracted managerial responsibility system in agriculture, industry and commerce, and after the central and local governments divided the revenue and expenditure, each being responsible for balancing their own budgets. Although foreign trade was faced with a constantly changing world market, it was an essential part of the national economy, and as such, its reform and development had to be in line with those of the domestic economy. Obviously, when every other industry or trade was implementing contracted managerial responsibility, foreign trade could no longer be centralized by the government with the proceeds distributed in accordance with a certain percentage between the central and local governments, which was a "dead-end street" because it was not conducive to the self-management of foreign trade enterprises and because the state could not afford the financial expenditure involved. Under such conditions, it was necessary to implement a contracted managerial responsibility system. This system, with the respective responsibility of central and local governments in terms of foreign trade earnings and their use, was in keeping with the financial policies of the central government. In a sense, this system changed the situation where foreign trade enterprises were responsible only for export but not for the gains or losses involved. Their rights, responsibility and profits were unified to a great extent, and the total amount of subsidies for export from the central government was brought under control.

The reform was proved to be a success on the whole. The reform policies encouraged local governments, departments, foreign trade enterprises and manufacturers to increase their exports, improve their operation mechanism, enhance their economic performance and expand their import and export on their own initiative.

In the period of the "6th Five-Year Plan" (1981 – 1985), the cumulative growth rate of export was 36.4%, and in the period of the "7th Five-Year Plan" (1986 – 1990), the cumulative growth rate was 76.5%. During the three years from 1988 to 1990, the cumulative growth rate was as high as 44%. Even when the prices were constantly rising in the domestic market and the exchange rate stayed unchanged, the subsidies from the state for exporting goods were still under control, which, to a great extent, helped reduce the pressure of the rising prices on exports. Although there were some deficits, the government adjusted the exchange rate accordingly to settle the problem. Besides, the cost of export commodities was not rising as fast as prices in domestic markets. Generally, foreign trade enterprises became stronger and made some considerable achievements in international operation.

But, as had been anticipated when designing and promoting the system, the actual implementation of contracted managerial responsibility from 1988 to 1990 was subjected to the restrictions of the financial system and the overall situation of economic reform. It could only be an alternative to be employed when all the advantages and disadvantages were weighed and considered, and a transitional and tentative plan formed. Therefore, it might foster, but could not avoid or settle the following problems:

(a) The financial system of dividing the revenue and expenditures between central and local governments brought along with it regional blockades and market segmentation, which were inevitably reflected in foreign trade.

(b) Inequality existed between different kinds of foreign trade enterprises in terms of financial conditions and competitive environments. Different governmental policies were applied to exports in different regions and different foreign trade enterprises. In other words, the system of subsidies for export goods and the system of foreign exchange retention were not abolished and the mechanism for foreign trade enterprises to assume sole responsibility for their own profits and losses was not established in the real sense.

（ c ） Examination and approval authority for establishing foreign trade corporations was devolved, in March 1988, on the governments of provinces, autonomous regions, municipalities directly under the central government or with independent planning status. Foreign trade corporations authorized by these local governments multiplied fast and the number was increased by over 2000. The operational order was made worse for the demand of these corporations went beyond the supply of export products and domestic human resources.

（ d ） Due to the unequal competitive conditions, which were not eliminated in the reform of 1988, the long-lasting problems of buying at a higher price and selling at a lower price in foreign trade remained unsettled. Most of the problems did not arise in foreign trade first, nor were they caused by the implementation of contracted managerial systems. The main point was that the roots of these problems were not eliminated, or in other words, the most unreasonable part of the old system stayed intact.

c. Improvement Stage: 1991－1993

This stage was characterized by the elimination of foreign exchange subsidies, reduction of restrictions on import and unification of foreign exchange rate. When the Contracted Managerial Responsibility System in foreign trade expired in 1993, the Ministry of Foreign Trade and Economic Cooperation （MOFTEC） pushed the foreign trade reform a big step further. As early as the latter half of 1989, MOFTEC started to prepare for further reform by investigating in different parts of the country and organizing over 100 meetings. Based on the ten-year reform experience, especially the experience of contracted managerial responsibility and the experience of enterprises in three industries responsible for their own gains and losses, MOFTEC made several proposals and reported to the State Council.

Then, on December 9, 1990, the State Council made the decision on several issues concerning the further reform and improvement of the foreign trade system. According to the decision, the government would eliminate export subsidies from January 1, 1991 and would establish responsibility mechanisms for enterprises to deal with their own gains and losses by themselves. This was a significant turning point for China's foreign trade management and could be considered a breakthrough in its history, because it changed the long-lasting situation that foreign trade enterprises depended on the financial subsidies of the state or "ate from the same big pot". The general principles for the reform in this stage were unified policy, equal competition, self-management, self-financing and promotion of agent system. The measures adopted were as follows:

(a) Abolishing financial subsidies for export, adjusting exchange rates accordingly and increasing the percentage of foreign exchange retained by the enterprises. Foreign trade enterprises, then, took the responsibility for their own profits or losses.

(b) Changing the original system of permitting a different percentage of foreign exchange retention in accordance with regions to a national unified system of permitting a different percentage of foreign exchange retention in accordance with the different classes of commodities exported.

One class, called special commodities, included oil and oil products. For such commodities, only a small percentage of foreign exchange was permitted to be retained by enterprises for the management and operation. Another class was called mechanical and electrical products. As manufacturers needed to import raw materials and spare and accessory parts, 10% of foreign exchange received was to be given to manufacturers, 5% was to be handed into the local governments, and the rest was to be retained by foreign trade enterprises. Still another class was called general commodities. Twenty percent of foreign exchange received was to be handed into the state, 10% was to be handed into the local governments, 10% was to be given to manufacturers and the rest was to be retained by foreign trade enterprises.

To guarantee the necessary use of the state, the national government was to buy from foreign trade enterprises and manufacturers 20% and 10% respectively of foreign exchange for the exports of mechanical and electrical products and general commodities at the average price in the swap market. The rest of the foreign exchange retained by foreign trade enterprises was mainly for foreign exchange swap and import.

(c) Cleaning-up and rectifying the operation of foreign trade enterprises as required by the State Council. After the cleaning-up, those foreign trade enterprises kept had to manage and operate in accordance with the approved scope of business. The national government would go on to support state-owned large and medium-sized manufacturers and tightly-knit groups of enterprises who used complex technology, exported their products in large quantities and conformed to the terms of exporting by themselves. Their rights to engage in import and export were examined and approved by the Ministry of Foreign Trade and Economic Cooperation. The government would continue to encourage and help the export of foreign-funded enterprises and reinforce the coordination and administration of imports and exports by foreign trade corporations and chambers of commerce.

(d) The governments of every province, autonomous region, municipality directly under the central government or with independent planning status and import and export corporations and enterprises contracted with the state government for certain quotas including the total volume of export, export collection and foreign exchange to be handed into central government. The quotas to be finished were approved annually in accordance with the demand of the 8th Five-Year Plan for the growth of foreign trade and the practical conditions of national foreign export.

(e) Improving import trade system. With the reform of prices and the increase of people's income, the government gradually abolished the subsidies for importing commodities, further decreased the import in the mandatory plan, narrowed the licensed import scope, and reduced tariff. The State Customs Committee significantly reduced the import tariffs on 225 kinds of commodities on January 1, 1992 and abolished the import regulation tax in April, 1992 so that the tariffs on 16 types of commodities were further reduced.

The reform made the following achievements. Firstly, it abolished the subsidies for export and relieved the financial stress on the government. Export was separated from the national financial restrictions and could develop on its own. Following the internationally common practice, foreign trade enterprises took the responsibility for their own profits or losses, which, on one hand, exerted some pressure on the management, and on the other hand, provided opportunities for them to act on their own initiative.

Secondly, it changed the system of retention which varied from region to region and created an environment for enterprises to compete on an equal footing. It facilitated the improvement of foreign trade operation and promoted the self-management of enterprises.

Thirdly, the government improved the macro-management system and began to employ such economic means as exchange rates, tariffs, taxes and credits for the regulation of foreign trade.

Fourthly, foreign exchange for the use of enterprises was expanded so that foreign products had more opportunities to enter Chinese markets.

Fifthly, the policies to encourage foreign trade and measures adopted for foreign trade management remained relatively stable and sustainable.

Meanwhile, great importance was attached to the foreign trade system of prefectures, cities and counties. The foreign trade enterprises at the grass-roots level formed an integral part of the state foreign trade system and played an important role in manufacturing and organizing commodities for export. The administration of these foreign trade enterprises were reformed accordingly to meet the requirements of the new system for enterprises to take the responsibility for their own gains and losses.

The reform proved to be a success. China's export kept a high growth rate and import picked up rapidly and grew in pace with export. The economic benefit of export was raised and the cost reduced and the turnover of current capital increased.

The structure of export commodities was further optimized; the percentage of manufactured goods for export was increased. The quality of export commodities and operation order turned better. The trade balance and international payment capacity improved.

But there were still some problems that needed to be settled. They were mainly as follows: a) Export rebates were seldom refunded in the full amount or in time. As a result, standardization and institutionalization were necessary in this area. Meanwhile, illegal acts such as tax fraud should be prevented and once such things occurred, the people involved should be severely punished. b) The management system of import could not meet the demands of foreign trade development and international norms. c) Operation management system of all kinds of foreign trade enterprises was far from perfect. d) Macro-management and coordinated service mechanism in foreign trade needed to be improved.

Ministry of Commerce, Department in Charge of Foreign Trade

d. Gradual Liberalization of Trade: 1994−2001

This stage was mainly characterized by the reform of the exchange rate system and sharp removal of tariff and non-tariff barriers to trade. The outstanding mark for the comprehensive reform of foreign trade was the practice of unification of exchange rates in 1994. The State Council made the decision on November 1,

1994 to deepen the reform of the foreign trade system, pointing out the goals of the reform were unified policies, open businesses, equal competition, enterprises' responsibility for their own gains or losses, integration of industry and commerce, promotion of agent system and establishment of operation mechanism conforming to the norms of the international economy. The main contents were as follows:

(a) Reforming exchange rate system and reinforcing foreign trade enterprises' responsibility for their own gains or losses. Since January 1, 1994, unification of the exchange rate began to be practiced in China. Based on the demand of the market, a single, managed RMB floating exchange rate was carried out; an inter-bank foreign exchange market was established; exchange rate formation mechanism was improved to keep the RMB floating exchange rate reasonable and relatively stable; foreign exchange settlement was put into practice and all types of foreign exchange retention by enterprises or local governments were abolished and the system for export enterprises to hand in a certain percent of foreign exchange was eliminated; foreign exchange was sold by banks from which enterprises could buy it with RMB in the current account with conditional convertibility.

Unification of exchange rate was both an important measure and a significant achievement of the reform of the foreign trade system. A single, reasonable exchange rate enabled foreign trade enterprises to be responsible for their own management decisions, profits or losses and to enhance their economic performance. It also facilitated the practice of an agent system in foreign trade to reduce the risks of foreign trade enterprises. After the unification, the state abolished the exchange retention for export and carried out a unified exchange settlement system. The establishment of a single, floating exchange rate system proved to be an essential element for the reform to be successful and a significant milestone in the transformation from the planned to the market-oriented foreign trade system.

(b) Reducing import tariff and adjusting policies for reduction or exemption of tax. With the deepening of the reform and the gradual establishment of a socialist market economy, the contradictions between high nominal customs duties and low actual customs duties levied, between different import duties for different enterprises or regions due to different policies, between China's policies for import duties and international economic norms and principles for equal competition in a market economy became more and more outstanding.

To solve these problems and contradictions, the government decided to reform and adjust the policies for import tariff. On the premise of significantly reducing import tax, it canceled many unequal policies for the reduction and exemption of import tax. It adopted unified, normative, impartial and reasonable policies for import tax in accordance with the requirements of a socialist market economy and international economic norms so that Chinese foreign trade enterprises could participate in international competition and international economic cooperation. The import tariff was reduced from 35.9% to 23% on April 1, 2006 and would be further reduced to the average of developing countries.

(c) Reducing export rebate rate. To settle the problem of too much export rebate and too little tax revenue, to prevent some foreign trade companies from defrauding the state of export rebate, the state decided to reduce the export rebate rate from July 1, 1995 and to further reduce it on January 1, 1996.

(d) Establishment of margin bank accounts in the processing trade. In order to prevent some enterprises from smuggling, and to facilitate the enterprises engaged in processing, the State Council decided to carry out nationwide margin bank accounts for imported materials in the processing trade including processing materials supplied by clients, processing with imported materials and the processing trade by foreign-funded enterprises; namely, enterprises engaged in processing, including manufacturers permitted to engage in processing materials supplied by clients, opened margin accounts at appointed banks in accordance with the customs documents and the amount of money spent on the imported materials. The manufactured goods were to be exported in a certain period of time and, with the verification of customs, the banks concerned would cancel the margin accounts. The margin accounts system excluded the imported materials for processing in bonded areas or bonded manufacturers with customs supervisors.

Through a series of reforms, the foreign trade system dramatically changed in China and gradually conformed to the international trade norms. The changes were as follows: tariff and non-tariff barriers were gradually broken down; multiple entities of foreign trade operation came into being with gradual improvement of the responsibility for their own profits and losses; foreign exchange management was market-oriented, and freedom of foreign trade was enhanced; the service system of foreign trade intermediary was basically formed; and the scope of foreign trade operation was widened. These achievements greatly enhanced the development of foreign trade and different types of economic cooperation.

7.4 Foreign Trade and Economic Growth

Openness is the basic development trend and feature of the present economic societies. The interrelationship between foreign trade and economic growth has increasingly become one of the research topics in economics. Since the reform and opening up to the outside world, China's economy and trade have both developed rapidly, and especially after the 1990s the national economy has kept growing at a relatively high speed. Foreign trade has played a more and more important role in the growth of the national economy.

7. 4. 1   The General Survey of China's Foreign Trade and Economic Growth

Since the founding of PRC, the economic power has increased considerably in the 60 years. The gross domestic product was RMB 67. 9 billion in 1952 and RMB 51,932. 2 billion in 2012. It increased 764. 8 times from 1952 to 2012, with an actual average growth rate of 13% per year. It amazed the world for a country to grow at such a high growth rate for such a long period of time. With the development of the national economy, the income of ordinary citizens also increased. The per capita gross domestic product was RMB 3,8354 in 2012, 325 times that of 1952 when the per capita gross domestic product was RMB 118, with an annual growth rate of 9. 2% .

Meanwhile, China participated more actively in international division of labor. The gross value of China's import and export in 2012 was USD 3,866. 76 billion, a 6. 2 % increase over the year before, of which the gross export was USD 2, 049. 83 billion with an increase of 7. 9% and the gross import was USD 1, 817. 83 billion with an increase of 4. 3% . The trade surplus was USD 231. 1billion, with a growth of 48. 1% . As the gross value of China's import and export exceeded that of the United States of America, China became the largest nation in terms of world trade. The growth of the economy and foreign trade is shown in Table 7. 4.

Table 7. 4   China's Foreign Trade and the Growth of Gross Domestic Product (GDP):
1990–2012

Year	Total Value of Import and Export (USD billion)	Growth Rate (%)	GDP (RMB billion)	GDP Growth Rate (%)	Per Capita GDP (RMB yuan)
1990	115. 44	3. 40	1,866. 78	9. 86	1,644
1991	135. 70	17. 55	2,178. 15	16. 68	1,893
1992	165. 53	21. 98	2,692. 35	23. 61	2,311
1993	195. 70	18. 23	3,533. 39	31. 24	2,998
1994	236. 62	20. 91	4,819. 79	36. 41	4,044

Cont.

Year	Total Value of Import and Export (USD billion)	Growth Rate (%)	GDP (RMB billion)	GDP Growth Rate (%)	Per Capita GDP (RMB yuan)
1995	280. 86	18. 70	6, 079. 37	26. 13	5, 046
1996	289. 88	3. 21	7, 117. 66	17. 08	5, 846
1997	325. 16	12. 17	7, 897. 30	10. 95	6, 420
1998	323. 95	−0. 37	8, 440. 23	6. 87	6, 796
1999	360. 63	11. 32	8, 967. 71	6. 25	7, 159
2000	474. 29	31. 52	9, 921. 46	10. 64	7, 858
2001	509. 65	7. 46	10, 965. 52	10. 52	8, 622
2002	620. 77	21. 80	12, 033. 27	9. 74	9, 398
2003	850. 99	37. 09	13, 582. 28	12. 87	10, 542
2004	1, 154. 55	35. 67	15, 987. 83	17. 71	12, 336
2005	1, 421. 91	23. 16	18, 321. 74	10. 4	14, 053
2006	1, 760. 40	23. 81	21, 192. 35	11. 6	16, 165
2007	2, 173. 73	23. 48	24, 952. 99	13. 0	18, 934
2008	2, 561. 60	17. 80	30, 067. 00	9. 0	22, 640
2009	2, 207. 20	−13. 9	33, 535. 30	8. 7	25, 575
2010	2, 972. 80	34. 7	39, 798. 30	10. 3	29, 524
2011	3, 641. 80	22. 5	47, 211. 50	7. 7	35, 181
2012	3, 866. 70	6. 2	51, 932. 20	7. 8	38, 354

Source: Calculated on the Basis of *China Statistical Yearbook of 2012* and Official Website of China's National Bureau of Statistics.

7. 4. 2   Interrelationship Between China's Foreign Trade and Economic Growth

Since the reform and opening up, China has made remarkable achievements in its economy and foreign trade. Economy and foreign trade promote and supplement each other. Such a relationship can be confirmed both by the changes in total volume and structure.

A. Statistically, Growth of Foreign Trade Promotes the Growth of Economy

Since the reform and opening up, China's foreign trade has developed at a higher speed than the gross domestic product, and has become an important promoter of the national economy. The relevant statistics of the years from 1990 to 2012 (see Table 7. 4) can attest to the positive effect of foreign trade on the growth of the economy.

China's foreign trade developed basically in line with the economic growth. When the economy fluctuated, foreign trade would be affected accordingly. In other words, when the economy kept developing at a high growth rate, foreign trade would develop rapidly, but when the growth rate of economy slowed down, foreign trade would be sluggish. This was obviously displayed by the growth of GDP and the increase of the total value of import and export. On the whole, the growing trend of the national economy and foreign trade between 1978 and 2012 was on the increase and displayed a close relationship of mutual dependency. This was in agreement with the observation of the academic world about the relatively fast post-war economic development of South Korea, Singapore and Malaysia. , namely, in the primary phase or "take-off" phase of a country's economy, foreign trade and national economy are mutually dependent.

In short, in an open economy, the growth of the national economy cannot be separated from the increase of foreign trade. Since the reform and opening up, China has developed its foreign trade, and made marked achievements in the use of domestic and foreign resources, the improvement of the allocation of domestic resources, and the promotion of economic development. The total value of China's national economy and the growth of foreign trade are highly interrelated and foreign trade has played an outstanding role in promoting the national economy.

B. Structural Changes of Foreign Trade Bring about the Fast Growth of National Economy and the Improvement of Export Product Quality

Dramatic changes have taken place in the structure of foreign trade since the reform and opening up. China has evolved from an exporter of primary products in the beginning of the reform into a large exporter of predominantly manufactured products, with an increasingly rising percentage of high-tech products. The marked optimization and promotion of the structure of foreign trade have contributed significantly to the growth of the national economy in terms of quality and benefits.

a. Influence of Structural Changes of Export Products on the Economic Growth

The percentage of manufactured goods in exported commodities is an important measurement of a country's industrialization and its optimization of the structure of exported commodities. The percentage of manufactured goods for export has steadily risen in China since the reform and opening up. The added-value of exported products has significantly increased with the transition from mainly primary products to predominantly mechanical and electrical products.

Table 7.5   Structure of China's Exported Products: 1980−2011   Measurement Unit: %

Year	Percentage of primary Products	Percentage of Manufactured Goods	Percentage of Machinery and Transport Equipemnt
1980	50. 3	49. 7	4. 7
1985	50. 6	49. 4	2. 8
1990	25. 6	74. 4	9. 0
1991	22. 5	77. 5	9. 9
1992	20. 0	80. 0	15. 6
1993	18. 2	81. 8	16. 7
1994	16. 3	83. 7	18. 1
1995	14. 4	85. 6	21. 1
1996	14. 5	85. 5	23. 4
1997	13. 1	86. 9	23. 9
1998	11. 2	88. 8	27. 3
1999	10. 2	89. 8	30. 2
2000	10. 2	89. 8	33. 1
2001	9. 9	90. 1	35. 7
2002	8. 8	91. 2	39. 0
2003	7. 9	92. 1	42. 8
2004	6. 8	93. 2	45. 2
2005	6. 4	93. 6	46. 2
2006	5. 5	94. 5	47. 1
2007	5. 1	94. 9	47. 4
2008	5. 4	94. 6	47. 1
2009	5. 3	94. 7	49. 1
2010	5. 2	94. 8	49. 5
2011	5. 3	94. 7	47. 5

Source: Calculated on the Basis of *China Statistical Yearbook* and Official Website of China's National Bureau of Statistics.

As is shown in Table 7. 5, from 1980 to 2011, the percentage of exported manufactured goods in the total volume of export rose by 45 percentage points from 49. 7% to 94. 7% , while the percentage of exported primary products dropped from 50. 3% to 5. 3% . It indicates that China is no longer a small exporter as it was in the beginning of the reform when it exported both primary and manufactured goods, but it has become a large exporter with the export of manufactured goods accounting for more than 90% of the total export products.

Meanwhile the internal structure of manufactured products has also changed considerably, showing an upgrading development tendency. This can be proved by the large increase of the percentage of technology-intensive machinery and transport equipment in the total volume of export. It can be clearly seen from the table that the percentage of machinery and transport equipment accounted for 4. 7% of the total volume of export in 1980 and rose by nearly 45 percentage points to 47. 5% in 2011.

From the above analysis, we have come to know that in a period of a bit more than 30 years, the structure of China's export has changed dramatically and has been steadily upgraded and optimized. It has witnessed the transformation from primary goods to manufactured products, and from resource-intensive products to labor-intensive products. The contribution of upgrading of export structure to economic growth is reflected in the structure of production and the total export volume.

Firstly, the transformation of export structure improved the structure of production. The transformation of export structure is the result of, and at the same time the external stimulus to, the transformation of production structure and promoted the latter's optimization and adjustment. Let's take China's industry for an example. The percentage of textiles dropped both in production and in export and it dropped faster in export than in production. The percentages of steel and other metals, machinery and transport equipment were on the increase both in production and in export, and they increased faster in export than in production. This suggests that for a rapidly changing industry, whether growing fast or declining, the transformation of export structure takes place faster than that of production structure. It is obvious that export structure leads the production structure and the upgrading of production structure provides a more spacious room for growth of the economy.

Secondly, the transformation of export structure expanded the total volume of export. The optimization of export structure led to the increase of total volume of export. Since export itself is an integral part of gross domestic production, the optimization of export structure will certainly promote economic growth. The expansion of the total volume of export brought about by the optimization of export structure leads to the increase of foreign exchange. The total foreign exchange of China was USD 0. 167 billion in 1978. With the rapid growth of export, the foreign exchange reserves multiplied fast. The national reserve balance added up to USD 3,311.6 billion at the end of 2012 and China became the first largest nation in terms of foreign exchange reserves. The foreign exchange reserves helped settle the problem of fund shortage in China's economic construction and enhanced China's import capacity. It played an immeasurable role in meeting the requirements of resources and technology that handicapped the economic growth and greatly expanded the total volume of the national economy.

b. Influence of Structural Changes of Import Products on China's Economic Growth

Before the reform and opening up, the proportion of primary goods was quite high among imported products. Basic food accounted for a high percentage of imported goods, the highest being 26%. After the reform and opening up, the percentage of imported primary products began to fall, among which the percentage of imported food and live animals for food dropped markedly. The proportion of imported inedible raw materials kept stable in recent years. Imported manufactured products kept increasing, and the import of machinery and transport equipment, in particular, rose markedly and the import of capital goods accounted for a rather high percentage, too, as is shown in Table 7.6.

Table 7.6   Structure of China's Import Products: 1980–2011 Measurement Unit: %

Year	Percentage of Primary Products	Percentage of Food and Live Animals for food	Percentage of Inedible Raw Material	Percentage of Manufactured Products	Percentage of Machinery and Transport Equipment
1980	34.8	14.6	17.8	65.2	25.6
1985	12.5	3.7	7.7	87.5	38.4
1990	18.5	6.3	7.7	81.5	31.6
1991	17.0	4.4	7.8	83.0	30.7
1992	16.4	3.9	7.2	83.6	38.9
1993	13.7	2.1	5.2	86.3	43.3
1994	14.3	2.7	6.4	85.7	44.5
1995	18.5	4.6	7.7	81.5	39.9
1996	18.3	4.1	7.7	81.7	39.4
1997	20.1	3.0	8.4	79.9	37.1
1998	16.4	2.7	7.6	83.6	40.5
1999	16.2	2.2	7.7	83.8	41.9

Cont.

Year	Percentage of Primary Products	Percentage of Food and Live Animals for food	Percentage of Inedible Raw Material	Percentage of Manufactured Products	Percentage of Machinery and Transport Equipment
2000	20. 8	2. 1	8. 9	79. 2	40. 8
2001	18. 8	2. 0	9. 1	81. 2	43. 9
2002	16. 7	1. 8	7. 7	83. 3	46. 4
2003	17. 6	1. 4	8. 3	82. 4	46. 7
2004	20. 9	1. 6	9. 9	79. 1	45. 0
2005	22. 4	1. 4	10. 6	77. 6	44. 0
2006	23. 6	1. 3	10. 5	76. 4	45. 1
2007	25. 4	1. 2	12. 3	74. 6	43. 1
2008	32. 0	1. 2	14. 7	68. 0	39. 0
2009	28. 8	1. 5	14. 1	71. 2	40. 5
2010	31. 1	1. 5	15. 2	68. 9	39. 3
2011	34. 7	1. 7	16. 3	65. 3	36. 2

Source: Calculated on the Basis of *China Statistical Yearbook* and Official Website of China's National Bureau of Statistics.

As Table 7. 6 indicates, in the initial years of reform and opening up, import products were, to a great extent, a measure taken to make up for the shortage of domestic means of livelihood. As a result, the role of import was restricted for production and thus for the promotion of economic growth. The total import value of primary products in 1980, for example, was USD 6. 959 billion, accounting for 34. 8% of the gross import value, of which the import value of food and live animals for food was USD 2. 927 billion, 14. 6% of the gross import value. The import value of inedible raw materials was USD 3. 554 billion, 17. 8% of the total import value. The import value of manufactured products in the same year was USD 13. 058 billion, accounting for 65. 2% of the total import value, of which the import value of machinery and transport equipment was USD 5. 119 billion, 25. 6% of the total import value.

Since the 1980s, the position and role of foreign trade was reconsidered and reevaluated. Foreign trade as an important force to promote the growth of economy was no longer treated as a means of compensation for the needed products. In the course of rapid economic growth, more and more capital goods were imported. By 2011, the import value of manufactured products was USD

1, 139. 215 billion, accounting for 65. 3% of the total import value, of which the import value of machinery and transport equipment was USD 630. 57 billion, accounting for 36. 2% of the total import value, 123. 2 times that of 1980. The import value of primary products in the same year was USD 604. 269 billion, accounting only 34. 3% of the total import value, of which the import value of food and live animals was USD 28. 774 billion, accounting for only 1. 7% of the total import value; the import value of inedible materials was USD 284. 923 billion, accounting for 16. 3% . The import of capital goods significantly improved domestic conditions of production and considerably enhanced the production efficiency. Meanwhile, the import of machinery not only promoted the development of the industrial sector, but also transformed agriculture and other traditional industries and enhanced the upgrading of industrial structure. The improvement of technology and upgrading of industrial structure contributed to the quality and efficiency of economic growth and added to the potential power of economic growth.

According to the figures by China's customs, the import of high-tech products was on the increase from 1991 on. The import value of high-tech products in 2012 was USD 506. 75 billion, an increase of 9. 5% over the year before. The import of high-tech products was mainly in the areas of electronic technique, computer and communication technology and computer-integrated manufacturing technology. The import of these high-tech products was of great significance to the transformation of insufficient mode of economic growth, the improvement of its quality and efficiency and sustainable development of the economy.

In a word, the influence of foreign trade on economic growth was reflected not only in the expansion of foreign trade that contributed to economic growth, but also reflected in the upgrading of foreign trade structure that promoted the expansion of economic growth and improved its quality and efficiency. From the perspective of sustainable development, the latter had far-reaching and more meaningful influence. Therefore, the upgrading of foreign trade structure and, on the basis of this, the expansion of foreign trade scope, were the main "driving motors" or "catalyser" of China's economic growth in the context of an open economy.

7. 4. 3   China's Dependence on Foreign Trade

Foreign trade in China evolved in keeping with, or in parallel with, its economic growth. But Kiyoshi Kojima, a Japanese economist, holds that if the increase of foreign trade keeps in line with national economy, it does not necessarily mean that, when viewed from a longer period of economic growth, the development of foreign trade has promoted economic growth. In other words, economic growth is not necessarily brought about by foreign trade. To reveal the impact of foreign trade on economic growth, it is proper to compare the increase of foreign trade with the growth of national economy. Therefore, the variation of a country's dependence on foreign trade can reveal the interrelationship between foreign trade and economic growth.

A. Definition of Dependence on Foreign Trade

Dependence on foreign trade refers to the radio of a country's total value of foreign trade to its gross domestic product in a certain period of time (usually a year). It is used to measure a country's economic dependence on the world market. It can be further classified into two subcategories: dependence on export and dependence on import. The former refers to the ratio of total export value to the total value of gross domestic product and the latter, to the ratio of total import value to the total value of gross domestic product.

B. Factors That Affect the Dependence on Foreign Trade

The following factors will affect a country's dependence on foreign trade.

a. Dependence on Foreign Trade and Scope of Economic Development

There is an inverse relationship between a country's dependence on foreign trade and the scope of economic growth. A small country usually depends more on foreign trade because its economic growth is mainly influenced by external markets and external liquidity. A large country's major driving force comes from internal markets and compared with small countries, it depends less on foreign trade.

b. Dependence on Foreign Trade and Stages of Economic Development

The economic development of countries in the present world can be classified into three different types in accordance with the stages of industrialization and industrial structures the countries find themselves in: primary development stage, intermediate development stage and high development stage. A country in the primary development stage has little connection with the outside world and depends less on export. A country in the intermediate development stage usually places heavy industry in the central position of its economic growth and the needed raw materials and fuel must be imported in great quantities. In order to balance trade, it has to export in great quantities accordingly. Such countries depend more on export. A country in the high development stage normally places high technology in the central position and its industrial structure is highly technology-intensive. Such countries earn profits through the output of capital, technology and management and depend relatively little on export.

c. Dependence on Foreign Trade and Foreign Policies or Foreign Trade System

The countries or regions that pursue the liberalization of trade emphasize the point of minimum interference from governments to maintain the most liberalization of international trade. For small countries, free trade policies will surely lead to relatively high dependence on foreign trade while for large countries, when free trade policies are adopted, dependence on foreign trade mainly involve other elements. The countries that practice protectionist trade policies are usually economically weak and their internal markets are far from perfect. They depend little on foreign trade.

For developing countries, if they depend more on export for economic growth rather than on domestic consumption and increase of investment, then they depend more on foreign trade. Once unrest occurs in the world market, especially when the price for export products at home drops sharply, domestic economy will be severely affected.

But if developing countries rely more on domestic investment and increase of consumption for their economic growth and ignore the positive effects of export, the economic growth will lack the driving force for international competition, and the result might also be destructive. Therefore, dependence on foreign trade should be brought under proper control.

C. Empirical Analysis of China's Dependence on Foreign Trade

China's dependence on foreign trade was 9.74% in 1978, of which export dependence was 4.60% and import dependence was 5.14%. Then in 2007, China's dependence on foreign trade was 66.82%, of which export dependence was 37.45% and import dependence was 29.37%. China's dependence of foreign trade in 2007 was 7 times that of 1978, of which export dependence was 9 times that of 1978 and import dependence was 7 times. The growth rate of export dependence was higher than that of import dependence, which indicates that in China's foreign trade, the role of export became more and more outstanding.

Since 2008, China's dependence on foreign trade dropped with each passing year. It decreased by 3.1% in 2012 compared with that of 2011 to 47%, back to the point of less than 50%, of which export dependence was 24.9% and import dependence was 22.1%, both declining to some extent (see Figure 7.3). It clearly indicates that China had made great achievements in transforming the economic growth mode from relying on foreign demand to relying on domestic demand.

What is noteworthy is that, at present, China is still in the primary stage in terms of international industry specialization. Its competitiveness is mainly in labor-intensive products or labor-intensive steps for making high-tech products. That means that there is still much room for China to transform its economic development mode. What can be foreseen is that by applying scientific outlook on development, carrying out economic restructuring and transforming the economic development mode, China's economy will depend more on domestic demand, and probably still less on foreign trade.

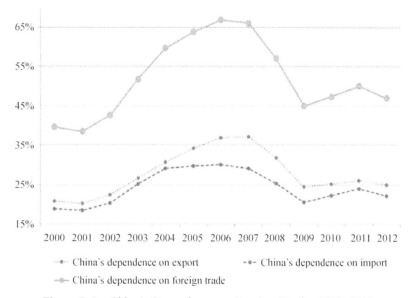

Figure 7. 5   China's Dependence on Foreign Trade: 2000-2012

Compared with other countries, China on the whole depends relatively more on foreign trade. But this is only at the superficial level. In reality, China's dependence is exaggerated to some extent for the following reasons.

a. RMB Exchange Rate

The undervalued Chinese currency (RMB) is the main factor that has brought about the overestimation of China's dependence on foreign trade. Since the reform of exchange rate in the mid -1990s, the RMB exchange rate has long been in an unbalanced state. The actual undervalued Chinese currency has brought about a long-term favorable balance of trade in China and, at the same time, an overestimation of China's dependence on foreign trade. Simply, China's gross domestic product in U. S. dollars will increase considerably and its dependence on foreign trade will decline by two-thirds if the equilibrium level of the RMB exchange rate is adjusted in accordance with the purchasing power parity and the calculation is done by the purchasing power parity of RMB (1 dollar =2 yuan) which is adopted by the IMF and widely used in the world.

On the other hand, China's export would be affected if the RMB exchange rate were adjusted in the direction of appreciation. In that case, China's products would be less competitive in the international markets, the foreign trade scale, especially export scale, would decline and China's dependence on foreign trade would also decrease. Therefore, when the RMB exchange rate was adjusted to the purchasing power parity level, China's dependence on foreign trade would be reduced by more than two-thirds. What is worth noting is that, compared with the purchasing power parity, the exchange rates of developing countries are generally undervalued while those of developed countries are roughly the same as the purchasing power parity. As a result, for most developing countries, the dependence on foreign trade is overestimated. Considering the above-mentioned, we can conclude that, on a conservative estimate, China's dependence on foreign trade is 100 percent overvalued.

b. Processing Trade

The study of China's dependence on foreign trade cannot exclude processing trade. The rapid development of processing trade in China has made great impact on its dependence because processing trade has become China's most important mode of foreign trade. Although the purchasing rate and value-added ratio of the products inside China have increased in recent years, the growth of processing trade has little connection with the operation of the domestic economy. As a result, the use of an index system including processing trade might overestimate the dependence of China's economy on international markets.

c. Composition of GDP

When we compare a country's dependence on foreign trade with other countries, we need to bring into consideration the different compositions of GDP in different countries. Generally, the tertiary industry is not as tradable as others. So the higher a country's percentage of tertiary industry in GDP is, the lower its dependence on foreign trade might be. Conversely, the lower a country's percentage of tertiary industry in GDP is, the higher its dependence on foreign trade might be. There is a great difference between countries in the composition of GDP. In the United States, for example, the tertiary industry accounts for about 80% of GDP, and in Japan, about 70% . But in China, the tertiary industry accounts for only about 33% . If we compare the different degrees of dependence on foreign trade between countries without taking into account the differences in their GDP compositions, we might get misleading conclusions.

Case 7. 1   Haier Group's International Strategy

Brief Introduction to the Case

The route of international operation Haier Group can roughly be divided into four periods: 1. Brand-making at home: 1984－1990; 2. Exploring international markets: 1990－1996; 3. Tentative overseas investment: 1996－1998; 4. Globalized development: 1999 － present. Through nearly a decade of exploration, Haier Group established a mature "three one-third's international market development strategy", namely, of the total value of sales, one-third comes from the domestic sales of the goods produced at home, one-third from international sales produced at home and one-third from international sales produced overseas.

Company Profile

Qingdao Refrigerator Factory, the predecessor of Haier Group, was founded in December, 1984. In the following three decades, Haier Group has grown from a small factory of collective ownership, with less than 800 employees, sales revenue of RMB 3. 80 million, and the deficit reaching as high as RMB 1. 47 million, into a large internationalized enterprise group integrating scientific research, production, trade and finance into one. At present, it is moving towards the goal of Fortune Global 500 Companies. Mr. Zhang Ruimin, Chairman of the Board of Directors and CEO, is one of the main founders of Haier Group.

Haier Group has established 21 Industry Zones, 5 Research and Development Centers and 19 Overseas Trading Companies around the globe. With more than 80, 000 employees, its turnover reached RMB 150. 9 billion in 2011, of which the brand value reached to RMB 96. 28 billion. For 11 years successively, it had been on the top of the list for the most valuable brand value in China. Haier Group has actively fulfilled its social responsibility by means of providing the fund for building 164 Hope Primary Schools and 1 Hope Middle School and making 212 sets of science and education animated films entitled Haier Brothers. Haier Group was the only white goods sponsor for the 2008 Beijing Olympic Games.

Under the guidance of the brand strategy put forward by Mr. Zhang Ruimin, Haier Group adopted one after another brand strategy, diversification strategy and internationalization strategy. Towards the end of 2005, Haier Group entered the period of the implementation of the fourth strategy—global branding strategy. As has been mentioned before, Haier Group made great achievements in

2011, with the turnover of RMB 150. 9 billion, its brand value RMB 96. 28 billion, and stayed on the top of the list for the most valuable brand value in China for 11 years successively. Nineteen kinds of goods produced by Haier Group such as fridges, air-conditioners, washing machines, water heaters, computers, mobile phones and smart home integrations were appraised as famous brands in China. Of these goods, the fridges and washing machines were named "first world famous brands in China" by the National Administration of Quality Supervision, Inspection and Quarantine.

Haier was chosen as one of the "Top Ten World Class Brands in China" by the Financial Times for the second time in March, 2008. Ranking the 13th on the Forbes list of the Top 600 World's Most Prestigious Enterprises in June, 2008, Haier Group was listed the highest of the Chinese enterprises. In the selection of "Top 200 Asian Enterprises" organized by The Wall Street Journal Asia in July, 2008, Haier Group was at the top of "Enterprise Leadership in Mainland China" for the 5th time. In a word, Haier has been among the ranks of world-class brands and its influence is increasing rapidly with the expansion of its global markets.

By June, 2011, Haier's cumulative applications for patents totaled 11, 315 in number, including 3, 666 patents for invention. As of June 2011, Haier Group applied for 671 patents in the first few months of the year, including 291 patents for invention, nearly 3 patents for invention for each working day. Based on proprietary intellectual property rights, Haier Group has actively participated in the formulation of 23 international standards, 7 of which, for example, about no-powder washing technology and electricity guard technology, have already been issued. This indicates that Haier's technological innovation is recognized in the field of international standardization. Haier has led or participated in the formulation and revision of 283 national standards, of which 267 have been issued, and 10 have won the National Standards Innovation and Contribution Awards. Haier has also participated in the formulation of 447 industry standards and other standards. Haier Group is the household appliance enterprise that has participated most in the formulation of international, national and industry standards. Haier Group is the only representative of enterprises from developing countries that has entered the International Electrotechnical Commission (IEC), the decision-making body in the industry. Haier Group was selected by IEC in June, 2009 to be the "practice base for standard innovation", the first in the world, and was chosen to be one of the 1st model enterprises for national technical innovation in China in 2011.

In the course of exploration and innovation, Haier Group has adopted "Overall

Every Control and Clear" Management Model, "Market Chain" Management Model and "Oneness of Person-Order" Development Model which have attracted the attention of international management. At present, special case studies have been done by Harvard University, University of Southern California, International Institute for Management Development (IMD), European School of Management, and Kobe University. More than 30 of Haier's management case studies have been incorporated into the case studies corpuses of 12 universities in the world. One of Haier's management cases—"Activating Stunned Fish", for example, has been incorporated into the case studies corpus of Harvard Business School and the "Market Chain" management has been incorporated into the management case studies corpus of the European Union.

Case Analysis

Haier Group's localization strategy regarding overseas direct investment can be summarized as "Three in One" and "Three and One". The former refers to the realization of local design, local production and local sales in one foreign country; the latter refers to the integration of local financing, local talents and local culture and the creation of localized famous brands.

The internationalization strategy of Haier Group includes an investment strategy in ten large economic zones around the globe. Haier Group has divided the world market into ten influential economic communities. They have chosen locations for their factories in each community so that when 60% of their products can be consumed locally, they could send their products to other member nations in the community to gain such preferential treatments as tariffs and to achieve more rapid development.

In the course of overseas investment and operations, Haier Group has followed the overseas investment principle of "Market Shares before Building Factories" and "Break-Even Point". In other words, Haier Group's overseas direct investment proceeds like this: exports → sales network → branding → achieving break-even point → investment in factories. It can be seen that Haier's decision to invest in factories in the local area depends on whether Haier's brand is accepted by the local market or whether Haier's products could find markets in the local area.

In the course of internationalization, Haier Group has put forward the idea of "choosing the difficult before the easy". Its export strategy is a typical example. Generally, any enterprise that attempts an international operation would start with the easy before the difficult, and then gradually gain experience and become stronger. But Haier has done just the opposite in its exports. Haier took the developed countries as its target market and exported their products there to establish their brands before it opened up the markets in developing countries. In this way, Haier has attained its goals of both establishing its brands and occupying the markets. It shows that Haier Group has not taken a normally progressive path in its growth, but it has taken a great-leap-forward path on the basis of its brand-making strategy and its own advantages.

Haier's internationalization strategy can be roughly divided into the above-mentioned three strategies: three one-third's strategy, localization strategy and ten large economic zones strategy. The key to Haier's success in its overseas direct investment is the implementation of its localization strategy, which is also the necessary path for Haier Group to go from "Globalized Haier" to "Haier International".

Case 7. 2   China Ocean Shipping Company: An Impetus for China's Foreign Trade Development

China Ocean Shipping

Brief Introduction to the Case

China Ocean Shipping Company (COSCO) is a multinational enterprise group whose main business is shipping and logistics. While devoted to shipping and logistics service for clients around the world, COSCO also provides quality services in the construction and repair of ships, ocean engineering, wharf, trade, finance and information technology. COSCO is people-and-market oriented, and relies heavily on science and technology for the best possible returns.

Performing its duties as an enterprise, COSCO keeps engaging itself in both production management and capital management. With international shipping as its main industry, it also attempts to expand its service in logistics, to develop the construction and repair of ships, and to explore energy resources so that it can turn from a global shipping carrier to a logistics service provider backed up by shipping and to a leader in international shipping and logistics.

Turning from a company engaged in multinational business to a multinational corporation, COSCO functions as a strong impetus for China's foreign trade growth.

Company Profile

China Ocean Shipping Company or COSCO is one of the super-large central enterprises controlled directly by the central government. COSCO has evolved from a small shipping company founded on April 27, 1961 when it had only 4 ocean ships with a total deadweight of 22,600 tons. By 2012, COSCO had become a multinational enterprise group with shipping, logistics and construction and repair of ships as its main businesses. Having established itself as a leader in international shipping, logistics and construction and repair of ships, COSCO is one of the Fortune Global 500 enterprises, ranking the 384th on the Fortune 500 list in 2012.

As of 2011, COSCO possessed and controlled nearly 800 modernized merchant ships with a total deadweight of 560 billion tons and the volume of cargo transportation per year reached more than 400 million tons. Its ocean-going shipping lines covered over 1,600 ports in more than 160 countries and regions. Its overall fleet size ranked 1st in China and 2nd in the world, of which the container ship fleet ranked 1st in China and 6th in the world, the dry bulk carriers fleet ranked the 1st in the world, and the general vessel fleet, multifunctional fleet and special transportation fleet were among the 1st in the world and the tanker fleet was one of the super tanker fleets in the world. COSCO invested in and operated 32 wharfs worldwide with 157 berths in all. According to the latest statistics published by Drewry in July, 2009, the throughput of container terminals in the Pacific owned by COSCO in 2008 stayed the fifth in the world.

With tremendous logistics resources—over 4,000 logistics vehicles including large carrier vehicles, each with 289 axes and a maximum loadability of 8,000 tons, storage yards covering 2.49 million square meters and storehouses covering 2.97 million square meters, COSCO provides clients with high value-added services in the fields of home appliances, chemical products, power and financing. It has provided logistics services, for example, for many important projects at home and abroad such as the Qinghai-Tibet Railway, Tianjin Airbus and India's Power Plant and has made a number of records in the industry.

According to the data collected from COSCO's official website in 2012, the multinational company possessed several ship-building and repair bases with 16 shipyards which were capable of building or repairing 300,000 or 500,000 tonners. Its business included construction, modification and repair of large-sized ships and ocean engineering. With leading production equipment and management, advanced technology, high production efficiency and relatively low cost of production, COSCO is the largest ship-repairing and the most advanced ship-building enterprise in China, capable of repairing and modifying 500 large ships, and building 840 tons of ships annually.

As of 2012, COSCO had established a global framework for businesses, with Beijing at the centre, and nine regional companies — Hong Kong, America, Europe, Singapore, Japan, Australia, South Korea, West Asia and Africa — outside. COSCO owns over a thousand enterprises and branches in more than 50 countries and regions with some 130,000 employees. More than 400 Chinese employees were stationed abroad and over 4,000 foreign people were employed. The gross value of assets amounted to RMB 300 billion. Its overseas assets and earnings added up to more than half of the total. It has formed a complete business chain of shipping, logistics, wharfs, ship-building and repair around the globe.

Graphical Symbol of COSCO

The graphical symbol of COSCO is a ship-like graphic formed with COSCO, the abbreviation of the company's English name. The symbol, widely used by COSCO in its business operations, reflects quite outstandingly the industry features and operation principles of COSCO. The blue color signifies the close connection between the company and the sea. With cleverly constructed patterns and far-reaching significance, the image symbolizes COSCO's spirit of riding the waves forward like a ship, with a determined mind, to the outside world.

Case Analysis

COSCO is one of the Chinese enterprises that gained the earliest access to international capital markets. As early as 1993, COSCO Corp came into the market in Singapore through back door listing. At present, COSCO is the dominant shareholder or equity participant of such listed companies as China COSCO, COSCO Pacific, COSCO-HIT, COSCO Corp, COSCOL, CIMC, and CMBC. On May 30, 2010, COSCO was selected as one of the Fortune Global 500 firms by Financial Times, a famous British business newspaper and was ranked the 450th. This was the third time that COSCO was selected since 2008.

Going global has become an outstanding and distinct feature of COSCO in the new period of development. Since the beginning of the 21st century, COSCO has sped up its globalization process with globalized operational service, capital management, cultural management, cooperative competition, social responsibility and diplomatic resources as its essential features.

As a Chinese multinational corporation, COSCO has paid great attention, from the early time in its history, to its corporate citizen's social responsibility. COSCO has put forward its definite goals "to develop and establish its leadership in the fields of shipping, logistics and ship-building and repair; to keep honest and mutually trusted relationships with customers, employees and business partners, and to pay back to the greatest extent the shareholders, community and environment. " COSCO established a comprehensive management system in 2001 including an international environment management system and occupational health and safety management system and became the first Chinese enterprise to obtain certificates of the three major management systems. It began to participate officially in the United Nations Global Compact in 2004 and took the initiative to carry out the ten basic principles listed in the Global Compact and made great efforts to realize sustainable development. Its sustainable development reports were recognized by the United Nations Global Compact as model reports for four years in a row and COSCO was the first Asian enterprise to win such honors.

Case 7. 3   Globalization of Jiangsu Sunshine Group

Brief Introduction to the Case

Based on the world textile market, Jiangsu Sunshine Group is an international brand group, characterized by prominent textile industry, outstanding brand, strong research and development team, and multi-industry production and operation. In the course of development, Jiangsu Sunshine Group applies the intra-industry trade theory and economics of scale theory, makes the best use of advantages of China's raw material quality, human resources and its own advanced technology and management, devotes itself to brand-building, and constantly cultivates new growth points. At present, its total assets amount to RMB 3.65 billion.

Company Profile

Jiangsu Sunshine Group, founded in 1986, is one of the national key enterprises and one of the 33 industries supported by the state. With 15,000 employees, it is the largest enterprise in China's textile industry, with the most variety of products, the best quality, the most advanced technology and the best equipment. It has formed a diversified production pattern including textile products, apparel, biomedicine, and thermoelectricity.

Jiangsu Sunshine Group is China's largest fine wool production and high-thin worsted manufacturing enterprise and high-thin worsted fabric production base.

The Group covers an area of 800,000 square meters. The total assets amount to RMB 4,000 million and the fixed assets add up to RMB 2,500 million. It has invested RMB 1.2 billion in complete sets of world-advanced equipment for spinning, weaving, dyeing, detecting, and clothes-making. The equipment was imported from dozens of countries in the world such as Germany, France, Italy, Switzerland, and Belgium. Now, with 115,000 worsted yarn spindles, 600 weaving machines and 2 high-end clothing production lines, the Group is capable of producing 22 million meters of worsted fabrics or cashmere, and 600,000 sets of high-end clothing a year.

The Jiangsu Sunshine Group has gained both ISO9002 quality system certification and ISO14001 environment system certification, and is at present the largest worsted fabric and apparel production base in China. Its scale of production ranks the 3rd in the world.

Case Analysis

According to the development goals of industries in the "10th Five-Year Plan", conventional industries should be made high-tech and high-tech industries should be scaled up. In such a context, Jiangsu Sunshine Group has strengthened its scientific management and oriented itself to the needs of global competition and to scientific and international operation. It has developed two sets of products. The first set is fabrics, which includes more than 6,000 kinds in 20 categories: woolen cloth series, suede series, TEN-CEL series, linen series, ecological silk protein series, novel synthetic fibers series, and cashmere wool series. 60 of these were recognized as national or provincial new high-tech products or newly-developed key products. The second set is apparel, which is targeted at white-collar workers. Now there are such brands as VENETIA (Suits), GEZELIA (Women's dress), POMPEI (Business wear).

Jiangsu Sunshine Group attaches great importance to research and development.

It has established one national technology research center, one wool spinning research institute, and one postdoctoral scientific research station, the only one in China's wool spinning enterprises. It has set up information agencies in foreign countries such as the United States, Italy, and Australia and also in big cities in China: Hong Kong, Beijing and Shanghai. By associating closely with more than 20 universities, the Group has formed a new product development mechanism that is leading in China and synchronous with the world's most advanced level, and a technology innovation system that integrates production, learning and research. At present, the Group is capable of developing 7 to 10 new products every day.

According to the intra-industry trade theory, it is possible for the same industry to exchange differentiated goods and intermediate goods. The success of Jiangsu Sunshine Group is that it makes the best use of the difference of factor endowment between China and other countries. The difference of factor endowment will necessarily lead to the difference of comparative cost, which constitutes the foundation and cause for intra-industry trade. Since the textiles made in different parts of the world are different, Jiangsu Sunshine Group takes advantage of the factor endowment of China's raw material and product differentiation, and has become the supplier of fabrics for several famous brands in the world. The Group also makes full use of its economies of scale and imperfect competition.

The development of economies of scale inside an industry leads to imperfect competition. Jiangsu Sunshine Group produces high-quality fabrics on one hand and on the other hand, it introduces advanced technology and equipment to produce garments. As its production has reached a considerable scale, it is in a favorable monopoly position in the world market. Textiles are labor intensive products. Jiangsu Sunshine Group has made use of the advantage of the factor endowment in Chinese human resources that gives it a competitive edge over its international competitors.

The theory of increasing returns to scale put forward by American economist Paul Krugman holds that when the production of a product increases in number or the scale of production expands, the unit product cost will decrease and the low-cost advantage will be achieved. As a result of this, favorable conditions for specialized production and export will emerge. Jiangsu Sunshine Group has positioned its products as high-grade fabrics and high-end clothing and determined its annual production scale as 22 million meters of fabrics and 600, 000 sets of clothing.

When the scale of production has reached that level, all factors of production have been brought into full play and division of labor on the basis of specialization has been strengthened. Jiangsu Sunshine Group, for example, has divided clothing into several featured products like VENETIA, GEZELIA and POMPEI. These featured products are manufactured with different technology and mode of management, but they are all quite advanced in international business.

There is no doubt that disadvantages would arise if these featured products were manufactured in a mixed manner. Economies of scale has also enabled Jiangsu Sunshine Group to make the best use of its own business environment such as transportation, communication facilities, financial institutions, and natural resources to obtain the benefits brought about by economies of scale.

Case 7. 4 Hangzhou Great Star Industrial Co. Ltd: Going from ODM to OBM

Brief Introduction to the Case

Hangzhou Great Star Industrial Co. Ltd. (stock exchange code: 002444, stock short name of its ordinary shares: "Great Star Industrial") is an enterprise that specializes in the development, production and sale of middle-and-top-grade hand-tools and electric tools. It is one of the leading enterprises in the field of hardware tools in China with the largest scale, most advanced technology, and the most advantageous channels. In terms of hand-tools, it is the largest in Asia and top six in the world. Compared with most domestic hardware tool manufacturers that still stick to the OEM business model, Hangzhou Great Star Industrial Co. Ltd. is already on its way from ODM (Original Design Manufacturer) to OBM (Original Brand Manufacturer).

Company Profile

Hangzhou Great Star Industrial Co. Ltd. , founded in 1993, has specialized in manufacturing hand-tools and electric tools that are closely related to our daily life. With a determined and innovative spirit, it has developed thousands of kinds of products that are sold worldwide and are favored by consumers at home and abroad.

Since its founding, Hangzhou Great Star Industrial Co. Ltd. has attached great importance to independent innovation. With a large research and development team, it develops hundreds of new products every year. It was one of the top 100 China national innovative enterprises in 2008 and patent model enterprise in Zhejiang Province and provincial enterprise technology center. Based on the core idea that details count, it takes on itself the responsibility of making China's hardware industry internationally competitive and building century-old brands.

Hangzhou Great Star Industrial Co. Ltd. has maintained rapid economic growth ever since it was founded. By the end of 2009, its total assets amounted to RMB 918. 81 million. Its net profits increased from RMB 72. 27 million in 2007 to RMB 219. 33 million in 2009, an increase of 203. 48 percent. Its earnings per share increased from RMB 0. 68 in 2007 to RMB 1. 13 in 2009. In addition, diluted net assets income rate for the recent two years was 57. 09% and 46. 21% respectively.

Case Analysis

Although hardware tools are in great demand, the hardware tool industry is a very competitive one. To succeed in the industry, an enterprise must be very competitive. Hangzhou Great Star Industrial Co. Ltd. will most probably become a century-old-brand hardware tools manufacturer in China for the following reasons: 1. The influence of rapid growth of the Chinese economy; 2. The benefits of marked advantages of China's manufacturing in the world; 3. The company's own outstanding core competitiveness.

Hangzhou Great Star Industrial Co. Ltd. has taken advantage of its core competitiveness: distribution channels, research and development, brands and products, and has quickly become a hand-tool enterprise that is the largest in Asia and the 6th in the world. Its distribution channels has now covered the surface of the globe and thousands of types of its products are now sold in over 20 thousand chain supermarkets around the globe every day.

With a strong research and development team the Group owns 235 patents at home and abroad; about 400 newly developed products are put on the markets for sale every year. The sales volume of new products accounts for about 70% of the total main business income. The continuous introduction of new products has promoted the company and, therefore, the rapid increase of profits in recent years.

The Group's products with world-class brand "Sheffield" are widely sold in the world's largest hardware chain stores and department stores. Products with its own brands had gotten a pretty high gross profit margin which was rising continuously in three years, to as high as 33% in 2009. It is expected that in the future, with the implementation of the brand strategy, the gross profit margin of the Group's products will increase further so that more profits will be gained.

Compared with most Chinese hardware tool manufacturers who still adopt OEM (Original Equipment Manufacturer) operation mode, the operation mode of Hangzhou Great Star Industrial Co. Ltd. is moving from ODM to OBM. The present operation mode of the Group is mainly ODM. In other words, the

Group conducts the research and development of new products, and then provides clients with the design of new products, which will be sold with the clients' brands. The Group guides and strictly supervises the production technology, technical processes, and production specifications in the upper section of the industrial chain. Since the Group's products contain its own designs and other innovative elements, it can achieve more profits than it would by means of OEM.

In recent years, Hangzhou Great Star Industrial Co. Ltd. has gradually improved its independent research and development and production techniques. The sales volume brought about by the ODM mode account for more than 80 percent of the total main business income. The sales volumes brought about by the combination of ODM and OBM in 2007, 2008 and 2009 are 96. 86%, 98. 61% and 98. 97% respectively.

In the future, Hangzhou Great Star Industrial Co. Ltd. will stick to the core idea that "details count" and will go all out, with persistence and innovation, to improve its core competitiveness so as to maximize the shareholders' benefits.

Questions for discussion

1. State briefly China's foreign trade development since PRC was founded.

2. State briefly the international status of China's trade in goods and service trade.

3. Sketch out the main reform stages of China's foreign trade system since the reform and opening up.

4. Summarize the main characteristics of China's foreign trade system reform.

5. Why do we say that China's economic growth and foreign trade development supplement and promote each other?

6. What's the meaning of dependence on foreign trade? What do you think of China's dependence on foreign trade, high or low?

Along with the development of the economy and the move into ranks of middle – income countries, China has not only become a power in the world in terms of its introduction and utilization of foreign investment, but also been accelerating investment abroad, which is approaching the turning point of the balance between ODI (outward direct investment) and FDI (foreign direct investment). This part elaborates on the practice and management of Chinese utilization of FDI and ODI in detail.

Chapter 8

International Direct Investment- the Practice in China

8. 1　The Practice of Chinese Utilization of FDI

8. 1. 1　The Process of Chinese Utilization of FDI

The 3rd Plenary Session of the 11th Central Committee in 1978 marked the beginning of China's great journey of reform and opening up, along with which the use of foreign capital was more and more valued. Foreign capital utilization is an important way to obtain comparative benefits as well as a basic policy of China's opening to the outside world. Since then, the attention on foreign capital has always promoted the development of the Chinese economy, which has 30 years of history up till now. For more than 30 years, China has responded appropriately to the situation, adapted to the changes in the global economy and made great achievements in the utilization of foreign capital. (see Table 8. 1)

Table 8.1   The Overall Utilization of Foreign Direct Investment(1979−2012)

Year	No. of Projects	Contractual Foreign Investment (100 million USD)	The Actually Paid-in Capital (100 million USD)
1979−1984	3,724	97.50	41.04
1985	3,073	63.33	19.56
1986	1,498	33.30	22.44
1987	2,233	37.09	23.14
1988	5,945	52.97	31.94
1989	5,779	56.00	33.92
1990	7,273	65.96	34.87
1991	12,978	119.77	43.66
1992	48,764	581.24	110.08
1993	83,437	1,114.36	275.15
1994	47,549	826.80	337.67
1995	37,011	912.82	375.21
1996	24,556	732.76	417.26
1997	21,001	510.03	452.57
1998	19,799	521.02	454.63
1999	16,918	412.23	403.19
2000	22,347	623.80	407.15
2001	26,140	691.95	468.78
2002	34,171	827.68	527.43
2003	41,081	1,150.69	535.05
2004	43,664	1,534.79	606.30
2005	44,001	1,890.65	603.25
2006	41,473	1,937.27	630.21
2007	37,871	−	747.68
2008	27,514	−	923.95
2009	23,435	−	900.33
2010	27,406	−	1,057.35
2011	27,712	−	1,160.11
2012	24,925	−	1,117.16
1979−2012	763,278	−	11,761.08

Source: *China Statistical Yearbook 2012* and the Official Website of the Ministry of Commerce.

Table 8. 1 reveals that, from 1979 to 1984, the number of Chinese projects utilizing FDI was only 3, 724, with USD 9. 75billion of contractual foreign investment and USD 4. 104billion actually paid-in capital respectively, which indicates that FDI was small in China at that time. Nevertheless, the table displays that the use of foreign capital spurted a climax in 1992. The projects utilizing FDI added up to 48, 764, 4 times that of the previous year, while contractual foreign investment and the actual use of foreign investment reached USD 58. 124billion and USD 11. 068billion respectively, 5 and 2 times than the previous year respectively. In the same year, Deng Xiao-ping gave a speech in south China, which theoretically cleared the barrier in the use of foreign capital. After the speech, there was an intermittent growth in China's utilization of foreign investment due to the change of international and domestic situations. At the end of 2001, after China's entry into WTO, the pace of its reform and opening up further accelerated and the utilization of FDI grew correspondingly. The use of actual foreign capital amounted to USD 53. 505billion in 2003, to USD 63. 021billion in 2006 and USD 105. 735billion in 2010, which increased by 67. 8% compared with the year 2006. Affected by the global economic environment, there were 24, 925 newly approved foreign-invested enterprises in 2012, fell by 10. 06% . The amount of actually paid-in capital totaled USD 111. 716billion, fell by 3. 7% . It should be said that foreign direct investment has promoted the process of reform and opening up in China and has contributed greatly to the development of the Chinese economy. According to figures from the National Bureau of Statistics, by the end of 2012, there had been 763, 278 foreign-invested enterprises nationally. FDI contributed more than 40% to the GDP of China that year. It can be concluded that FDI has brought huge benefits to China, including a great promotion of the economic growth, employment, technology and independent innovation.

A. The Early Stage—from 1979 to 1984

The 3rd Plenary Session by the end of 1978 summed up the historical experience and lessons in time and made the basic state policy of opening up based on the over-all international and domestic situation, in the hope of making full use of the favorable condition of economic globalization to introduce international capital into Chinese construction. Therefore, after formulating new relevant regulations, policies and measures, China also improved the investment environment gradually and mobilized the initiative and enthusiasm of foreign merchants in investment. China's utilization of foreign capital achieved a preliminary development during this period. On July 1, 1979, the 2nd Plenary

Session of the National People's Congress passed and promulgated *The Sino-Foreign Joint Venture Law of the People's Republic of China*, which marked the historic inflow of FDI in China. From 1979 to 1980, special economic zones were set up successively in Shenzhen, Zhuhai, Shantou and Xiamen. Foreign direct investment enjoyed special preferential policies in the special economic zones.

In this initial phase, Deng Xiao-ping regarded, firstly, the capital and technology of overseas Chinese as a breakthrough to introduce foreign investment. He pointed out that: "The present construction requires more than one road. We can make use of foreign funds and technology. Overseas Chinese and their descendants can also come back to set up factories. " Deng Xiao-ping proposed to attract talents and intelligence of overseas Chinese and their descendants and to introduce capital from overseas Chinese and their descendants, Chinese in Hong Kong, Macao and Taiwan, which made a breakthrough in the initial use of foreign capital. However, since the introduction of the investment had just begun, China lacked relevant legislation and experiences. Besides, foreign businessmen harbored concerns. As a result, the investment amount was not too much. In 1983, the first foreign capital conference summed up the experience in time and made the deployment in improving legislation and adopting more liberal policies. Meanwhile, 14 coastal cities were opened, including Shanghai, Guangzhou, Tianjin, Dalian and Qingdao, which, as a result, speeded up the pace of introducing foreign investments.

From 1979 to 1984, contractual foreign investment in China reached USD 9. 75 billion, and the actual paid-in capital figured up to USD 4. 104 billion, USD 6. 84 billion annually. China broke the ice in the preliminary introduction of foreign capital during this period. But in this stage, the foreign capital mainly came from Hong Kong and Macao and was invested in labor-intensive industries in Guangdong, Fujian and other coastal provinces and cities. Nevertheless, the foreign capital of this phase played a positive part in making up the deficiency of the capital in Chinese construction, introducing advanced technologies and promoting scientific and technological progress and employment

B. The Stage of Sustained Development—from 1985 to 1991

In October of 1986, the State Council promulgated *The Regulations for the Encouragement of Foreign Investment* and some measures for the implementation of this act. The act was significant in the improvement of operating conditions of foreign enterprises. Furthermore, the act gave preferential treatment to foreign invested exporting enterprises and technologically advanced enterprises. In

December of 1987, the relevant departments of the state formulated provisions to introduce foreign investments. In 1988, the Central Committee of the Party and the State Council extended the coastal economic open area to Liaodong Peninsula, Shandong Peninsula, cities and counties of other coastal areas and approved the establishment of Hainan province and Hainan special economic zone. In April of 1990, the revision of *The law on Sino-Foreign Equity Joint Venture in China* by the National People's Congress improved the provisions concerning the joint venture. In the same month, Shanghai Pudong New Area was approved to enjoy some of the policies of economic development zones and special economic zones. The implementation of a series of policies greatly improved the foreign investment environment for the utilization of foreign capital. During this stage, China also achieved a faster development in introducing and utilizing foreign investments.

From 1985 to 1991, contractual foreign investment in China reached USD 52. 592 billion, USD 7. 513 billion annually. The actual paid-in capital amounted to USD 25. 057 billion, USD 3. 58 billion annually. The data had been greatly improved compared with that of the first half of the 1980s. During this stage, as to Chinese absorption of foreign capital, Taiwan funded enterprises became a newborn main force in addition to Hong Kong and Macao. Foreign funded industries also extended to manufacturing projects and export-oriented enterprises, which laid a solid foundation for China to expand its market.

C. The Stage of High-speed Development—from 1992 to 1995

At the beginning of 1992, Deng Xiao-ping visited south China and delivered an important speech, affirming the market as the means to allocate resources in a socialist economy. In October of the same year, the 14th Party Congress proposed " the establishment of the socialist market economy ", theoretically clearing the barriers in the utilization of foreign investments. These were all good news for the opening and the utilization of foreign capital in China. At the same time, as to the policy of opening up and the introduction of foreign capital, the Chinese government further opened 6 ports along the Yangtze river, 13 inland cities and 18 inland provincial capitals, established 52 high-tech industrial development zones, 11 tourism resorts, advancing from coastal areas to inland areas. In 1994, China realized the two-track exchange rate and began to implement a unified market exchange rate. In June of 1995, the State Council promulgated *The Interim Provisions Guiding the Foreign Investment and Industrial Catalog for the Foreign Investment*, in which the industrial categories were divided into the encouraged, the permitted, the restricted and the prohibited, which greatly improved the transparency of the policy. These policies created a favorable new situation for the opening up and promoted the investment introduction greatly, both in breadth and depth.

During the four years from 1992 to 1995, contractual foreign investment in China reached USD 343. 522billion USD 85. 88billion annually, and the actual paid-in capital came up to USD 109. 811billion, USD 27. 453billion annually, which was a qualitative improvement compared with that of early 1980s. It was noteworthy that sources, the regions and the industries of foreign investments underwent great changes in this stage. In terms of sources of foreign investments, more and more multi-national corporations in developed countries began to enter China and set up branches. Regions of foreign investments were no longer limited to the coastal special economic zones and coastal open cities. Foreign merchants also began to enter Midwest China. Industries of foreign investments shifted from labor-intensive industries to capital, technology intensive industries like large-scale chemical, electronic, services, infrastructure projects etc.

D. *The Stage of Improvement and Adjustment—from 1996 to 2001*

After Deng Xiao-ping's southern tour speech in 1992, while the influx of foreign capital in China promoted the rapid development of the Chinese economy, it also exposed many problems, such as the imbalance among investment industries and regions. Therefore, after 1995, China made a strategic adjustment, introducing foreign capital selectively, shifting from the pursuit of quantity to the pursuit of quality, so as to make foreign capital subject to the adjustment of the economic structure in China. In 1997, as the Southeast Asian financial crisis broke out, China also encountered a hitherto unknown pressure in the use of foreign capital and faced many complex problems. At the end of 1997, the Party Central Committee and the State Council held a national work conference on the utilization of foreign capital. Based on the experience of twenty years' use of foreign capital, the conference put forward further opening to the outside world, raising the level of foreign capital utilization, combining the investment and the current development of Chinese national economy while continuing to maintain the scale and level of foreign capital utilization and paying more attention to regions and industries of investments while introducing foreign investments so as to enable foreign capital to contribute to Chinese economic restructuring. In October of 1999, the central economic work conference further emphasized "the large-scale development of western regions". The government encouraged foreign merchants to invest and build factories in the central and western regions and would provide more preferential policies. In this phase, foreign capital utilization was marching toward a new multi-level, all-round and focused pattern.

During the 6 years from 1996 to 2001, the contractual foreign investment in China reached USD 349. 179billion, USD 58. 197billion annually and the actual paid-in capital amounted to USD 260. 358billion, USD 43. 393billion annually. It can be seen that the utilization of foreign capital in this stage and previous stage shared not much difference. Moreover, the contractual foreign investment presented a negative growth over the previous stage. However, owing to the central government's policy adjustment, the quality of the foreign capital utilization was improved, including the optimization of investment regions and industries.

E. The Stage of Steady Growth—from 2002 to 2008

In 2001, China officially became a member of WTO, which suggested that the reform and opening up of China embarked on the international road, which had a great influence on the investment introduction. In the first place, at the time of foreign merchants' access to Chinese market, its transparency had been improved, because the entry into WTO forced China to provide an operating environment consistent with WTO rules and international practice for these foreign merchants. In the second place, the admittance into the market was expanded, business, banking and other fields of services and trade were opened gradually, introducing more and more foreign capital into China. In the third place, foreign merchants were given national treatment. At the time, foreign merchants had been in China for 10 years and had acquired enough knowledge of Chinese laws, customs, market rules and so on, which also helped them gain a profound understanding of the potential of the Chinese market

Since 2002, foreign direct investment in China remained a relatively stable growth rate. In 2002, the actual utilization of foreign capital amounted to USD 52. 743billion, topping USD 50billion for the first time. In 2004, the number totaled USD 60. 63billion, smashing through the USD 60billion barrier. In 2007, the number was USD 74. 768 billion, topping USD 70billion. In 2008, it reached USD 92. 395billion, topping USD 90billion.

F. The Stage of Further Adjustment—from 2009 to the present

Affected by the 2008 global financial crisis, some foreign companies withdrew capital from China, which resulted in a temporary decline of foreign investments in China. In 2009, there were 23, 435 national newly approved foreign-invested enterprises, dropped by 14. 83% . The actual paid-in capital amounted to USD 90. 033billion, fell by 2. 56% . However, the Chinese government handled the situation properly, implementing a series of policies which helped to maintain the macro-economic development. Therefore, many foreign enterprises viewed China as the best harbor of refuge, and poured investments into China to escape the financial crisis. This also partially resulted in a small climax of the actually utilized foreign investments in 2010. In 2010, 27, 406 national newly approved foreign-invested enterprises were set up, increased by 16. 94% , the actual paid-in capital figured up to USD 105. 735billion, up by 17. 44% . In 2011, Chinese utilization of FDI continued to rise. 27, 712 national newly approved foreign-invested enterprises were set up, with an increase of 1. 12% and the actual paid-in capital amounted to USD 116. 011billion, with a growth of 9. 72% . In 2012, 24, 925 national newly approved foreign-invested enterprises were set up, with a decrease of 10. 06% . The actual paid-in capital added up to USD 111. 716billion, down by 3. 7% .

During this period, foreign direct investment mainly came from large multi-national corporations. Investment industries mainly covered the automobile, steel, machinery and petrochemical field. Investment regions had remained predominantly in coastal open cities, with a large number of foreign investment enterprises in the central and western regions. In general, China's utilization of foreign capital still maintained an upward tendency.

8. 1. 2　The Characteristics of China's Utilization of Foreign Direct Investment

A. A Higher Proportion of Sell-back of the Products of Foreign Enterprises

The proportion of sell-back of foreign enterprises can be obtained by dividing their industrial output by its exports from 1990 to 2012. The proportion was quite high, which remained at 40% . Although we lack the data of the 1980s, this ratio was expected to be higher than that of recent years. because in the beginning of reform and opening up, foreign direct investment were more often in forms of "processing trade", "compensation trade" and "processing, sample processing, assembly and compensation trade".

B. New Investments Constituted the Main Part in the Foreign Investment

The foreign investment that China utilizes has always been new ones. In recent years, the proportion of mergers and acquisitions in the investment is still quite small although mergers and acquisitions of multi-national corporations in China have achieved some development due to the loosening of policy.

According to the statistics of World Investment Report by the UN World Trade Development Conference, mergers and acquisitions of multi-national corporations in China grew from USD 8 million to USD 13. 721billion from 2000 to 2008, which still shared a very small proportion in the total investment. It is worth noting that, since the financial crisis in 2008, Chinese companies continue to accelerate the pace of mergers and acquisitions. In 2011, the quantity and amount of overseas acquisitions of Chinese mainland enterprises broke the record, with 207 transactions, amounting to USD 42. 9billion. In fact, mergers and acquisitions had become the quickest way to expand for Chinese enterprises. According to the data from Thomson Reuters, since 2012, the total amount of mergers and acquisitions Chinese enterprises involved in had amounted to USD 61. 7billion, with a total of 689 cross-border mergers and acquisitions, up 43. 8% compared with 2011. The domestic merger and acquisition accounted for 60% of the total, with 1, 803 transactions, amounting to USD 92. 5billion.

C. The Gradual Increase of the Ratio of Foreign-owned FDI

Foreign invested enterprises in China can be divided into Sino-foreign joint ventures, Sino-foreign cooperative enterprises and wholly foreign-owned enterprises. From 1995 to 1998, with the narrow appreciation of exchange rate of RMB, FDI of foreign-owned enterprises and Chinese foreign cooperative ventures presented an upward trend while FDI of Sino foreign joint ventures decreased continuously. From 1998 to 2002, while RMB exchange was fixed against the dollar, FDI of Sino foreign joint ventures and Sino foreign cooperative ventures was on decline, and the trend was particularly evident. Only FDI of wholly foreign invested ventures achieved accelerated and constant growth, and surpassed other types of FDI, accounting for about half of total FDI in 2002. Since 2002, the FDI proportion of wholly foreign-owned ventures had been on the increase year by year, and reached as high as 78. 6% in 2011.

D. Imbalance in the Industrial Distribution

There was an obvious imbalance in the industrial distribution of Chinese FDI utilization. Foreign investments mainly poured into the second industry, especially the industrial sector, and a relatively smaller proportion into the first and third industry. In 2011, the manufacturing industry in China actually utilized USD 52. 1billion foreign direct investment, accounting for 44. 9% of the total, while the agriculture, forest, animal husbandry, fishery, mining industry actually utilized USD 26. 2billion foreign direct investment, accounting for 2. 3% of the total. The third industry actually utilized USD 61. 28billion foreign direct investment, accounting for 52. 8% of the total. The vast majority of FDI centered on the general processing industry and labor intensive industry, which was not conducive to the adjustment and upgrading of Chinese industrial structure and tended to lock China to the bottom of the value chain in the international division of labor.

E. Differences in Investment Regions

Since the reform and opening up, the eastern region had always been the focus of foreign direct investment. The formation of this situation was mainly affected by historical and natural factors, geographical location, and many other factors such as the policies of the opening up. At the beginning of the reform and opening up, China first developed the eastern region which took the lead in the development of infrastructure and economy. Because of the cluster effect of the investment, the eastern area had been a magnet for foreign direct investment for a very long period of time. The unbalanced regional distribution of FDI expanded the difference in growth rates between western and eastern regions, which led to the imbalance in the regional economic development and to the widening of income gap, which was not beneficial to the coordinated development of the region.

8. 2   China's Policy on the Utilization of Foreign Direct Investment

8. 2. 1   The Evolution of China's Policy on the Utilization of the Foreign Investment

FDI policy belongs to the typical public policy. FDI policy is the product of the political system, and usually appears in the form of regulations, laws, decrees, the court ruling and administrative decisions.[1] FDI policy has broad and narrow definitions. The broad one refers to all policies related to foreign investments. The narrow one covers the principles and measures about the management of FDI made by host governments on the basis of the national goal. It is an important component of a country's economic policy. Policies and laws analyzed in this chapter are mainly centered on the utilization of FDI, including the national laws and local regulations. The general principle of China's policy on foreign capital is subject to the guidelines of the national reform and opening up and the economic

---

1   Earl R. Kruschke & Byron M. Jackson. *Public Policy Dictionary*. Translated by Tang Li-bin, Shanghai Far East Press, 1992, page 32.

development, and has its own features at the same time. Since 1978, the concept and arrangement of FDI policy have experienced obvious changes with the adjustment of national economic development strategy. China's policy on foreign capital has undergone the following three stages.

A. The Stage of Cautious Approach in the Opening up—from 1978 to 1985

At the beginning of reform and opening up, China was relatively backward in economic development and people's living standard was generally low. The planned economic system, having been in the dominant position since the founding of PRC, determined that China adopted the trade development strategy of import substitution before the reform and opening up. China had repeatedly refused the entry of foreign capital. It was not until the 3rd Plenary Session that it was established that China would take economic construction as the central task, adhere to the four cardinal principles and follow the route of the reform and opening up. It was the first time that the important effect of introducing foreign investments on China's economic development was affirmed. The party and state leaders liberated strategically the undue attention given to the foreign capital, freed people from the distress about whether the road was capitalist or socialist and furthered people's understanding of the introduction of foreign capital to a new height. Overall, the FDI policy in this phase had made some achievements. Nevertheless, China's poor economic foundation and its lack of charm made the investment still very difficult.

B. The Preferential Policy Stage—from 1985 to 1992

In the late 1980s, the market economy gradually developed in China. On the whole, the enterprise could arrange production activities independently according to market signals, which changed the situation of passive obedience to the government arrangement. Simultaneously, China's neighboring countries, especially Southeast and South Asian countries, had also developed their own policies and measures to introduce foreign investments, constantly adjusted the policies and regulations on the utilization of foreign investments, and encouraged the entry of foreign investors. Hence, the increased inflows of foreign capital in peripheral countries and regions weakened China's utilization of foreign investments, forming a rivalry with China.

In October of 1986, the State Council promulgated *The Regulations on the Encouragement of the Foreign Investment*, in which foreign invested enterprises, especially those with advanced technologies, were permitted to enjoy special preferential tax, fee, profit distribution and land use fees and to enjoy rights of automatic and independent operation. Subsequently, the local government introduced various preferential policies successively. A competition of preferential policies for foreign invested enterprises arose in the nation.

In order to stop the irrational and malicious competition, from 1987 to 1992, the central government made two major adjustments of FDI policy, with the focus on the clear principle, objective and way of introducing and utilizing foreign capital. During that time, the central government formulated a series of laws and regulations on utilizing foreign investments, so as to regulate the behavior of local investment. The relevant policy during this stage aimed at an adjustment to the previous short-term policy which jumped on the bandwagon and sought no benefits, ideologically advocated an active utilization of foreign investments and did a spade work for the subsequent investment.

C. Mutual Benefits and Win-win Stage—from 1992 to 2001

Since the goal of a socialist market economy reform was set in 1992, the government had been continuously adjusting the policy on foreign capital. China approached actively to the international norms and improved the transparency of its policy. Moreover, it reduced the administrative intervention of the state and relaxed control over the management of large amounts of goods. With the strengthening of market mechanism, large foreign multi-national corporations began to invest and build factories in China. In 1999, the development strategy of "going out" was put forward. China began to implement a proactive fiscal policy to deepen the reform and further relax the policy over the use of foreign capital.

Under the guidance the "going out" strategy, in the late 1980s, new changes to the Chinese foreign direct investment policy emerged. The first one was to attract boldly and guide actively multi-national corporations to invest in China. The second was to start to use the international securities market to introduce foreign capital. The third was to emphasize the national treatment of foreign investment enterprises. The Chinese government in this stage tended to be more rational in the formulation of the policy on foreign capital. The government no longer pursued the absolute growth in quantity, but focused on improving the quality and efficiency of the national economy and valued the mutual benefit and win-win situation of the domestic economy and foreign capital.

D. The Stage of Scientific Development—from 2001 to the Present

By the end of 2001, with the entry into WTO, China's opening up entered a new historical period. The introduction and utilization of foreign capital was designated to optimize the domestic industrial structure by the use of foreign capital, technology and management experiences. The policy on foreign capital had been adjusted correspondingly, shifting from funding the capital gap to introducing high-tech technologies. "Going out" and "bringing in" were viewed as two inseparable parts in the introduction and utilization of foreign capital. The one-way flow of foreign direct investment was changed into inward and outward flow of the investment. In this stage, our government could take into account both the social construction and the economic development, continuously improved the quality and level of foreign capital utilization and perfected the policy on foreign capital, making a significant leap in the quality of the policy.

8. 2. 2   The Prospect of China's FDI Policy

To introduce foreign investments is a significant issue that our country faces in the process of reform and opening up. In order to introduce foreign investments, the policy on foreign capital in our country develops from nothing and from cautious opening to the scientific development. The continuous improvement of the policy on foreign capital reflects the Chinese government's efforts and exploration in a scientific utilization of the foreign capital. But in terms of the effects of the policy, the quality of the investment doesn't make people feel optimistic. Furthermore, the domestic technology and industrial upgrading are still under great pressure. For one thing, China's economic foundation is weak and the core technology is deficient. For another, China can find problems in its foreign capital policy by comparing the above four stages. For instance, the evolution of the policy values more of its concept and discourse than the policy implementation tools and the evaluation of the effects of the policy, which limits the optimization and upgrading of the policy on foreign capital to the simple change of its form. This is largely due to the great influence of the change of the international environment on the foreign investment policy. Therefore, the government needs to pay special attention to the overall arrangement and scientific combination of the policy tool in the formulation of foreign policy, strengthen the enforcement of the foreign investment policy, fully develop the market mechanism of the foreign investment policy and promote public participation continuously.

8.3   The Practice of Chinese Outward Direct Investment

The outward direct investment constitutes an essential part of the strategy of Chinese opening to the outside world. It is a major part of the "going out" strategy. ODI, coupled with the utilization of FDI, forms an inflow and outflow pattern in the aspect of international migration of Chinese capital. These years, more and more Chinese enterprises begin to go abroad to invest and run enterprises overseas. The set-up of overseas enterprises plays a positive role not only in promoting the development of domestic state-owned enterprises but also in boosting the domestic economy. To safeguard the healthy development of outward investment, the government conducts scientific macro management and regulation over it through various means. This section elaborates on the characteristics, the possibility and the management of Chinese ODI.

8.3.1   The Development of Chinese ODI

Since the founding of PRC in 1949, Chinese ODI has experienced several stages of development.

A. The Initial Stage of Development—from 1949 to 1978

During the 30 years from the founding of new China to the implement of the reform and opening up, Chinese enterprises made some direct investment in the overseas market. During this period, in order to explore the international market and develop the trade with other countries, various foreign trade companies set up overseas branches in Paris, London, Tokyo, New York, Hamburg, Hong Kong, Singapore and other international metropolises respectively and started a number of trading companies. Meanwhile, some of the trade related Chinese enterprises invested overseas to run some ocean shipping and financial enterprises. They were the first group of overseas enterprises run by Chinese domestic enterprises after the inland Chinese government took over a number of Chinese enterprises in Hong Kong. The investment was generally small in scale and trade-related in nature. These enterprises were located in some well-known ports and big cities in the world and mainly engaged in trade activities. The start of this group of overseas enterprises exerted a positive influence on the development of foreign trade in PRC.

B. Further Development Stage—from 1979 to 1985

Since China implemented the policy of reform and opening up in 1979, ODI of domestic enterprises have developed rapidly. In November of 1979, Beijing Friendship Commercial Service Company and Japanese Tokyo Maru Trading Co. , Ltd jointly ran the Jinghe Incorporated Corporation, which was the first overseas joint venture after the reform and opening up of China. The main business of the enterprise covered introducing technologies and equipment for the renovation of food enterprises in Beijing, running Beijing flavor restaurants and providing chef service in Japan etc. In March, 1980, Chinese Ship-building Industry Corporation, China National Chartering Corporation and Hong Kong Global Shipping Group jointly invested 50 million USD to start the International United Shipping Investment Company Limited, which was based in Bermuda, and establish International United Shipping Proxy Companies in Hong Kong, engaging in deputizing the business of import and export of Chinese ships and marine equipment and managing the international shipping business. China accounted for 45% of the investment, which was the biggest one in amount by then. In that stage, Chinese invested enterprises abroad included CCIC Finance Limited, a financial business enterprise in Hong Kong, Jingda Limited by Share Ltd, an economic and technical service consulting enterprise started in Japan, Sino-Yemen Construction and Engineering Company Limited, a project contracting enterprise in Yemen in Arabia, Transocean and Yuantong shipping Service Corporation, enterprises set up in Holland engaging in the ship agency business and shipping supplies respectively , Star Shipping Agent Limited by Share, an enterprise started in Australia engaging in the shipping agent business.

C. The Stage of Accelerated Development—from 1986 to 1992

During this period, Chinese ODI underwent rapid development, which was mainly reflected in the increase in the type of domestic enterprises participating in the overseas investment. Not only foreign trade enterprises, but also industrial enterprises, commercial enterprises, science and technology enterprises and financial and insurance enterprises were involved in overseas investment. The field of overseas investment was expanded. Overseas enterprises were set up in the industries of service, industrial and agricultural production and processing and resource development. The number of overseas enterprises was increased. By the end of 1992, the overseas non-trade enterprises had reached 1,360, foreign trade enterprises amounted to 2,600 or so. Chinese investment in foreign trade enterprises and non-trade enterprises totaled over USD 400million. Overseas enterprises were distributed more widely in different countries and regions. By the end of 1992, Chinese enterprises had set up overseas enterprises in more than 120 countries and regions in the world.

D. The Stage of Adjustment and Development—from 1993 to 1998

Due to the overheated economy, the unreasonable investment structure and excessively rapid rise of prices, in the beginning of 1993, the state decided to implement an adjustment of economic structure and monetary tightening so as to enable the overheated economy to land softly. Correspondingly, overseas investment business also entered the clean-up and rectification period. The competent authorities of the State implemented strict control over the approval of the new overseas investment, and undertook a re-registration of overseas enterprises which had been set up by various departments and local areas. As a result, overseas investment began to slow down. During the 6 years, Chinese ODI added up to USD 1. 278billion. Around 1, 500 overseas enterprises were approved. Based on the previous overseas investment experience and the analysis on the international competitiveness of Chinese enterprises, at the end of this phrase, the Chinese government put forward a new strategy, aiming at encouraging the development of outward investment which could exploit China's comparative advantages, better using the two markets and two kinds of resources, forming cross-industry, cross-department and cross-region multinational groups, organizing and supporting step by step a group of powerful and advantageous state-owned enterprises to invest overseas (mainly to Africa, Central Asia, the Middle East, Eastern Europe, South America and other places), while actively expand exports at the same time. New strategies indicate that ODI would experience a new round of rapid development.

E. A New Stage of Faster Development—from 1999 to 2008

In order to promote the development of export trade, speed up the adjustment of the industrial structure and to transfer the domestic mature technology and industry to overseas markets, the Chinese government, starting from 1999, has proposed to encourage competent enterprises to invest abroad, stimulate the export of domestic equipment, technology, materials and semi-finished products and expand foreign trade through the promotion of overseas processing and assembly and local production and on-site sales or sales to neighboring countries. This new policy is systematically summarized as "going out" strategy. In order to speed up the implementation of the strategy of "going out", the Ministry of Commerce awarded successively more than 200 companies

"The certificate of approval of processing trade of enterprises abroad". ODI prompted by overseas processing trade will become a new growth point in China's foreign investment. The rapid development of this type of overseas investment will lead to new changes in the investor, the mode and the industry structure of ODI. In addition, after the entry into WTO, while foreign enterprises and products enter the China market, Chinese enterprises should also stride abroad to grasp the opportunities and make full use of other rights granted by other contracting parties. During this stage, overseas investment is more reasonable with the blind investment being reduced. Being market-oriented and benefit-centered has gradually become a basic principle that China enterprises follow in overseas investment. With the increase in the amount of overseas investment and the number of overseas investment enterprises, Chinese multi-national corporations also come to the stage. China has already had a number of multi-national corporations that match the definition.

According to the statistics from the Ministry of Commerce and the State Administration of Foreign Exchange, in 2008, Chinese ODI amounted to USD 52. 15billion, of which, non-financial direct investment was USD 40. 65billion, accounting for 78% and financial direct investment was USD 11. 5billion, accounting for 22%. In 2008, Chinese ODI ranked tenth or so in the world. By the end of 2008, more than 5,000 Chinese domestic investors set up about 11,000 outward investment enterprises overseas, locating in 173 countries or regions. The accumulated balance (stock) of ODI amounted to USD 169. 4billion.

F. Further Adjustment Stage after the Financial Crisis—from 2008 to the Present

In 2008, the global financial crisis caused by the American subprime crisis spread to the world, exercising a great impact on the world economy, which marked the end of the international investment boom since the beginning of 2003. Global ODI moved into the adjustment period.

In 2007, America's subprime crisis began to emerge. Under the background of economic globalization, the subprime mortgage crisis rapidly transformed into a global economic crisis. The financial crisis led to a large reduction in private equity funds, which resulted in the decrease in the related global transnational mergers. In addition, the financial crisis led to the collapse of a large number of financial institutions and the shortage of capital, making the rise in financing costs of multi-national corporations and the decline in corporate profits, and resulting in the difficulty in the financing of multi-national corporations, curbing their large scale transnational investment. Meanwhile, international investors were concerned about the serious economic recession that developed countries had been suffering and were reluctant in investing. The financial crisis brought about a lack of confidence in the investment and financing of multi-national corporations. The uncertain economic conditions and the collapse in global demand worldwide led to the lack of confidence in the transnational investment in the host country. Even multi-national corporations with sufficient funds would be careful of transnational investment for fear of the increase in the investment risk. *The World Investment Report 2012* of UNCTAD indicated that, in 2011, the world foreign direct investment outflows reached USD 1,690billion at the end of the year with the stock of USD 21.17billion. According to the data, in 2011, Chinese ODI accounted for 4.4% and 2% respectively of the global flow and stock. In 2011, China ranked the 6th in the global ODI flow and the 13th in the stock.

In 2012, Chinese ODI flow and stock hit an historical high. Investors within the territory of China directly invested in 4,425 overseas enterprises in 141 countries and regions in the world with the cumulative non-financial direct investment of USD 77.22billion and a year-on-year growth of 28.6%. Among the total investment, the equity investment and other investments added up to USD 62.82billion, accounting for 81.4%, the profit reinvestment figured up to USD 14.4 billion, accounting for 18.6%. The rapid increase of Chinese ODI in recent years was related to the increased ODI motivation of Chinese enterprises, the demand by other countries for external financing after the global financial crisis and the "going out" strategy actively implemented by Chinese government.

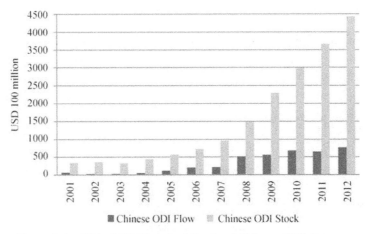

Figure 8.1   2001–2012 Flow and Stock of Chinese ODI Overseas

Source: UNCTAD, the Ministry of Commerce.

Although at the end of 2012, the stock of Chinese ODI accounted for less than 2% of global ODI stock, the ratio rose rapidly in recent years, from 0.5% in 2012 to 6% in 2003. In 2011, Chinese ODI flow accounted for about 3.8% of the global flow. The ratio rose to 6% in 2012, which was partially a consequence of a strong growth of ODI of Chinese enterprises, and also resulted from the relatively slow growth of global ODI flow due to the impact of the global financial crisis.

8.3.2   The Characteristics of Chinese ODI

A. The outward investment is fast in the expansion of the scale and main body.

Since the reform and opening up, Chinese ODI has gained rapid development on weaker foundation and has built up to a certain scale, with a great number of overseas investment companies and a high average annual growth rate of ODI. In recent years, some large and pioneering domestic enterprises, technologically advanced enterprises and excellent enterprises with famous brands has joined the ranks of outward investment. In 2012, Chinese outward investors continued to maintain a diversified pattern. The top three were limited liability companies, accounting for 43.3% of the total investment, the state-owned enterprises, 19.7%, private enterprises, 11%. While the investment subjects continued to be optimized, the average investment scale of outward investment enterprises was expanding. According to the statistics of the Ministry of Commerce, the average investment was over USD 10,000,000.

B. The Wider and More Diversified Regional Distribution of ODI Enterprises

By the end of 2012, there had been 10 thousand or so Chinese ODI enterprises in 141 countries or regions, which covered 71.2% of the world countries and regions. The investment coverage rate in Asia and Africa reached 90% and 81% respectively. The number of Chinese overseas enterprises in Asia accounted for 50% of the total overseas enterprises, with 16.8% in Europe. Among the countries and regions, Chinese Hong Kong, Russia, USA, Vietnam, Japan, Arabia, Germany, Australia, the United Arab Emirates, Singapore aggregated 50.2% of foreign enterprises. Chinese overseas enterprises in Hong Kong accounted for 16.7% of the total number, America 9.6%, Russia 5.3%, Vietnam 3.9%, Japan 3.4%, the Emirate of Arabia and Germany 3.1% each, Australia 2.8% and Singapore 2.1%. On the whole, Chinese overseas enterprise distribution has a certain link with the market structure of Chinese foreign trade.

C. The Distribution of Overseas Enterprises in All Three Industries

The manufacturing enterprises accounted for 31.8% of the total number of overseas enterprises, wholesale and retail trade 19.4%, business service industry 15.1%, construction industry 7%, mining industry 5.4%, agriculture, forest, animal husbandry and fishery 4.7%, transportation, storage and postal industry 4.1%, residents services and other services 3.1%, and scientific research, technical service and geological exploration industry 2.7%. In recent years, the overseas processing trade and resource development became important fields of Chinese outward investments due to the encouragement of national policies and, therefore, enjoyed a rapid development in investment. In terms of the industry distribution of ODI stock, business services, wholesale and retail trade, finance, mining, transportation, storage and postal industry totally accounted for about 80%, among which, the business services sector accounted for 25.9%, wholesale and retail trade 17.2%, financial industry 14.2%, and mining industry 12.7%. In the investment stock, other industries sharing large proportion were as follows. Transportation, storage and postal industry accounted for 10.2%, the manufacturing sector 8.1%, the real estate industry 3.8%, information transmission, computer and software industry 1.6%, and the construction industry 1.4%.

D. Various Modes of Investment, a Majority of Joint and Cooperative Enterprises, both Startup and Acquisition of Setting up

ODI modes of Chinese enterprises (or investment ways) became more and more diversified. Some invest in cash (including their funds and domestic loans), some with foreign loans, some with the domestic machinery, equipments and other materials, and some others with domestic technology patents or proprietary technology (including services). Concerning the ownership structure of Chinese outward investment enterprises, overseas funded enterprises accounted for about 30% of the whole, the joint venture and cooperative enterprise co-organized with the host country or a third country accounted for about 70%. These outward investment enterprises were in the form of companies limited by shares and companies with limited liability. Most Chinese overseas enterprises were newly founded (including additional equity investment, profits reinvestment and other investment). In the past, companies through acquisition and merger, which is prevalent in the world (including the stock exchange) had been few. But there were more and more of them in recent years, Take 2012 for example, foreign investment through mergers and acquisition accounted for 23.8% of ODI flow.

E. Close Relationship between Overseas Enterprises and Domestic Parent Companies

95% of the overseas enterprises were overseas subsidiaries or branches. 5% of them belonged to the associate companies. Currently, the business of some Chinese overseas enterprises was mostly controlled directly by the domestic company, which had no marketing networks and channels of information in the local area overseas. Moreover, a number of overseas enterprises contacted only with the parent company. There were little or no connections among investment enterprises abroad and between investment enterprises and local enterprises overseas. These companies developed no awareness of autonomous operation and didn't have independent brands of their own. What's more, they didn't regard the whole world market as a business and the profitable stage, and had not yet implemented any strategies to optimize the allocation of resources on a global scale.

8. 3. 3 The Possibility and Condition for Chinese ODI

At present, the possibility and conditions for Chinese enterprises to invest overseas to start enterprises mainly include the following.

A. A Number of Powerful Enterprises Enjoying a World Reputation

On the 500 largest global companies list released in 2012 by American *Fortune Magazine*, the number of Chinese companies had been on the rise for 9 years. In 2012, in China (including Mainland China, Hong Kong and Taiwan), a total of 79 companies were on the list, exceeding Japan for the first time in history (68 Japanese enterprises were on the list), second only to America (132 American companies on the list), [1] see Table 8. 2.

About 20 years ago, only Bank of China, Chinese Chemicals Import and Export Corporation and Chinese Grain and Oil Import and Export Corporation were on the list. Since China's entry into WTO from 2001, the rank of Chinese enterprises on the list has continued to rise. In 2001, 11 companies in Chinese mainland were on the list. In comparison, there were 197 in the USA and 88 in Japan. In 2006, 5 years after the entry into WTO, 22 Chinese mainland enterprises were on the list, with 162 American ones and 67 Japanese ones. It

---

1 The world's 500 companies of *Fortune Magazine* is the most famous and authoritative list measuring large firms in the world. The list is released by the magazine annually. "The world's top 500" is its commonly accepted name in China.

was notable that after the international financial crisis, the Chinese economy stood out in the world while the position of the Chinese enterprise rose sharply on this list. In 2009, 42 mainland companies got onto the top 500 of *Fortune Magazine* with 139 American ones and 71 Japanese ones that year. In 2010, 57 Chinese mainland companies were on the list, with 133 and 68 American and Japanese ones respectively. In 2011, Chinese mainland companies numbered 69 on the list.

The above facts demonstrate that China has a number of powerful and influential enterprises in the world. Those enterprises have scientific management, advanced management and good reputation, have acquired some international operation and overseas investment experiences and enjoy obvious comparative advantage. They can raise funds in the international financial market and invest overseas with their funds as well. Additionally, a majority of large enterprises or groups in China have already created internationalization strategies, which will effectively promote and facilitate the development of Chinese overseas investment.

Table 8.2   Chinese Enterprises on the Top 500 List of *Fortune Magazine* in 2012

2012 Ranking	2011 Ranking	Name	Proceeds of business (million USD)
5	5	China Petrochemical Corporation	375,214
6	6	China National Petroleum Corporation	352,338
7	7	National Electric Net Ltd	259,141.8
43	60	Hon Hai Precision Industry co., Ltd.	117,514.4
54	77	Industrial & Commercial Bank of China	109,039.6
77	108	China Construction Bank	89,648.2
81	87	China Mobile Communications Corporation	87,543.7
84	127	Agricultural Bank of China	84,802.7
91	139	Noble Group	80,732.1
93	132	Bank Of China	80,230.4
100	–	China Construction Engineering Corporation	76,023.6
101	162	China National Offshore Oil Corp	75,513.8
111	–	China Railway Construction Corporation	71,443.4
112	95	China Railway Group Limited	71,263.4
113	168	SINOCHEM GROUP	70,990.1
129	113	China Life Insurance (Group) Company	67,274

Cont.

2012 Ranking	2011 Ranking	Name	Proceeds of business (million USD)
130	—	SAIC Motor	67,254.8
142	145	DONGFENG Motor Group	62,910.8
152	149	China Southern Power Grid Corporation Ltd	60,538.3
165	197	China First Automobile Group Corporation	57,002.9
169	229	China Minmetals Corp	54,509.1
194	221	China CITIC Group Co. Ltd.	49,338.7
197	212	Baosteel Group Co., Ltd.	48,916.3
205	250	China North Industries Group Corporation	48,153.9
216	211	China Communications Construction Co	45,958.7
221	222	China Telecom Group Company	45,169.8
233	346	Chinese Huarun Corporation	43,439.5
234	293	Shenhua Group	43,355.9
238	227	China South Industries Group Corporation	43,159.5
242	328	Ping An Insurance (Group) Co., Ltd.	42,110.3
246	276	Chinese Huaneng Group	41,480.6
250	311	Chinese Aviation Industry Corp	40,834.9
258	343	Chinese Post Group	40,023.3
269	279	Hebei Iron and Steel Group	38,722.4
275	320	Jardine Matheson Group	37,967
279	247	Quanta Computer	37,770.3
280	297	Chinese Metallurgical Group Co., Ltd.	37,612.6
292	289	Chinese People's Insurance Group Co., Ltd.	36,549.1
295	326	Shougang Group	36,117.1
298	331	Aluminium Corp	35,839.2
318	431	China Aviation Oil Holding Co	34,352.4
321	341	Wuhan Iron and Steel (Group) Company	34,259.5
326	398	Bank of Communications	33,871.6
330	458	Jizhong Energy Group	33,660.8
333	371	China United Network Communications Limited by Share Ltd.	33,336.1
337	350	Taiwan Petro China Limited by Share Ltd	32,768.9

Cont.

2012 Ranking	2011 Ranking	Name	Proceeds of business (million USD)
341	405	Chinese Guodian Corporation	32,580
346	367	Jiangsu Shagang Group	32,096.8
349	430	China Railway Materials Limited by Share Ltd.	31,991.1
351	352	Huawei Klc Holdings Ltd.	31,543.4
362	362	Hutchison Whampoa Limited	30,022.9
365	485	Chinese Building Materials Group Co., Ltd.	30,021.9
367	435	China National Machinery Industry Corporation	29,846.3
369	375	China Datang Corporation	29,603.2
370	450	Legend Group	29,574.4
384	399	Chinese Ocean Shipping (Group) Corporation	28,796.5
390	—	Chinese Electric Power Construction Group Co. Ltd.	28,288.6
393	366	Cofco Corporation	28,189.7
397	446	Henan Coal Chemical Industry Refco Group Ltd.	27,919.2
402	475	China National Chemical Corp	27,706.7
408	410	Formosa Petrochemical Co	27,178.6
416	508	TEWOO Group	26,410.9

B. China's Acquisition of Certain Financial Firepower

In 2012, Chinese exports reached USD 2,049.83billion. The country's foreign exchange reserves amounted to USD 3,311.6billion by the end of the year. The per capita GDP in China was RMB 38,354. These figures suggested that it was possible for China to spend a part of the capital investing overseas and setting up overseas companies. It could be said that in China, the inflow of international capital was greater than the outflow, which was expected to last for years. However, this situation was gradually changing and the difference between the outflow and inflow was shrinking. China was changing from a big trading country to an investment power, and from a potential power of outward direct investment to a real one. China was moving into a new stage in which it should speed up the overseas investment properly. Capital inflow and outflow was an international trend of economic development and could achieve mutual development.

C. China's Comparative Advantage in terms of Technologies and Equipment

A comparative advantage, not necessarily the absolute advantage, in technologies and equipment would make overseas investment completely possible. As long as China enjoyed a comparative advantage over the host country, the investment could be feasible. In some fields of technology, China had reached advanced international level. Furthermore, China possessed a large number of appropriate technologies, special technologies and traditional technologies, whose prices were relatively cheap. These technologies were popular in developing countries. Similarly, China also had relative advantage in individual equipment and complete sets of equipment. Especially, in recent years, many domestic products in China were in excessive supply. Many enterprises had unutilized capacity. Therefore, it was an urgent need to use foreign investment to transfer competitive equipment and technologies overseas.

D. China's Advantages in the Management and the Talent

Although there was a gap in the overall level of management of Chinese enterprises compared to that of the companies in developed countries, in some regions and industries as well as some enterprises, the management was still relatively advanced. For instance, in recent years, China Qingdao Haier Group Company became internationally famous with its effective management, whose management experiences and case entered the classroom and textbooks of famous business schools overseas. In the process of reform and opening up, some Chinese enterprises had cultivated and trained a number of personnel familiar with the international practice and market environment, and were able to engage in overseas production, operation and management.

In short, taking into account the objective and subjective conditions, it can be safely concluded that it is possible for Chinese enterprises to invest overseas and manage transnational business. A more positive attitude should be held to promote the development of this promising cause and promote more Chinese enterprises to go out to play a more significant part on the international economic stage.

8. 4   Chinese ODI Management

8. 4. 1   Macro-management of Chinese ODI

The macro-management of ODI mainly refers to the management conducted, under Chinese laws and the current policy, through the administrative, economic and legal means of competent authorities at all levels of government, over Chinese party of joint ventures and cooperative enterprises and Chinese enterprises overseas. The above-mentioned government departments include departments directly under the function of the State Council as follows: the Ministry of Commerce, the National Development and Reform Commission, the State Owned Assets Supervision and Administration Commission, the Ministry of Finance, the State Administration of Foreign Exchange, the Ministry of Human Resources and Social Security, the General Administration of customs, as well as the Administrative Departments of Foreign Trade of the provinces, cities, autonomous regions and municipalities. The macro-management is multi-leveled, mainly covering outward investment promotion, support, approval, protection, rewards, restriction, supervision, inspection, punishment and revocation. At present, the macro-management of outward investment can be cataloged into comprehensive centralized management, professional management, the management of local government and the management of Chinese embassies and consulates.

The Ministry of Commerce and the National Development and Reform Commission are the administrative department authorized by the State Council, managing outward investment. Their main functions involve formulating the relevant management measures for outward investment, collating and releasing statistics about outward investment according to relevant rules, supervising outward investment enterprises, making nation and industry oriented catalog for outward investment and formulating measures to encourage and support outward investment. Centralized management of the Ministry of Commerce constitutes an important part of the macro-management. Over years, the Ministry of Commerce has formulated a series of provisions and measures concerning the management of outward investment, such as provisions on the approval of the establishment of outward investment enterprise and the statistical system of ODI. So far, systems concerning outward investment related management, laws and regulations, promotion, service and security have been established or are under construction.

Professional management of outward investment involves foreign exchange management, the management of the state-owned assets and labor wage management. The State Administration of Foreign Exchange, Bank of China, State-owned Assets Supervision and Administration Commission, the Ministry of Human Resources and Social Security assist in the management of Chinese outward investment, responsible for outward investment related foreign exchange transfer, capital investment, wages and the formulation, implementation and supervision of overseas assets management policies. In recent years, special regulations like *The Offshore Investment Management, On Encouraging and Regulating Offshore Investment, Offshore Investment Foreign Exchange Management, Interim Measures on the Management of Property Right Registration of State-owned Assets* were enacted and implemented, which enables the relevant management to be conducted under the law and to produce positive effects.

The management, carried out by the provinces, cities, autonomous regions, cities specifically designated in the state plan and relevant departments of the State Council over outward investment in accordance with the relevant regulations of the state, also belongs to the macro policy management and control. The major function of local governments and relevant ministries is to determine the major investment direction and field in the range of the national unified plan, in consideration of the comprehensive advantages and the characteristics of local area and industry, and to formulate specific measures relating to outward investment management.

The Economic and Commercial Counselor's Office (room) of Chinese embassies (consulates) is responsible for the guidance and management of Chinese outward investment enterprises in the country (region). The specific content of the management covers safeguarding the legitimate rights and interests of Chinese enterprises and Chinese part of joint ventures, supervising and inspecting the implementation of national policy and the observance of local laws and regulations of Chinese enterprises and Chinese part of joint ventures overseas, and coordinating the relationship between Chinese overseas enterprises and the local government, making their production and business activities conducive to promoting the healthy development of the economic relationship between the two countries.

Generally, there are five major objectives of national macro management over outward investment. The first is to regulate the scale and total amount of outward investment. The second is to adjust and optimize the investment areas, country, the industries (field), subjects, modes and structures. The third is to improve the benefits that outward investment brings for the economy and society. The fourth is to ensure that the value of overseas state-owned assets is preserved and increased. The fifth is to provide various services for outward investment and outward investment enterprises

8. 4. 2   Industry Guidance for Chinese ODI

In view of the possibility of Chinese ODI at present and new features of the world ODI development, as well as the goal of Chinese domestic industrial structure adjustment and optimization, key industries for Chinese outward investment at the present stage are listed below.

A. The Processing and Assembling Manufacturing Industries

The start of this type of enterprise can not only break through the trade protectionist policy of the host country, promote and expand the export of domestic technologies, equipment, semi-finished products, components and raw materials, achieve the goal of local production, local sales and the third-country market sales, but also can gain comparative benefits by making full use of the comparative advantages of China in equipment, technologies and human resources. Currently, the state offers key support for outward investment in this industry and has formulated a series of preferential policies. The processing and assembling manufacturing industry involves mechanical industry, electronic industry, light industry, clothing industry, building materials industry and electrical equipment manufacturing industry.

B. The Resource Development Industries

The resources development project is generally long in construction cycle and large in the amount of investment. The resource development project became a focal Chinese ODI in the past decade, and will still be so in the future. This is due to a small amount of per capita resources in China. In the overseas investment for China's shortage of resources project will help to break the monopoly of resources and thus, carries an important strategic significance.

C. The Science and Technology Development Industries

Such enterprises fall into three categories. One is to invest and co-manage the technology intensive enterprises in the host country in order to learn from their advanced technology which China lacks or fall behind and bring the technology back for domestic application. Another kind is to set up new high-tech product development companies in developed foreign countries and then hand over newly developed products to the domestic enterprises for production and finally sell products abroad. Still another kind refers to the domestic high-tech enterprises which are encouraged to enter the international market, invest overseas, expand the export of high-tech products and internationalize technology products. The development of highly technological overseas investment projects is encouraged and supported by the State.

D. Project Contracting and Labor Cooperation Businesses

China is rich in labor resources. Chinese labor contracting enterprises are fairly competitive in the international market. Therefore, labor contracting enterprises are supported by the government to set up related enterprises overseas to expand Chinese overseas project contracting and labor cooperation businesses.

E. Trade and Service Industries

These kind of enterprises includes those providing service for finance and insurance, the import and export trade, the wholesale business, information consulting, transport and communications, health care, tourism, advertising and repair service industry. Through the establishment of Chinese owned enterprises or joint ventures in the service industry, China can directly expand service export, and can indirectly promote the export of the tangible commodity.

Case 8. 1   Wanxiang Group "Married" A123 at the Cost of USD 2. 56 Million

Basic Facts

After 5 months of efforts, Wanxiang Group's transnational acquisition of USA Lithium Battery Company finally drew to a close. News from the Wanxiang Group headquarters said that, in the evening of January 28, 2013, America local time, the Committee on Foreign Investment America (CIFUS) officially announced approval of Wanxiang Group's acquisition of American A123 Systems.

Wanxiang Group would work with A123 on the acquisition, which was expected to be completed shortly. This once again marked Chinese private enterprises' successful acquisition of one of America's famous companies. Wanxiang Groups also said that it would accelerate the development of the clean energy industry on the base of its traditional manufacturing industry.

The Background and Process

Which kind of company was American A123 Systems? Why did it attract the attention of Wangxiang, a large private company?

It was reported that, A123 was set up at the Massachusetts Institute of Technology in 2001 and was named by *Fortune Magazine* as "one of the 15 companies which will change the world". In 2009, A123 was listed on the NASDAQ in America. It was once known as the largest and most technologically advanced lithium battery manufacturer in the USA. Capital adsorption ability of A123 was very impressive. Before the listing, A123 raised twice the issue price and enlarged the scale of issuing. Even so, its performance on the market was better than expected. After 2 days on the market, the company's share price soared by 54%. A123 eventually raised 3.8 billion USD, and at the same time, gained USD 249million of governmental financial assistance.

To Wanxiang, who had an ambitious dream about electric cars, what struck their fancy was the lithium battery technology of A123. The lithium ion battery, produced by A123, had high power and high energy density, long service life and excellent safety performance, which made it lead the lithium ion battery market. Its technology was oriented towards the next generation product in traffic and transportation, power grid energy storage and consumer applications. Besides, its customers comprised General Motors, BMW, Fisk and SAIC. Its business covered the American and Chinese markets.

However, such a star company was stuck in trouble 3 years after its establishment. The weakening of the USA market demand for batteries and hybrid caused great economic pressure to battery suppliers like A123. In March, 2012, the A123 Company fell into a crisis because of battery recall. Just then, Wanxiang Group put forward the investment proposal. After several rounds of consultations, the two sides signed a strategic investment agreement on August 16, 2012.

Although the investment met the wish of both sides, things hadn't gone smoothly. A123 failed to obtain follow-up investment because it was unable to meet the conditions stipulated in the agreement. In October of that year, A123 submitted a bankruptcy application to American bankruptcy court. American JCI, Germany Siemens, Japanese NEC participated in the bidding successively.

On, December 8, in A123 bankruptcy auction, Wanxiang Group successfully bid USD 256.6million for all A123 assets except governmental and military ones, beating the joint bid of USA Johnson Controls and Japanese NEC. Relevant personnel of Wanxiang Group disclosed that, according to the transaction, Wanxiang would acquire the car, grid energy storage and commercial assets, including not only all of the technology, product, customer contract and facilities in America's Michigan, Massachusetts and Missouri, but also a cathode powder manufacturing factory in China and the equity of a joint venture with SAIC, namely, Shanghai Advanced Traction Battery Systems Limited.

As the largest auto parts enterprise in China, starting from 1999, Wanxiang has begun the research on the clean energy industry, and has made remarkable achievements in high power and high energy polymer lithium ion power battery, integrated motor and drive control system, vehicle electronic control system and automobile engineering integration technology. It has acquired industrial capacity of 0.12 billon ampere hours lithium ion power battery and 2,000 sets of electric powertrain. The acquisition will further establish the leading edge of Wanxiang Group in the global clean energy industry. Holding A123 is a shortcut to the access to international host plant supporting, American electric vehicle market and the promotion of its status in the Chinese market.

Case 8. 2   Geely's Acquisition of Volvo

Basic Facts

At 21: 00, March 28, 2010, Zhejiang Geely Holding Group Company Limited and American Ford Automobile Company formally signed the final share purchase agreement in Goteborg, Sweden. After more than a year of arduous negotiations, Geely , a Chinese private enterprise acquired, at the cost of USD 1. 8 billion, 100% of the shares and related assets (including intellectual property rights) of a luxury car brand Volvo (the Volvo cars) , which had a history of over 80 years.

The stock purchase agreement still needed regulatory approval of China. After routine adjustment to the purchase price based on the accounting of pension gap, debt, cash and capital, Geely and Ford completed the delivery in the third quarter of 2010. Geely would retain the present plant of Volvo cars in Sweden and Belgium and would also build new factories in China at an appropriate time, making its production close to the Chinese Market

Details

Geely's acquisition of Volvo is of great significance. The acquisition is significant for the development of Geely Holding Group itself. Firstly, Geely will own 100% of the Volvo brand of cars, 9 series of products of Volvo cars, the intellectual property of 3 new platforms, nearly 600,000 units of production lines with high capacity and high degree of automation, and more than 2, 000 global networks and related talents and important supplier systems. Secondly, it can rapidly expand the scale of the production and sale. In 2009, the total business income of Geely was RMB 4. 289billion while the gross income of Volvo cars was about RMB 100billion, which was over 20 times that of Geely. Thirdly, Geely is one of the fastest growing Chinese automobile manufacturers and a leading enterprise in Chinese automobile industry. The successful acquisition of Volvo is a Shortcut to a technology leapfrogging of the Chinese automobile industry and is beneficial to improving the soft power of the Chinese automobile industry. The acquisition will help to change the image of Chinese vehicles on the international market, which can promote the expansion of domestic automobile brand towards the international market as soon as possible. Moreover, the acquisition serves as a role model for Chinese private enterprises to carry out overseas mergers and acquisitions. In the international financial crisis, the value of many foreign enterprises' assets is underestimated, which is a good chance for Chinese enterprises. Through overseas merges and acquisitions, Chinese enterprises can obtain competitive international brands as well as core technologies and international marketing channels at relatively low costs. Geely's successful merger agreement will stimulate Chinese private enterprises' mergers and acquisitions overseas.

It is noteworthy that Geely still faces many challenges. Geely's acquisition of Volvo is only a start, after that there is still a very long and arduous road. An overseas merger and acquisition transaction is only the first step, while the integration after the transaction afterwards can be very long and hard. To measure the success of overseas mergers and acquisitions, the effective integration, smooth operation, profitability and the increase of the value are more significant than the merger and acquisition itself. Geely will face tough challenges in the following operation. Geely promised to keep Volvo R&D headquarters and production base in Sweden. The opposition from the Labor Union eased significantly after Volvo gained independence. In the specific operation, Geely has little experience in overseas sales, not to mention carrying out important production and business operation in Sweden which is thousands of miles away and totally different from China. While managing Volvo, such a high-end automotive product and brand, Geely's lack of global stature, and its past reputation for making low-end vehicles will make it difficult to maintain its good reputation for quality and performance. Chinese management culture and western corporate culture are not easy to converge. Chinese corporations generally lack experience in international management. In terms of money, Geely needs large-scale financing. Volvo cars needs Geely to ensure adequate investment in research and development after the merger to maintain its position as a world-class safe car manufacturer. The merger agreement is USD 1.8 billion. According to the valuation of Rothschild, the overseas operation is expected to need USD 1 billion. When Ford took over Volvo cars for USD 6.45 billion in 1999, Volvo Group, which was manufacturing trucks, was trying to break away from the car business, which was, at that time, profitable, but had been a loss since then. At present, Geely does not say how it plans to finance the deal. But according to inside information, Geely will be financed through the company's own funds, state-owned enterprises and establishments and banks. As to market, Geely also faces uncertainty. America, Sweden, Germany, Britain and Russia are the main market for the Volvo car. In

2009, Volvo's global sales were 334, 800 vehicles, dropped by 10. 6% , while Sales in China were 22, 400, increased by 88% in the same year. Normally, Volvo's global sales are about 400, 000 vehicles, with the highest up to 470, 000, with Europe and the United States as its major market, not China.

According to relevant statistics, if products after mergers and acquisitions are mainly sold to the Chinese market, the Chinese side can prevent sales decline with their familiarity with the Chinese market and its capacity to control the market and may even further expand sales, so as to compensate for the overseas loss. Geely successfully signed the merger agreement, largely because Volvo was attracted by the potential growth of the Chinese market. There are many uncertain factors concerning whether the Chinese automobile market can provide enough space for the future development of Volvo cars and become its important market

In the aspect of technology, the digestion and absorption process of Geely will be long. The acquisition involves all the shares of Volvo cars that Ford Motor owned, including two Volvo car factories in the world and all intellectual property rights of products, research and development institutions, national sales center and storage center etc. However, according to Booth, chief financial officer of Ford, the intellectual property rights agreement was signed between Ford and Volvo, therefore, the use of relevant technology by other companies would be limited (other companies clearly refer to Geely) . In addition, Ford and Geely signed separate agreements covering intellectual property, which was to facilitate the current business operation of Volvo. In fact, this was mainly to alleviate the concern that the technology that Ford and Volvo jointly developed would soon fall into the hands of a Chinese company, and this Chinese Company was expected to compete with Ford in Europe and the North America market.

Case 8. 3   CNOOC's Acquisition of Nickerson: Stimulate Chinese Enterprises to Go out

Basic Facts

On December 7, 2012, the Canadian government announced the approval of CNOOC Limited's application for the acquisition of Canada's Nickerson at USD 15. 1billion. CNOOC completed the biggest overseas acquisition of Chinese enterprises.

The Background and Process

CNOOC had planned to acquire overseas oil companies for a long time. In 2005, CNOOC planned to acquire the Unocal Corp, an American company, but failed because of strong political resistance in America. 7 years later, CNOOC finally succeeded in Canada. Under the deal, CNOOC paid USD 15.1 billion in cash to acquire 100% of Nickerson's ordinary shares and preferred stock, but had to take over Nickerson's USD 4.3 billion debt. Prior to the deal, many people felt keyed up about the new acquisition, for the transaction would need the approval of the Canadian, European and American governments. From CNOOC's announcement of the final deal on July 23, 2012 till the day, this acquisition lasted five months in the government approval process. The Canadian government announced twice prolonging the examination and approval. Moreover, the problem of insider trading discovered in the American capital market overshadowed the takeover for a time. Even so, CNOOC's confidence to purchase Nickerson was not shattered. CNOOC's determination to buy Nickerson was a long-term result of consideration, and would not be changed in any case. CNOOC was confident about the deal, and believed in Nickerson's promising team.

Details

After the acquisition of Nickerson, CNOOC would further expand its overseas business and resource reserve, in order to realize a long-term, sustainable development. Assets of Nickerson contain conventional oil, oil sands and shale gas resources, which are distributed in western Canada, British Beihai, Mexico Bay and Nigeria Ocean, the world's major producing areas. The combination of superior assets of the company not only is a good supplement to CNOOC resources, but also enhances CNOOC's globalization layout. CNOOC is the largest Chinese offshore oil and gas producer. After the acquisition, the ratio of CNOOC petroleum resources in the land will be increased greatly. In the second quarter of 2012, the average daily output of Nickerson was 207,000 barrels of oil equivalent. In 2011, the annual average output of CNOOC was 909,000 barrels of oil equivalent. After the acquisition, CNOOC's daily oil and gas production is expected to increase nearly by 23%.

Furthermore, Nickerson's rich resource reserves will become the apple in the hand of CNOOC. By the end of 2011, Nickerson had acquired 900 million barrels of proven reserves of oil equivalent, 1,122 million barrels of probable reserves of oil equivalent and 5,600 million barrels of potential oil equivalent mainly in the form of Canadian oil sands. Additionally, the expansion of the oil and gas resources makes good preparation for CNOOC to march into the refinery and sales market. The expanded exploitation will contribute to the development of its refinery and oil product sales channels. So far, CNOOC has acquired a number of local refineries in Shandong, and has established a sales company of oil products in Shandong to expand its sales network.

In order to speed up the pace to go out and to enhance the international management capacity of enterprises, cultivating a number of world-class multi-national corporations has become the consensus of the Chinese economic community. What's more, the situation in the Middle East has become unstable. America, EU and other countries impose an oil embargo on Iran and Syria, which forces China to shift to other oil markets. North America is likely to become a new hot region for Chinese energy acquisition overseas. Going out of the country means risks as well as opportunities. The acquisition in the field of energy involves not only the issue of funding but also political risks and operating risks, which should be taken into account cautiously. From the viewpoint of Li Xiangyang, the director of the Institute of Asia-Pacific Studies of Academy of Social Sciences in China, the current price of assets in developed countries is reduced, coupled with the relatively lenient policy about the entry of foreign capital. Nevertheless, he warns that successful bargain-hunting is only the first step. The future management will be very difficult. After going out, Chinese enterprises need to further improve their international business concept and organization and management ability.

Questions for discussion

1. Briefly describe characteristics of Chinese FDI utilization.
2. Briefly describe the evolution of Chinese policy concerning the utilization of foreign capital.
3. Briefly describe the possibility and condition for Chinese ODI.
4. Briefly describe the industry guidance for Chinese ODI.

China officially became the 143rd member country of the World Trade Organization on December 11, 2001, after 15 years'great efforts and continued negotiations. China's accession to the WTO, on the one hand, has had a huge impact on the world trading system and international economic system; and on the other hand, it has made a thorough and profound change to Chinese economic and social development. The accession, considered by many Chinese scholars as the "second" reform and opening up in China, is a major event during China's reform and opening up process. Therefore, if we intend to gain a complete understanding of China 's economy today, China 's accession to the WTO is an issue which cannot be avoided.

Chapter 9

WTO and China

9. 1　Review of the History of China's Accession to the WTO

9. 1. 1　The Historic Origin of World Trade Organization

In the course of the evolution of the modern world economy, the trend of free trade constantly alternated with trade protectionism, either of which held a leading position in turn in economic policy-making of a country. The theoretical basis of free trade can be traced back to British economists Adam Smith's and David Ricardo's theories. Powerful theories of economics have been developed to back the free trade theory. Although many governments have realized the significance of free trade, there is no country willing to unilaterally reduce trade barriers, because they worry that other countries would not follow accordingly. The core of this problem is the lack of trust: the governments of all countries are aware of the fact that all economies will benefit from lower trade barriers, but because of fears that other countries will not lower their trade barriers, they are unwilling to lower trade barriers of their own.

What can be done to break the deadlock? One of the solutions is to develop a series of rules concerning cross-border trade between countries to reduce trade barriers. But who is to play the role of supervising governments to ensure that they indeed obey the game rules? And who is to impose sanctions against the government that has violated the rules? Could it be possible to set up an independent organization whose role is to supervise international trade, to ensure no breach of rules and to impose sanctions in the event of breach? Although governments would not abide by the arrangement in case of damage to the national sovereignty, yet since the Second World War, the framework of international trade with such a property has begun to develop.

A. The General Agreement on Tariffs and Trade (GATT)

The stock market crash in the United States in 1929 led to a severe global economic depression. In order to protect domestic industry and secure job opportunities, the U. S. Congress passed the "Smoot Hawley Act" in 1930, which significantly raised U. S. import tariffs, reaching a record level of 30% − 50%. The tax benefits of the Act almost covered all the domestic industries. Needless to say, in order to cope with the Act, other countries were compelled to improve their tariffs, and then the U. S. launched a counter-attack in a hurry, the consequence of which led the world economy further toward recession.

The economic losses caused by these selfish trade policies beginning from the "Smoot-Hawley Act" have had a far-reaching effect on economic organizations and ideology after the Second World War. After the end of the recession, the U. S. Congress was suddenly in favor of free trade from its originally wavering attitude. In 1944, 44 allied nations held a rally in Bretton Woods, New Hampshire in North America, with an aim to build three international economic organizations: the International Monetary Fund (IMF), International Bank for Reconstruction and Development (IBRD) and the International Trade Organization (ITO). After a period of hard work, the first two finally got to be established as expected. However, the U. S. Congress rejected the "Havana Charter" after it was submitted to allied nations for approval as an international law to establish the ITO. So, the ITO eventually failed. Such being the case, the countries had to draft a separate agreement, which combined the portion of tariff and trade policy in the Charter with an agreement consisting of 123 tariff concessions already reached by allied nations. And this agreement is the "General Agreement on Tariffs and Trade (GATT)".

From the background, we can see that GATT is a multilateral agreement. Its goal is to realize free trade through the elimination of tariffs, subsidies, import quotas and similar trade barriers. The GATT rules are implemented based on mutual supervision mechanisms. If a country considers that its trading partner has violated GATT rules, it can apply to GATT's regulatory body for an investigation. If the investigators found the complaint based on evidence, the regulatory body would require member countries to put pressure on the country in breach to force it to change its current policy. Generally, this kind of pressure is huge enough to make the country change its policy. If not, the breaching country may be expelled from the GATT. Overall, GATT is surely a success. For example, in the eight rounds of negotiation to establish the GATT framework, the average tariff dropped substantially. Just take the U. S. for an example. From the Geneva Round in 1947 to the Tokyo Round in 1979, the average tariff imposed by the U. S. fell by 92%. The rapid growth of world trade over the same period greatly promoted the world economy.

B. World Trade Organization (WTO)

In 1986, the rise in trade protectionism forced the GATT members to start the 8th round of negotiation, known as the Uruguay Round. One of the outcomes of the Uruguay Round was the foundation of the World Trade Organization (WTO). The WTO plays a role of supervision for the implementation of the GATT rules and principles in a more effective way. In addition, the WTO also oversees the administration, implementation and operation of the General Agreement on Trade in Services (GATS) and the Agreement on Trade-Related Aspects of Intellectual Property Rights (TRIP), both of which were reached in the Uruguay Round. The WTO has some enforced means which GATT never had. For example, in the settlement of trade disputes, members can no longer reject an arbitration report. If the breaching member fails to act according to the arbitration decision, other members have the right to punish it and impose trade sanctions as the last resort.

By February, 2013, WTO had 159 members, including China. As an advocator and supervisor of free trade, the WTO regulatory and operation mechanism has gained positive results. Take the dispute settlement mechanism as an example. From January 1995 to February 2013, 456 cases of disputes arising between members had been submitted to the dispute settlement organization of the WTO for mediation. In contrast, GATT had handled only 196 dispute cases in nearly half a century. The fact reflects that the individual member is very willing to resort to the WTO. It also shows that the WTO has gained the members' confidence in dispute settlement.

C. The Basic Principles of Operation of the World Trade Organization

The World Trade Organization and the GATT are operated based on the following basic principles: the principle of non-discrimination, the principle of trade liberalization, the principle of predictability, the principle of fair trade and the principle of encouraging the development and economic reform. Among them, the non-discrimination principle has two components: the national treatment policy, and the most favored nation rule. National treatment means that imported goods should be treated no less favorably than domestically produced goods after the foreign goods have entered the market. The most favored nation rule requires that a WTO member should treat the other WTO members the same as its most preferential trading partners. The principle of trade liberalization aims to reduce trade barriers through a continuous push of members' negotiations (including not only tariffs and duties, but also quantitative restrictions of import prohibitions and quotas, even extending to the issues of administrative procedures and exchange rate policy). The principle of predictability means that through regulating each member and increasing the transparency, it is expected to realize the stability and predictability of the trade environment of the global multilateral trade system, and to further promote trade. The principle of fair trade means that the WTO does not completely rule out trade "protection". More precisely, in some cases, the WTO does allow trade protection. The WTO advocates open, fair and non-distorted competition. The principle of encouraging development and economic reform is mainly linked to the developing members. The WTO, following the principle of GATT, allows giving special help and trade concessions to the developing members with an aim to encourage their economic development.

9. 1. 2   The Motivations and Benefit-Cost Analysis of China's Accession to WTO

A. The Motivations of China's Accession to WTO

A government or policy makers' decision to join such a trade organization or agreement as the WTO results from a great number of economic and political considerations. Case in point, according to the research, the motivation for China's accession to the WTO can be attributed to two aspects: The first is to seek greater market for its exported products, namely the improvement of international trade policy environment; the second is to deepen the opening up and further promote the system reform by a commitment to free trade and the pressure from trade partners.

Owing to restraints and suppression the planned economy policy brought to China's economic development, China has been dedicated to the reform of economic policy and the opening up since the late 1970s (which is called the Policy of Reform and Opening up). The Policy has greatly liberated the productive forces, and opened a new era for the rapid growth of the Chinese economy. As early as 1986 China suggested the proposal of rejoining the GATT. China at the time was in the early period of reform and opening up, and still followed the planned economy policy. China's purpose of joining the GATT was very obvious, which was to expand the export volumes and develop foreign trade. In the 1990s, China introduced the export-oriented trade development policy to solve the trade insufficiency and to further promote economic growth. In the context, the GATT or WTO well catered to this policy. It is safe to say that the accession to the WTO would maximize the strength of the export-oriented trade policy. Interestingly, while China was aspiring to exploit export to "conquer" the world, it found itself excluded from the world's largest international trade and economic organization, which already had 142 members with China becoming its 143rd member. Another interesting fact is that the Congress of the U. S. , which is the most important trading partner of China, carried out intense debate every year over whether or not to give China the most favored nation treatment. Such an issue, since 1989, has had a negative effect on Sino-US relations. If China became a member of the WTO, the issue, which was standing in the way of China's export trade, would be definitely resolved automatically. Under these circumstances, it is not difficult to understand China's perseverance and determination to join the GATT or WTO. To improve the international trade policy environment for Chinese exported products was the driving force for China to accede to the WTO.

Then let's discuss the second motivation, namely, to urge a political reform through the commitment to free trade. In essence, the WTO regulates the behavior of the government, rather than enterprises; therefore, the political motivation of the accession to the WTO is to reduce governmental intervention in the economy with the result of the government's commitment to free trade. The marketization principle the WTO pursues will play a positive role of pushing forward China's marketization as well as reducing government administrative monopoly. This political motivation is not only a consideration of China's pursuit of deepening reform and opening up, but also a consideration for other countries, especially the U. S. , when they decided to make China become a member of the international trade system, the key of which is the WTO. For example, in 2000, in a speech American President Clinton made trying to persuade the Congress to approve China's entry into the WTO, he said, "China's entry into the WTO will have a profound impact on its political system", which was a powerful argument for President Clinton to successfully eliminate doubts and to win support. In short, whether China's entry into the WTO could exert its due influence on political reform, to deepen the reform by entry into the WTO was undoubtedly an initial desire and a significant drive as well.

B. The Benefit-Cost Analysis of China's Accession to the WTO

From China's decision to resume the contracting nation status of the GATT till China's admission to the WTO, more than 10 years had passed. The benefit and cost of the admission of China to the WTO had been a hot topic at home. The varied views of the benefits and cost of China's entry into the WTO are summarized below from three aspects: economic benefits, system benefits and costs.

a. The Analysis of Economic Benefits of China's Entry into the WTO

The benefits of free trade: The very core and the operation mechanism of the WTO is to prompt individual members to gradually remove trade barriers through multilateral trade negotiations so as to liberalize international trade. China's entry into the WTO meant China could get a greater market access to other member countries' markets, and at the same time China was required to grant foreign exports a greater market access too. This is what is called liberalized trade. The issue of benefits of free trade is considered one of the oldest in economics. It can be traced back to 1776 when Adam Smith clearly put forward in "*The Wealth of Nations*" that free trade offers a country the greatest interest. After 200 years' development of economics, almost all economists support the idea of opening markets and improving trade. The benefits of free trade to a country can be divided into two kinds, one is static benefit, which is brought through the comparative advantage of the resources in efficient use and allocation; the other is dynamic benefit. More trade requires a further division of labor, which may increase the possibility of more innovation and higher technology, and therefore the productivity can be improved. The free trade benefit was regarded as a "bonus" of China's entry into the WTO. It was particularly important to China's export-driven development strategy.

Helpful to improve economic efficiency: To efficiently allocate and use resources can be made possible not only by means of free trade, but also by the operation mechanism of the WTO. Some basic principles of the WTO help to create a more equitable, fair, objective and transparent environment for trade between member countries, which can assist enterprises in the member countries to reduce huge costs and high risks due to great differences in national trade laws, regulations and policies. In this way, enterprises can allocate more resources to production technology, and therefore, can enhance economic efficiency and productivity. In addition, greater market access also means more competition in the domestic market, which in turn lead to lower production costs and prices.

Helpful to increase employment: International trade benefits most people in an economy. For example, the increase in exports will directly increase jobs, but it does not always benefit every individual in the society; the workforce unable to participate in the competition may be forced to find new jobs or to accept lower wages. However, the WTO can promote technology progress and improve labor productivity through trade liberalization and expansion, so as to provide more jobs by the adjustment of industrial structure and employment replacement. Taking into account the comparative advantage of China, the increase in exports in the long term will tend to offset a negative impact on employment owing to increased imports.

Helpful to solve the dual economic structural problem: After a period of rapid economic development, regional disparities in China are gradually becoming wide with absolute and relative poverty on the rise. A great number of people are denied employment. They are demotivated in taking part in social and economic activities. The dual economic structure results in overall underdevelopment, as shown in the fact that the economy in the eastern coastal areas are advanced, industrialized and urbanized, whereas the mid and west areas backward and rural. Such a big gap in development is the root of the current social instability. Rural poverty is not the agricultural problem but the problem of farmers. The stagnation in rural urbanization and industrialization is attributed to the dual economic structure. Therefore, in order to solve the rural problem, it is fundamental to turn the rural population into an urbanized and industrialized population, which is an extremely tough task. Such being the case, China's entry into the WTO offers a rosy prospect for the country's transformation of its industrial structure, and also offers an excellent opportunity for turning the rural population into an urbanized and industrialized citizenry.

b. The Analysis of System Benefits of China's Entry into the WTO

Helpful to Chinese market reform: As discussed above about the motivations of China's entry into the WTO, the entry would be great help to deepen China market reform in an external manner. In effect, the marketization principles the WTO would play a positive role in accelerating China market reform and reducing government administrative intervention. In addition, the government's commitment to free trade would decrease its involvement in economic activities.

Helpful to the settlement of trade disputes: Frictions and disputes in trade are inevitable between countries. How to address trade disputes between countries and regions fall into two approaches: multilateral and bilateral. The multilateral approach is to address the disputes through the international economic rules and organizations while bilateral is through mutual negotiation and compromise. Obviously, if a trade dispute arises between a developing country and a developed country, the bilateral approach naturally renders the developing country at a disadvantage, because the bilateral approach favors the one with great strength. Compared to the developing country, the developed country is stronger both in economic strength and trade sanction revenge. So the outcome by the bilateral approach is obviously more favorable to the developed country. At present the multilateral economic system — the WTO dispute settlement mechanism — provides an effective way for developing countries to resolve international economic frictions. It could be forecast that the growth of the Chinese economy and the increased exports due to the adoption of an export-oriented strategy would inevitably lead to the increase in the trade frictions between China and other countries. Entry into the WTO would furnish China with a vital solution to address these trade disputes in a fair and reasonable manner.

c. The Costs Analysis of China's Entry into the WTO

The protection of infant industries: The theory of infant industry protection maintains that when a new industry in one country is in its starting stage, it is normally unable to compete against the same foreign industry. But its competitiveness and future comparative advantage can be improved by the transitional protection strategy and support policies. After the admission to the WTO, China was required to enhance the market access of certain industries, which was a fatal blow to enterprises in the infant industries. However, the theory of infant industry protection itself is very controversial, for example, how do we judge whether an infant industry surely has "a promising future"? How long should the protection period be? In fact, when we review the WTO practices, no instance of economic collapse because of following the WTO rule to open the market could be found in a single country or area. A study of Japanese companies shows that the high production cost and poor innovation ability generally exist in the industries with a high degree of protection, while efficient production and frequent innovations prevail in the industries with a high degree of opening and fierce competition.

The issue of national sovereignty: National sovereignty is the country's right to exclude other countries' intervention in its internal affairs. The worry or complaint about international economic organizations is mainly linked to the fact that the organizations may enforce some unnecessary policies, with the result of sovereignty violation. In the negotiations of the WTO, the economic strength of developing countries is obviously lower than that of developed countries like the U. S. and EU countries in terms of hiring lawyers, specialists and lobbyists, which put developing countries at a distinct disadvantage. Actually, China's entry into the WTO was interpreted as a partial transfer of its national sovereignty.

9. 1. 3 China's relations with the WTO and the GATT: From "Rejoining the GATT" to "the Entry into the WTO"

Jeffrey Gatel, who was responsible for drafting all the legal documents concerning China's entry into the WTO, once made a comment, "No single country is like China when it comes to the entry into the WTO. China's experience is so unique and tortuous that a book can be written about its entry process. " Indeed, after China regained its status in the International Monetary Fund and the World Bank in 1980, China decided to resume its seat in GATT. From that moment till China's entry into the WTO on November 10, 2001, exactly 21 years had passed.

A. The Review of China's Rejoining GATT

As early as 1947, China, as one of the 23 original contracting countries of GATT, signed the relevant agreements. But due to various historical reasons, China was disconnected from GATT for over 30 years. Then the difficult course of rejoining GATT and admission to the WTO began. From the beginning of 1986, China determined to seek its resumption of status as a GATT contracting country. The negotiations were mainly a struggle in diplomacy. The purpose was to make China return to the last and also most important international economic organization.

The first difficulty of China's rejoining GATT laid in the fact that GATT gave market economy a top priority and strictly followed this principle when it formulated its international economic and trade policies. However, China was at the time cagey about market economy. Owing to being unable to make a breakthrough in this fundamental issue of market economy, negotiations were only limited to discussion of the change to policies or the usage of certain wording, which definitely led to the continued negotiation deadlock. Not until

China introduced the economic reform based on market principles, did the "Chinese working group", set up in November 1987, take a substantive step of identifying the qualification of China's rejoining GATT and assessing China's economy and trade system.

In 1992 the negotiation went into the essential phase. Because the U. S. and EEC (European Economic Community) both required China to reduce the tax of thousands of goods with tax ID, China had to drive a hard and lengthy bargain with major GATT contracting countries. While China was having tough bilateral negotiations with major GATT members, the 8th round of multilateral negotiation, the Uruguay Round negotiation, drew to an end. China was granted observer status to participate in this round of negotiation. By December 1993, the Uruguay Round negotiation, which lasted for 7 years, finally came to an end, with the result that the General Agreement on Tariffs and Trade (GATT) was replaced by the World Trade Organization (WTO).

Under these circumstances, China was compelled to expedite the negotiation of rejoining GATT, because according to the WTO agreement, if China wanted to become a founding country of the WTO, it should not only sign all the agreements in the Uruguay Round, put forward its own tariff concession schedule and service trade concession schedule, but also achieve the rejoining before January 1, 1995 when the Uruguay Round Agreement would come into effect. Therefore, in order to meet with the requirements of rejoining GATT, China then rushed into the last-minute negotiations with major individual members. But regrettably China failed to achieve the substantial results, and the hope for rejoining GATT was crushed.

B. China's Negotiations for the Entry into the WTO

In January 1995, the WTO was established in place of GATT. The same year, China decided to apply for entry into the WTO, and according to the requirements, started the lengthy and bitter bilateral negotiations with 37 WTO members. From the first agreement reached with Hungary in May 1997 to the last agreement with Mexico on September 13, 2001, and later on to the legal documents of China's entry into the WTO approved by the 18th meeting of the Chinese Working Group of the WTO on September 17, 2001, the whole process was full of ups and downs and intricacies. Of all the negotiations China had, the negotiations with the U. S. and EU were the toughest and most tiresome. China held 25 rounds of negotiations with the United States, and 15 with the EU.

During the negotiations for China's entry into the WTO, the disagreement between China and the western developed countries focused on the issue of China's status as a developing country. For China, it was of great significance to be admitted to the WTO as a developing country, because the WTO multilateral trading system granted developing countries special status and treatment, which directly affected the extent of obligations China had to undertake and the rights it could enjoy. The western developed countries were against China's entry into the WTO with the status of a developing country. Among their diverse reasons, there were two typical ones: one is that if China was entitled to privileges of developing countries, its commitment to market opening would be meaningless; the other is that China did not meet half of the requirements put forward in investment measures, protection of intellectual property rights and the policy in service trade before its entry into the WTO. So, if they admitted China with developing status, they feared that China would retain the original approach after its entry.

The relevant WTO agreements, although often mentioning developing countries, did not define the concept. Based on the Gross Domestic Product (GDP) per capita, China was without doubt a developing country, but the developed countries led by America presented some standards like providing foreign aid as evidence to oppose China's developing country status. After the bitter negotiations, both sides eventually compromised — China agreed not to write clearly in the legal document that it enjoys special treatment for developing countries, while the developed countries agreed to "address the issue of China's status as a developing country in a flexible and pragmatic manner". The outcome of the negotiations was that China promised to abide by the rules, to fulfill its obligations, and meanwhile to enjoy most of the interests due to developing countries during the transitional period.

9. 1. 4　China's Commitments to the WTO: Fulfillment and Controversy

When enjoying the rights as a WTO member, China also should assume its responsibility. China's responsibilities and obligations are stated in the legal documents of China's entry into the WTO, which consist of *Accession of the People's Republic of China*, *Protocol on the Accession of the People's Republic of China and 9 appendices*, *Report of the Working Party on the Accession of China*. The fundamental content of these documents is a series of commitments China made based on the WTO rules to the formulation and implementation of the trade-related laws and policies. China's commitments consist of two types: one is of very specific and practical commitments, such as tariff reductions and so on; the other is of the principled terms and conditions, such as commitment to economic policies.

A. The Controversy of China's Commitments to the WTO

Protocol on the Accession of the People's Republic of China aroused a widespread debate in China, which falls mainly into two aspects: one concerns the issue of China's status as a "non-market economy country"; the other is linked to the "Special Safeguard Clause". Some Chinese criticized the excessive concession China made to the interest exchange in the negotiation in the two aspects with WTO members, especially the U. S. and EU.

a. The status of "non-market economy country". For a long time, the developed countries led by the U. S. treated China as a "non-market economy country" in trade practice. According to the WTO rules, "surrogate country system" was allowed to be used in the anti-dumping investigation and recognition of Chinese exported products, which has long been regarded as an unjust and unfair trade treatment. However, *Protocol on the Accession of the People's Republic of China* permits this system to continue, and to be kept for 15 years. After the entry, China was still the country most suffering from anti-dumping measures. The relevant research demonstrated that discrimination against Chinese products in terms of anti-dumping measures was indeed on the increase. Therefore, *Protocol on the Accession of the People's Republic of China* was severely criticized at home. As a matter of fact, the severity of the issue of "non-market economy country" was overestimated by some domestic scholars. First of all, after the entry, the rise in anti-dumping investigation for China's exports was closely related to the improvement of market access to China's trading partners and China's soaring export volumes. An empirical study showed that the intensity of anti-dumping cases for China's exports (the ratio of the anti-dumping cases to the total export volume) was not enhanced. The status of "non-market economy country" had a far less unfavorable impact on trade than some scholars had imagined. Secondly, after the expiration in 2016, even if all WTO members would admit China's status as a "market economy country", China can be expected to continue its unfair treatment in anti-dumping investigation, which is connected with the developed countries' legal system and its operation. Furthermore, even if the anti-dumping measures are considered less desirable, there will also be new measures to replace it to satisfy the need for trade protectionism; for example, countervailing duties are increasingly adopted.

b. "Special Safeguard Clause". During the negotiations in China's entry into the WTO, some WTO members feared that the rapid growth of Chinese exports after its entry would do harm to their domestic markets and industries. For an exchange of interests, China made a commitment in the *Protocol on the Accession of the People's Republic of China* that provided China's exports were increasing so strikingly that "a serious injury" or "a threat to serious injury" was caused to related industries in those WTO members, they could take individual safeguard measures against Chinese exported goods. This commitment triggered a domestic outcry, because it meant that other members could unilaterally and arbitrarily use this clause to take special safeguard measures against Chinese exports, which obviously would be a terrible blow to China's exports in related industries.

B. The Fulfillment of China's Commitments to the WTO

According to a white paper, *China's Foreign Trade*, published in 2011, in the past decade, China's commitments to the WTO were largely fulfilled. In terms of tariff reductions, China's general import tariff level was reduced gradually from 15.3% in 2001 to 9.9% in 2005. By January 2005, a vast majority of commitments to reductions had been delivered. In terms of commitments to the removal and reduction of non-tariff measures, since January 2005, China has eliminated all the import quotas, import licenses and other non-tariff measures like specific bidding for 424 products with tax file numbers. It has only reserved the import license management for controlled products according to the international conventions and the WTO rules for ensuring life safety and environmental protection. In terms of market access, China has fully relaxed its control over foreign trade rights, expanded the opening up of the service market, and to a certain extent, created a more equitable market environment. However, some commitments to the WTO have not been delivered; for example, there is still a gap in law enforcement as requested by the developed countries. China therefore has received criticism from WTO members.

9.2 The Influence on China after its Entry into WTO

More than 10 years has passed since China entered the WTO at the end of 2001. Around the 10th anniversary of China's entry into WTO, a great number of literature research in domestic academic circles summarized and discussed the "gains and pains" of China's entry. The research had come to a basic conclusion that China's entry into the WTO had a comprehensive and profound influence on Chinese society and its development. This section discusses the influence of China's entry in both economic and political terms. The discussion about economic influence is further divided into macro and micro levels. At the macro level, economic growth, international trade, international competitiveness of industry and foreign investment are analyzed, while at the micro level, investigation about trade frictions between China and other trading partners is examined.

9. 2. 1   The Economic Influence

A. The Analysis at the Macro Level

a. Economic growth: The decade after China's entry into the WTO had witnessed the fastest economic growth as well as a more stable one. Calculated in accordance with the World Bank database, GDP data, during 1978−2001 before China's entry into WTO, China's annual growth rate was 9. 6% on average. In contrast, during the 10 years after its entry, despite the most serious global financial crisis after the Second World War, China still managed to keep the average annual economic growth rate at 10. 45% , which is very exceptional in the history of economic development in the world. In addition, the economic growth was not only faster, but also more stable. The amount of fluctuation had greatly reduced. For example, even in 2009 when hit most by the global economic crisis, China still managed to keep the economic growth at a rate of 9. 1% , only 5. 1% lower than that in 2007 when economic growth was the fastest in the same period. In contrast, the difference between the annual maximum speed and minimum speed in the 1980's and 1990's was respectively 11. 1% and 10. 4% . After the entry, China's economy showed a rapid but more stable progress, mainly because China had greatly improved the global division of labor. Therefore, resources had been better allocated around the globe, which not only enhanced the efficiency in the use of resources, but at the same time increased the space for maneuvers. This is virtually one of the most fundamental reasons. Naturally there has always been a view that the more a country participates in the global labor division, the more external shocks it will be subject to and thereby its economic stability may be on the decline. But it should be noted that both domestic and foreign markets can do better with the reduction of economic fluctuation than a mere domestic market. The system theory proves that a large system is more stable than a small one; an open system is more stable than the closed. Ten years' economic growth after China's entry had fully supported the theory, that is, the more participation in global labor division, the less economic fluctuation and the more stability.

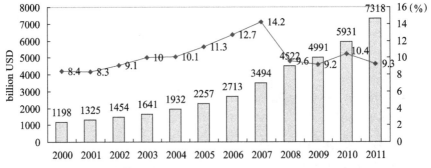

Figure 9.1   China's GDP and GDP Growth Rate from 2000 to 2011

Data source: World Bank, World Development Indicators, 2013.

b. International trade: During the 10 years after China's accession to the WTO, China had participated more in the global division of labor, and fully displayed its comparative advantages. The international trade including trade in goods and services had achieved outstanding development. Foreign trade had continued to expand with the improved trade quality. The dependence on foreign trade had risen from 44% in 2001 to 57% by the end of 2010.

(a) The trade in goods: The 10 years after the entry is considered the golden period of Chinese goods trade. In 2001 when China just entered the WTO, China's international trade totaled USD 510 billion, 4.4% of the total volume of global trade, of which export volume was USD 266.1 billion and import volume USD 243.6 billion, accounting for 20% and 18% in the proportion of GDP respectively. China at the time was the world's 6th largest exporter. In the following 10 years after the entry into the WTO, China's export and import each year kept growing at an average rate of 18.3% and 17.6% respectively, much faster than the global annual average growth rate of 8.9% and 9% in the same period, also faster than China's economic growth rate of the same period. In 2012 China's goods export and import was 4.9 times and 4.7 times of those in 2001 before the entry. It was the period of the fastest growth since the reform and opening up. The export had contributed over 20% on average to the domestic economic growth. China had leaped to the world's 2nd largest country by GDP, the world's largest exporter, the world's 2nd largest importer. Its trade volume accounted for 9% of the total global trade.

(b) The trade in services: China's trade in services had also made considerable progress. From 2001 to 2010, the total value of China's service trade climbed fourfold to USD 362.4 billion from USD 71.9 billion. Exports in

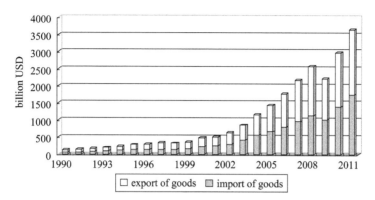

Figure 9. 2   Chinese Export and Import of Goods in 1990−2012 (in current USD)

services Data source: World Bank, World Development Indicators, 2013

trade rose from USD 33. 34 billion in 2001 to USD 193. 3 billion in 2010, an average annual growth rate of 18. 38% ; imports from USD 39. 27 billion in 2001 to USD 171. 2 billion in 2010, an average annual increase of 19% . The export and import in service trade jumped from the 12th place and the 9th place in 2001 to the 4th and the 3rd place in 2010 respectively. From the perspective of the static effect, the development of trade in services had reduced the service prices, and improved the welfare. From the perspective of the dynamic effect, the fast development of the trade in services was normally accompanied by a technology spillover, which had promoted the efficiency of production factors and increased wealth. Overall, the expansion of service trade played a significant role in China's economic acceleration.

(c) The trade structure: China, after its entry into the WTO, optimized its goods trade structure. The primary products in the goods export dropped from 10% in 2001 to 5. 2% in 2010. The Chinese government made remarkable progress in export of large mechanical and electrical products and complete sets of equipment such as automobiles, ships, aircrafts, railway equipment, and communication products by means of trade restructuring and change to the growth mode of foreign trade. Notably, the export of high technology products had gained a great momentum. Its export accounted for 17. 5% of the total goods export in 2001, and 31. 2% in 2010. Meanwhile, the import of advanced technology, equipment, key parts and components as well as bulk resources had also expanded on a continued basis.

c. Foreign direct investment (FDI): There has been an increasing concern among economic scholars about the relations between foreign direct investment and economic growth. They have reached a common understanding that foreign direct investment has a positive effect on a country's economic growth through capital accumulation effect, technology diffusion effect and institutional change effect. According to the statistics issued by China's Ministry of Commerce, in 2001 when China just entered the WTO, the inflow of foreign direct investment was USD 47 billion. In 2010, the figure soared to USD 105.7 billion. The annual growth rate was 9.5% on average. The UN statistics revealed that the stock of China's absorption of FDI jumped from USD 193.3 billion in 2000 to USD 578.8 billion in 2010. In the period after the entry into WTO, foreign direct investment had maintained a relatively stable growth, which contradicted many scholars' predictions that the wider opening of investment fields after the entry would lead to the flood of FDI. As a matter of fact, the data based on the United Nations Conference on Trade and Development indicated that the stock of Chinese absorption of FDI accounted for only 3% of global stock, merely up 0.4 percentage point compared to that in 2000, and accounted for only 9.7% of the stock of FDI in developing countries, even lower than that in 2000 before the entry. Thus, it is safe to say that the entry has had little effect on China's absorption of foreign direct investment. In reality, the commitments to foreign direct investment China made in *Protocol on the Accession of the People's Republic of China* are mostly principled, rather than the substantive opening up and policies.

In short, during the 10 years after China's entry into the WTO, trade in goods and services achieved a remarkable accomplishment. The scale and quality of foreign capital utilization improved. The rapid development of foreign trade made a great contribution to economic growth and social development. At the same time, China's economic growth also played a significant role in world economic recovery. However, China's foreign trade had been beset by a number of problems as well, such as extensive mode of development, exported products with low added value, no fundamental improvement in trade terms, and the continued imbalances in international balance of payments.

B. The Analysis of Trade Frictions at Micro Level

As mentioned earlier, one of the main motivations of the entry into WTO is to improve international trade policy environment. A potential benefit is that China can use WTO mechanisms such as the dispute settlement mechanism or consultation mechanism to resolve the trade frictions between trading partners and to reduce the trade protection implemented by other members. This section analyzes the influence of the entry into WTO on China through the examination at the micro level of trade frictions between China and its trading partners. We mainly study two types of trade friction: the anti-dumping measures and specific safeguard mechanism, because they have attracted the most domestic concerns and have the greatest impact on the trade relations between China and its partners.

a. Anti-dumping measures

China is the country most subject to anti-dumping [1] investigations and anti-dumping measures. For example, according to the WTO website database, from 1995 to the first half of 2012, there were 643 cases of anti-dumping measures against Chinese exports, accounting for 24.2% of the total global cases; 884 cases of anti-dumping investigations against Chinese exports, accounting for 21.4% of the total. Through a data comparison of anti-dumping investigations and measures China suffered prior to and after the entry, the absolute number of the cases involved in both anti-dumping investigations and anti-dumping measures were on an apparent rise after the entry, instead of a decline. Based on the WTO website database, the number of anti-dumping cases filed against Chinese exported products surged from 32 in 2001 to 56 in 2009, up 75%. The number of anti-dumping investigation cases against China accounted for 14.75% of the total global investigations in 2001, but 43% in 2010. The rise of the proportion showed that discrimination against China's export products through anti-dumping measures had further increased. Such a result is not difficult to understand. Prior to China's entry, if a foreign government was under political pressure caused by Chinese import, it could discriminatory treat the Chinese products simply by adopting the approach to unilateral tariff improvement. However, after China's entry, in the face of the rapid growth of the China's exports, the members could only choose the policy tools allowed by the WTO rules. Obviously, anti-dumping was just the ready and "legitimate" tool to serve the purpose.

In addition, the increased discrimination against China also reflects the tool of trade protection is especially "useful" to China. In the bilateral negotiations for entry, China attached great importance to the issue of "whether to grant China the market economy status". One of the reasons behind it is that if China were identified as a non-market economy country, many members, especially the U.S., would use the "surrogate country" system when judging the existence of

---

[1] Dumping refers to the export to a country in the world market at a price lower than its normal value. Since dumping is identified by WTO as "unfair", the WTO allows the member suffering dumping adopts anti-dumping measures to "correct" the price to the normal. Because of the legitimacy of anti-dumping measures, antidumping measures are abused excessively as a tool of trade protection.

dumping of Chinese exports. This system will place Chinese export enterprises in a very disadvantageous position, because it can very easily identify the Chinese exports as dumping and therefore permit members to take anti-dumping measures against China's exports. In the *Protocol on the Accession of the People's Republic of China*, regardless of how the WTO members will identify China, the country's market economy status will be automatically confirmed 15 years after its entry. Yet, before 2016, anti-dumping measures are still regarded as an easy-to-use and successful tool for trade protection against Chinese exports.

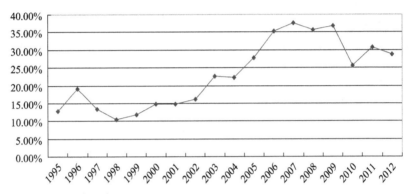

Figure 9.3   The Percentage of Anti-dumping Investigations against China in the Total Global Investigations

Data source: WTO Antidumping Database Website.

b. Special safeguard clause

During the negotiations for China's entry into the WTO, in order to make other members compromise on some issues, and finally meet the goal of joining the WTO, China had to make some concessions. One of them was to accept the "Transitional Product-Specific Safeguard Clause" (hereinafter referred to as "Special Safeguard Clause"). The clause provides that if the amount of increase in Chinese products[1] exported to other WTO members is so large as to cause "serious injury" or "a threat of serious injury" to the related industries of those members, then these WTO members can take individual safeguard measures against Chinese products. The "Special Safeguard Clause" remained effective from December 11, 2001 to December 11, 2013. Because of the fewer barriers in the

---

1   Chinese products here do not include textiles and apparel. The trade in textiles and apparel between China and the U. S. and EU has not been fully integrated into the WTO multilateral trade system even after China's entry into the WTO. Fundamentally speaking, the trade conflict in textiles and apparel is solved through bilateral means.

use of the Special Safeguard Clause compared to anti-dumping measures, Special Safeguard Clause against Chinese exports to some extent could replace anti-dumping measures.

During the 10 years after China's entry (mainly from 2002 to 2009), the WTO members initiated 28 investigation cases on Chinese products through the Special Safeguard Clause, of which the developed countries (the USA, the European Union and Canada) initiated 9 cases and the developing countries or regions 19 cases. In terms of the finally imposed cases, the U. S. imposed the Special Safeguard Clause only on 1 case, while the developing countries 14 cases. The U. S. initiated the most cases of the Special Safeguard Clause against China. Of the 6 cases on which the Clause had not been imposed, there were 5 cases which the agency concerned confirmed "market disruption", but the American President decided not to impose trade restrictions, reflecting the important role of the American head of state in trade policy decision-making. The 2009 "tires safeguard case" was the first "case against China under Special Safeguard Clause" after President Obama took office. The pressures from the related interest groups forced President Obama to approve the 3 - year import surcharge on Chinese tires, which triggered the Sino-US trade war . Although there was only one case on which the Special Safeguard Clause was imposed finally, the effect was great with the significance far beyond the Clause itself.

From the view at the micro level, China's trade frictions with other members after its entry have shown an upward and varied tendency. But the increased trade frictions do not mean the deterioration of Chinese trade policy environment. Instead, Chinese exports after the entry is on a significant rise, which will surely lead to increased trade frictions with other trading partners.

9. 2. 2   The Influence of Market-oriented Reform

As discussed above, an important motivation for the entry into the WTO was to take advantage of market-based principles the WTO pursues to speed up the market economy process, to reduce the government intervention in the market, and to break the administrative monopoly, and therefore to promote the system reform "in reverse". However, compared with the achievements of China's opening up and economic growth since its accession to the WTO, the progress in market-oriented reform seems to have stirred more controversies. On the one hand, during the ten years since the accession to the WTO, China indeed had established the legal system in accordance with the WTO requirements, abolished more than 3, 000 laws, regulations and rules, adjusted the trading system and policy in a relatively comprehensive way, increased transparency, and regulated government behavior. Some scholars through empirical study found that since entry into the WTO the government and state-owned enterprises have withdrawn orderly from some areas and the percentage of private and foreign-funded enterprises in the national economy have steadily improved. The competition is evidently enhanced, and the market mechanism has played a fundamental role in resource allocation in most departments and industries.

However, on the other hand, the state-owned enterprises are still in a dominant position in the public utilities, finance as well as other industries beneficial to the national economy and the people's livelihood. Many studies suggest that the degree of monopoly in these departments shows an upward tendency opposite to the requirement of free market reform. Monopoly of state-owned enterprises after the entry does tend to be reinforced. Thus, "a dual market" has come into being — the market level has been greatly enhanced in competitive sectors, and at the same time accompanied by the monopoly in fundamental sectors. Such a dual market indicates that the standard of China's market economy is not satisfactory, in other words, the target of market-oriented reform in reverse through the entry into the WTO has still not been fully realized.

9. 3　The Chinese Role in the WTO: Conversion and Prospects

9. 3. 1　China's Demand for Interests in the WTO

After more than 10 years of development, China's status as a large trading nation has been established (China's trade accounts for more than 10% of the total world trade.). However, there are still more uncertainties in the current world economy: the impact of the global financial crisis is still lingering; rising trade protectionism is a threat to the existing international trading system; in addition, the issue of RMB exchange rate, as well as trade frictions also makes China's international trade environment more complex and unpredictable. In order to coordinate with the opening up strategy of mutual benefits and win-win clearly put forward in the "12th Five-Year Plan", and to further practice the "export-oriented" strategy to achieve high economic growth, China needs a more stable, open and fair international economic and trade environment. Having become a WTO member, China is committed to the pursuit of the following objectives in the current international trade system:

A. The Greater Market Access to More Members

After entering the WTO, China gained greater market access to other members through automatically enjoying the "the most favored nation treatment" and other benefits. However, China's abandoning in the *Protocol on the Accession of the People's Republic of China* of the "chips" (mainly including the issues of "market economy status" and special safeguard clauses) will have a negative impact on the pursuit of greater market access in a certain period of time. Admittedly, the *Protocol* has provided the validity [1] of the terms. But it should also be noted that even after the expiration, these terms would continue their influence on the degree of market access for a while and other members would very probably employ alternative terms or measures allowed by the WTO to fill the "time gap". To achieve greater market access to more WTO members, China has to offer a greater market access of its own in exchange on the one hand; on the other hand, it has to seek for communication, policy coordination and cooperation with other members under the WTO framework and request other members to conform to the WTO rules and to strengthen self-discipline with regard to special safeguard, anti-dumping, countervailing discriminatory measures against China.

B. The Opposition of Trade Protectionism in order to Maintain the Global Trade Order

After the financial crisis, international trade protectionism has started to spring up. Nowadays global economic and trade protectionism is flooding; Doha Round of negotiations has not made a substantive breakthrough, therefore the global trading system featuring the WTO has been threatened. Since the WTO offers China, the world's largest exporter, a more effective mechanism and method to settle the trade disputes with other countries, China will do its utmost to maintain the WTO stability and guarantee the efficient operation of the rules.

C. The Wise Adoption of Industrial Policy

The entry into the WTO has limited China's trade policy. In order to realize the industrial structure adjustment and industrial upgrading, Chinese enterprises strived to transform from labor-intensive to capital and knowledge intensive, and therefore China began to increasingly adopt the related industrial policies. But,

---

1   The valid periods of "non-market economy status" and "special safeguard clause" are 15 and 12 years respectively.

the adoption is subject to two aspects: one is the WTO relevant rules, for example, the non-discriminatory principle has a restriction on government's supportive policy; the other is that Chinese related industrial policies have received fierce criticism from the developed countries, the U. S. in particular, which believe that certain of China's industrial policies have violated the entry commitments. It can be expected that China's adoption of certain industrial policies will definitely be in conflict with other members. China needs to not only create a more relaxed environment for the adjustment and upgrading of industrial structure, but also search for alternative methods to industrial policies.

9. 3. 2   The Key Issues China Faced

China committed to assume more than 20 duties under the WTO multilateral agreements, covering all areas in trade. After entering the WTO, China fulfilled its commitments to the WTO: gradually expanded the market access to agriculture, manufacturing, and services; loosened the control over foreign trade rights; further simplified import management; further improved the import promotion system; and substantially reduced tariffs. China's general tariff level dropped from 15. 3% in 2001 to 9. 6% in 2010. The average tariff rate for agricultural products was down from 18. 8% to 15. 6% and for industrial products to 8. 7% . After China reduced the import duties of 6 tax items such as fresh strawberry in 2010, China had fulfilled all its commitments to the WTO. During the 10 years after entry, China gave an excellent performance in removing non-tariff measures, canceling the import quota and import license of 424 tax items, and calling off in turn the management of more than 800 tax items. Trade investment was liberalized, and convenience significantly enhanced. Despite of the good performance in delivering the promises, China still had disagreements with other members on intellectual property rights, industrial policy, trade rights and distribution services, transparency and services.

A. Anti-dumping

As we mentioned earlier, China remains the country most suffering from anti-dumping measures and investigations. The discrimination against China has not been weakened because of China's entry into the WTO, but has gotten even worse. China's "non-market economy" status is regarded as the primary cause for the ineffective prevention of anti-dumping against it after entry. In order to deal with the adverse situation, China has begun to tackle it by actively seeking other members' recognition of China's "market economy" status before the expiration and deterring other members who use anti-dumping against China by using anti-dumping measures against them. At present China has become one of the countries most frequently using anti-dumping measures. China's exports will certainly be affected in the long run by anti-dumping measures. Even if China's market economy status is fully acknowledged, this problem is unlikely to be completely resolved.

B. Intellectual Property Rights

There is an increasing concern about the protection of intellectual property rights. The 1995 Uruguay Round Package also included an agreement about the protection of intellectual property rights, i. e. TRIPS (Agreement on Trade-Related Aspects of Intellectual Property Rights). The TRIPS requires that members agree to and insist on the patent protection period and copyright protection period of at least 20 years and 50 years respectively. Since joining WTO, China has taken a number of steps to protect intellectual property rights in accordance with the relevant requirements in the agreement, and established the basic legal framework, but the enforcement of the laws and regulations is still facing challenges. One of the particular problems is serious counterfeiting and piracy. The protection of intellectual property rights has become the focus of dispute between China and the developed countries. The U. S. maintains that China has made little progress in the protection of intellectual property rights. In the annual Special 301 Report, it included China in the watch list several times. Therefore, it can be predicted that in the future the developed countries will take more stringent measures to force China to improve the enforcement of protection of intellectual property rights.

C. The Industrial Policy

At present China's industrial policy is still the focus of Europe and America in trade policy review. The developed countries accuse China's industrial policy of violating the WTO rules and directly or indirectly affecting the competitiveness of some industries. The questions about China's industrial policy mainly concentrate on the national treatment, market access, export restrictions, technology transfer and subsidies. Industrial policy has become the main focus of Sino-US and Sino-EU trade frictions.

D. The Issue of Transparency

Developed countries think that the Chinese government imposes selective intervention on agriculture, and that China has the worst transparency and is the most difficult to predict in the market of primary produce. In addition, they blame the non-transparent management system of Chinese customs and inspection and quarantine organizations, and the arbitrary taxation in anti-dumping investigations.

E. The Market Access to Services

After joining the WTO, China has positively and orderly expanded the service sector to the outside world. According to the commitment, China has fulfilled its WTO obligations in many services departments including business, communications, construction, distribution, finance, tourism, transport services. In addition, the Chinese government has promulgated laws and regulations on market access for foreign investment in some important fields of the service trade. China has further perfected the legal system in absorbing foreign investment in the services sector, enhanced the transparency, made the sector open wider to the outside world and increased foreign direct investment. However, all of these still cannot meet with the requirements of European countries and the U. S. For example, the U. S. frequently complains that the permits and operation requirements in China are so bureaucratic and complex that foreign service providers such as banks, insurance, express delivery, construction and engineering find it very difficult to realize their potential in the Chinese market. China is under pressure for market access in many service sectors.

9. 3. 3 China's Role in the WTO: Important Participant and Active Builder

Pascale Lamy, WTO director-general, once said, "China' entry into the WTO is a big event and of particular significance for China itself, for the WTO and for its more than 150 members. " China, as a WTO member, is always active in participating in all trade activities within the framework of the WTO and in making constructive achievements. This is mainly reflected in the following aspects. Firstly, China has provided a more open market and more market access for other members' exports. From 2001 to 2010, China's imports grew at an annual rate of 20% ; Secondly, in accordance with the WTO commitments China has considerably reduced the tariff, making the current tariff rate generally lower than that of the other members, which led to a clear recognition from members having trade relations with China that doing business with China is not only based on WTO trade rules, but also becoming completely transparent; Finally, many members follow the successful case of China. The successful experience of China's entry into the WTO is a good example for other developing members, especially for those developing countries in the Asia Pacific, Africa, and Latin America.

At the beginning of the accession to the WTO, China was basically a "recipient of the rules"; gradually, with the rapid growth of the Chinese economic aggregate and trading, the status and influence of China in the WTO is changing. China has become one of the few important WTO members. The WTO expects China to play the role matching its economic power. The developed countries expect China to further open up its market, and the developing countries also hope that China's entry can improve the negotiating ability of the developing countries with the developed countries, and can promote WTO reform. In the future China will play a greater role in the WTO: Firstly, at present in the process of the Doha Round negotiations, there would be no substantive progress without China's participation. Therefore, to promote progress in the Doha Round negotiations, China should be more involved in the negotiations, more active to open the market to the outside world, and provide leadership, especially in the formulation of the 21st century global multilateral trade regulations. Today's economic challenges need an innovative global solution, and China will play a leading role in this process. Secondly, China will deepen the opening up and reform. At the beginning of the accession, China's reform focused mainly on the reduction of tariffs and non-tariff barriers, which fell within the "the border policy", a slight open category. Later on, China should continue to promote the opening up and reform, such as industrial policy, transparency and service trade access. China's reform and opening up can lay a foundation for the WTO members to form an integrated world market. Finally, China should be fully involved in the research of some of the new issues, and strive to become a leader among the WTO members, for example, China is currently negotiating the "government procurement agreement" (GPA), as well as the cross-cutting issue: trade and climate change. China is on the rise, starting to bring a profound influence to the global trading system. It is believed that China will eventually become the backbone in promoting global trading system progress.

Case 9. 1   American Special Safeguard Measure against Chinese Tires

The case of American special safeguard measure against Chinese tires is regarded as the first Sino-US trade friction since President Obama took office. At the beginning of 2009, based on Section 421 of Trade Act of 1974, the United

Steelworkers Union of America applied to the U. S. International Trade Commission for the special safeguard measure against the commercial tires China exported to the U. S. The Union requested that the American government impose import restrictions on China's tires used for passenger cars, light trucks, mini vans and sports cars. In June the same year, the International Trade Commission recommended special duties of 55%, 45% and 35% respectively for 3 consecutive years on China's tires for passenger cars and light trucks. The Chinese government hoped to settle the case through bilateral negotiations. At the time, the related enterprises responded to the suit; the relevant industry association lobbied the American government extensively; even the government bodies concerned acted as a mediator. However, in September 2009, President Obama finally approved the proposal that the restrictive tariffs would be imposed on the import of Chinese tires for a period of three years, specifically, a tariff of 35% for the first year, 30% for the second year and 25% for the third year. The same year the Chinese government appealed to the WTO. In December 2010, the WTO dispute settlement mechanism published a panel report, saying that the American practice was not in conflict with the WTO rules. China expressed its dissatisfaction to the conclusion. In June 2011, China filed an appeal to the WTO related institution for a review of the panel report. On September 5, 2011, the WTO appellate body issued a 123 – page ruling report, the core contents of which still supported the conclusion drawn in the panel report. The ruling report also deemed that the American special safeguard measure against Chinese tires was in accordance with the WTO rules and that Chinese tires did cause damage to the American related industries. Finally, China gave up appealing.

The WTO award was mainly based on Article 16 of the *Protocol on the Accession of the People's Republic of China*. The Article states that in cases where products of Chinese origin are being imported into the territory of any WTO Member in such increased quantities or under such conditions as to cause or threaten to cause market disruption, the WTO Member so affected should pursue application of a measure under the Agreement on Safeguards.

The Sino-US trade dispute over tires aroused the widespread attention because since the U. S. was in favor of China's entry into WTO in 2001, it was the first time for America to make use of the "special safeguard clauses" among Chinese commitments to the WTO to impose punitive tariffs on Chinese products (Although there were 4 cases of investigation using the special safeguard clause in the Bush administration, all of these investigations were finally settled by bilateral negotiations. The "punitive tariff" was avoided at the last minute.) Regrettably, according to the relevant WTO rules, the countries in a similar case can directly invoke the American sanction proposal and impose sanctions against China's tires.

The approval of the proposal by the Obama Administration can be regarded as the outcome of the pressure from domestic trade protectionism. In fact, the reasons for using special safeguard against Chinese tires were not sufficient. First of all, since 2007 the export growth of China's tires had not been obvious. The export in 2008 was only 2. 2% more than that in 2007, while the export in the first half of 2009 was 16% less than that in the first half of 2008. So there was no "heavy imports in a short time"; second, Chinese tires concerned were mainly for the American repair market, while the made-in-America tires were for the original accessory market and the replacement market. So there was no direct competing relation between the two; third, the American tire industry had shown little change before and after China's tires entered the market. Even in 2007 when the export of Chinese tires increased most, the American tire industry was also profitable. Therefore the factual damage did not exist; fourth, the purpose of American tire businesses shutting down factories and production equipment was to make industrial structure adjustment in order to enter into the high-end market. It had nothing to do with the import of China's tires. Even if America stopped the import of Chinese tires, it still had to import large quantities from other countries to replace the Chinese products.

In fact, over the three years, the punitive tariffs on China's tires offered no more related job opportunities. On the contrary, the negative impact on the American economy was increasingly evident. Above all, there were 4 American tire production businesses in China, accounting for more than 2/3 of China's exported tires to America. The punitive tariffs directly affected the interests of these American businesses. Some of them were forced to fully bear these tariffs in order to keep the market share of their products in America. Secondly, taking special safeguard measures against China's tires could not solve the problem of the applicants' so-called unemployment of 20, 000 tire manufacturing workers, and even would seriously affect the employment of 100, 000 staff engaged in tire imports and sales that was greatly dependent on China's tires. The strong opposition from the American tire industry such as American Tire Industry Association and the American Tire Free Trade Alliance was clear evidence. Thirdly, to restrict imports from China would not alleviate the domestic industry competition, or ultimately solve the industry problem. In the place of Chinese tires, America had to seek imports from a third country. As a matter of fact, tire imports from China was decreased but the imports from Korea, Malaysia and other places were on the rise. Fourthly, the restrictive measures had greatly added to the car purchasing cost for American consumers and weakened the effects of a series of measures the American government put forward in order to revitalize the auto industry. The punitive tariffs led to the increase in tire price. In turn, the price rise might even have influenced a number of consumers to consider postponing tire replacement, which posed potential threat to driving safety.

Surprisingly, the impact of punitive tariffs on Chinese enterprises was far less than had been expected. First of all, though the punitive tariffs did make China's exports to the U. S. decline, the decline did not reach the very bottom. Actually the imposition of punitive tariffs in the first year did force China's exports to drop more than 20% , but later on the exports began to gradually restore year by year. Secondly, Chinese enterprises just took this opportunity to move into the "high-end" market. The export price for China's tires export over the past few years had not fallen, but risen.

In September 2012, a special ad valorem tariff levied on China's tires came to an end after the expiration of three years. The special safeguard measures have become meaningless following the removal of the pressure from the domestic trade protection and political concerns. It can be said that there are no winners in this trade dispute between China and the United States.

Case 9. 2   Jintan, Jiangsu Province: A Small Southern City's Bonus and Worries after the Entry into the WTO

Jintan County, Changzhou, Jiangsu Province, China, is well-known as "A Manufacturing Place of Chinese Exported Clothing" despite its humble location. There are over six billion people on the globe and if we calculated the total number of Jintan-made clothing in 2011, one out of twenty people in the world was wearing clothing made there. Jintan's clothing industry started in the 1960s, grew in the 90s, and boomed after China's entry into the WTO. In 2012, there were more than 800 textile enterprises in Jintan with the total assets surpassing more than RMB 1 billion. More than 500 of these enterprises were engaged in clothing manufacturing. The number of workforce now is beyond 50, 000. The explosive growth of Jintan's textiles industry can be considered as the positive results of China's entry into the WTO.

The textiles trade has been long outside the GATT. Since 1974, the international textiles trade has been under control of the quota system of *Multi Fibre Arrangement* (MFA), which is intended to protect the developed countries' trade in textiles from foreign competition, and imposes quotas on the amount that developing countries could export to developed countries. The quotas put restrictions on textiles export of some countries such as China, but on the other hand help the establishment of textile industries in emerging countries, such as Bangladesh, Sri Lanka and Kampuchea, which took advantage of favorable quotas to setup large-scale textiles industries for export. China has comparative advantage in the textiles industry, but is greatly restricted by the quota system. Under the MFA, Chinese textiles and garment manufacturing businesses have to obtain the quotas before taking orders from Europe and America, which is troublesome and cost-consuming. For example, Chenfeng Group, the leading enterprise in Jintan, regarded the annual application to Department of Foreign Trade and Economic Cooperation of Jiangsu Province for quotas as the top priority. Sometimes it even had to apply twice a year, which cost so much labor and energy. It may in some cases encounter discrepancy between quota variety and exported products, which would be even more troublesome.

In 1995, the WTO had a great influence on the situation. According to the package of the Uruguay Round negotiations, the WTO members agreed to abolish the MFA on December 31, 2004. Many textile exporters in developing countries hoped to benefit from the elimination of the quota system. In 2001 China joined the WTO, which prompted textiles export to increase strikingly. China's textiles had very obvious competitive advantages in the international market — cheaper labor with high productivity, the economies of scale for Chinese exporters secured by mass production was difficult to imagine in other developing countries. In addition, Chinese factories had good infrastructure, making possible rapid and timely transportation. In the clothing industry, this is crucial, because fashion requires the products to change quickly. China's exporters could shorten the cycle of export far more than other manufacturers in developing countries could offer. Furthermore, in terms of the perspective of contractual commitment, Chinese textiles manufacturers had much better reputation than other manufacturers in developing countries such as Bangladesh, which were dishonored by "poor quality and late delivery" which offset their low price advantage. The abolition of MFA was deemed as an excellent opportunity to greatly improve Chinese textiles export share in the international market, because Chinese manufacturers would make use of the elimination of quotas to expand the exports to America and EU, and then gain a large edge over textiles exporters from other developing countries. Because of the typical competitive advantage owned by textiles and clothing enterprises, the sales in clothing and textiles industry in Jintan from 2002 to 2006 were breaking the record and profits also reached an all-time high. At the time, the products covered an almost complete clothing category of a variety of fabrics, such as business suits, fashion garments, children's apparel, casual wear, underwear, down jackets.

After 2006, the textiles and clothing exports in Jintan, like the overall Chinese textiles industry, encountered some obstacles. China's surging exported textiles caused unease in developed countries. The *Protocol on the Accession of the People's Republic of China* states that if Chinese exports soar in the short term and cause damage, then other countries can cite "special safeguard clause" to Chinese exported products. In December, 2004, in order to partly relax the pressure from trade protectionism due to the possible soared Chinese textiles exports after the abolition of MFA, China decided to impose tariffs on textile exports, which was aimed at increasing the export cost of Chinese textiles so as to reduce the demand from overseas. The ratio was very low, approximately 4%−6% , and most tariffs were collected according to the low value. In the first half of 2005, the textile exports to the EU and America increased sharply, but notably, USA and EU textile imports over the same period remained the same, which indicates that the surge was because of the import source transfer from other manufacturers to China, instead of an absolute import increase. To handle the flood of Chinese textiles, the USA and the EU imposed a quota system again on Chinese textiles. To deal with such a situation, the USA, EU and China held several rounds of negotiations, and finally reached an agreement that China should make a restriction on its textile exports with an annual growth rate of around 15% , and in 2008, the restriction would be completely revoked.

After a series of ups and downs, Chinese textile exports more than quadrupled from USD 53. 28 billion in 2001 to USD 247. 89 billion in 2011. Over the same period, the textile and clothing production in Jintan rose from less than RMB 1 billion in 2001 to more than RMB 11 billion in 2012, which became one of the mainstays for the local economy. Like the overall Chinese textile and clothing industry, the industry in Jintan experienced a rapid and slow rise after the entry and fully showed its comparative advantages.

However, after the full enjoyment of the WTO bonus, the development of the textile and clothing industry in Jintan also faced "potential threats". First of all, its clothing manufacturing is mainly OEM and ODM. Although the brand is often prestigious globally, the added value for factories is quite low. For example, local manufacturers may only earn one or two euros out of a garment sold in Europe at the price of 50 euros. What's more, the long-term OEM production almost deprives the local businesses of their initiative of creating an independent brand. They are often trapped in a dilemma of "being the cat's paw".

In the background of the WTO bonus decreasing gradually, the worries and threats the textiles and clothing industry in Jintan is facing mirrors those in the overall Chinese industry. Meanwhile, it also reflects the embarrassment of Chinese manufacturing under the export-oriented strategy.

Case 9. 3   The Anti-dumping Case of "Ao Kang" Shoes: A Contest Between "Egg" and "Stone"

China has been most hit by anti-dumping investigations and anti-dumping measures. The situation has not improved even after China's entry into the WTO. Traditionally, the European footwear industry, called "sensitive industry", has been the target of trade protectionism. During the bilateral negotiations for China's entry, the EU had footwear products included in the list of four types of products on which quotas continue to be imposed for 3 years even after China's entry into WTO, so by January 1, 2005, after the 3 - year expiration, the European Union cancelled the quota in accordance with the agreement.

The European consumers' fascination with handmade footwear leads to small-scale and workshop production, which also results in the high cost of making shoes. It is opposite to low-cost and large-scale production by machinery in China. Under the pressure of competition, it is inconceivable for the European footwear enterprises without the quota protection.

At the beginning of 2005, as one of the largest markets for China's footwear exports, the cancellation of the EU quota greatly stimulated the Chinese footwear industry. The total output of China's leather shoes in 2005 hit the record of 2. 53 billion pairs, an increase of almost 40% compared to two years before. Exports only for the EU market reached 196 million pairs, equivalent to two times the total exports of leather shoes to Spain, the leading leather shoes country in Europe. Chinese shoes exported to Europe sold for mainly between 50−60 euros, while the same type of shoes made in Spain and Italy sold at 80−100 euros. The impact of quality and inexpensive Chinese shoes was very considerable. In 2005, more than 200 Spanish businesses closed down, accounting for almost 1/10 of the total number of Spanish footwear businesses. The unemployed workforce reached over 400, 000. In contrast, the shoes imports in Spain in 2005 grew 30. 5% compared to the year before. The Chinese shoes solely exported to Spain exceeded 21. 59 million pairs. Similar cases could also be seen in Italy, France, Germany and other countries.

In May 2005, in order to cope with the influx of Chinese shoes, European Confederation of the Footwear Industry (CEC) made a complaint to the European Commission. The European Commission subsequently initiated an anti-dumping investigation on Chinese and Vietnamese exported leather shoes. From putting on record to investigation and then to sentence, the EU displayed a rare high efficiency. On October 16, 2006, the European Commission announced it would levy an anti-dumping duty of 16. 5% for a period of 2 years on the leather shoes exported from China and Vietnam. But after the expiration of the anti-dumping duty, the EU launched the "sunset review", extending the anti-dumping measures for another 15 months until March 31, 2011.

Obviously, the levy of anti-dumping duty gave a huge blow to the Chinese shoe-making industry as a whole. In 2006, the number of Chinese exported shoes to the EU fell by 15% , from 2. 08 billion to 1. 78 billion pairs. More than 1, 200 Chinese footwear businesses and 2 million people were affected. The anti-dumping duty led directly to the shutdown of a number of footwear businesses on the southeast coast which mainly exported to the EU. At the time Ao Kang undertook OEM orders from a number of EU enterprises. Its export volume to the European market accounted for 70% of its total export volume and over 20% of its total sales. After the levied anti-dumping duty, Ao Kang had to terminate contracts with quite a few EU partners. The exports to the EU shrank sharply.

With the coordination of the Chinese Leather Association, of more than 1, 200 affected Chinese footwear businesses, 154 joined the defense against the decision made by the European Union, but the European Commission rejected their defense later. In October 2006, 5 Chinese footwear businesses including Ao Kang hired lawyers to sue the European Commission to the EU General Court for the illegitimate anti-dumping duty.

Ao Kang's legal team put the focus on the mistake made in the procedure of anti-dumping investigations initiated by the EU on Chinese footwear businesses. Since the EU did not recognize China's market economy status, Chinese enterprises did not enjoy the market economy treatment (MET) in the anti-dumping investigation, which made product cost and domestic selling prices unable to be used to make a comparison and estimation of the "dumping margin" (a standard to recognize a dumping action). Therefore, the EU would refer to the price in the third country as the "normal value" of the product being investigated to determine the dumping margin. Technically it was extremely unfavorable to Chinese businesses. Normally, for anti-dumping investigations like this, Chinese enterprises as requested would ask the EU to have a separate review of MET, i. e. an application for a review of market economy treatment, and the EU was accountable for responding to such an application. But in this case, though Ao Kang and other businesses submitted an application to the EU for a MET review, the European Commission did not give a response. On January 13, 2006, the legal group further urged the European Commission to respond to the application. The Commission said in a statement four days later that because the investigation was ongoing, it was unable to make a comment. Therefore, Ao

Kang and other businesses considered the procedure of the anti-dumping investigation faulty and sued the EU General Court. However, the European Commission believed that it did not violate Anti-dumping Law, because according to Article 17, sampling method is also applicable to the businesses applying for MET. In this case, it could not respond to a large number of applications for MET. "It will create unnecessary burdens for the investigation, and lead to the delay in completing the investigation or make the anti-dumping investigation data not representative and therefore invalid". In March 2010, the EU General Court supported the Commission's claims, and rejected the litigation request from 5 Chinese footwear businesses.

In May 2010, of the five footwear businesses, only Ao Kang continued to sue the EU High Court. In the second trial, Ao Kang's defense lawyer put great weight on the issue that the sampling the European Commission used on the Chinese footwear businesses lacked representativeness. Earlier, the EU used a unified anti-dumping rate as a substitute for a separate rate without carefully examining the Chinese footwear businesses. After the European Commission initiated the anti-dumping investigation in May 2005, there were 154 Chinese footwear businesses responding to it. Owing to the large number of the investigated businesses, the Commission adopted by law the method of sampling survey to determine the dumping margin. According to the court ruling, the Commission chose 13 businesses (exclusive of Ao Kang) to carry out the sampling investigation. Sampling investigation means that the investigation result of the 13 businesses can be applied to others investigated. Anti-dumping duty is calculated on basis of the weighted mean of the dumping margin. Afterwards, the 13 sample businesses were not identified as MET. So the EU Commission selected the data from 3 businesses in a third country, Brazil, as a reference of "normal value".

Ao Kang argued in the appeal that the General Court confused the concepts of "individual dumping margin" of the EU *Anti-dumping Law* with that of dumping margin of non-sample businesses with market economy treatment (MET/IT), and then the court calculated the dumping margin based on the data of sample businesses. Actually the calculation of "individual dumping margin" is completely different from the MET review. The sampling techniques clearly showed their difference. This time the High Court was in favor of Ao Kang's claim based on mainly two reasons. Firstly, according to the relevant articles of the EU *Anti-dumping Law,* in the anti-dumping investigation, if the products are imported from China, the "normal value" should be determined according to the material allegation of those investigated businesses, and the investigation standard and procedure should be established according to the production and sales of similar products in the market economy. In this regard, the European Commission has the obligation to evaluate whether the evidence submitted by exporters is sufficient to help them to enjoy MET, and also has the obligation to review the aforesaid evaluation. The High Court maintained that Article 27 of Anti-dumping Law only states how to determine the "normal value" while Article 17 states how to determine the dumping margin by means of sampling. Therefore the two articles are different both in content and purpose. In this case, the European Commission evidently did not respond to application for individual MET from individual businesses, but directly adopted a sampling method according to the related articles. Secondly, the EU General Court made different decisions on cases of the same type. On February 2, 2012, in a lawsuit of a Hongkong footwear business with the EU, the General Court wrote in its ruling that according to the related articles, the Commission had the obligation to examine the MET application from a trader. "The obligation has no relations with how to determine the dumping margin", and should be fulfilled within 3 months after the investigation.

In view of the above, on November 15, 2012, the High Court pronounced the judgment that the first trial of the General Court in March 2010 was wrong and should be rejected; the European Commission should compensate Ao Kang for its legal cost to the EU General Court and High Court amounting to over RMB 5 million. The importers and exporters which had done business with Ao Kang could obtain the refund of the anti-dumping duty imposed for 6 years from the EU organizations concerned.

Ao Kang's success in the lawsuit had a tremendous influence in China. Its significance lies not in the financial interest the decision brought, but in the symbolic sense. Since China joined the WTO, it has been involved in more than ten cases of anti-dumping and countervailing measures, but did not win a single case. The successful case of Ao Kang with the EU Commission is believed to have tackled the related legal issues, to have found the relevant legal basis for future international trade disputes like anti-dumping for Chinese businesses, and have provided a stronger legal guarantee for the internationalization of Chinese enterprises. In addition, it also set a model for the domestic enterprises: in case of international trade disputes, Chinese enterprises can use legal means to protect their own interests; sometimes the egg also can have a victory over the stone!

Questions for discussions

1. What are the main principles of the GATT and WTO?

2. What are the main motivations of China's entry into the WTO?

3. What are the benefits after China's entry?

4. Does the entry help China to create a better international trade environment?

5. What is the influence of China's entry on the trade frictions with other countries?

6. Why is the issue of anti-dumping so controversial in China?

7. What are the impacts of the entry on the Chinese economy?

Acknowledgments

The compiling of this book and the course construction on China's economy are in compliance with the internationalization of the university's operations model put forward by Professor Liu Shuhan, the former president of Tianjin University of Commerce. The book is written by the teachers of School of Economics

The authors and translators for each chapter are:

Chapter 1 Liang Chen, Liu Yanxia

Chapter 2 Jiang Dayang, Meng Qingsheng

Chapter 3 Guo Xiaoying, Xu Yi

Chapter 4 Shao Yongtong, Xu Yi

Chapter 5 Chang Shuyu, Yang Huiyuan

Chapter 6 Wang Wenjing, Feng Donglin

Chapter 7 Liu Huiqun, Wang Yongxiang

Chapter 8 Liu Huiqun, Wang Xiaobo

Chapter 9 Wang Xiaowen, Hu Yinpeng

The proofreading and verification of the Chinese version was conducted by Wang Yujing and Jiang Dayang, while the English version was proofread by Professor Zhu Hong, Professor Wang Yongxiang and Ms. Dawn Davis.

We wish to take this opportunity to tender our gratitude to Professor Liu Xiaojun, Dean of the School of Economics.

When writing the book, the authors did their utmost to apply and to demonstrate the latest research at home and abroad. We wish to pursue new perspectives and information as well as being easily understood. We also warmly welcome criticisms and corrections from readers. For the references, if any author was neglected, please accept our apologies.

The research on the evolution of China's economic policy, theory and practice, achievement and problem, is a vigorous and new economics field worthy to explore. The authors will continue probing into the meaningful issues regarding China's economy and world economic development and will contribute to global economic circles.

Editor email: wyj714ivy@126. com

This book is the result of a co-publication agreement between China Financial and Economic Publishing House (China) and Paths International Ltd (UK).

Title: Economics of Contemporary China: Policies and Practices
Editor-in-Chief: Wang Yujing
Deputy Editor-in-Chief: Liu Shuhan, Zhu Hong
ISBN: 978-1-84464-526-8
Ebook ISBN: 978-1-84464-527-5

Paths International Ltd

Published in the United Kingdom
www.pathsinternational.com

CPSIA information can be obtained
at www.ICGtesting.com
Printed in the USA
LVHW060622100320
649471LV00006B/88